Recent British Sociology

Recent British Sociology

John Eldridge

M

First published 1980 by

THE MACMILLAN PRESS LTD
London and Basingstoke

Associated Companies throughout the world

ISBN Hardcover 0 333 266390
Paperback 0 333 266404

Printed in Hong Kong
Typeset by Leaper and Gard Ltd, Bristol

CONTENTS

ACKNOWLEDGEMENTS

This book has grown out of a report that I first wrote for the Sociology Committee of the SSRC. It is now a very different product but I wish to thank the SSRC for permitting me to build upon that work and proceed with this publication. I also wish to mention that I have drawn upon material from two previous papers. These are 'Panaceas and Pragmatism in Industrial Relations' and 'Industrial Relations and Industrial Capitalism'. These references may be located in the bibliography.

I have been fortunate to work in the congenial atmosphere of the Sociology Department at Glasgow University. A number of colleagues have discussed various matters arising in the text with me and I have appreciated that. The responsibility for what follows, however, is mine alone.

I want to record my thanks to Margaret Hall for her immense help in the preparation of the typescript of this book, especially the bibliography which was a very demanding assignment. I also appreciate the courtesy, care and efficiency with which the editorial and production staff at Macmillans have approached their task.

Finally, personal thanks are due to Rosemary Eldridge and our children Paul, Elizabeth and Alison. They tolerate the presence of a sociologist in the house with great humour. They have been very patient and a delight to live with. I dedicate this book to them.

PART I YESTERDAY

In the past thoughts were too real to be kept like a cultural
portfolio of stocks and bonds. But now we have mental assets.
As many views as you like. Five different epistemologies in an evening.
Take your choice. They're all agreeable, and not one is binding or
necessary or has true strengths or speaks straight to the soul.

Saul Bellow, *Humboldt's Gift*

INTRODUCTION: NOT WAVING BUT DROWNING?

Sociology has typically been in an unstable state, alternating between planes of extravagant optimism and extravegant pessimism amongst its cultivators about its capacity then and there, or at least very soon, to find abinding solutions to the problems of human society and the problems of human sociology, that is, solutions to the major social problems and the major cognitive ones.

(Robert Merton in Peter M. Blau, *Approaches to the Study of Social Structure*, Free Press, 1975, p. 22)

In 1946, T.H. Marshall gave his inaugural lecture at LSE and called it 'Sociology at the Crossroads' (reprinted in *Sociology at the Crossroads*, Heinemann, 1963). It may be recalled that he noted two routes pointing in opposite directions and suggested an alternative 'middle way'. The 'way to the stars' was the way of attempting to formulate universal laws of historical development or general principles of human behaviour and perhaps attempting to relate them to 'ultimate values'. The 'way into the sands' was the collection of facts without any sense of purpose as to why they were being collected. The first way, thought Marshall, could lead to a sociologist becoming a slave to his concepts and the second a slave to his methods. These points, although only briefly elaborated, anticipated the kind of ground that Wright Mills was to explore in *The Sociological Imagination* (1959) with his attacks on grand theory and abstracted empiricism. And the middle way? 'It leads into a country where sociology can choose units of study of a manageable size — not society, progress, morals and civilisation, but specific social structures in which the basic processes and functions have determined meanings' (op. cit., p. 21). This may well have been a remark directed in part at his colleague Ginsberg, who was pre-eminently concerned precisely with morals, progress and civilisation. But he did nonetheless call Durkheim, Weber, Mannheim and even Hobhouse as witnesses for his case that this was the way forward. Furthermore, thought Marshall, there could be a practical relevance in such sociological work.

In choosing topics it is natural that we should be influenced by the

> nature of the practical problems that face us. Sociology need not be ashamed of wishing to be useful. There are real advantages in relating research to current issues. In the first place, it is stimulating and purposeful and less likely to lead to random investigations. In the second, facilities may be available which are lacking in other cases. Much of the data now needed can be collected only by public authorities, and when the needs of the moment urge them to action social scientists can reap the benefits.
>
> (op. cit., p. 22)

W.J.H. Sprott offered a cheerful rejoinder to Marshall in his Hobhouse memorial lecture *Sociology at the Seven Dials* (1962). Rather than picturing sociologists marching towards a crossroads and faced with a decision, Sprott thought it was more apposite to think of groups coming from various directions and, upon meeting, arguing furiously with each other. So he differentiates: the fact gatherers; the methods men; the historical sociologists; the sociological birdwatchers (ethnographers); the middle-range theorists (testing manageable hypotheses); the analytic theorists (model-builders like Parsons and Merton); and the dynamic theorists (such as Marx, Weber and Pareto). Sprott accepts that there may be useful communication between them but that it is also in the nature of the case that one has to live with a plurality of approaches: 'Owing to the vast range of the subject and the various pre-dilections of those who pursue it, Sociology will always be an untidy subject but I do not see why we should be dismayed by that' (op. cit., p. 17). This may help to put the arguments in some sort of perspective but it does not stop them. It may also indicate the amorphous nature of the subject which is not infrequently commented upon (cf. Runciman, 1970). It will not dampen the fire of debate: '. . . according to the interests of the individual sociologist, whether, for example, he views the model of his own society with curiosity or criticism, or whether he is interested in the very process of model improvement itself he will have his own view of what sociology ought to be, and will tend to deplore the activities of those whose views and interests are different from his own' (op. cit., p. 7).

I find it refreshing to read again these lucid voices of yesterday. And yet, as one contemplates the deluge of sociological writing since then, it is to sense that the homely metaphors of crossroads and seven dials are inadequate. If one was to stay with directional metaphors perhaps one should think in terms of radar screens. To read some sociology today is (almost literally) like reading another language. We may be informed that sociological concepts have to obey a double hermeneutic; or it may be suggested that it is only possible to do sociological theory with the aid of video tape. We will certainly be warned of the dangers of 'positivism' and we might be encouraged to think of the sociological task as reflexive and emancipatory. We may be challenged to say whose side we are on; we will be made aware of the difference between normative and non-normative sociology. Sturdy distinctions between bourgeois and Marxist sociology dissolve under a welter of comment about structuralism, existentialism, phenomenology and symbolic interactionism. We may wonder whether a critical sociology is the same as a sceptical sociology.

Inserted into all the above will be an unavoidable encounter with paradigms. Undeterred by the philosophers of science who write about each other as Popper (1), Popper (2), Popper (3), as they get locked in epistemological combat about the possibilities of the growth of knowledge and undismayed by the many meanings of the term that have been unearthed, we proceed. Is sociology a pre-paradigm science? Are we moving towards a single paradigm? Is this possible and if so is it desirable? And do paradigm shifts occur in sociology and does the Kuhnian scheme apply to sociology anyway? Is this a recipe (or an excuse) for methodological anarchism or can we judge between the forms of life which each paradigm represents?

In the wake of these questions and the uncertainties they point to I should like to make a number of observations by way of introduction to the review that follows.

When Berger and Luckmann wrote *The Social Construction of Reality* (1967) they concluded (p. 209): 'In contrast to some of the dominant fashions of theorising in contemporary sociology, the ideas we have tried to develop posit *neither* an ahistorical "social system" *nor* an ahistorical human nature . . . We cannot agree that sociology has as its object the alleged "dynamics" of social and psychological "systems" placed *post hoc* into dubious relationship.' The concept of system has come under severe attack from this influential quarter and the call is to study social processes and social interaction. This brings into focus the work of people such as Mead, Blumer and Goffman. We can readily appreciate how worries about the reification of systems can arise from such an approach. However, the processual approach does not ignore the problem of constraint in social relations and it does not hang together ultimately without a concept of structure. This point comes through very well in Brittan's *Meanings and Situations* (1973). After an illuminating discussion on the varieties of interactionist approaches he states:

> All the models of interaction that we have discussed in this book are subject to the same stresses and strains. To consider social life as drama, as a game, as exchange, is to be guilty of an obsessive interest in the momentary, episodic and situational aspects of social relationships. Paradoxically, in spite of claims to the contrary, each one of these interaction models is intimately tied up with general models of society. The dramatic metaphor lends itself to the view of society as a network of interlocking roles, the game model is linked to a model

> of social conflict, the exchange model is easily assimilated into modern systems theory. Hence it is probable that the problems intrinsic to 'everyday life' are not only contextual but transcend the 'immediately given'. (op. cit., p. 203)

If one accepts the burden of the above argument, as I do, then *a fortiori* it is not possible to concede the ethnomethodological case in so far as it rests upon the context-specificity of meaning. In its exclusive focus upon members' methods, its apparent unwillingness to abstract from concrete particulars, its exponents seem to me to condemn themselves to endless description and to turn their back upon the activity of theorising. (A number of papers on ethnomethodology are to be found in Turner, 1974; for instructive critiques see Lassmann, in Rex, ed 1975; McSweeney, 1973; and Goldthorpe, 1973.)

I think that through the thicket of positions and perspectives it is possible to see how individual sociologists come to articulate their positions. In some cases one can see where a person stands by examining what he is denying. I think that the work of writers as diverse as Bernstein, Goldthorpe, Rex, Bottomore and Gellner shows through in this way.

Finally, despite the experiences of false starts and blind alleys I think that it is appropriate to think of knowledge as cumulative. If it were not so, there would be little point in writers such as Frankenberg (in Barker and Allen, 1976) and Brown (in Allen and Barker, 1976) telling us about the neglect of gender differences in community studies and industrial sociology respectively. They point not only to gaps in knowledge, but deficiencies in explanations that might be made good in some future work.

In what follows I have sought to examine what has been accomplished in recent British sociology. After some brief comments on the development of the subject in Britain, I focus on what has been attempted over the last twenty to thirty years. My purpose is to outline and illustrate what I think to be some of the main debates. From time to time I have indicated my own standpoint. I cannot claim to have 'covered the ground' in any exhaustive sense but rather to have cut a swathe through the field. Naturally I hope that what is harvested gives a reasonable appreciation of the subject as practised in Britain. I suspect, however, that the distinction between wheat and tares may not be as clear-cut as it was to the farmer in the parable. There is, after all, more than one way of seeing and judging British sociology.

2 NOT SO RECENT BRITISH SOCIOLOGY

From 1929 to 1954 Morris Ginsberg was Professor of Sociology at the London School of Economics. With the important exception of T.H. Marshall he stands as the representative figure of British academic sociology during that period. He succeeded L.T. Hobhouse who, in 1907, had been jointly appointed with E.A. Westermarck to the Martin White Chair. Since Ginsberg was highly sympathetic to Hobhouse's approach to sociology and indeed, with him and G.C. Wheeler, had co-authored *The Material Culture and Social Institutions of the Simplier Peoples* (1915) there was almost an element of apostolic succession at LSE in the teaching of sociology. Through them generations of students were taught the roots, tasks and scope of sociology.

In his inaugural lecture, published as *The Roots of Sociology* (1907), Hobhouse had listed four main sources: political philiosophy, the philosophy of history, the growth of the physical sciences and particularly biological theories of evolution, and the development of social-survey methods of investigation designed to uncover the facts of social life. These four points were to be recapitulated by Ginsberg and one oberves that they are carried through into Bottomore's text book *Sociology* (1962). Hobhouse related them to a programmatic statement of the sociological task:

> We have . . . to form a coherent conception of what progress means for us. We shall then it seems, have need not only of a scientific account of the fact of change, but also of a philosophical investigation of social values — that investigation which we found at the outset underlying the work of political philosophers. The ethical conception of progress once formed, we have to confront it with the facts; we have to ask ourselves how the various combinations that we find in experience arrange themselves in relation to it, whether they can be placed on the line of advance, or fall on some side path or blind alley. We have to ask ourselves how the movement of history comports itself, whether we find that civilisation, or any particular form of civilisation, does in fact move in this direction as the ages pass, and if so, we have to ask what are the conditions on which this advance depends. If again, we can assign them, we have finally to determine the point at which we ourselves stand the conditions of

subsequent advance. Thus for the completion of our task we need both a science and a philosophy, and it is only through the union of the two that we can bring the certainty and precision of systematic thought to bear upon the problems of practical life.

(reprinted in *Sociology and Philosophy*, 1966, p. 19)

This then was the vision and the promise, with its suggestion that relating sociology to immediate practical and social problems entailed a long route march. His sociology was comparative, developmental and evolutionary, perhaps most satisfactorily expressed in *Morals in Evolution* (1906) and synthesised in *Social Development* (1924). His own political liberalism was reflected not only in his journalistic work with the *Manchester Guardian* but notably in his instructive book *Liberalism* (1911). There he advocated a definite move away from laissez faire liberalism to a 'liberal socialism' in which some measure of state regulation of social and economic life was seen as necessary and desirable for the protection of individual liberty and the full development of the personality.

It has been suggested by Philip Abrams that Hobhouse's orientation to his subject was decisive for British sociology as a whole: 'Whatever others might have done in the way of spelling out new methods of empirical research, or deriving policy proposals from surveys of poverty or *a priori* accounts of social evolution, it was Hobhouse who made possible a convergence of amelioration and sociology by finding a way to stand Herbert Spencer on his head' (*Origins of British Sociology*, p. 87). What Hobhouse had to do was to show that his concerns for freedom and the rational good, whilst linked to an analysis of the evolution of societies, did not entail a policy of non-interference: that there was a positive role for the state to play.

Spencer, on the other hand, had such a pre-occupation with the unplanned consequences of planned human action that he advocated non-interference. In *The Study of Sociology* (1873) he had deployed his famous example of the wrought-iron plate which needed flattening. He describes what happens if the offending protusion is hit with a hammer: it does not work and only produces a further warped effect on another part of the plate. If therefore the process of dealing with a mis-shapen iron plate is more difficult than might be first imagined, how much more so is society. Is humanity, he asks, more readily straightened than an iron plate? Hence it is a form of political bias to argue that legislation is the way to solve social problems. It turns sociological inquiry away from the phenomenon of social evolution and gives too much credence to a conception of society manufactured and controllable by statesmen.

What Hobhouse contested was not the need to study social transformations over extended periods of human history, but the social Darwinism of Spencer's philosophy — a survival-of-the-fittest doctrine which simply assumed that the self-regulating character of social evolution was ultimately on the side of progress. Spencer did in an abstract way see social change as inevitable and leading to 'progress' but his immediate and practical case for sociology appeared to reside in the conviction that it moderated the hopes and fears of 'extreme' political views:

> After clearly seeing that the structures and actions throughout a society are determined by the properties of its units, and that (external disturbances apart) the society cannot be substantially and permanently changed, it becomes easy to see that great alterations cannot suddenly be made to much purpose . . . Evidently so far as a doctrine can influence general conduct (which it can do, however, in but a comparatively small degree) the Doctrine of Evolution, in its social application, is calculated to produce a *steadying* effect, alike on thought and action.
>
> (*The Study of Sociology*, Ann Arbor, 1961 ed, p. 365)

Against this view Hobhouse reflects on the value of altruism which he sees increasingly expressed in the growth of democracy and the extension of the rights of citizenship. His analysis of property rights and his support for the public ownership of industry represented a view that social justice and the rights of individuals depended for their accomplishment on the community control of resources.

Does this brief recollection of Spencer and Hobhouse simply serve to underline their contemporary irrelevance? Spencer is sometimes seen, I suspect, as something of an embarrassment in the history of British sociology. What can properly be recalled, however, is that his treatment of social evolution was path-breaking, his use of the organic analogy, which in his better moments he treated as scaffolding to his analysis, rather than literally, was far reaching in its influence on sociology. Moreover, he was a figure of sufficient substance to be treated by Durkheim as someone to be refuted before his own views on social evolution could be substituted. When Talcott Parsons wrote *The Structure of Social Action* (1937) he asked the question: 'Who now reads Spencer?' Then as now the answer must be: very few. Yet it was a question that was to rebound on its author whose later study *Societies: Evolutionary and Comparative Perspectives* (1966) is grounded in an evolutionary sociology among whom Spencer must be numbered.

As for Hobhouse, whilst he gets credit for opposing the social biology of Spencer, he is not usually rated very highly today. The Comtean style of sociology mixed with elements of Hegelian philosophy suffices to classify him as a 'positivist' and an 'idealist' and who can survive such pejorative adjectives today? Yet *Morals in Evolution* is a considerable essay in comparative sociology. In particular, it is worthy of note that his treatment of the concept of citizenship in relation to the growth of democratic societies pre-dates T.H. Marshall's significant essay *Citizenship and Social Class*, which is discussed below. Hobhouse's work is relevant to Marshall's thesis and it would be surprising if Marshall had not taken it into account.

Again, Hobhouse does take as a central problem the role of the state in industrial societies. Whatever reservations one may have about an over-harmonistic view of social life and a somewhat benign image of the state in Hobhouse, at least it merits his close attention. This is a subject which sociologists tended to neglect in later years, only to be sharply reminded of it recently, notably by Marxist scholars, and well illustrated in the Miliband/Poulantzas debate.

Hobhouse, the optimistic liberal humanist, may well have been disillusioned personally and politically as a result of World War I. At the same time it is relevant to recall that he did not lose himself in sociological schematising to the exclusion of reflecting on contemporary issues. His analysis of industrial relations and the relations between industry and the state gave rise to cogent tracts for the times from a liberal perspective. In their general thrust they have much in common with the more well-known work of R.H. Tawney (of whom more below). As an example of what I have in mind the essay 'Industry and the State' may be consulted (reprinted in *Sociology and Philosophy*, 1966). Many writers on the 'reformist' wing of industrial relations would still, today, find themselves sympathetic to the general stance taken up.

More generally, the comparative method linked to a concept of development, which Hobhouse proposed and illustrated in his own work, is a reminder of the need for an uncramped sociology with space to breathe and room to move. And, as we shall see, the question of 'development' re-appears on the sociological agenda in various forms and guises.

Geoffrey Hawthorn has suggested, in *Enlightenment and Despair*, p. 111, that the evolutionary conception of the subject embraced by sociologists at the London School of Economics 'committed the subject itself to lasting intellectual oblivion in England, the object of indifference and even scorn' (op. cit.). That is a severe judgement. Abrams takes a different view and is I think nearer the mark:

> It is above all unfortunate that the effort of Hobhouse and Tylor to pull together a theory of social evolution, anthropological data, and statistical techniques in a systematic sociology of development was allowed to languish. At the end of *German Sociology* Raymond Aron observes that a comparative sociology of national development pursued in different countries is one of the more important tendencies in modern sociology displacing the old national schools. It is ironic that British sociologists should have pioneered this sort of work only to abandon it because of its historical involvement with a

> difficult moral philosophy . . . We could do worse than re-discover Hobhouse and Tylor.
>
> (*Origins of British Sociology*, p. 152)

It is true that, so far as the academic stream of sociology was concerned, very little happened until after World War II and at first only slowly after that. There were of course relatively few people involved. As far as Ginsberg's contribution goes what he mainly did was to write a series of lucid and unpretentious essays. These sought to clarify what was involved in the understanding of social evolution, the diversity of morals and the idea of progress. In addition he offered various expository papers on Comte, Durkheim, Hobhouse and Weber. References to Marx are limited and are mostly remarks in passing. The overall effect, however, is I think to convey the impression of watching from the sidelines rather than actively pushing forward the research activity. To be fair Ginsberg did undertake a modest piece of research on social mobility — 'Interchange between Social Classes', *Economic Journal*, (1929). To a limited extent that can be seen as a precursor of the collective efforts of David Glass and his colleagues, *Social Mobility in Britain* (1954). That study was probably, however, more directly encouraged and guided by T.H. Marshall.

The Hobhouse–Ginsberg lineage never was the whole story, of course, although for an extended period it projected the image of sociology in Britain. Even that may be putting it too strongly. The social-survey tradition of Booth, Rowntree, Bowley and the Webbs went alongside and was to be intertwined with Fabian socialism. Indeed, this strand has itself sometimes been identified with British sociology almost to the extent of forgetting the evolutionary system-building approach. So John Rex, for example, in *Key Problems of Sociological Theory* (1961), tends to view the British sociological tradition as an empiricist fact-finding activity with no serious theoretical concerns. In large measure this turns out to be an attack on the social administration approach to research.

The social administration wing never really was quite consistent with stereotypes of dull, pedestrian fact-finding inquiry in any case. The Webbs at their worst could approach this and *Methods of Social Study* (1932) does not exactly catch the imagination. But some contributions were of great sociological interest. This is pre-eminently the case with T.H. Marshall. Marshall, having been trained as a historian, joined the London School of Economics in 1925 and applied himself to the study of social policy and welfare. This he combined with an incisive appreciation that the study of social stratification was central to sociological inquiry. His whole approach is conveniently illustrated, though not exhausted, in *Sociology at the Crossroads and Other Essays* (1963). 'Citizenship and Social Class' is included in that collection. It is a product of the Alfred Marshall lectures given at Cambridge in 1949.

Modest in scale, this nevertheless proved to be a seminal work. As is now well known, Marshall looked at the evolution of citizenship in English society — in its civil, political and social elements. The rights that these encompassed tend to involve different institutional spheres: civil rights involve equality before the law; political rights entail electoral equality in parliamentary and local elections; and social rights equality of access to the educational system and the social services. Marshall's historical survey led him to conclude that the formative period for civil rights was the eighteenth century, for political rights the nineteenth century and for social rights the twentieth century. However, this development of citizenship with its emphasis on equality coincided with the growth of capitalism which was based on class inequalities. How could this be so? Partly because some citizenship rights were based on individualist premises which were not inconsistent with capitalism. Partly because the growth of some rights, especially in the political and welfare spheres, took the sharp edge off economic inequalities and permitted a measure of social stability rather than revolution. Partly because the equality entailed in citizenship does not entail egalitarianism.

What Marshall discerned was the co-existence of conflicting principles in social life and of the indeterminacy which this gave to the future:

> Apparent inconsistencies are in fact a source of stability achieved through a compromise which is not dictated by logic. This phase will not continue indefinitely. It may be that some of the conflicts within our social system are becoming too sharp for the compromise to achieve its purpose much longer. But, if we wish to assist in their resolution, we must try to understand their deeper natures and to realise the profound and disturbing effects which would be produced by any hasty attempt to reverse present and recent trends.
>
> (op. cit., p. 127)

The fruitfulness of Marshall's work is I think plain to see, although I am not sure that its influence has always been appreciated. He shows in practice what an historical sociology can accomplish. Although the main focus of his attention has been English society this has been a stimulus to more comparative work. The American sociologist Reinhard Bendix for example wrote *Nationbuilding and Citizenship* (1964) with Marshall's work as a pivotal reference. Moreover, Marshall's teasing out of the ways in which forms of social equality and inequality can coexist has promoted a sensitive approach to the analysis of social stratification in industrial societies. This can be clearly observed in the writings of younger contemporaries including Dahrendorf, Lockwood, Goldthorpe and Giddens. His general perspective does suggest a response to the question why class revolutions do not readily occur in capitalist societies. As such it provides a continuing challenge to Marxist theory and certainly offers an illuminating comment on the so-called incorporation thesis (to which I shall return).

The interest in social mobility, its bearing on class analysis and particularly perhaps the part played by the education system is easily traced in his work. These were two areas of study which did get off the ground in the early post-World War II period. Not least was Marshall's encourgement to those in the social administration field to think sociologically. A testimony to his continuing influence in that respect is summed up in the very title of Julia Parker's text book *Social Policy and Citizenship* (1975). There she explores with more recent data how far citizenship rights have reduced in any substantial way the effects of gross inequalities of income and wealth.

Marshall's successor to the Chair of Social Administration at LSE was Richard Titmuss. Again he brought a lively sociological imagination to the analysis of social policy. One only has to read *Essays on the 'Welfare State'* (1958) to see this. His over-riding interest was in the nature of social inequality and his general orientation is one of radical functionalism. Much of the flavour and scope of his work is brought out towards the end of his 1951 inaugural lecture, 'Social Administration in a Changing Society':

> We know little . . . of the forces that are shaping the norms of family life. We do not understand the fundamental reasons for the falling birth rate; for the greater popularity of marriage, for the rising esteem of children in our society, or the significance of the large increase in the number of married women who now leave their homes to work in factory and office. On the surface there are contradictions here; just as there are when the problem of incentives, perhaps the crucial problem in economic inquiry today, is considered alongside these trends. Maybe there is in process a new division of labour in the family, a re-arrangement of role, of function; a new calculus of effort and reward in which the frontier between workplace and home is becoming blurred. Such processes, which may upset current theories about industrial productivity, may also lead to situations of stress in the home and in the factory; new situations of dishonesty in which men find their inherited systems of norms no longer rewarding. But while families may be hurt by these stresses, people rarely die from them. The maladjustments in society do not now kill as they did in the nineteenth century. Medical science at least keeps people alive. Our old indices of social disorder are now less useful. We cannot so easily measure the complex sicknesses of a complex society; the prevalence of stress diseases of modern civilisation, the instabilities of family relationships or the extent of mental ill-health in the community. Difficulties of accurate measurement should not prevent us, however, from seeking to extend our knowledge of the causes at work.
>
> (*Essays on the 'Welfare State'*, pp. 32-3)

Here we have an explicit recognition of the inter-relations between work, family and health and complex and changing industrial societies, which is a continuing reminder of the dangers of getting imprisoned in the specialisms of a discipline. Titmuss explores these issues further in essays on the position of women, industrialisation and the family and in path-breaking studies in the sociology of medicine in which he examined aspects of the National Health Service. In his comments on the division of labour and on the professions we find him quoting Durkheim with approval. There is also, as in Marshall, a sense of paradox as to how developments which brought about the welfare state have continued to co-exist with class inequalities. Just as Galbraith was to draw attention to poverty in the midst of plenty in the United States of *The Affluent Society* (1958) so Titmuss was to 'rediscover' poverty in the full-employment Britain of the 1950s. Hence the conventional wisdom of what the welfare state did for the population was challenged, notably in *Income Distribution and Social Change* (1962). While the technical problems of measuring income distribution are recognised Titmuss's argument was that the trend towards equality of personal incomes had come to a halt in the 1950s.

The examination of the distribution of wealth and income led in its social-administration aspect to a re-examination of poverty and indeed to bringing the topic back on to the political agenda. In this work Titmuss was to be joined by a number of painstaking researchers including Townsend, Abel-Smith, Wedderburn and Coates. Peter Townsend's newly published study, *Poverty in the United Kingdom* (1979), stands as an imposing testimony to the way in which close-grained empirical study can pose a challenge to the prevailing orthodoxies of the political parties as regards their existing social policies.

In the early days of the social administration department at the LSE R.H. Tawney was involved. He was of course later to become Professor of Economic History at the school so his work is not to be encompassed in a single label. Here was a talent of the first order who was to become the conscience of the British Labour Party and a social scientist whose influence on sociology cannot be disputed. Tawney's wide-ranging historical studies and his immediate social and economic concerns were marked by an enduring interest in the causes, forms and consequencies of social inequality. *Equality* was first published in 1931. The fourth edition, revised and with a new chapter covering the period 1938-50 was published in 1952. When a paperback edition of the book was published in 1964, after Tawney's death, it was fitting that Richard Titmuss should write the introductory essay. In the book Tawney noted that whilst legal inequalities had been abolished in the wake of the French Revolution and in the early industrial societies, other forms of inequality remained — of wealth, economic circumstances, education and access to culture. Indeed, since such inequalities were seen as the reward for individual effort or punishment for the lack of it, they received moral approval from the Church and the State. Instead of the growth of an industrial community, where life chances are broadly similar and access to the goods and services of society open and available to all who need them, we have class division. With detail, illustration and irony, Tawney shows what this means in terms of education, health, housing and working conditions. More generally he insists that conditions of inequality to which he has drawn attention are a threat to social democracy.

> The sense of the dangers confronting it is not difficult to discern. It consists of a conflict between the claims of common men to live their lives on the plane which a century of scientific progress has now made possible and the reluctance of property to surrender its special privileges. The result is a struggle which, while it lasts, produces paralysis, and which can only be ended by the overthrow either of economic and social privilege or of political equality. Democracy, in short, is unstable as a political system, as long as it remains a political system and nothing more. The politics of our age, not only domestic but international, are variations on that theme.
>
> (op. cit., 1964 ed, p. 196)

Tawney's political advocacy of greater social equality led him to produce pamphlets and books that concentrated especially on the two areas of education and industry. *Secondary Education for All* (1922) is a good example of the first and *The Acquisitive Society* (1921) of the second. The education topic provided a continuing theme for political debate and later sociological analysis — what is involved in equality of opportunity in the sphere of education? The second contains a description of the emergence of 'functionless property' and discusses how industry can be accountable to the community. Although he saw public control and supervision as a pre-requisite for industrial re-organisation, he did not think that nationalisation would automatically bring industrial democracy. The administrative bureaucracy would have to be tamed and made accountable to those it served — employees and consumers.

Tawney looked for a non-Marxist solution to the transendence of class divisions: a common interest based on a common humanity in which power was responsibily exercised because it was accountable and grounded in equality of respect. This view of an ethical community based on a vision of social justice is in the tradition of English social criticism which still finds expression in writers such as Raymond Williams today. If liberty and equality were to Tawney compatible principles, it was in a community marked by fraternity (or fellowship) where this would occur. This value position provided a basis for his critique of capitalist society and which was re-affirmed by A.H. Halsey in his 1977 Reith Lectures. A capitalist society based on competition, exploitation and rivalry was not consistent, claimed Tawney, with a fraternal society of equals. Market forces could not generate social co-operation. Either the unfettered power of the market must be held in check or the vision would perish:

> So to those who clamour, as many now do, 'Produce! Produce!' one simple question may be addressed: 'Produce what?' Food, clothing, house-room, art, knowledge? By all means! But if the nation is scantily furnished with these things had it not better stop producing a good many others which fill shop windows in Regent Street? If it desires to re-equip its industries with machinery and its railways with wagons, had it better not refrain from holding exhibitions designed to encourage rich men to re-equip themselves with motor cars? What can be more childish than to urge the necessity that productive power should be increased, if part of the productive power which exists already is mis-applied? . . . Yet this result of inequality, again is a phenomenon which cannot be prevented or checked, or even recognised by a society which excludes the idea of purpose from its social arrangements and industrial activity. For to recognise it is to admit that there is a principle superior to the mechanical play of economic forces which ought to determine the relative importance of different occupations, and thus to abandon the view that all riches, however composed, are an end, and that all economic activity is equally justifiable.
>
> (*The Acquisitive Society*, 1961 ed, pp. 39-40)

One sees in Tawney's concern for the establishment of a just moral order in capitalist society something of a parallel with Durkheim. For Durkheim the question is raised: how can the appetites which a capitalist society engenders be regulated? In *Professional Ethics and Civic Morals* and *Lectures on Socialism* there are instructive comparisons, particularly perhaps in his attitude to inherited wealth and the institution of property. Durkheim also has a vision of social life as a harmonious community of endeavours in which the economic function is subject to moral control. 'Society has no justification if it does not bring a little peace to men — peace in their hearts and peace in their mutual intercourse. If, then industry can be productive only by disturbing their peace and unleashing warfare, it is not worth the cost' (*Professional Ethics*, p. 60).

But it is the comparison with Weber that is the more frequently recognised. Tawney's historical studies have continuing significance. Accounts of agrarian changes, commercial revolution and the rise of the gentry in sixteenth and seventeenth-century England remain of lasting interest to scholars exploring the transition from late feudal to capitalist society. His most celebrated historical study *Religion and the Rise of Capitalism* (1926) overlaps with and explicitly considers Weber's *The*

Protestant Ethic and the Spirit of Capitalism (1920). In the preface to the 1937 edition of the book, Tawney modified his earlier criticism of Weber. He continued to maintain, however, that Weber exaggerated the uniqueness of Calvinist social theory and did not take sufficiently into account the changes that took place in Calvinism in the century following Calvin's death. Yet the drift of Tawney's thesis is much the same as Weber's. Calvinism encouraged the breakdown of Catholic social ethics and was consistent with the growth of economic individualism. Puritanism made its contribution to political freedom and the growth of democracy. It also emphasised the virtues of diligence, enterprise and thrift. These qualities remained as a foundation for capitalist society as the religious underpinnings weakened or disappeared. And his conclusion is reminiscent of the closing lines of Weber's essay. Tawney says:

> 'Modern capitalism,' writes Mr Keynes, 'is absolutely irreligious, without internal union, without much public spirit, often though not always, a mere congeries of possessors and pursued.' It is that whole system of appetites and values, with its deification of the life of snatching to hoard, and hoarding to snatch, which now, in the hour of its triumph, with the plaudits of the crowd still ringing in the ears of the gladiators and the laurels are still unfaded on their brows, seems sometimes to leave a taste as of ashes on the lips of a civilisation which has brought to the conquest of its material environment resources unknown in earlier ages, but which has not yet learned to master itself.
>
> (op. cit., Penguin ed, p. 280)

In short, Tawney contributes to a sociological understanding of religion, class, property, education and industry. There is also the moral concern of the social critic, in his case stemming from Christian socialism. Whereas he sought to outline an alternative social organisation to capitalism, his historical studies showed how frequently economic power triumphed over moral principle. Therein lies the tension of his work. At the personal level one is not surprised to discover that he turned down a peerage. His letter to the then Prime Minister Ramsay Macdonald was as brief as it is memorable: 'Thank you for your letter. What harm have I ever done to the Labour Party? Yours sincerely, R.H. Tawney.'

The argument I have been advancing is that whilst one can recognise the Hobhouse—Ginsberg line in Britain with its explicit sociological claims — broadly located in theories of social evolution and the ambiguous legacy of Comte and Spencer — other fruitful lines of sociological activity can also be traced. Whatever the current status of evolutionary theory in sociology (and it still has some distinguished protagonists) one cannot dismiss the British tradition either as anti-theoretical or narrowly empiricist as if it were a trail of worthless social surveys. Moreover, the work of Marshall and Tawney constitutes an active example of historical sociology concerned to explain particular developments in particular societies. The evolutionary theorists can reasonably be called 'positivists', but it is not sensible to describe Marshall or Tawney in such a way. So the background to British sociology is not encompassed by single terms such as 'positivist' or 'empiricist'.

One somewhat elusive character on the sociological scene in Britain during the 1930s and 1940s was Karl Mannheim. Mannheim had a distinguished academic career in Germany, first at Heidelberg, where he was a contemporary of Alfred Weber and later, from 1930 to 1933 at Frankfurt, where he was Professor and Head of the Department of Sociology. In 1933, when Hitler came to power, Mannheim joined the London School of Economics as Lecturer in Sociology. A number of his Frankfurt colleagues chose to go to the United States and set up the Frankfurt school in exile. But Harold Laski apparently told Mannheim that it would be his job with Ginsberg to establish the position of sociology in the academic life of England. His professional relationship with Ginsberg however appears not to have been fruitful and his stay in England is usually regarded as something of an anti-climax after his earlier academic eminence.

Mannheim was on the LSE staff from 1933 to 1946. In 1940 he also did some part-time lecturing at the Institute of Education in London. In 1946 he was appointed to the Chair of Education at the Institute, the year before his death in 1947. During this period the English version of *Ideology and Utopia* (1936) was published — revised to take account of a new reading public in the English-speaking world. *Man and Society in an Age of Reconstruction* was published in 1940, again revised and enlarged compared to the earlier edition. In 1943 he published *Diagnosis of Our Time. Freedom, Power and Democratic Planning* was published posthumously in 1951. He was also the first editor of the Routledge & Kegan Paul International Library of Sociology and Social Reconstruction. This was a pioneering activity in the publishing field and became well established and extensive.

Ideology and Utopia is unquestionably a landmark in the sociology of knowledge. It is the centrality of that study, with its pre-emptive definition of what constituted the sociology of knowledge, that created an obstacle for Berger and Luckmann when they came to re-consider the scope of the subject in *The Social Construction of Reality*. In the British context *Ideology and Utopia* was not ignored. It was an object of attack by Karl Popper in *The Open Society and its Enemies* (1941), partly because he opposed holistic categories of the type employed by Mannheim and partly because he saw the sociology of knowledge as an illegitimate substitute for epistemology. More sympathetic, though not uncritical, comments on Mannheim's treatment of objectivity are to be found in Rex's *Key Problems of Sociological Theory*. The sociology of knowledge has not, however, been a major pre-occupation in Britain. Some revival of interest over the past decade can be detected with the publication of *The Social Construction of Reality* and with a renewed interest in the work of the Frankfurt School.

Mannheim did to some extent turn away from the academic world in England to other intellectual support. For many years he met with a group of Christian thinkers including T.S. Eliot, J. Middleton Murray and J.H. Oldham. According to Mannheim, the group met four times a year for a weekend to discuss contemporary social changes and their relevance for Christianity. An essay emerging from this context is 'Towards a New Social Philosophy' in *Diagnosis of Our Time* (1943). What the essay does bring out is his conviction concerning the strategic role of the intelligentsia in a mass society:

> If we fail to replace the vanishing old social controls by new ones, we can be quite sure that substitute controls will emerge, but it is very doubtful that these haphazardly emerging controls will be more adequate than those which could be provided by the co-operative thinking of the best brains among our scientists, theologians, philosophers, educationists, social workers etc. If in our mass society neither the school nor the church and religion provide codes, patterns of action and paradigmatic experiences, it is the cinema and other commercialised institutions which take over the role of teaching people what to strive for, whom to obey, how to be free, how to live (op. cit., pp. 148-149).

Mannheim stresses what he terms the need for a Third Way — the social democratic option of planning for freedom. Not laissez faire liberalism, not totalitarianism but an accountable system of government based on a working consensus. The role of the intelligentsia is to foster and sustain values which make such co-operation possible. Sociology has a place in this task. It should be taught in schools and universities as a way of helping people to make creative responses to the decisive issues of the day. 'Today it is becoming evident that it is impossible to expect a democracry to survive if the science of society is neglected in it, both as an aid to those who govern and to those who have to judge their achievements as parts of a coherent scheme of reform' ('Youth in Modern Society', op. cit., p. 43).

Mannheim does offer a critique of capitalism: it is centred on the meaninglessness of much modern work, the routines of the division as buttressed by Taylorist principles of scientific management, and the emptiness of leisure. 'The Capitalist commercialisation of leisure with its fostering of, and endless craving for, new sensations is as much responsible for the new type of mind as the wrong type of division of labour and social functions which creates partial tasks almost devoid of meaning' ('Towards a New Social Philosophy', op. cit., p. 138).

Mannheim's diagnosis is reasonably clear, his solutions less so. His critique of mass society can be seen alongside the contributions from the Frankfurt School. In Britain, mass society analysis has not been much of a home-grown product with the exception of cultural critics such as Leavis, Hoggart and Williams. At a later stage the writings of Mills, Kornhauser and Marcuse were to receive attention, but at the time of writing *Diagnosis of Our Time* Mannheim's contribution was not easy to situate. His treatment of the role of the intelligentsia is ambiguous — it ranges from a notion of making constructive use of experts in society to the idea that the intelligentsia are the carriers of high culture who will, through education, uplift the masses. He does not give much attention to questions of the ownership and administration of the economy, nor does his analysis connect with an appraisal of the role of the political parties. What one is left with is a flavour of Comte and Durkheim — the need for a guiding intelligentsia (surrogate priests) and the need for social reconstruction. A new social order in times of change can be accomplished by creating an over-arching hierarchy of values and reaching a working consensus. The consequent emphasis on the importance of education is very Durkheimian in spirit. Without such a process of education guided by a cultural elite the irrational forces of an untutored mass penetrated by capitalist values in the spheres of production and consumption will triumph over rational and orderly life.

The anonymous reviewer in the *Times Educational Supplement* said of Mannheim that 'no man is doing more . . . to illumine with thought the darkness of our time and to point the way to a new social order based upon a democratic concept'. That is a generous judgement. In any event the impact on British sociology appears somewhat marginal. The episode of his presence in Britain, however, cannot pass unremarked and would probably repay further consideration.

So far I have made no mention of social anthropology and yet of course its inter-twining relationship with sociology cannot be ignored. Comte, Marx, Engels, Spencer, Durkheim and Hobhouse all wrote about 'primitive', 'simple', or 'traditional' societies within some general evolutionary framework. Weber wrote extensively on agrarian societies, ancient Judaism and the religions of China and India. In Britain, there were some writers in the late nineteenth and early twentieth centuries whose dominant interest was in 'primitive' societies. Tylor, Frazer, Westermarck and Rivers were notable contributors. However these were to be superseded in large measure by the twin influences of Malinowski and Radcliffe-Brown. The story of the development of British social anthropology over the fifty-year period 1922-72 has been well told by Adam Kuper in *Anthropologists and Anthropology* (1973). My purpose here is simply to indicate some of the ways in which developments in social anthropology have impinged upon sociology.

The internal debates between the evolutionists, the diffusionists and the functionalists were sharp. After Radcliffe-Brown and Malinowski, the diffusionist presence in British social anthropology was minimal. Its continuing influence in archaeology is another story. As for the evolutionist/functionalist dispute, the difference in part was one of emphasis. Both sides shared the organic metaphore of society. Both were interested in principle in explaining social change and social stability, although in their more descriptive snapshot studies functionalists do not display much of a pre-occupation with social change. Nevertheless, Robert Nisbet in *Social Change and History* (1969) is surely right to remind us that all the central premises of the classical evolutionary theory of change — immanence, genetic continuity, differentiation, directionality and uniformitarianism — are also to be located in functional analysis. And the emphasis in the explanation of social change tends to be on sources within rather than outside the system. The dispute between the evolutionists and the functionalists was on other grounds. The functionalists stressed the importance of ethnographic field work in contemporary societies in place of the evolutionists' emphasis on the search for the origins of human society which Radcliffe-Brown contemptuously dismissed as 'conjectural history'. The functionalists' stress was on the inductive method of gradually piecing together how a society functioned and this was seen by them as preferable to a deductive method of charting stages of evolution in societies — a method which in any case was sometimes not more than illustrative rather than systematic in approach because of the problem of obtaining reliable evidence. It could be argued that the functionalist approach in practice was less ethnocentric than the evolutionists, some of whom tended to see the liberal democracies of Western Europe as the high-water mark of moral progress and rank other societies as somewhat inferior. The functionalists stressed the diversity of culture and respect for this diversity carried with it a moral and cultural relativism. This usually underscored a view that 'simple' societies should be preserved. Obviously it also made things methodologically easier if outside influences on a society could be kept to a minimum. The ambivalence of such field workers to colonial administrators can therefore well be imagined. Malinowski himself was to acknowledge that his failure to take into account European influence on the Trobrianders was a serious shortcoming in his work. Yet the colonial adminstrators must in practice often have been the gatekeepers so far as access to the tribal groups was concerned.

The influence of functionalism in society was immense and much of this was stimulated by Malinowski and Radcliffe-Brown. One can see for example the appreciative judgements which Parsons makes on Malinowski. When Merton produced his celebrated functionalist paradigms both of the anthropologists were of direct interest and relevance to his exercise. Homans too, notably in *The Human Group* (1950) was much influenced by this tradition, although always retaining some doubts as to how far the functionalist method could be satisfactorily validated.

Radcliffe-Brown and Malinowski were by no means at one on what constituted the appropriate mode of functionalist analysis. Malinowski focused upon psychological needs — what beliefs in magic and religion for example could do for the individual. For him patterns of culture could ultimately be traced back to the biological needs of sex and hunger. Hence, in the vocabulary of this kind of functionalism, 'needs' related to individuals and 'vital functions' are related to them. For Radcliffe-Brown the level of explanation is typically at the sociological and there is characteristically a very explicit borrowing from Durkheim. He makes it clear that for him one can indeed have 'a natural science of society' and in that respect he reinforces the positivist element in British sociology. It was conceptual analysis at the level of social facts that was the heart of the matter for him.

His view of social facts and of social structure is, however, more realist and immediate than that of Durkheim. Social facts are, he maintains, in principle directly observable rather than inferred. Social structure consists of the sum total of all the social relationships of all individuals at a given moment in time. Not all of these will actually be observed but Radcliffe-Brown insists that the phenomenal reality is there. Hence in a letter to Levy-Strauss he writes: '. . . while for you, social structure has nothing to do with reality but with models that are built up, I regard the social structure as a reality' (cited in Kuper, op. cit., p. 70).

The functionalist tradition in British social anthropology can be said to have reinforced the positivistic view of sociology (particularly in the Radcliffe-Brown version) to have kept alive the organic view of society with its consensual view of purpose and values, and to have maintained a language-in-use of structure, function, adaptation and survival. This remained much in evidence in British community studies after World War II. These were often undertaken by anthropologists rather than sociologists (see Frankenberg, *Communities in Britain*, 1966) and significantly were usually located in villages and peripheral areas.

The British school of social anthropology kept alive the Durkheimian approach to social theory which was to find more widespread acceptance after World War II in British sociology, notably in the work of Basil Bernstein on language and socialisation and in the quite different area of the sociology of industrial relations with contributions from Fox, Flanders and Goldthorpe among others. More particularly Malinowski's work represents an ethnographic approach to language in use which still commands attention in the writings of sociolinguists. *Foundations in Sociolinguistics* (1977) by the American Dell Hymes serves as a significant example. The issue of rationality raised by the ethnography of Malinowski and later Evans-Pritchard has provided a seed-bed for continuing discussion and is well illustrated in Bryan

Wilson (ed.), *Rationality* (1970).

The relative absence of concern, however, with relationships between the colonial powers and the colonised cannot go unremarked. It was responded to at a later period — the 1940s and 1950s — by pluralist analysts like Furnivall and M.G. Smith. Not until the 1960s, however, do we get a sociology of the third world. Peter Worsley's over-view *The Third World* (1964) stands as strategic shift of emphasis. With this and various neo-Marxist approaches to the sociology of development, which I discuss elsewhere, the functionalist tradition was seriously eroded. Indeed the future of social anthropology itself has been called into question — hence the apocalyptic title of Peter Worsley's paper to the Sixth World Congress of Sociology in 1966: 'The End of Anthropology?'

3 WHEN WE WERE VERY YOUNG

In May 1960 *The Twentieth Century* devoted an edition to sociology in Britain. It appeared at the beginning of a decade in which the subject was to extend into higher education as never before. Donald MacRae's claim for sociology in his essay could have served as a good text to support the advance:

> Sociology can provide an admirable education. Its theoretical classics are as difficult as bracing and as rewarding as those of modern philosophy; its concern with the practical and present involves commitment to reality of a profound character; its difficulties are of a kind to encourage both intellectual rigour and a healthy scepticism about the limitations of human knowledge and capacity; its concern with justice and values restores the sociology student to a central and generous area of philosophical concern; its techniques are useful for the ordinary business of life and involve some understanding of the powers of both quantitative and comparative reasoning.
>
> ('Between Science and the Arts', p. 442)

MacRae mused upon the question how and whether the opportunities that seemed to be opening up for sociology would be seized. The same question was followed by two American contributors with some knowledge of the British scene, Edward Shils and Norman Birnbaum. Shils did not have much on the credit side to say for British sociology. He referred to 'a number of modestly undertaken local surveys, some interesting work on educational selection, a judicious study of children and television, an austere review of social mobility in Britain, a study of the black-coated worker made, in the largest assemblage of black-coated workers in the world, without a single interview, a few suggestive surveys of university students, some solid studies of Negro immigrants and dock thefts in Liverpool' ('On the Eve', op. cit., p. 451). What was needed, Shils argued, was in the first instance a need to study British society. There was no exclusive method for studying how people live in a wide range of social situations but 'a new regime of British sociology which does not give primacy to intimate and intensive interviewing might just as well spare itself the pains of birth' (p. 458). Shils maintained that in this way comparative study and general sociological theory would be enriched by such empirical studies of contemporary Britain.

Birnbaum also thought that contemporary British society would repay study — but since this has to do with the analysis of class structure and with the distribution of power and cultural values there was an element of controversy that inevitably surrounded the subject. Does that make the position of sociology in effect a sophisticated way of encompassing one's ideological preferences? Birnbaum thinks not because empirical findings are accumulated and have to be tested against rules of evidence. That does not mean sociologists are non-ideological animals, rather they are learning to live with a paradox: 'Ideological interests produce the most objective sort of sociology, provided that the sociologist is reasonably self-conscious about his ideology. The tension between ideology and science, then, remains sociology's fatal and recurrent crux; the effort to overcome it is the source of such intellectual and spiritual dignity as it possesses' (op. cit., p. 470).

In each of the three essays mentioned there are some common points of reference. There is a common view that Oxford and Cambridge by their opposition hindered the development of the subject. The future of sociology was seen in some important respects as bound up with its future in these two places. Birnbaum however was shrewd enough to see that while sociology had enemies, notably among philosophers, historians and political scientists, it might also be endangered by its friends. He had in mind the social anthropologists. The three writers naturally all make reference to the LSE. MacRae, for instance, says that four main strands intermingle in British sociology and all find expression in LSE. (These are social administration; investigation by means of surveys into social problems; empirical research into areas such as education and industry; and theoretically informed comparative sociology.) A litany of names from the past is uttered. Whatever their formal disciplinary allegiance their work was sociological in character: the Webbs, Hobhouse, Tawney, Laski, Malinowski, Ginsberg and Mannheim. Their intellectual descendants were located in such as Titmuss, T.H. Marshall and Glass. Birnbaum took the view that British sociology had retained its reformist bias. This, he thought, might be changing: 'In the younger generation of university teachers, partly as a result of Mannheim's influence, that bias has given way to a more sophisticated and modernised interest in Marxism' (p. 466). Writing of the same group, MacRae notes the emergence of what he regarded as a depressing neo-Marxism. Birnbaum is clearly more cheerful about the prospect: 'Marx — after a century of refutations — is the one sociologist who cannot be ignored. His notions of class conflict, on the process of change in society, on the conditions for the emergence of ideology and social awareness, his general and ill-specified view of "alienation" as the human condition in capitalist society, have infused all of sociology' (p. 464). Shils comments on the New Left who he saw as struggling against Marxian cliches and to some of them offers a tribute mixed with prophecy: 'They still have their strong political interests but they are open enough, honest enough, and human enough to be curious. It is among them that some of the success of good fortune for British sociology should be sought' (p. 452). So the outline emerges of a subject with a reformist tradition in Britain, and with some growing awareness of Marxist thought but which on either count might lead to an unquietness of mind among those touched or challenged by it.

In the same edition of *The Twentieth Century* there are a number of papers which do reflect on empirical work being carried out at the time. Henriques in 'The Miner and his Lass' dwells on a subject that had formed part of the study *Coal is Our Life* (Dennis, Henriques and Slaughter, 1956). This was a study of a working-class community to which the adjective traditional was almost inseparably attached. The picture drawn was of a society that would just as automatically today be labelled male chauvinist:— 'a male-dominated society where women reach their peak of sexual attractiveness early and swiftly decline into the monotony of marriage, where the pit sets the stage and compels the action' (p. 406). In passing, Henriques points to the lack of a developed understanding of working-class life in Britain — also to the limited literature on the sociology of the family at any class level. A contribution to both of these was made by Ferdynand Zweig. His paper 'The New Factory Worker' was a preview of his book *The Worker in an Affluent Society* (1961). The indefatigable Dr Zweig, we learn, interviewed 675 workers in 5 large industrial firms in Sheffield, Workington, Luton, Birmingham and Mitcham. Here the gauntlet was thrown down: 'The whole working class finds itself on the move towards new middle class values and middle class existence. When I compare this situation with what I saw ten years ago, the change can only be described as a deep transformation of values, as the development of new ways of thinking and feeling, a new ethos, new aspirations and cravings' (p. 397).

We are told that the British working class is losing its proletarian character. Its members are involved in 'the revolution of rising expectations' and are concerned with actively improving their living standards, are more money-minded, more concerned with family life, with the advancement and bringing up of his children and with security of employment. The new working class was less imbued with the ethos of class solidarity. Actually there are some anticipations of Marcuse's view of the working class, notably I think in the following:

> He [the worker] is more subtly managed than ever by new inducements and incentives, by the social atmosphere of the works, by works routine moving targets and time schedules and general style of living — all without the whip which previously hung over him. He is manoeuvred into positions where he is required, often with his tacit or overt consent, though the consent is often more formal than

> real. The new forms of social discipline, the new human relations techniques of modern management are the necessary counterpart of the new working man who is now emerging. The working man of old probably could not have been handled in such a subtle way as the working man of today. The new working man is a self-disciplined man, is much more thoroughly industrialized, more smoothly adjusted, as part of the smoothly working industrial machine. He is no longer bullied because it is no longer necessary to drive him. He is a willing player of that game.
>
> (pp. 403-4)

This kind of talk constituted a challenge to the neo-Marxists and to other professional sociologists who were to participate in the discussion of embourgeoisement. The traditional working-class portrait of the mining community with its work-centred, trade-union conscious, male-dominated organisation is in effect counterpoised against the individualised, family- and leisure-centred, pecuniary new working class in the two papers cited and that certainly forms much of the backdrop for discusssions on stratification and the working class in Britain.

The implicit or explicit contrast of the working class with the middle class in relation say to values and aspirations does not easily handle the differences within classes. This actually comes out so far as the middle class is concerned in Watson's paper 'The Managerial Spiralist'. A minority of that middle class was becoming involved in managerial positions in large organisations. What he suggested was happening so far as that particular segment of the middle class was concerned was a form of social mobility in which a manager's careeer and social standing progressed and was essentially linked to residential mobility. This, in Watson's view, tended to minimise the social and cultural connections of such people with the local community. They did not have the same interest in the local community as members of the aristocracy or local capitalists and small businessmen. This spiralist concept has not I think been much examined subsequently but it did throw some light on community life and more generally on social mobility. Bell in *Middle Class Families* (1968) is one of the few sociologists actively to follow this lead.

Some of the intricacies of analysing social mobility are discussed by J.A. Banks in 'Moving up in Society'. Since one of the landmarks of British sociology in the immediate, post-war period is D.V. Glass *et al.*, *Social Mobility in Britain* (1954), a failure to discuss this topic would have been an omission. In thinking of British society as socially mobile are we under an illusion?

Banks makes the simple but often ignored point that opportunities for mobility may be growing wider in some respects but narrowing in others. Social mobility has been made possible by class differences in family size and by changes in the occupational structure (i.e. the old manual working class is shrinking in size relative to other groups). At the same time, notwithstanding the extending provision of state education through the century, equality of opportunity does not exist as between classes. Working-class children tend to leave school at the earliest permissible moment. They are under-represented amongst the population of university students.

It is not only the sources of social mobility (whether inter- or intragenerational) that require analysis it is the meaning attached to the reality. Banks in a concluding comment (p. 426) provides an example of the critical potential of sociology to which other writers in *The Twentieth Century* collection had alluded:

> While we continue to pride ourselves on the opportunities for mobility which we provide, so long shall we continue to value and preserve the barriers between the classes which give meaning to the whole concept of mobility, and so long will parents seek to ensure that *their* children do not suffer from the consequences of other people's mobility. A society which faces the significance of the slogan 'equality of opportunity', where that opportunity is intended to select people for unequal destinies, is a society without illusions. We cannot pretend to be that.

4 THE SOCIOLOGY OF THIS AND THAT

'The metaphor I had long used for the state of sociology was the hollow frontier . . . The fact was that the centre was hollow. There was no central area of agreed upon intellectual organisation of the massively important but obvious and unexciting findings. In its absence consolidated growth could hardly be maintained' (George Homans in I.C. Horowitz (ed.), *Sociological Self-Images*, 1967, p, 27).

There is almost no end to the words that complete the phrase 'the sociology of . . .' Here is a goodly number that are located without difficulty: art, literature, communities, culture, cities, planning, crime, law, deviance, education, family, fertility, housing, industry, work, sex and gender, knowledge, beliefs, ideology, language, communication, leisure, media, medicine, organisations, politics, poverty, welfare, professions, race, religion, science, sport, youth stratification, war, military, social movements, development, industrial relations, occupations, modern Britian, the Third World, peasant societies, industrial societies.

Clearly 'the sociology of . . .' carries with it a connotation: it is not 'the economics of . . .', 'the history of . . .', 'the philosophy of . . .'. But to put the matter like that gives pause for thought: what kind of expectation is built into the sociological enterprise; how does it relate to 'the history of . . .' or 'the philosophy of . . .', or whatever, in looking at particular issues, topics or areas? Since one may observe that the practitioners within any one of these disciplines have disagreements which may revolve around epistemology, methodology, theorising, interpretation and even ontology the attempt to fit one kind of disciplinary activity with another is not like trying to fit a jig-saw puzzle togther, however difficult that can sometimes be. Rather the perceived relationship between the activities differs among and between its practitioners. These may vary from hostility, or indifference to a sense of complementarity and necessary interconnectedness. Indeed some sociologists may well feel more at home intellectually with say philosophers or historians than with some of their fellow sociologists. To speak therefore about 'the sociology of . . .' cannot, whatever it may denote, refer to a fixed division of labour between disciplines, nor to an orderly view of knowledge acquisition.

The existence of sociology (notwithstanding its hybrid origins and present plurality of perspectives) does stand to remind us of societies as totalities and of the interconnectedness of the parts. Sub-divisions of the subject may specify a topic, segment of society, or process. While these point to a focus of attention they should recall us to a sense of society as a totality. Thus the sociology of religion will not be a self-contained entity that will offer explanations of religious behaviour and practice solely with reference to the sphere of religion but will link its topic with other parts of social structure. (Max Weber's *Protestant Ethic and the Spirit of Capitalism* serves as an important exemplification of this precept, despite those who dismiss it as a slight essay.) Given this awareness the sub-division of the subject need not imply a fragmentation which, as it were, betrays the rationale of sociology's concern with the societies as wholes. If the sociologists' study of 'the social' is taken seriously then it encompasses all human activity in society. If we ask what sociologists actually do then one way of approaching this is through the sub-divisions of the subject — what is being emphasised, in what ways and to what purpose? What is being neglected or scarcely regarded?

One might imagine that sub-divisions of a subject are merely matters of convenience — education, industry, the family, religion — but that is not altogether so. For example, in outlining their interest in the sociology of work, Esland and Salaman distinguish it from industrial sociology, occupational sociology, the sociology of organisations and the sociology of the professions. Among other things they suggest: industrial sociology usually concentrates on work in industrial settings, occupational sociology on clearly demarcated occupations: therefore both ignore the work of many in society. The sociology of professions tends to be concerned with the pre-occupations of professionals themselves (e.g. what are the 'attributes' of a profession?) and the sociology of organisations rarely mentions workers. The label 'sociology of work' therefore is an attempt to counteract those tendencies. Not only so, a particular label may carry a perspective that the writer wishes to oppose. For example Esland and Salaman state: 'On the whole occupational sociology, with its emphasis on *occupation* rather than *work*, its commitment to a consensual model of society and focus on occupational *roles* with all the barrage of concepts that typically follow that conceptual orientation, seems unlikely to be able to consider the sorts of issues raised by the early theorists' ('Towards a Sociology of Work' in Esland, Salaman and Speakman, 1975, p. 24). Somewhat similar objections are raised in connection with the sociology of the professions and organisations. The choice of the label then becomes a strategic choice and the writer may implicitly or explicitly explicate his concepts against the available alternatives and, like a good examination candidate, giving his reasons. In a way this is like abandoning territory to the enemy. It is also possible to say 'This is good territory, let's repossess it'. That I think characterises Johnson's book on the professions

(Johnson, 1972) and Silverman's book on organisations (Silverman, 1970). The aim is to challenge prevailing orientations and offer an alternative perspective. This is something which needs to be reckoned with as well.

If the sub-division of the subject does not result in a loss of the sense of society as interconnected, then we would expect some kind of recognition that what is accomplished in one sphere may be relevant for another or even dependent upon another. There is some evidence that this kind of awareness exists. For example, Tunstall (1970) presents a Reades which integrates mass media and leisure. This is scarcely surprising given the amount of leisure time which people in industrial societies spend watching television and listening to the radio. Parker (1971, 1975, 1976) takes the view that the sociology of leisure is complementary to the sociology of work: work and leisure take on their meaning in relation to each other. Moore (1971) claims: 'A sociology of knowledge is a pre-condition of the sociology of race relations and a pre-condition of all sociology' (p. 99). So we can see here indications of overlap complementarily and dependence as between different sub-divisions.

When one comes to consider the range of sub-divisions in sociology, a somewhat curious feature emerges. Writing from inside their respective specialist focus, there is a tendency to suggest that their sub-division is not well connected with the 'mainstream'. The reasons given vary to some extent, but the phenomenon is worth illustrating and commenting upon. Bernstein refers to the neglect of the study of speech by sociologists ('A Socio-linguistic Approach to Learning', in Bernstein, vol. 1, 1971):

> The origins and consequences of forms of saying, linguistic forms, their conditions, formal patterning, regulative functions, their history and theory are not included in the sociologists' analysis. And yet long ago both Durkheim and Weber drew attention to the social significance of language.
>
> (p. 119)

He continues:

> Sociologists have studied the major complexes of social forms which shape the social order, their inter-reactions, and the factors responsible for their shape. Language is seen as an integrating or divisive phenomenon; as the major process through which a culture is transmitted; the bearer of social genes. However, this has rarely given rise to a study of language as a social institution comparable to the analyses made of, say, the family, religion, etc.
>
> (p. 119)

Here the view put forward is that what should be a central area of sociological inquiry and is formally recognised by sociologists to be such is insufficiently studied. But what about religion and the family, to which he refers by way of contrast? David Martin, in an amusing but seriously intentioned paper, wrote of the sociology of religion as a case of status deprivation (Martin, 1966):

> As one of the mainstream practitioners put it to me: do you have a real subject? . . . Nobody supposes that an interest in industrial sociology creates a problem (apart from the boredom of organisation 'theory') but to care about religious phenomena argues an abnormality, an intellectual perversion. In other words the sociologist of religion is an academic deviant living by a non-existent subject!
>
> (op. cit., p. 354)

Obviously Martin could appeal to Durkheim and Weber as Bernstein did for language to argue the centrality of religion as an object of study. But one can see that in practice he does not feel able to identify it with mainstream sociology. The sociologist of religion on this reading is seen as on the edge of the stream.

When we turn to the sociology of the family this is offered as another example of status deprivation in relation to mainstream sociology by Allen and Barker (1976):

> In this area it might be expected that work on gender relationships would be the most advanced and the theory most critical. However, it suffers from a marked lack of status in British sociology, deriving from its lack of 'theory' — except for Parsonian functionalism, its concern with the non-work/non-market area of social activity and its attention to women and children.

The low status is here linked with what is regarded as a low theoretical input. A very similar point is made about the sociology of race relations; Zubaida (1970) and Rex (1973) regard it as a field neglected by sociologists (as Bernstein claims is language). Lockwood (in Zubaida, 1970) points out (p. 57) that: 'Despite the dominating importance of the racial problem in both national and international affairs, the concept of race has not played a central role in the development of modern social theory.' The lack of theoretical integration with general sociological theory and the tendency to separate race relations from their general social context so far as sociology in Britain is concerned is likewise argued by Moore (1971). This all builds up to a sense of the neglect of the topic (despite its social problem characterisation), the lack of 'theory' and again its separation from the 'mainstream'.

No less surprising is the case of urban sociology in this self-depreciating down-grading activity. Mellor (1975), for example, considers that sociologists generally have little interest in urban affairs, even though there is widespread comment, public and political on the 'urban problem'. Pahl (1975) if anything puts the point (p. 198) more strongly: 'We have a situation in Britain today where students read in the newspapers of the urban crisis, the urban programme and the need for urban renewal but are told in the lecture hall that urban sociology does not exist.' The subject is not responding to the challenge of felt public need. Urban sociology like the sociology of religion is appaently denied valid existence. These views would appear to emanate from fellow professional sociologists. This is similar to Parker's (1975) observation on attitudes to the sociology of leisure. Just as urbanism may be seen as having a dependent status in the social structure, so too may leisure. Just as religion may be regarded as peripheral to more 'serious' concerns of the sociologist, so too may leisure.

Laments in other areas may be likewise located. The sociology of literature is 'analytically vague' and does not seem to have got off the ground according to Forster and Kinneford (1973). The sociology of education is 'one of the major examples of an area of enquiry in which both explicit "theory" and theoretical debate have been noticeably absent' (Young, 1971). Crewe, editing the first *Yearbook of Political Sociology* (1974) takes the view that British political sociology as an organised academic activity can hardly be said to exist. Reviewing the book Susanne Wood said 'The essays . . . do not unite around a coherent body of theory or set of concepts' (*BJS*, vol. XXVI, no. 1, 1975, p. 131).

One might have supposed that, with the growth of interest in the sociology of deviance over the past decade in Britain, such comments as those already noted might not be found. Indeed, given that deviance is about rule infraction it has some in-built colonising tendencies. Political, industrial, religious deviance are obviously all grist for the mill as well as criminal behaviour and law-breaking. Nonetheless the cry goes up: 'The boundary between orthodox sociology and the sociology of deviance has retained rigidity and impermeability. While it might be a matter of professional shame for a sociologist to be ignorant of the sociologies of religion, politics or development, a bland indifference is often displayed towards the social analysis of rule-breaking' (Rock and McIntosh, 1974, p. xii). In the light of preceding opinions one might suppose (*pace* Rock and McIntosh) that professional shame amongst sociologists is a scarce commodity! It is worth noting Rock and McIntosh's own labelling activities embodied in the juxtaposition of orthodox sociology and the sociology of deviance. It suggests a solidarity, a cohesion and exclusiveness which constrains the study of deviance to the margins. The difficulty, however, is in locating this 'orthodoxy' or 'mainstream'.

The question of the relation between 'theory' and the specialist sociologies has already been touched upon but may be pursued a little further. The issue of 'theory' appears in slightly different forms.

1. One may argue for the importance of empirical studies in particular areas as a necessary condition of theory development: 'The sociology of religion, and perhaps any other sort of sociology, is only as good as the first hand empirical studies, historical and contemporary, permit it to be. Such studies need not, of course, be themselves sociological, but they are a pre-requisite for any analysis and theory which is more than mere word-spinning' (Wilson, 1967, p. 303). This stresses the area — religion — as the object of theory.

2. One may claim that a particular field has been dominated by 'rigid empiricism' and that this has been at the expense of 'theory'. Hence, for example, one may have many readership surveys but no adequate sociology of literature. The volume of work accomplished in any area would not of itself tell us about the theoretical developments. Thus Mellor, writing of urban sociology, notes that there has been 'an accumulation of raw data in planning studies and historical monographs, but without any attempt to pull them together into . . . comparative study' (Mellor, 1975, p. 290).

3. The view may be propounded that 'theory' is impeded where a specialism is swayed by policy questions. The concern with immediate or short-term answers to problems may also be associated with a notion of rigid empiricism. Criticisms of this form have been made, for example, in the race relations field, as we have seen.

4. At the same time the point has been made by Peter Townsend that the study of social policy as such concerns itself with 'the means whereby societies prevent, postpone, introduce and manage changes in structure' (Townsend, 1975, p. 2). His view is that such study is essential to the development of adequate theories of social change. He suggests that in so far as 'social problems' have usually had any theoretical underpinning they have been over-generalised and inadequate versions of functionalism. Townsend's view is not really to be seen as opposed to that in the previous paragraph. The study of social policy does not have to be based on a client relationship and therefore does not have to take the 'problem' as a given to be solved in the terms that the policy-definers lay down.

5. The notion 'inadequate theory' comes up from time to time as in the preceding paragraph. It also was represented in Allen and Barker's comment on the sociology of the family. In both cases as it happens the objection was to 'functionalist theory'. The implication as I understand it is that such theory is in the nature of the case bound to be inadequate because of its over-emphasis and pre-occupation with concensus and equilibriating processes and insufficient appreciation of conflicts of interests and factors promoting change.

6. Another way of approaching the relationship between sociological theory and 'special sociologies' is to argue that the major concern of sociological theory is with the problem of order. How is society

possible? One then considers how far particular specialisms have concerned themselves with this question. This it may be held will serve as a check on the theoretical input. Thus Young maintains that serious theoretical debates may be located in the fields of stratification, deviance, politics and organisations but not in education. He continues: 'The major contemporary debates among sociologists about "functionalist" and "conflict" models and "structural" and "interactionist" levels of explanation hardly make their appearance' (Young, 1971, p. 1). Whether or not this is a correct view of the sociology of education may be contested. But the need is to recognise that there are approaches to theory which have been developed at a general level of discourse to guide and inform the conduct of studies in particular areas. What is implied is that the object of investigation is *society* and that particular pre-occupations in selected spheres must throw some light on the interconnections of the spheres with each other. At the same time particular perspectives, such as system or action approaches may be utilised as selected topics are analysed. This is a point emphasised by Parker (1975) in his discussion of the sociology of leisure.

7. A good summary statement, made in connection with the sociology of religion, but having more general application in my view is given by David Martin (1966, p. 359). It touches on the relationship between the particular and the general in sociology, the theoretical and the empirical and the different approaches that may be taken in sociological study:

> The defining characteristic of sociology ought to be a special tension beteen a critical attitude to the broad frameworks available and an imaginative approach to sheer data. Neither the unexamined frameworks nor the watertight empirical compartment are satisfactory . . . We cannot live in sealed off compartments but it is the task of sociology and of the sociology of religion in particular to think in terms of dialectic and synthesis.

As a coda to the above discussion I append five figures (Figures 4.1—4.5). The first is the simplest. It suggests a straightforward interchange between general sociological theory and each special sociology (education, industry, etc.). If only everyone would agree on a common framework — Parsonian, Marxist or whatever — that would be that. The second figure reminds us that there are competing sociological theories. It suggests that each might impinge on the special sociologies. Whether or not they are differently utilised by the sub-areas would be a matter for inquiry.

The third figure adds to the notion of competing sociological theories by drawing attention to other disciplines. Psychology and economics serve in an illustrative way here — others could be added or substituted. They also have competing general theories which permeate

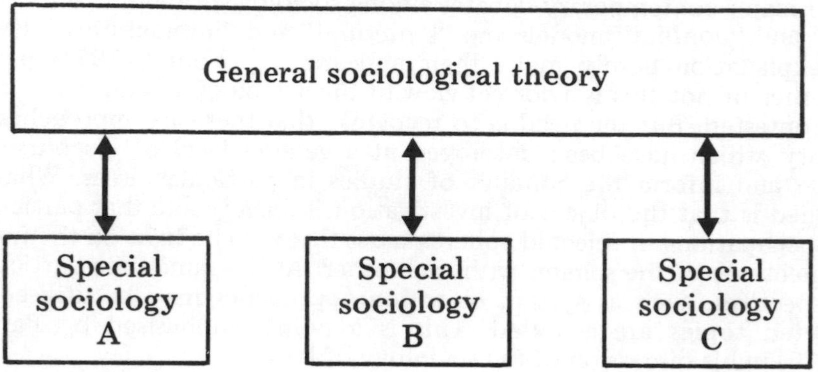

Figure 4.1

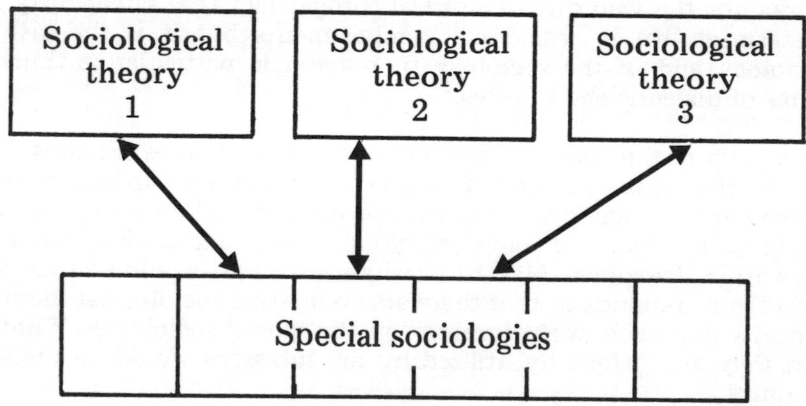

Figure 4.2

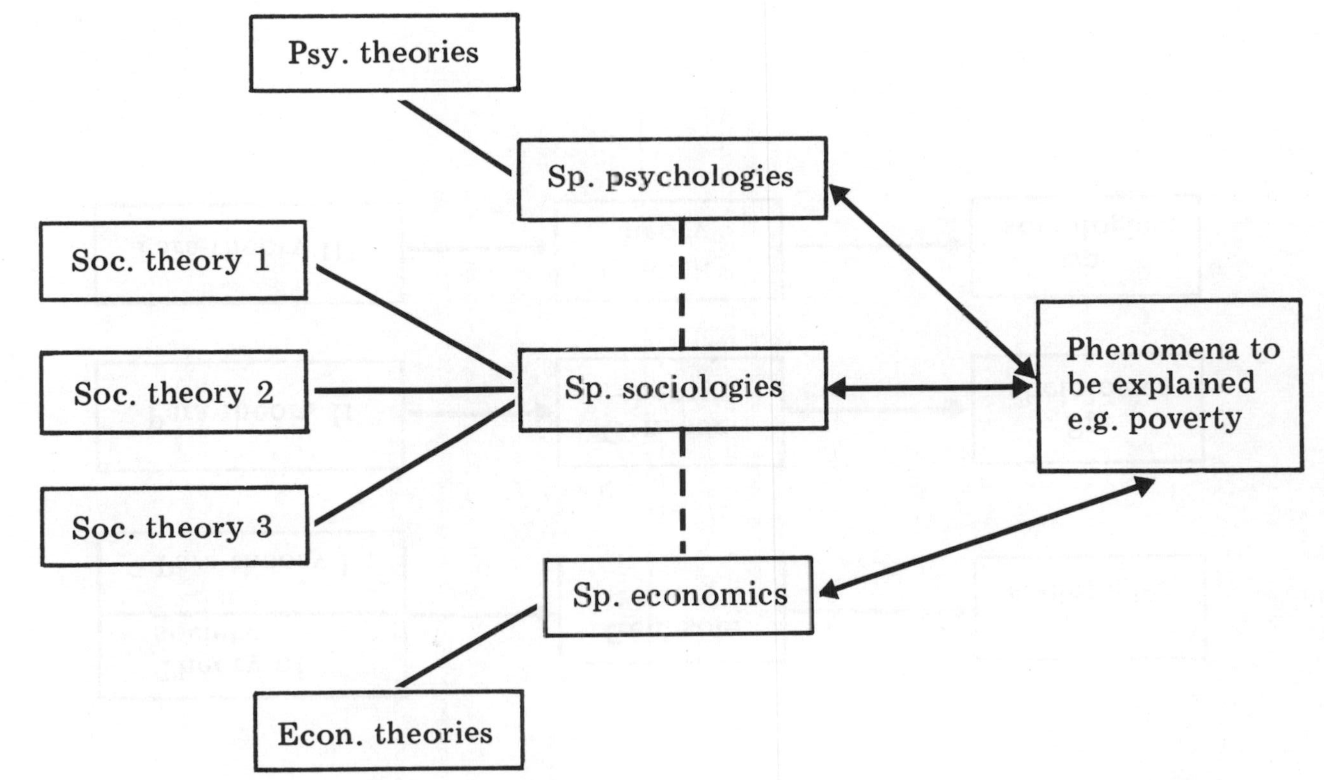
Psy. theories
Sp. psychologies
Soc. theory 1
Soc. theory 2
Soc. theory 3
Sp. sociologies
Phenomena to
be explained
e.g. poverty
Sp. economics
Econ. theories

Figure 4.3

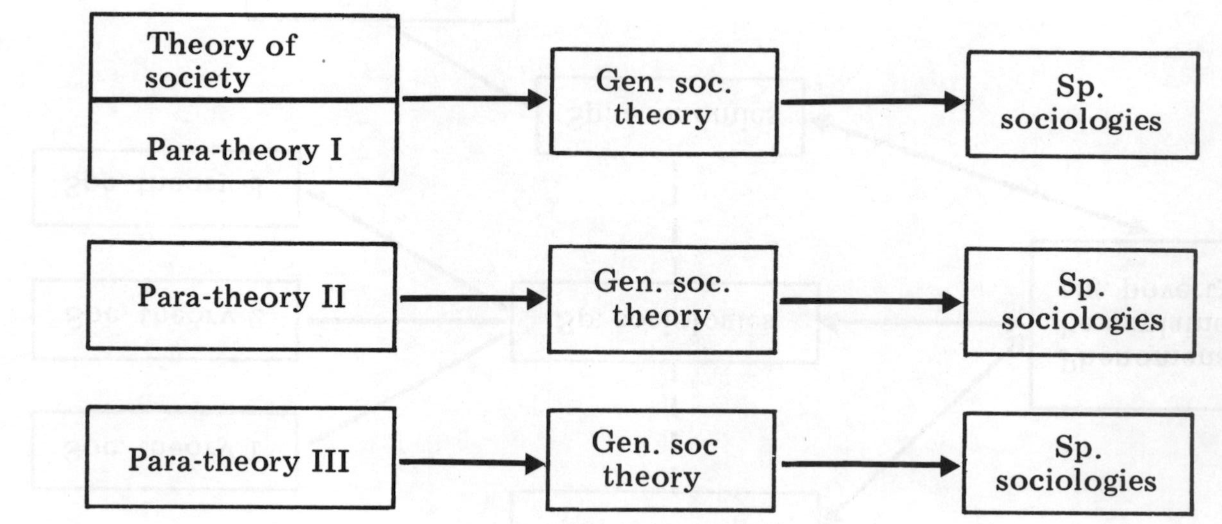
Theory of society
Para-theory I
Gen. soc. theory
Sp. sociologies
Para-theory II
Gen. soc. theory
Sp. sociologies
Para-theory III
Gen. soc theory
Sp. sociologies

Figure 4.4

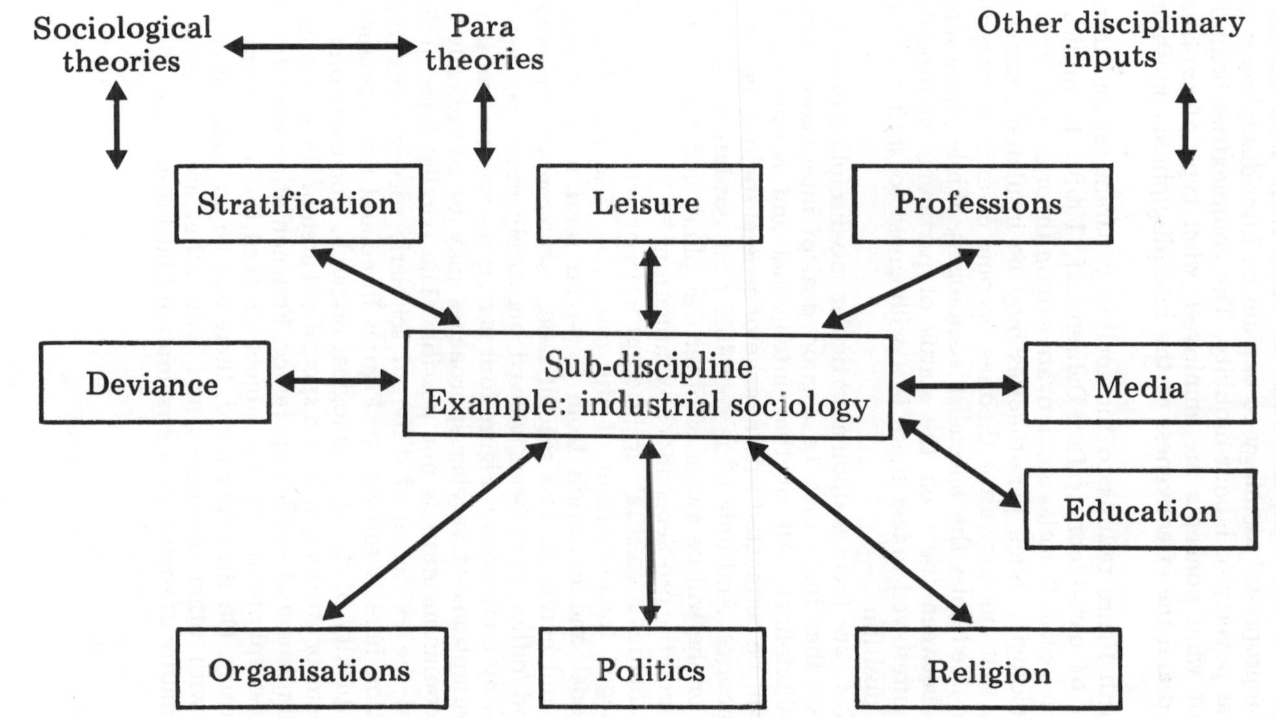
Sociological theories
Para theories
Other disciplinary inputs
Stratification
Leisure
Professions
Deviance
Sub-discipline
Example: industrial sociology
Media
Education
Organisations
Politics
Religion

Figure 4.5

their specialisms. Attempts are made to bring them into relationship with the 'appropriate' sociology to explain an inter-disciplinary 'problem' such as poverty or labour mobility. The complexities behind that in terms of what concepts are employed, what type of explanation propounded and the effectiveness of the inter-disciplinary meshing are enormous.

The fourth figure returns to the sociology parameter and turns on the notion of para-theory (after Dahrendorf, 1968). It implies that general sociological theories are derivative upon theories of society held by the sociologist. Such para-theories may be insulated against each other such that the derivative theories become co-existing paradigms. These then feed into the specialist sociologies. While there may be arguments between them on the status of particular methodologies these are unresolved unless there is a willingness to shift one's para-theoretical position.

The fifth figure focuses upon a particular sub-discipline in sociology. This suggests that there may be a good deal of interchange between other sub-disciplines. All of that intellectual and research activity, however, will be permeated with a range of general sociological theories and para-theories. And unless the sociologist has got into a disciplinary cocoon he or she will be aware of other disciplines and their inputs as they bear upon the problems under examination.

The five figures suggest rather different ways of defining and evaluating the alleged fragmentation of the discipline. The first figure is a unitary model and deviation from it would tend to be defined as schismatic and heretical. The second recognises competition between theories and rather than being viewed negatively could be seen as a sign of healthy controversy. Figure four carries the implication that the domain assumptions of varying approaches may be so radically different that communication is not possible. The parallel lines in figure four suggest the existence of different scholarly speech communities. Fragmentation here is separation. Figures three and five represent the untidy complexity of doing sociological research. Focussing on a particular problem or working within a specialised area of the discipline can become a limiting and sterile experience. Fragmentation would then be a meaningless splintering of the subject or even the loss of any disciplinary identity. On the other hand, there can be an imaginative interplay both with other disciplines and with other areas of sociology. It is to the nature of sociological imagination that I now turn.

PART II ALL THINGS NEW?

'The history of the social sciences is and remains a continuous process passing from the attempt to order reality analytically through the construction of concepts — the dissolution of the analytical constructs so constructed through the expansion and shift of the scientific horizon — and the reformulation anew of concepts of the foundations thus transformed. It is not the error of the attempt to construct conceptual systems *in general* which is shown by this process — every science, every single descriptive history, operates with the conceptual stock-in-trade of its times. Rather, this process shows that in the cultural sciences concept-construction depends on the setting of the problem, and the latter varies with the content of the culture itself. The relationship between concept and reality in the cultural sciences involves the transitoriness of all such syntheses. The great attempts at theory construction in one science were always useful for recording the limits of the significance of those points of view which provided their foundations. The greatest advances in the sphere of the social sciences are substantively tied up with the shift in practical cultural problems and take the guise of a critique of concept construction.'

Max Weber,
Objectivity in Social Science and Social Policy

5 A NEW SOCIOLOGY? CATCHING THE MILLSIAN IMAGINATION

In 1960 sociology in Britain was beginning to spread into a number of universities. In addition to the LSE the subject was taught already in various places including Birmingham, Edinburgh, Leeds, Leicester, Liverpool and Nottingham. The decade that followed was to see the new universities give plenty of room for what was to prove, for a period, a fashionable subject. Essex, Kent, Lancaster, Sussex and York were all cases in point.

In the 1940s and 1950s C. Wright Mills produced a number of books and many articles. Some of these were to become very well known to sociologists and to a wider reading audience. In 1959 he gave a series of talks on the BBC under the general heading 'Culture and Politics'. In 1969 he was visiting professor at the LSE. In 1962 he died at the age of 46. Yet the imprint of his influence, both direct and indirect, remains and not least in Britain. There are various reasons for this, some I suppose more obvious than others.

Mills stood foursquare for the sociological enterprise. It was for him a vocation. *The Sociological Imagination* (1959) saw him fighting for the cause: challenging those who occupied the territory in the American sociological establishment. The 'abstract empiricists' and the 'grand theorists' were brought to ironic account. Accusations of triviality, pretentious jargon, parochialism, a neglect of history, unreflective use of methods and narrowness of vision were made. He was calling social scientists to repentance:

> All classic social scientists have been concerned with the salient characteristics of their time — and the problem of how history is being made within it: with 'the nature of human nature' — and the variety of individuals that come to prevail within these periods. Marx and Sonbart and Weber, Comte and Spencer, Durkheim and Veblen, Mannheim, Schumpeter and Michels, each in his own way has confronted these problems. In our immediate times, however, many social scientists have not. Yet it is precisely now, in the second half of the twentieth century, that these concerns become urgent as issues, persistent as troubles, and vital for the cultural orientation of our human studies. (op. cit., p. 165)

Mills always conveyed this double sense of the living tradition of social science which could be creatively developed and the recognition that new problems confronted new generations and called for an imaginative response. His own work was grounded in the tradition. Weberian themes of bureaucracy, Marxist theories of class and the elitist theories of Mosca and Pareto are all critically reconstructed. It is this active theorising on new materials which make studies like *The Power Elite* (1956), *White Collar* (1951) and *The New Men of Power* (1948) still worth reading.

Mills's sociology of power and his substantive studies of its facets — in politics, the military, the business corporation, the unions and the media — showed how sociology might be practised. It was an alternative to Parsonian sociology. Although often pessimistic in his judgements Mills was guided by a humanistic concern — he sought to understand the conditions in which people could be agents rather than victims of history. Despite his pessimism and his awareness of the fateful forces in history that restrict human choice, there is residual hope. The future for Mills is not structurally determined: 'We study history to discern the alternatives within which human reason and human freedom can now make history. We study historical social structures, in brief, in order to find within them the ways in which they are and can be controlled. For only in this way can we come to know the limits and the meaning of human freedom' (*The Sociological Imagination*, p. 174).

It is not difficult to see the affinity between Mills's humanistic sociology and the ethos of the New Left in Britain — Marxists, who, despite the horrors of Stalinism, continued to believe in the possibility of socialism with a human face. Mills's analysis of the Cold War as a form of 'crackpot realism', his critique of elite domination and militarism in the East and West, his support for the Cuban Revolution, and his discussion of consumerism in the West, found a receptive audience. Within this orbit of the New Left were scholars in the social sciences, history and cultural studies who have themselves made substantial contributions to social theory or historical studies. T. Bottomore, S. Hall, A. MacIntyre, R. Miliband, J. Rex and E.P. Thompson are cases in point.

Mills's paper 'The New Left' (first published in *New Left Review*, September 1960 and reprinted in *Power Politics and People*, 1963) is a useful point of reference. He attacks the 'end of ideology' thesis as proclaimed by the Congress of Cultural Freedom in Milan in 1955 and relayed by *Encounter* magazine. It actually consists, Mills claims, of a group of Western intellectuals who have given up their commitment to socialism and replaced it by another ideology — that of the mixed economy and the welfare state — which, they assume is the road to prosperity. In their support for the world as it now is Mills portrays them as the mirror image of the socialist realist intellectuals of the Soviet Union.

His remarks addressed to colleagues on the left are perhaps even more interesting. In particular his doubts as to whether the working class can be regarded as the historic agency of change are not disguised. What was once an historically grounded hope in Marx has now become ahistorical and unspecific. His general view is that only in the early stages of industrialisation in a political context of autocracy do wage workers tend to become a class-for-themselves. Mills, in 1960, looks to the young intelligentsia as an agency for radical change in the first, second and third worlds. Against the complacency of the end of ideology intellectuals he looks to the young intelligentsia to develop a movement 'out of apathy'. I should make clear that Mills's essay by no means encompasses the end of ideology debate. A convenient summary of much of this debate, including contributions from leading figures such as Aron, Shils, Lipset, Bell, Horowitz, Harrington, as well as Mills, is to be found in Chaim I. Waxman (ed.), *The End of Ideology Debate* (1968).

Mills's 1958 BBC talks in similar fashion to his New Left essay called for intellectuals to repossess their own cultural apparatus and use it to show the Cold War establishment views of the world do not exhaust the possibilities for the future:

> The thing to do with our own alienation is to stop whining about it long enough to use it in the formulation of radical critiques and audacious programmes. If we do not do these things who will? We should conduct a continuing and uncompromising criticism and we should do so from standpoint of explicitly utopian ideals if need be. Unless we do this, we have no chance to offer alternative definitions of reality. And that of course is our major business. If we as intellectuals do not define and re-define reality, who will?
>
> ('The Decline of the Left', *Listener*, 2 April 1959, p. 548)

These alternative definitions of reality were to be developed and to become more widely available in the 1960s and to become embodied in new social movements: the civil rights movement and later the women's movement; in opposition to the Vietnam war; in the events of May 1968 which moved the immovable de Gaulle; and in the Prague Spring which did not move Breznhev, only his tanks.

Mills was not a Marxist in any orthodox sense of the term. I think this comes out clearly enough in his book *The Marxists* (1963). There he questions Marx's labour metaphysics — the view that the working class is the historic agency of change in capitalist societies — and concludes that there are theoretical deficiencies in his categories and in his general model of capitalism. He does not pull his punches:

> Behind the labour metaphysics and the erroneous views of its supporting trends there are deficiencies in the marxist categories of stratification; ambiguities and mis-judgments about the psychological and political consequences of the development of the economic base;

errors concerning the supremacy of economic causes within the history of societies and the mentality of classes; inadequacies of a rationalist psychological theory; a generally erroneous theory of power; an inadequate conception of the state.

(Penguin edn., p. 127)

Yet Mills still felt able to conclude that Marx's method was 'a signal and lasting contribution to the best sociological ways of reflection and inquiry available' (p. 128). Even Marx's errors and theoretical inadequacies were fruitful. But his work constitutes a beginning and not a sacred text as we try to understand our world today. So, for example, Mills argued, following Weber, that one must look not only at changing forms of economy and their effect on the distribution of power but also on the ways in which military organisation, bureaucratic administration, political struggle and the means of communication have their effects. One should not assume that the analysis of economy suffices to tell us what are the implications for the rest of society, even in capitalist societies. It is an important part of method, but the possibility that other spheres of social life, such as the military or the political, may operate autonomously has to be recognised and not ruled out by fiat.

This kind of position accomplished several things in my view, so far as the future development of sociology is concerned. It trades on a view of a living tradition in which writers such as Marx and Weber were treated as inspirational but not infallible. On the Marxist side Mills, in his rejection of economic determinism, strengthened the voluntaristic version which was to become associated with a renewed interest in 'the young Marx'. Alongside this goes the requirement to re-examine the appropriateness of the base-superstructure metaphor in Marx. In so far as a question mark was put against the usefulness of the distinction or it was dissolved by a thousand qualifications, fresh analyses involving conceptual, empirical and theoretical reformulations are called forth. It is the kind of thing one can observe in Herbert Marcuse and Alvin Gouldner, both of whom acknowledged very explicit intellectual debts to Mills.

Marcuse's *Soviet Marxism* (1958) parallels Mills's *Power Elite* (1956) although it is not especially dependent upon it. But it does involve a severe critique of the Soviet state. He argues, for example, that the base-superstructure distinction can be used for ideological purposes and that social realism in the Soviet Union must be so understood: it negates human freedom and conforms to the pattern of the repressive state. In *One Dimensional Man* (1964) he makes clear that Mills's work is highly relevant to his thesis. Similarly Gouldner, in *The Coming Crisis of Western Sociology* (1970), is highly critical of Soviet sociology and regards it as an unacceptable form of social engineering. In other words, such sociology does not make room for alternative definitions of reality which can question the working assumptions of the society in which it operates. In later essays, Gouldner, like Mills, reveals a double-edged attitude to Marxism. His essay 'The Two Marxisms' (in *For Sociology*, 1973) questions the historical agency of the working class in terms similar to Mills. And in his most recent study *The Future of Intellectuals and the Rise of the New Class* (1979) he develops this position and indeed labels himself a left neo-Hegelian.

It is in *The Dialectic of Ideology and Technology* (1976) that Gouldner (p. xiv) makes explicit his relationship to Mills's intellectual position on Marxism. 'At its most fundamental levels, my standpoint remains very much that of C. Wright Mills whose own radicalism and reflexivity was never expressed as a commitment to Marxism.' Gouldner describes himself as a Marxist outlaw, holding that even Marxism must be subject to critique. This uncomfortable position is reckoned by Gouldner to be important precisely because Marxism today, considered as a real historical movement, has not produced the human liberation it promised. However, in place of the Cold War when Mills was writing, Gouldner refers to the more recent period of *detente* between the USA, the USSR and China and suggests that this undermines still further the demystifying role of Marxism. For reasons of *detente*, it is argued, 'a powerful sector of the Marxist community throughout the world is disposed to repress or modify definitions of social reality at variance with the maintenance of that alliance' (op. cit., p. xiii). The task of the Marxist outlaw is to hold to the critical method which has its antecedents in Gouldner's view in the Socratic method. To apply it to Marxism and to the practical outworkings of Marxism is, as Gouldner puts it, to explore the dark side of the dialectic. 'Only those who can move without joining packaged tours of the world can afford such a journey' (op. cit., p. xvi).

Within the British context one can see the way in which writers in the New Left mould have created space to do their own scholarly work — mindful of Marx, but prepared to amend, to reconsider and to subject to critical scrutiny Marx's own work. This is very evident in the writing of Tom Bottomore. In his latest study, *Karl Marx* (1979), he makes damaging criticisms of Marx's theory of social classes. 'It is plain enough', he writes, 'that the growth of working class consciousness in the most advanced capitalist countries during the twentieth century has not followed the course that Marx anticipated, at least in his earlier writings' (p. 26). Bottomore is sceptical of much that is done in the name of Marxist theory, sensing the emergence of new dogmatics and sterile methodological disputations. He takes the view that there are no empirical Marxist studies that approach anything like the stature of *Capital*. He contemplates (p. 41) a possible way forward, but one that is surrounded by doubt:

Only as the inspiration of a 'critical outlook' not as a science of

> society, does it [Marx's thought] seem to bear upon the real features of social development in the present age. If the intention of Marx's thought can properly be interpreted (and this is my own view) as the foundation of a general social science — a sociology, then it must be said that this Marxist sociology has still to be constructed. *The task may prove impossible and may lead in the end to a scheme of thought quite different from Marxism* [my italics J.E.T.E.] and if the construction is to be attempted at all a profound re-orientation of Marxist thought as it now exists will be needed.

Notwithstanding Bottomore's strictures, one of the things that can be detected in British sociology, among those with a critical respect for Marx, is the attention this is paid to the superstructure of society. If the relative autonomy of law, culture, politics and the state is recognised, then what takes place in those spheres is worthy of investigation in its own right. Raymond Williams's treatment of the base-superstructure problem and his cultural analysis is an important example. His interest in the dynamic relationships of art, literature and systems of communication with man's productive activity has led to a series of impressive studies including *Culture and Society* (1958), *The Long Revolution* (1961) *Communications* (1962) and *The Country and the City* (1973). Similarly the work of Stuart Hall and his colleagues in cultural studies can be cited. *Policing the Crisis* (1978) is perhaps the most developed example of the genre. And in the field of political sociology Miliband's *The State in Capitalist Society* (1973) is very much in the spirit and tradition of *The Power Elite*.

Mills's pivotal influence also has to be understood in terms of his Weberian scholarship. This is most clearly evidenced through the book edited with Hans Gerth, *From Max Weber* (1948). This book has now been widely read and used by successive generations of students in Britain. The illuminating introductory essay presents a view of Weber that emphasises the ways in which his work amplifies that of Marx. In particular, the approach of Weber to the analysis of social stratification is highly commended and Weber's essay 'Class, Status and Party', included in the collection, has become a standard reference. The role of political action, the relationship of ideas to interests and social action, are central themes in Gerth and Mills's discussion of Weber. All in all it adds up to a formidable sociology of power. One can see the unmistakable contours of this approach in the work of British sociologists such as Lockwood, Rex, Goldthorpe, Runciman, Giddens and Parkin, most of whom I judge would not be unhappy to call themselves neo-Weberians. In Rex's work particularly, one senses an intellectual sympathy with Mills. *Sociology and the Demystification of the Modern World* (1974) is very much a book in the Mills mould. Rex frequently cites Mills and even has an essay entitled 'Public Issues and Private Troubles', which is a commentary and an 'updating of Mills's original essay on this theme.

In the early 1960s two edited collections were published and dedicated to Wright Mills: *The New Sociology* (1964) edited by Irving Horowitz and *Sociology on Trial* (1963) edited by Maurice Stein and Arthur Vidich. The second of these had an American audience primarily in mind but the book arrived on the scene as sociology was about to be pursued on a large scale in the new British universities. From the United States, where the subject had been established in the universities for many years, came the warning against turning the activity into just another profession, against being too willing to take up 'practical' projects that the critical edge of the subject is blunted: 'Simply by presenting radically different perceptions of a world that is otherwise taken for granted, society is irked, irritated and perhaps threatened as well. Analysis exposes the glue that holds the joints of society together and it forces people to view themselves within what is at best a fairly precarious social order' (p. 1).

This re-examination of the taken-for-granted world could of course serve as something of a slogan for sociology by quite diverse practitioners of the subject, and certainly not only Marxists. Peter Berger's delightful and witty *Invitation to Sociology* (1963) stands alongside Marxism as a radical phenomenological critique of society and has been widely read in the Penguin edition in Britain.

Sociology on Trial consists in part of an attack on the predominant forms of sociology in the USA, where Parsons and Lazarsfeld are seen as representative figures. So warning bells are sounded which certainly reach the ears of young British sociologists: do not treat the prevailing orthodoxy of American sociology as the mature specimen to which the subject in Britain should aspire. It is important to add that the suggestions as to what sociology should be like were not all of a piece and were not intended to be. *Sociology on Trial* was certainly not a monolithic take over bid for the subject but rather a call for some of the self-imposed chains — conceptual, methodological and theoretical — to be cast off. Gouldner's article 'Anti-Minotaur: the Myth of a Value-Free Sociology' perhaps symbolised the mood. This was also printed in *The New Sociology* and has appeared in various other books of readings. The essay was a sharp reminder that value freedom in Weber is not to be equated with moral indifference. Interestingly, Gouldner draws attention to other strands in American sociology outside the Harvard and Columbia orbit, notably the Chicago school. He sees Howard Becker and Erving Goffman as significant contemporary representatives of this style of sociology. In a prophetic moment he suggests that Goffman may become the William Blake of sociology. Be that as it may both Goffman and Becker were very much in the thoughts of the 'new criminologists' who surfaced in Britain in the mid-1960s and whose work I will discuss later.

Alternative ways of doing sociology may be glimpsed once the metaphorical character of many of its concepts are re-called. This is brought about particularly well in Stein's essay 'The Poetic Metaphors of Sociology'. His point is that the concept of system has tended to dominate sociology to the exclusion of other concepts. The concept of system, he protests, is only one metaphor among others. The classical social theorists used it but they also responded more imaginatively to the demonic quality of history. Stein rejects a sociology that squeezes out history and has no room for drama. Yet the concept of system in its modern usage, he claims, has done just that: 'Viewed as an observational attitude, system implied orderliness, certitude, objectivity, detachment, neutrality and mechanical reproducibility. Viewed as a quality of objects being studied it suggests inter-connectedness, comprehensiveness, generalisability, and impersonality. It smothers all consciousness of the terrors and the thrills, the heights and depths that mark the concrete life of man in human society' (p. 173).

If one is able to use the system metaphor in the context of history and drama then, in Stein's view, this makes for a creative and imaginative sociology. And among the exemplars of this approach, alongside such writers as Paul Goodman, Herbert Marcuse and Hannah Arendt, he cites Raymond Williams. With the precarious but definite establishment of cultural studies in Britain, a conversation with sociology has begun. This has been mutually enriching. It is somewhat ironic in view of this heritage that some cultural studies contributors, having recently discovered Althusser, have discovered system with a vengeance and are in some danger of becoming ahistorical. But perhaps it will not endure for as Tennyson once put it 'our little systems have their day, they have their day and cease to be.'

Irving Horowitz, in his introductory essay in *The New Sociology*, makes clear that its newness has to be seen against prevailing tendencies in American sociology, whilst in reality it is in the intellectual tradition of classical sociology. It is a challenge to examine the master problems among which are cited the social costs and benefits of economic development, new nationalisms, varieties of socialist and capitalist societies, the relation of racial competition to democratic norms, the connection between industrial life and anomie, population and health, and international conflicts. The gauntlet (p. 23) is thrown down:

> A society cannot long endure scientific cant when there is better sociology being written in the popular press than in the professional journals. This is plainly an absurdity. What does one read to find out about problems of unemployment in West Virginia — of what happens to coal miners in an affluent society where oil and gas have replaced coal as a fuel source? Must we turn to the popular media for an analysis of the costs as well as the benefits of social change?

The collection of essays in *The New Sociology* is indeed wide ranging, including three by British authors — Miliband, Bottomore and

Worsley. Here however, I want to emphasise only one aspect of the collection. Mills himself was very interested in the 'underdeveloped' societies and their relationship with the advanced industrial societies of the world. Schematically this is reflected in his essay 'Culture and Politics' in *Power, Politics and People*, where he distinguishes between underdeveloped, properly developing and overdeveloped societies. The very act of reclassifying does tend to shift the frame of reference somewhat and the essay treats critically of overdeveloped societies, whereas in more conventional analyses of modernisation the likelihood is that they are defined as goals for the 'underdeveloped' to aim at. More extensively he wrote about Cuba, expressing a sympathy for the Cuban Revolution that made him very unpopular in his own country. One recalls this twenty years on as Castro, now an acknowledged leader of the Third World group of nations is warmly welcomed and applauded when he speaks to the United Nations Assembly in New York and when the United States's own Carribean and Latin American policies are looking extremely fragile and vulnerable. Mills's interest in the sociology of development touches on a field of study that is also involved in its own debate with Marxism, which I will discuss more fully subsequently. For the moment it is pertinent to observe that Mills's work on Cuba is nicely paralleled in Paul Baran's 'Reflections on the Cuban Revolution' in *The Longer View* (1969). Significantly, John O'Neill, in his editorial introduction to Baran's work entitles his essay 'Marxism and the Sociological Imagination'. In any event, Mills's interest in Latin America can be seen as having affinities and intellectual links with the work of Horowitz, Baran and Frank.

The sociology of development is still quite modest in accomplishment so far as British sociology is concerned, although there are some recent hopeful signs. But it is noteworthy that Worsley's essay in *The New Sociology* deals with a Third World theme — bureaucracy and decolonisation — although the principal illustration is the historical one of North Saskatchewan in North America. More important his book *The Third World* (1964) seems to me to constitute a large-scale sociology in the Mills style. Indeed he cites Mills's warning on abstracted empiricism and grand theory saying that the point applies equally to British sociology. The challenge is to think on the major movements of our time and so (p. ix) he sets his terms of reference accordingly: 'I am writing . . . to try and help stimulate a dialogue with those who become increasingly concerned with the central world-fact of the gulf between what, for shorthand, I have called Euro-America (i.e. *North* America) and the rest of the world. The only other problem of this scale of importance is the existence of the Bomb: a subject equally untouched by orthodox sociology.

I have been arguing that Mills's work serves as a signpost for sociology at the beginning of the 1960s just as British academic sociology was expanding. It suggested alternative ways of doing sociology that dissented from pevailing forms of academic sociology in the USA. His work provided a stimulus to rediscover classical sociology, whilst at the same time calling for an analysis of contemporary problems. Critical in spirit, Mills's studies ranged over a number of substantive areas of sociology and a variety of topics. There were sufficient affinities with both Marx and Weber in Mills to provide encouragement to neo-Marxists and neo-Weberians. He conveyed a fresh sense of the possibilities of a truly historical sociology as against descriptive functionalism and he gave a different emphasis to comparative sociology than that normally found within the evolutionary perspective.

It would be idle to pretend that the story of the 1960s and 1970s in British sociology was a triumphant celebration of the sociological imagination. I have suggested that there are notable traces and illustrations of this spirit. Alongside this, however, was a crisis of confidence and at times what looked dangerously like a failure of nerve: new forms of trivialisation, new expressions of dogmatism, new ahistorical analyses of society, coupled with a reluctance to do any actual research. The kind of 'new sociology' which Mills represented does have a generosity of spirit and vision that many of us could with benefit seek to recapture.

6 THE SOCIOLOGY OF ECONOMIC LIFE: A GROWTH INDUSTRY?

The development of industrial sociology in Britain

Industrial sociology is a well-established sociological specialism in Britain, in terms of teaching and research. I should like to offer some observations on the character of its development. These will not be in any strict chronology, but may serve as notes towards a sociology of knowledge.

Throughout the 1950s the two most conspicuous groups for industrial sociology were the Tavistock Institute and Liverpool University. The approaches of these two groups have been reviewed in two critical papers by Richard Brown ('Participation, Conflict and Change in Industry', *Sociological Review*, 1965, pp. 273-95; and 'Research and Consultancy in Industrial Enterprises', *Sociology*, vol. I, 1967, pp. 30-60.) What one finds in both instances is a focal interest in technology, its relationship to plant social structure and particularly the impact of technical change on the employees. In W. Scott *et al.*, *Technical Change and Industrial Relations* (1956), the reason for this interest is explicitly (pp. 5-6) indicated:

> The selection of technical change seemed to combined both theoretical and practical requirements. The technical organisation of production in a factory is therefore indispensable for the advancement of our basic knowledge of the social system of the plant; at the same time the maintenance and if possible the acceleration of the rate of technical progress in industry is generally considered to be one of Britain's main problems in the post-war years. Since resistances to change are to a large extent social in origin, it appeared that a study of technical change in relation to social structure might make a useful contribution to the development of industrial policy . . . We wished to access how a particular structure influenced attitudes to a possible or impending change and when a major change had been effected, to ascertain the consequent changes in structure and whether these had modified attitudes to change. In this way we hoped to throw light on the factors which by influencing attitudes promote and impede technical change.

This was a study which took hold of an issue that had come to be defined as a problem — the adaptation of workers to technical change — and seeking to provide information which, while it would not determine industrial or social policy was intended to be of relevance for policy-makers.

The topic of resistance to change, combined with a study of plant social structure, was one which had already been explored by American industrial sociologists. One could cite, for example, Roethlisberger and Dickson *Management and the Worker* (1939), Warner and Low *Social System of a Modern Factory* (1946), Walker's *Steeltown: an Industrial Case History of the Conflict between Progress and Security* (1950) and *Towards the Automatic Factory* (1957). The last two named were also located in the steel industry and the themes are very similar to that of the Liverpool study. The case-study approach also marks the American and British studies. Why did the Liverpool group adopt the case-study approach? Again (p. 10) they are admirably clear on the matter:

> In social research we are usually faced with a complex of many, an and not simply one or two, interacting factors. It is therefore important in the present state of knowledge to seek to unravel the complex to identify its component elements and to assess their relative significance in given conditions. Many studies have suffered from a premature endeavour to limit their scope to the analysis of one or two factors in a number of situations before the more significant variables have been defined, and thus it is possible with assurance to select certain factors to be studied and others to be 'controlled'.

The ordering of the case study was based on a straightforward treatment of the plant as a social system. Basically four categories were used: formal structure, informal structure, occupational structure and tradition. This commitment to a case-study approach with the plant as a social system was precisely the view located in George Homans's essay 'The Strategy of Industrial Sociology' in *Sentiments and Activities* (1962). This was his response to the question 'whether more enlightenment would be achieved by getting for a few plants some crude notion of the balance of many factors than by getting for many plants the correlation of a few factors, not necessarily the most important' (p. 265). The emphasis on the case-study approach and the plant conceptualised as a social system did not mean for the Liverpool researchers (or for Homans) that social factors outside the plant should be ignored. For example, in Scott's *Technical Change and Industrial Relations* the information is offered that a third of the melters in the plant when interviewed about their attitudes to the introduction of continuous shift working expressed dissatisfaction with the change, despite the fact that the actual number of hours worked per week declined. The explanation offered was in terms of the pattern of values associated with their leisure-time activities and particularly the significance of the weekend. Hence the loss of a weekend day was for such people not compensated by the gain of a weekday. This indeed is a good example of the idea of the social origins of resistance to change.

The Liverpool sociology department at this time was headed by T.S. Simey. The main research workers during the period in industrial sociology were W. Scott, J. Banks, O. Banks, T. Lupton and J. Woodward. To the subsequent work of J. Banks, Lupton and Woodward we must return. But apart from the intrinsic merit of the Liverpool studies one can see the situation as a seeding operation so far as British industrial sociology is concerned. The Tavistock Institute in its industrial research shared with the Liverpool researchers an enduring interest in technical change. The idea of socio-technical systems encapsulates a concern with linking together in a good 'fit' the employee's psychological needs and the organisation of tasks within a particulaar technological situation. Early examples of this genre are Rice's *Productivity and Social Organisation* and Trist and Bamforth's much quoted paper, 'Some Social and Psychological Consequences of the Longwall Method of Coal-Getting (*Human Relations*, vol. iv, 1951) which was a forerunner of *Organisational Choice: Capabilities of Groups at the Coal Face under Changing Technologies* (1963).

As with the Liverpool group, one can see the interest in the factors promoting or inhibiting productivity and one can also see the case-study method employed. In the Tavistock approach, however, consultancy is built in and the attempt is made to identify resistances to change with the aim of removing or modifying them. The focus is on the behaviour of small groups and distinctions are drawn between task groups and sentient groups and much attention is given to how these should be meshed together (the answer varies between 'early' and 'late' Tavistock). This interest in monitoring change and organisation design, which of course also characterised the Tavistock-inspired Glacier Project reflects a different attitude to research. It is client-orientated and this constitutes its relevance to policy. This leads to a collaborative relationship between client and researcher and serves as an early example of action research in British social science. Since the clients tended to be management groups the criticism was levelled from time to time that this was managerial sociology. So while the style and stance of the Tavistock research was different from the Liverpool group, its topic of interest was very similar. Both groups were interested in knitting together 'theory' and 'practice' but they interpreted the quest differently. However enough has been said here to set the scene on what follows as British industrial sociology expands its activities.

Let me turn next in the narrative to the Joan Woodward phenomenon. Having displayed an interest in technology and technical change, she was to pursue this in her South-West Essex study, the outline of findings being published in the DSIR research pamphlet

Management and Technology in 1958. The impact of this study on management studies, industrial relations and sociology was considerable. Why should this have been?

1. The work itself consisted of a survey of 203 manufacturing firms in South-East Essex. This extensive kind of inter-firm survey was a new departure for British sociologists. It was different from the one-off case studies of either Liverpool or Tavistock. This did not of course prevent Woodward from supplementing her survey findings with case-study material which she did more particularly in the full study *Industrial Organisation: Theory and Practice* (1965).

2. Technology (i.e. the collection of plant, machines, tools and recipes available at a given time for the execution of the production task and the rationale underlying their utilisation) is classified on a scale of increasing complexity: unit and small-batch production, large-batch and mass production, and process production. It is treated (*Management and Technology*, p. 4) as a critical variable in explaining organisation structure and behaviour': . . . technical methods were the most important factor in determining organisational structure and in setting the tone of human relationships inside the firms.' It appeared that different technologies imposed different kinds of demands on individuals and organisations, and that these demands had to be met through an appropriate form of organisation.

Among the factors associated with increasing technical complexity were: decreasing labour costs, increasing ratios of indirect labour, administrative and clerical staff to hourly paid workers, increasing proportion of graduates among supervisory staff and widening span of control of the chief executive. In other respects there were similarities between firms at either end of the technical complexity scale that contrasted with the centre (mass production). In the centre there was less evidence of worker autonomy and responsibility in task performance and smaller spans for first-line supervisory control.

Explicit in the Woodward approach was the suggestion that firms with given technologies might need to develop certain kinds of organisational arrangements if they were to be successful. This was of obvious practical interest to managers. Her work became treated as an effective demolition job on 'the one best way' of management myth. Principles of scientific management, the practice of which would lead to good management and successful business performance were directly challenged. The message permeated into technical colleges, business schools and management training courses. The social science alternative was that principles need to be be modified to meet cases. Indeed, instead of starting with the principle, one starts with the situation. But it was not just a matter of treating every case on its merits in an *ad hoc* way. Rather one could discern family resemblances between cases with similar technologies.

Here was something that social science could do for managers. It could replace arid abstract principles of management by a concrete situational approach which was more 'realistic'. It was also in some respects reassuring for managers. They could come to recognise that some of the 'problems' they faced were not unique to them, they were endemic to firms with particular kinds of technology. Furthermore this could diminish the scape-goating of managers when things went wrong. If certain problems are built into the structure and are endemic to that kind of technology then it is no use blaming Tom, Dick or Harry or even yourself. It is a 'given' that one simply has to recognise and come to terms with a part of the situation. So a given technology will imply certain kinds of organisation structures as being more appropriate than others. Within those structures there will be typical problems and points of friction that one may learn to expect and live with. To that extent managerial uncertainty is reduced.

3. The influence of Woodward's work on fellow sociologists has been varied and quite far-reaching.

(a) The typology of technology (whose scale of complexity was seen as mirroring the chronological development of industry towards increasing mechanisation and product standardisation) takes its place alongside comparable developmental classifications such as Blauner in *Alienation and Freedom* (1964) and Touraine *et al.* in *Workers Attitudes to Technical Change* (1965). I do not, however, see this as a central focus in Woodward's work as it is in the American and French contributions I have cited. However it perhaps served to reinforce views of the chemical industry as proto-typical of the future. Arguments about the industrial relations and class implications of this contention are noted in chapter 13 p. 181 ff.

(b) Work is undertaken broadly within the Woodward framework. An early example was Thurley and Hamblin, *The Supervisor and His Job* (DSIR, 1963). This was a study of 137 supervisors in 5 firms using the methods of direct observation and activity sampling. It was concluded that the importance given to such supervisory tasks as planning work, checking on work progress, dealing with production contingencies and reporting back to managers varied in different technological situations. But technology was not seen as the sole determining factor on supervisory behaviour; it was suggested that training affected supervisory styles ('autocratic'/'democratic'/'laissez faire') and management practices also affected supervisory practices. For a useful overview John Child's paper 'The Industrial Supervisor' (in Esland, Salaman and Speakman, *People and Work* 1975) may be consulted. As with *Management and Technology* such work could be seen to have lessons that could be drawn about supervisory training and went well beyond general presumptions about the appropriate role of the supervisor.

At the Industrial Sociology Unit, Imperial College, Woodward and her colleagues continued to consider the significance of technology in relation to organisation structure (Woodward, 1965; and Woodward (ed.), 1970). Three things occur which are instructive in that I suspect they are paralleled in other sociological research activities. First, if 'technology' is a variable affecting organisation structure and functioning then attempts may be made to refine the concept so that differential effects may be more precisely traced and measured. This is all the more tempting with a hardware concept like technology where precise definitions seem more possible to obtain. This is discussed in Woodward (1965) and attempts to make precise operational measurements of technology are spelled out in an instructive appendix. However we learn that 'a sustained attempt to measure technical variables was eventually abandoned. This gave rise to two developments: a broadening of the concept of technology, and a consideration of the concept of control' (Davies, Celia, Dawson, Sandra and Francis, Arthur, 'Technology and Other Variables: Some Current Approaches in Organisation Theory', in Woodward (ed.), 1973, p. 151). The quotation makes reference to the two other points I have in mind. The concept is broadened (p. 151), as opposed to being refined. This was primarily to take into account non-manufacturing organisations:

> Because of the overtones of manufacturing and machine tools that technology as a concept has, we now find it more useful to talk in terms of 'tasks'. For a working definition of task we have adopted Perrow's definition of technology, making it more flexible so as to include both 'doing' and 'thinking' tasks. Tasks then are the actions that an individual performs upon an object, or the thoughts applied to problems, with or without the aid of tools or machines, in order to make some changes in the object or solve the problems.

Certainly the definition is more elastic and presumably seeks to ease the way for comparative organisation studies not necessarily within the industrial sphere. The reference to 'thinking' and 'doing' reminds one however that objective and subjective elements occur in the definition. Indeed elements of belief systems and even ideology may be located. Actually this is also written into Woodward's definition of technology which, as we have seen, includes the notion of rationales for the utilisation of plant machines, tools and recipes for production. This may help to account for the difficulties of sharpening the variable when into the hard entity of technology beliefs and ideologies are written in.

The introduction of another concept — in this case 'control system' — is another way of trying to complete unfinished business. 'Two elements of the control system are salient for our attempts to explicate the link between task and structure. One is the making of decisions about the design and programming of the varying tasks involved in production. The other is ensuring that people actually do the work necessary to perform the programmed tasks' (Davies, Dawson and Francis, op. cit., p. 151). The control system (and predictably in this kind of conceptual activity the researchers go on to develop a typology of control systems) serves as an intervening variable between task and organisation structure. In particular it is suggested that the type of control system will influence the degree of uncertainty in the organisation. Again one can see the managerial implications. Just as the original typology of technical complexity was seen as increasing the measure of managerial understanding of organisations (as opposed to the formal management principles) so the intention of looking at control systems is to indicate which are the best fit for particular situations. The 'best fit' will obviously be those that reduce uncertainty. Although the concept of control system is derived from operations research it is clear from the definition that its expression, content and effectiveness will be based on the distribution of power in the organisation. Yet this does not itself surface as a central question for analysis. The political element in organisational life and the processes involved is in my opinion very muted in the Woodward framework. It is all rather bloodless. Yet in so far as this kind of study attempts to understand in order that managers may control uncertainty the existing distribution of power is taken as given. The significance of the relationship between power and uncertainty has of course been suggestively traced by Crozier in *The Bureaucratic Phenomenon* (1964).

(c) Work was also stimulated among researchers who saw Woodward's work as a challenge to develop organisation theory, but which entertained doubts as to the central role of technology in the analysis. This was not just a shift in emphasis as in the later work of the Industrial Sociology Unit but an alternative attempt to analyse organisational structure whilst acknowledging the stimulus of Woodward's work. It also accepted the organisation as the focus for analysis. I refer primarily to the work of Pugh, Hickson and colleagues.

What about the Aston school? We now have in book form a report on its work, Pugh and Hickson *Organisational Structure in its Context* (1976). After the first chapter, the rest of it consists of mildly edited versions of conceptual and empirical papers written in the 1960s (and in the main first published in the *Administrative Science Quarterly*).

Anyone who has met members of the Aston group will know with what energy and enthusiasm they went about their research. The account of the formation of the group in 1961 in what was Birmingham College of Advanced Technology, later the University of Aston, conveys this sense of seizing the opportunity to do pioneer work with both hands. Under the general guidance of Tom Lupton, who had a large research grant from the Human Sciences Committee of the DSIR, we learn that the four first researchers began 'in the basement of a condemned office block several hundred yards from the main college buildings. Its members sat with their desks touching one another, cramped in a small room with sky-lighting on to the pavement outside through which the wheels of Birmingham's city buses could be seen rolling by' (p. ix). We learn that the group appreciated this physical isolation. They had a sense of autonomy and purpose and all participated in the design and work of the project. It was in short a genuinely collective enterprise. One consequence was that the actual topic of research changed. From an initial purpose of looking at explanations of factory worker performance (Lupton's original interest and very well exemplified in *On the Shop Floor*), the focus shifted. 'The day came when it was realised that the worker worked in an organisation with a management control structure, and that this had not been included in the potential explanations'. This thought governed everything afterwards. With the conviction growing that 'no-one had any idea how to compare the structure of one organisation with that of another' the embryonic Aston school decided to remedy this forthwith. Bliss was it in that dawn to be alive!

Early on in the account we learn that the researchers came to think that the basic control structure of organisations has five primary dimensions: specialisation of activities, standardisation of procedures, formalisation of documentation, centralisation of authority and autonomy from any owning organisation. The first three of these, it is suggested, can be subsumed under the concept structuring of activities (which can be measured) and the last two under the concept concentration of authority. Before long we are invited to consider 'context'. Contextual factors may in various ways be related to structural factors. This however is not as one might suppose a consideration of organisation in their environment: 'The structure of an organisation functions in a setting of potentially related factors. Any or all of the factors such as an organisations' size, relationships with other organisations (dependence), technology, charter or purpose, ownership, location and origin may have some link with the form taken by its structure. As with structural concepts, these factors are operationalised as measurable variables' (p. 9). What this does suggest is that the term structure is used in a restricted and somewhat idiosyncratic way by the Aston researchers. Many of the contextual factors are understandably defined by others as structural. Why were these distinctions made? I find it more confusing than enlightening.

The working assumption is that one can trace associations between variables. As these are brought to light an empirical taxonomy of work organisations can be constructed. There are four main empirical types suggested: workflow bureaucracy, personnel bureaucracy, full bureaucracy and non-bureaucracy (that is low in structuring and low in concentration). Let no one doubt the ambition behind that typology: 'In terms of structural characteristics, it can be suggested that these are the principal forms of organisation of which late twentieth century organisational society is composed' (p. 16). 'Structural' in the above quote must mean 'contextual' and 'structural' since the taxonomy is constructed from a combination of typical contextual and structural arrangements. The elaborated definitions of these types also makes that clear.

As one now reflects on the work of the Aston school there are I think a number of points worth emphasising:

1. The original group was quite strongly guided by Pugh's approach factor analysis to research design (derived from his background in psychology). Hence we have an array of factors brought into the reckoning. These are operationalised into variables and the extent to which the variables are negatively or positively associated reported on. The opening-up of the range of factors gave rise to a growing uncertainty as to the importance of technology as an explanatory factor in determining organisation structure.

2. The work described is basically a cross-sectional study. It is thus a static picture that we have. This I think is readily conceded by the authors but it does mean that questions of organisational change are very much on the margin. This is incidentally one reason why I think the authors' criticisms of Max Weber are misguided. The purpose of his ideal types (not empirical types) of bureaucracy was to develop a comparative sociology that was centrally concerned with examining social change. The consequence of the Aston research strategy is that we never see organisations in action. I think this may be because the authors decided to set their faces against ethnographic processual studies on the grounds that first one had to operationalise all the relevant variables, then do static comparisons and only after that go for longitudinal studies to measure change. Even then the analysis would not be processual and the question is whether this self-denying ordinance in the name of methodological rigour is justified. An alternative strategy is to undertake comparative case studies. If these are chosen with particular problems in mind then it should be possible to consider the constraints on human action in particular contexts and the ways in which change and innovation take place in organisations.

In his paper 'Recent Trends and Possible Future Trends for Sociology of Organisations', (in Archer, Margaret S. (ed.), *Current Research in Sociology*, 1974, pp. 407-41) Crozier argues that the significant issues thrown up in the 1960s in the study of organisations as intellectual and practical questions were twofold. First, what is the meaning and what are the limits of what we call rational when considering men's action and how does the organisational phenomenon structure rationality? Second, how can we achieve change in a world of organisations? Yet in the Aston studies neither of these areas seem to be illuminated.

Perhaps the ever-present question is not whether we should measure, but what we should measure and for what purpose. Always there is the inbuilt tendency to trivialisation in the search for more and more precise measures and we end up with sawdust and not the elegant object we thought we were constructing.

Something should be said about the Aston school's original data base, It relates to 46 firms in the Birmingham area stratified by size and product or purpose (as defined by the Standard Industrial Classification). Another six organisations were also referred to 'because it formed a larger pool of data' (p. 44). The researchers write of the Birmingham organisational units which means that some were parts of larger enterprises and authorities and others were whole organisations. Curiously the question of what is or is not an organisation seems to be rather unclear and that must be written through all that follows. It might be added that from the way the information is processed we have no way of knowing whether the organisations are located in Birmingham, England, Birmingham, Alabama, or for that matter Hong Kong. This reflects the formalism into which, for better or worse, this kind of analysis leads us. It is worth recalling a very different kind of sociological study conducted in Birmingham at more or less the same time, Rex and Moore's *Race, Community and Conflict*. There can be no doubt in anyone's mind as to what city that data was collected in, even while the authors were seeking in some ways to generalise their findings about race relations to other urban centres.

The data was collected from interviews with the chief executives of the organisational units and with 'departmental heads of varying status' to obtain the required information (the composition and numbers of the latter by organisation are not I think specified but the substance of the interview schedule is given in an appendix). Pugh and Hickson write: 'Since the research strategy was to undertake a wide survey to set the guidelines, the result was superficiality and generality in the data. The project deals with what is officially expected *should* be done, and what is in practice *allowed* to be done; it does not include what is *actually* done, that is, what "really" happens in the sense of behaviour beyond that instituted in organisational forms' (p. 45). While this is stressing formal organisation characteristics it must be insisted that this data is not simply descriptive as the authors appear to claim. It contains an evaluative element. So far as I can see we are not told what the researchers did when accounts from different managers in an organisation disagreed nor how they coped with any discrepancies between verbal accounts and documentary information. Furthermore one may wonder, when differences between practice and precept were uncovered, how these affected the scoring on the many scales constructed for measurement.

In fairness to the Aston researchers and to Pugh and Hickson's book, readers should be directed to their concluding chapter. There they examine some of the criticisms that have come their way (not altogether identical with those I have mentioned) and respond to them. What they have to say about the meaning and validity of their measures and the possibility of causal inferences is of interest. In case any of us had missed the message their own view of the Aston work is summarised:

'The Aston studies are attempts to estimate atemporally the relationships between stable and meaningful characteristics of organisations which have been operationalised defined and measured' (p. 187). Despite the fact that this work is formalistic the question remains: to whom are these characteristics of organisations meaningful? Sooner or later we have to bring people back in with their skills and interests, resources and strategies. I suspect this is why many of the Aston researchers have moved on to recognise the centrality of the concept of power in explaining behaviour in organisations. That is a concept which doesn't even appear in the index of *Organisational Structure in Its Context*.

While it may be appreciated that the work of Woodward and her colleagues, and that of the Aston school have somewhat different emphasis, they have both contributed to what has come to be called strategic contingency theory. In general this is contrasted with approaches to 'scientific' management which were based on the premise of the 'one best way' to design efficient organisations:

> This newer approach has grown out of a body of social science research which has reported statistical associations between organisational characteristics and statistical variables. It represents, in fact, one of the simplest theoretical models which such results could support, namely that situational characteristics predict dimensions of organisations because they present requirements which act as moderately severe constraints upon the choice of an organisational design conducive to high performance. The major difference of this newer approach from earlier organisational theories lies in its acknowledgement that the process of designing organisation involves the selection of a configuration that will best suit that particular situation which prevails.
>
> (John Child, 'Organisation: A Choice for Man' in Child, J. (ed), 1973 p. 237)

Child's paper serves as a trenchant appraisal of the limitations of this development in organisation theory. He allows that, for managers, contingency theory may well be more useful than scientific management theory because it is more sensitive to a range of considerations pertaining to the enterprise in its environment. At the same time it is, he thinks, an exercise in 'fine tuning' in that it treats constraints as given by the situation and the aim is to respond to the constraints to accomplish effective economic performance. Behind this concept of the organisation and its environment is the notion of functional imperatives. Child's view is that this approach is not a technically neutral approach to organisation design any more than scientific management was (despite the claims of both). It is unecessarily conservative in its treatment of organisation change. Child (p. 247) summarises his critique of contingency theory as follows:

(1) it overlooks the fact that political and ideological referents already operate in the process of organisational design in addition to the 'technical' referent emphasised in administrative theory;
(2) the standards of economic performance against which the consequences of adopting different organisational forms are assessed, are themselves open to some degree of discretion or choice;
(3) there is evidence to suggest that within given situations an important degree of choice is available between different modes of organisation, without serious diseconomies being incurred;
(4) some degree of choice may also be available to organisational decision-makers in the long term with regard to situational factors themselves.

What this critique does is to cast doubt on the underlying logic of contingency theory in terms of the posited relationships between organisation structure effectiveness and the environment. It seeks to propound a view of social action which takes account of the realities of constraint without reifying the concept. It touches on the relationship between theory and practice and implies that if sociologists want their work to have practical relevance this may include showing that available choices for 'rational' action are wider than imagined, certainly wider than the contigency theorists allow for. What Child is proposing is a less fixed way of dealing with organisational behaviour. But the linkage between theory and practice actually implies a shifting definition of the client. It is not only managers who would need to be involved in effective strategies for change. Light is thrown on the value component implicit in 'action research' which connects 'pure theory' with normative applications. Child argues that the formulation of organisational strategy would have to include an extension of participation, which would embrace employees and possibly other interested parties: 'If such a process were extended through the various sections and levels of organisations so that it was founded upon a framework of opportunities for direct participation, then this development would itself probably represent a substantial long term social gain in terms of widely held values such as involvement in democratic processes and the opportunity to assume responsibility' (op. cit., p. 255). The critique of the logical status of contingency theory stands separately from this last point but indirectly it serves to remind us that certain kinds of 'theory' can be seen as nestling in snugly with perceived applications by specific interest groups. Others are more diffuse and raise questions of application that are more difficult to answer and hence apply to concrete situations. This is partly because they take the political dimension of human activity (with their choices and conflicts of interests) into account and partly because assumptions are scrutinised that less demanding theories take for granted.

Burns and Stalker's, *The Management of Innovation* (1961), was, and in my opinion continues to be, one of the most important British contributions to industrial sociology and the sociology of organisations.

> The core of all the twenty studies on which the book is based is the description and explanation of what happens when new and unfamiliar tasks are put upon the industrial concerns organised for relatively stable conditions. When novelty and unfamiliarity in both market situation and technical information become the accepted order of things a fundamentally different kind of management system becomes appropriate from that which applies to a relatively stable commercial and technical environment.
>
> (Burns's preface to second ed, 1966, p. vii)

The way in which these twenty cases (which were essentially extended interviews with managers in firms across a range of industries) came to form a coherent sociological study is described in the Introduction and is instructive. Early work, limited and only partially successful, stimulated questions and raised problems of conceptualisation that encouraged further inquiry and some redirection of original interests. The distinction eventually formulated between mechanistic and organic forms of management now almost has the status of 'what-every-sociologist-knows'. A detailed typology is given of each — the first system being seen as appropriate for stable conditions and the second for changing conditions where fresh problems constantly have to be faced and unforeseen contingencies dealt with. As with Woodward's claim that management principles could not be enunciated independently of particular contexts of operation, so too Burns and Stalker argue that 'the beginning of administrative wisdom is the awareness that there is no one optimum type of management' (p. 125). So mechanistic and organic management systems are represented as being at either end of a continuum, from the most stable and predictable environment to the most unstable and unpredictable.

Now at once this touches upon the question of 'organisational rationality' as the authors (p. 119) recognise and the following quotation links the administrative issue with objective sociological analysis.

> The case we have tried to establish . . . is that the different forms assumed by a working organisation do exist objectively and are not merely interpretations offered by observers of different schools. Both types represent a 'rational' form of organisation, in that they may both, in our experience, be explicitly and deliberately created and maintained to exploit the human resources of the concern. Not surprisingly, however, each exhibits characteristics which have been hitherto with different kinds of interpretation. For it is our contention that empirical findings have usually been classified according to

> sociological ideology rather that according to the functional specificity of the working organisation to its task and the conditions confronting it.

These fighting words follow a review of theories which concentrate variously upon 'formal organisation', 'informal organisation' (and various prescribed relationships between the two), 'machine models' and 'organic models'. The claim is that much of what takes place under such analyses tells us more about the standpoint of the writer than the operation of working organisations.

From what has so far been discussed it might be supposed that the alternative form of theory put forward by Burns and Stalker is an interesting variant of functionalism in which the rate of technical and commercial change are the independent variables (external to the firm and therefore 'environmental') and the form of management system as the dependent variable. The fit between the two then becomes appropriate or not appropriate (functional or dysfunctional) according to the system's response to the environment. In times of movement to or from stability or unpredictability when there is mis-match between environment and management system then one might offer a diagnosis as to the ways in which the management organisation needs to be adapted. But reality turns out to be more complex. This is because the working organisation is not the only 'system'. Explanations of organisation and of behaviour in organisations have to take into account the 'political' and 'status' systems. The first concerns the competing demands for resources, and the second with the rights, privileges, duties and obligations, distributed among organisational members. Neither of these systems can be fully understood by internal studies or organisation but need to be related to the wider society (see Burns and Stalker, op. cit., pp. 144-54).

At one level of analysis the discussion of political and status system carries with it the implication that behaviour that has to be understood as related to these systems may distort and create 'malfunctions' in the working organisation. And indeed at the level of top management action the task is to subordinate and mesh in political and status concerns so as not to distort the working organisation. This is how the book concludes: 'There is an obligation on management not only to interpret the external situation to the members of the concern, but to present the internal problems for what they truly are: the outcome of the stresses and changes in that situation and in markets, technical requirements, the structure of society itself' (op. cit., p. 262). For the sociologist however, the question of rationality is not so easily disposed of and Burns in his later preface makes plain that patterns of social action which may give rise to 'dysfunctional' management systems may nonetheless be rational in terms of other means and preoccupations of people at work. Indeed what is interesting and I think missing in the first edition of the *Management of Innovation* is the conceptualisation of a plurality of social systems built out of the actions of individuals and groups with varying commitments. While all of this may be seen as structured in organisational forms, the reality is more elusive:

> Besides commitments to the concern, the 'political' group and to his own career prospects, each member of a concern is involved in a multiplicity of relationships. Some arise out of incompatibilities of social origin, sub-culture and age. Others are generated by the encounters that are governed, or seem to be governed, by a desire for the comfort of friendship or the satisfaction of popularity and personal esteem, or those other rewards which come from inspiring respect, apprehension or alarm. All relationships of this sociable kind, since they represent social values, involve the parties in commitments.
>
> (op. cit., p. xiv)

Now what is of relevance for present purposes is the way in which a structural-functional study contains within it the seeds for a reinterpretation of behaviour as variously oriented forms of social action. Furthermore it leads to a view of sociology which has implications for transcending industrial sociology or the sociology of organisations:

> We are, I believe, closer to the study of the social world as a process, instead of an anatomy frozen into 'structured' immobility; closer to the identification of the abstraction, society with the empirical fact, behaviour, if we accept the essential ambiguity of social experience and organise interpretation of it in dynamic rather than structural terms. It is in this way, by perceiving behaviour as a medium of the constant interplay and mutual re-definition of individual identities and social institutions, that it is possible to begin to grasp the nature of the changes, developments and historical processes through which we move and help to create.
>
> (op. cit., p. xvi)

An anthropological dimension

I began the account of the development of industrial sociology with a reference to the Liverpool school. One of the members of that group was Tom Lupton. Apart from his more entreprenurial role in relation to the Aston group, noted earlier, his connection with the Manchester school of social anthropology is of particular interest. Enriched no doubt by the participant observation approach of anthropological field studies, Lupton and other colleagues applied them to factory-based inquiries. Lupton's own work was exemplified in the two detailed case studies reported in *On The Shop Floor* (1963).

Lupton's overall preoccupation was with the social factors affecting production and the case studies of the garment and engineering factories seek to show what are the conditions in which control of output by workers may be accomplished or impeded.

The general anthropological orientation incorporates a Gluckman-esque approach to the social functions of conflict. Furthermore he makes use of V. Turner's work on conflict regulation in an African tribal situation. While in a number of respects Lupton may be said to have a functionalist orientation to the treatment of conflict there can be no doubt that he sees it as inevitable and reflecting real conflicts of interest between managers and workers. This informs his treatment not only of overt disputes but also absenteeism and labour turnover.

It is also the case that Lupton draws upon the American tradition of participant observer studies in industry. While he makes several incisive criticisms of the Hawthorne Western Electric studies of Roethlisberger *et al.*, his own work deals with similar matters: the nature of work groups and clique formations, the influence of normative patterns on individuals' behaviour. These matters are considered clearly on connection with the actual production system and the methods of wage payment. Another obvious source of inspiration was the work of Donald Roy, whose participant observation studies in American engineering shops continue to serve as exemplary models to would-be researchers. The more recent work of Jason Ditton on 'fiddling' and 'time-manipulation' in bakeries draws upon the same tradition to great effect (Durham University Papers in Sociology Nos 2 and 6). Lupton also makes direct reference to the influence of George Homans. Homans of course had direct knowledge of the industrial sociology scene in the USA and his book *The Human Group* (1950) is a work of synthesis that draws heavily upon it. In that book he makes a conceptual distinction between external and internal social systems and that distinction is taken up by Lupton in *On The Shop Floor*. The external system for Lupton incorporates: the market situation (stability and size), relations with competitors, location of industry, trade union organisation (national and local) and type of product. These are economic, technical and industrial relations factors.

Lupton's Manchester colleague Sheila Cunnison undertook a similar study: *Wages and Work Allocation: A Study of Social Relations in a Garment Workshop* (Tavistock, 1963) and both of them reflected in a joint article on the utility of their systems approach ('Workshop Behaviour', in Gluckman, M. (ed.), *Closed Systems and Open Minds*). One conclusion was that the treatment of external factors was less well done in the nature of the case because participant observation focuses on the immediate site of study. The implication was that for greater rigour the participant observer's study needed to be supplemented by a more sophisticated understanding of the economic system of which the factory is part and a thorough exploration of the significance of 'overlapping systems'. They argue that 'there are segments of other social systems which are latent within a single workshop. For instance, a man's role as a father, or as a member of a social class, may effect his behaviour in the workshop' (op. cit., p. 125). To get information about overlapping systems would involved 'intensive interviews with the families of workers . . . to map out kinship networks, to discover financial obligations to him, and the present occupation, educational and occupational histories, and leisure time activities of the worker and his family' (op. cit., p. 125). These factors concern the worker's location in the wider society. The point is an enlargement on what the authors of *Management and the Worker* had written long before: 'The relation of the individual employee to the company is not a closed system. All the values of the individual cannot be accounted for by the social organisation of the company . . . The ultimate significance of his work is not defined so much by his relation to the company as by his relation to the wider social reality. Only in terms of this latter relation can the different attitudes of satisfaction or dis-satisfaction of individuals who are presumably enjoying the same working environment be understood' (pp. 375-6). In so far as one begins to contemplate structural factors inside and outside the place of work which may interrelate and affect attitudes to and behaviour at work then one has really arrived at a social action perspective by another route.

This I think is reflected in the fact that the way is charted out not only for in-plant behaviour studies but for labour mobility studies. Once one gets out of the bind of studying the plant as an internal or closed social system, contributions can be made to an area that has for long interested labour economists. The latter have often bewailed the need for psychologists and sociologists to help them in the area to provide explanations of non-economic factors. But it is to the social action perspective in industrial sociology that I now turn.

The social action pivot

I begin with reference to two studies, one explicitly in the area of industrial sociology, the other more general, but of considerable relevance: David Lockwood's *The Blackcoated Worker* (1959) and John Rex's *Key Problems of Sociological Theory* (1961).

What Lockwood did pre-eminently in *The Blackcoated Worker* was to argue for the utility of the distinction made by Weber between class and status as a way of explaining the absence of class consciousness among clerical workers in Britain. This is what informs his discussion of 'market situation' and 'work situation'. The work situation was seen as a crucial mediating variable affecting the presence or absence of class consciousness. Thus it was held that the work situation of clerks in small personalised offices structured their perception of themselves as extensions of management. It promoted an individualistic attitude and a negative attitude to trade union membership. It also supported a status view of society with its complex hierarchies of prestige (to some extent based on occupational differentiation) rather than a class view of conflicts of interest between 'workers' and 'employers'. Naturally work situation and market situation could change and one of the strengths of Lockwood's study is a historical consideration of those changes. This explores the growth in office work and its bureaucratisation (again the selection of a Weberian pre-occupation) and the likely effect on unionisation and class consciousness which such structural changes might engender.

What one can clearly recognise in Lockwood's work is an attempt to apprehend the relationship between objective class position and subjective perception of class position. It is, furthermore, an attempt to replace the 'black box' Marxist concept of 'false consciousness' with what he holds to be an account of the discrepancy between objective situation and subjective perception. This, in principle, is ascertainable and open to empirical inquiry and, it is claimed, has greater explanatory power. This is so, not least because such questions can be historically and structurally located.

Key Problems of Sociological Theory, while not centrally concerned with industrial sociology, did have a tone-setting effect with its explicit advocacy of the action frame of reference. This is based very closely on the kind of approach first outlined by Weber in *Economy and Society* and is used to serve as a critique of functionalism in general and Parsonian functionalism in particular. At the same time, dissatisfaction is expressed with the conflict theories of Coser, Gluckman and Dahrendorf. The general stance of Rex is that the action frame of reference takes explicitly into account the possibility of actors in conflict over desired ends and that this provides a more realistic basis for analysing social change. What begins as a micro-account of social interaction by way of a Weberian appreciation of the concept of 'legitimacy' develops into a macro-sociology of social systems. The action and limits of the approach as envisaged by Rex are well summarised in the following:

> The emphasis which we have planned on 'ends' however, led us to agree with the explanation of particular historical situations, rather than seeking to verify general laws about social systems by the comparative study of different social systems. The general model of conflict which we have propounded is not a general theory of social systems in this sense. It is merely a guide for the formulation of particular models applicable to particular social systems. It is these particular models which have to be proved and tested by comparing their predictions about various sorts of social activity with the actual course of events. A general theory of social systems could only be

> established if it could be shown that there were recurring elements in the ends which were sought through various social systems.
>
> (op. cit., p. 184)

It will be noted that in his formulation of the action frame of reference Rex does not reject the terminology of social systems. What he does is to maintain that rather than being organised around a consensus of values, social systems involve conflict situations, the character of which may range from open violence to peaceful bargaining. In a somewhat similar way to Dahrendorf he introduces (p. 129) the notion of pluralism at the societal level: 'The existence of such a [conflict] situations tends to produce not a unitary but a plural society in which there are two or more classes, each of which provides a relatively self contained social system for its members. The activities of the members take on sociological meaning and must be explained by reference to the group's interests in the conflict situation'.

There is one other element in Rex's approach which may be mentioned here. It is his view of the relationship between sociology and social policy. Here he follows Weber's view (most fully expressed in 'The Meaning of Ethical Neutrality in Sociology and Economics'). The sociologist qua sociologist cannot posit what social ends are desirable. He can seek to show linkages between social means and social ends. What can the public expect of the sociologist:

> They may . . . expect him to express more sharply the real, as distinct from the utopian, value choices which face them as participants in a particular society. But they should not expect him, nor should he claim, to be competent to make those value choices for them.
>
> It is in this sense, and in this sense alone, that sociology may be thought of as a radical critical discipline. It will simply fall into bad repute if it fails to recognise this and seeks to compensate for the conservative ideological commitments of its recent past by embracing a new political radicalism.
>
> (pp. viii-ix)

In terms of some later developments in sociology generally and industrial sociology in particular this was a timely comment and provides a context for understanding some of Rex's later battles.

The action frame of reference approach during the 1960s not only provoked theoretical discussion but also empirical work. In the field of industrial sociology this was notably exemplified in the affluent worker study. The whole study is reported in three volumes (Goldthorpe *et al.*, vols 1 and 2 1968, and vol 3 1969) and spans the areas of industrial and political sociology, with an overriding interest in social stratification. For immediate purposes I will drawn attention to the first of these volumes *The Affluent Worker: Industrial Attitudes and Behaviour* and I think also that should be coupled with Goldthorpe's paper 'Attitudes and Behaviour of Car Assembly Workers: A Deviant Case and a Theoretical Critique' (*BJS*, 1966).

In one way it might seem surprising that volume 1 received the attention it undoubtedly did. After all it is explicitly presented as a by-product of a study with a different focus (namely the examination of the embourgeoisement thesis). Indeed the authors (pp. 6-7) themselves were aware of limitations of their work as a contribution to industrial sociology and, say so plainly without equivocation:

> Considered as a study in industrial sociology it is certain that this monograph suffers from various shortcomings through its dependence on research in which the industrial attitudes and behaviour of subjects of investigation were but one of several areas of interest. On almost every topic discussed in the pages which follow it is not difficult to think of further information which it would have been desirable to have but which our enquiry neglected. Furthermore, our research methods were not as rigorous as might have been possible in a more restricted project. For example, a study concerned with 'attitudes' should, ideally, have used more sophisticated methods of ordering and measuring these than we were able to apply across the variety of issues our interviews covered. And, similarly, to study behaviour in the most satisfactory way would have called for more systematic observational studies, in addition to interviewing, than we were able to carry out. Finally, there is, of couse, the point that the workers we studied were — with the central objectives of our research in mind — a highly selected group. It is particularly important that this should be remembered wherever material concerning our sample is used as a basis for the discussion of general theoretical issues: the significance of the sample must always be that of a special rather than a typical case.

These cautionary words regarding methodological adequacy and theoretical applicability are I think not unwarranted. Yet, as the first fruits of the affluent worker project whose findings were being awaited with interest at least by professional sociologists, surely there was more than self-criticism on offer. Certainly there was and among the more salient points I would list the following:

1. First, such evidence as is provided is deployed to support a theoretical critique of writers in the 'human relations' and 'technological implications' approaches respectively. The first of these goes back to Mayo but is intended to cover more recent contributions such as those of Maslow. It is partly the 'universalist' treatment of human 'needs' in industry (which, as we have seen, also draws the fire of contingency theorists). The alternative emphasis is on the view that individuals' wants and expectations are culturally determined variables not psychological

constants. Rather than start with the assumption that the factory or work situation should be a source of group solidarity and social satisfaction and defining situations where this does not happen as 'pathological', the alternative approach is that one should find out empirically what people want and expect from their employment and how their situation fits in with these preferences. Hence it is suggested: 'It is possible for work not to be a central life interest and to be given largely instrumental meaning without the individual being thereby virtually deprived of all social activities and relationships which are rewarding in themselves. Rather . . . the readiness to adopt an orientation to work of the kind in question would appear often to indicate a commitment to the interest of one primary group — the conjugal family — which is of an over-riding kind' (op. cit., p. 180).

The critique of the 'technological implications' approach was essentially an attack on Woodward's position and that of the socio-technical systems perspective of the Tavistock Institute. This was partly another attack on a version of structural functional analysis. But the refutation was seen as based on empirical evidence. It was accepted that technology was a major factor affecting the degree of intrinsic job satisfaction and influencing patterns of social relations and group formation at work. At the same time it was stated that on a whole range of industrial attitudes and behaviour there was no clear relationship with employees' work situation. Thus the 'instrumental orientation' to work was reported as existing in different technological environments.

2. Both of the above critiques were put forward as a challenge to what were treated as established orthodoxies in industrial sociology and both focused on the inadequacies of treating the place of work as a closed social system. Against this the alternative development of the action frame of reference is propounded. To be faithful to the authors' own intentions I think two points need to be stressed. The first is that in part they were offering methodological advice on where the study of industrial work should begin: namely with the actors' own definitions of their situation. This could refer to such things as relationships with others at work, their view of the firm, of the unions and of their own life 'prospects'. But this was a starting point which would enable researchers to establish empirically the variety of meanings held by workers. This is clearly linked with the view that a fuller explanation has to inquire into the sources of these orientations:

> The values and motivations that lead workers to the view of work they have adopted must be traced back, so far as this is possible, to typical life situations and experiences. In this way, therefore, the possibility — indeed the necessity — arises, as it does not with other approaches we have considered, of explaining and understanding the social life which goes on within the enterprise by reference ultimately to the structure and processes of the wider society in which the

enterprise exists.

(op. cit., p. 185)

Although it is conceded that their own study made only tentative steps in that direction it is for such reasons that the 'social correlates' of the instrumental orientation to work are investigated.

3. The third feature of the study which served to promote discussion was the authors' suggestion that the affluent workers they studied were 'prototypical'. Thus it was argued that industrial workers, particularly the unskilled and semi-skilled would increasingly come to view their work in instrumental terms: as a means to ends which were extrinsic to their work situation. This was related to such structural factors as urban redevelopment and the decline of 'traditional' working-class communities; with increased geographical mobility; with changes in the character of the working-class family; with workers' planning more actively for the future for themselves and their families rather than embracing a fatalistic attitude to the future as some of their 'traditional' forebears had done. These changes, it was argued would be accompanied by changes in attitude to trade unionism:

> To the extent that events and expectations from work are confined to high-level economic returns, so the meaning of trade unionism will tend to be interpreted in a similar instrumental way. And to the extent that individuals' central life interests are to be found in the cultivation and enjoyment of their private, domestic lives, commitment to trade unionism understood as a social movement or as an expression of class or occupational solidarity, is unlikely to be widespread. On the other hand, where there is a strong drive to increase the material rewards of work, and thus consumer power, their involvement in union activity concerned with matters of wages and conditions of service of immediate interest to workers may, of course be expected — and involvement, perhaps, of some intensity. While militancy directed towards such ends as greater worker control may well become more difficult to sustain among home centred employees, we would regard greater aggressiveness in the field of 'cash-based' bargaining as a very probable development.
>
> (op. cit., pp. 176-7)

The argument surrounding 'prototypicality' is understandable, not only because the authors were trailing their coats at that point but also because of the political implications that might be thought to follow if the claim was correct. Certainly it becomes clear in all three volumes of the *Affluent Worker* that while the embourgeoisement of the working classes is an incorrect description, changes of various kinds were taking place. It is the significance and generality of these changes that remains a central question. What the prototypicality claim helped to do was to remind other sociologists of the interconnectedness of social life and the range of vision that this required if adequate work was to be done. It also rested on the premise that such work could take social action and relate it back to social structure. This sociological work would be done by empirical study and this separated it from philosophical speculation about society.

The social action perspective in industrial sociology gave rise to a number of empirical studies. Among the book-length examples one can cite are Ingham's *Size of Industrial Organisation and Worker Behaviour* (1970); Beynon and Blackburn's *Perceptions of Work: Variations in a Factory* (1972); and Martin and Fryer's *Redundancy and Paternalist Capitalism* (1973). And Fox's text book *A Sociology of Work in Industry* (1971) is based on the action frame of reference. The price of such recognition is that the 'new' approach will itself be subjected to critical scrutiny. There was a robust debate in the *Journal of Management Studies*, Daniels (1969 and 1971) and Goldthorpe (1970). Daniel's viewpoint is further represented in his paper 'Understanding Employee Behaviour in its Context: Illustrations from Productivity Bargaining', in Child (ed.), (1973). On the basis of his empirical work in a chemical plant Daniel argued that to write of say an instrumental orientation to work as fixed and to be accounted for by social factors outside the plant was misleading. This was because at different times and in different contexts workers could exhibit different orientations. In the bargaining context it could be instrumental whereas in the work context it could be geared to intrinsic features of the job. Hence the demands for intrinsic rewards in the job situation may not be an alternative to the demand for extrinsic rewards. They may co-exist and demands of both kinds increase. In part this can be treated as a refinement of Goldthorpe *et al.* in so far as the notion of orientation to work is not rejected as a methodological starting point but more emphasis is put on looking at the work situation as a process and with various facets. Daniel concludes that while variations in priorities and attitudes occur within the work context, there is a spectrum. At the one end will be workers who give exclusive importance to extrinsic rewards and at the other end those who treat intrinsic rewards in like manner. In one respect Daniel's challenge is not to the social action perspective but to the 'prototypicality' argument and also to what he regards as an over-crude application of orientations to work which too rigid to do justice to all that takes place in the work situation.

A similar refining intention permeates Brown's paper 'Sources of Objectives in Work and Employment', in Child (ed.), (1973). He also is not convinced by the prototypicality argument and shares Daniel's view on the importance of 'context'. He extends the point about context to apply to community as well as work: sudden changes in context may, he suggests, give rise to marked changes in expressed objectives. He argues that the concept of 'orientations to work' has been regarded as relatively unproblematic and that the accompanying explanatory model has been too simple: 'Once the notion itself is questioned, and its relationship to other factors seen as reciprocal rather than one-way, the sources of variations in orientations to work, and the significance of such variations, becomes more difficult to determine' (op. cit., p. 36).

In developing the social action approach Brown argues both for a more rigorous treatment of the actors' definition of the situation. How are systems of meaning created, sustained and changed? But he does not fall into subjectivist error. Research should not lose sight of 'the distribution of resources, of power and authority and of physical and technological conditions in industry, which form some of the more intractable "conditions of action" for those pursuing their individual and/or shared objective in work' (op. cit., pp. 36-7).

A more hostile evaluation of the social action approach in industrial sociology is made by Baldamus in *The Structure of Sociological Inference* (1976). The affluent worker study is described as a case of conspicuous trivialisation'. The essense of the argument is that the initial focus on the embourgeoisement thesis was macro- rather than micro-sociological, was exploring a dynamic developmental process, and was a sociological rather than an economic theory. Yet it became micro-sociological, subjectivist, static and economic as it proceeded. Thus he regards the study (and this really has particular application to vol. 1) as a case of psychological reductionism in the mould of neo-classical economics with an inadequate appreciation of the dynamics of industrial conflict: 'Labour conflict is . . . reduced to nothing worse than the contrariety of buyers and sellers, which in turn evaporates into individual subjective interests and notions' (op. cit., p. 64). Baldamus goes on to maintain that this 'distorted' theory is in tune with a public opinion which in a sense it may feed. Thus 'the idea that no real substance adheres to the economic reality of contemporary society commands increasing acceptance in public opinion. Accordingly, the physical aspects of economic activities, of wages, incomes, prices, effort, hours of work and so on, are redefined as relatively unimportant. They are only in the mind. Just as the trained sociologist is able to create this idea simply by the method of *defining* (and re-defining) the objects of his study, so the larger public can cope with unacceptable or vexatious realities by the use of selective definitions of their own situation' (op. cit., pp. 65-6).

Baldamus, incidentally, is not the only one to voice this kind of criticism (which although stringent, it should be added, was used as an example of the inherent difficulties of doing sociological work). In his generally more sympathetic paper 'The Affluent Worker: An Evaluation and Critique', in Parkin (ed.), (1974) Gavin Mackenzie writes: 'What does need to be emphasised . . . is that the adoption of an action perspective in connection with a "by product" of a study of changes in class structure entails a serious dilution of the authors' earlier conceptualisation of class and class structure. For whatever the merits of focusing on "prior orientation" in the examination of industrial behaviour, the analysis of the class structure of capitalist society requires an examination of structured inequality and life choices — which as Goldthorpe and Lockwood argued earlier, typically depend upon position in the division of labour' (op. cit., p. 242).

Baldamus clearly takes the affluent worker project as an example partly because of its professional standing but mainly, I think, because he wants to show how this represents a movement towards a phenomenological sociology (notwithstanding its tabulated statistical findings). This is why he proceeds to fire away at Beynon and Blackburn's *Perception of Work: Variations within a Factory* (1972). Baldamus's criticisms are not easy to summarise in that he attempts to show with extensive textual references how *Perceptions of Work* hangs together as a study. But the centre point of the matter does I think come through. It is that everything about the study is transformed into discussions of 'perceived' or 'experienced' phenomena. This is because everything is put on the plane of how the actor sees the world. Work, pay, power structures are perceptions rather than physical realities. What one has therefore are accounts of how far expectations which workers bring to the factory are congruent with their perception of reality and what adjustments or accommodations they make when there is incongruence. He suggests that in the end the authors have some difficulty in being consistent in their phenomenological presentation in that they offer an observer's view. When the main findings are evaluated, Baldamus suggests,

> The earlier euphemistic terms ('satisfactions' etc.) are re-interpreted, and replaced by distinctively negative evaluations. Industrial work, as perceived in the observers' own world view, now turns out to be 'alienating', 'highly exploited', 'coercive', 'frustrating', 'deadly monotonous', 'repulsive', 'oppressive'. For instance, in the final explanation of the day men, relatively the most discontented of the four groups, discontent is interpreted as a result of 'utopian' expectations in the sense of unsuccessful accommodation. Conversely, complete adjustment under such conditions where utopian expectations 'were beaten down by experience' is now described as 'resignation'. In other words, the researchers' expectations, superimposed upon the respondents' perceptions, are even higher than those of the most alienated groups.
>
> (op. cit., p. 7)

Now part of Baldamus's aim here is to support a 'realist' view against a 'subjectivist' view of industrial life. Blackburn and Beynon's own inconsistency with the phenomenological method is seen as evidence of the power of 'recalitrant observation' — that reality will, as it were, break through almost in spite of the authors. If the phenomenological paradigm is applied to the world it will, the argument runs, be revealed as inadequate and containing irreparable methodological errors.

It should be said that since elsewhere Goldthorpe has attacked phenomenological sociology (1973), Blackburn has written accounts of trade union structure (1968) and Beynon a study of Fords (1973) with a strong appreciation of power structures, one obviously needs to be aware of inadequate labels. My own gloss on this would be that the social action perspective was embarked upon as a reaction to other perspectives in industrial sociology. It had roots in Weber (and linguistic affinities with Parsons). Its focus on the actors' definition of the situation did not have to exclude consideration of social structure (and certainly in the case of Goldthorpe *et al.* did not wholly do so) but by focusing on the actor could (and did) leave many things unsaid. This was partly a problem of following research through given the usual story of limited time and resources so that the established links with the wider social structure were implied and/or tenuous. This is somewhat similar to the kinds of problem raised by Lupton and Cunnison about how to research the external system when the participant observer spends all his or her time in the factory.

What the social action perspective did do was to give impetus to approaches that focus upon the actor as agent and the social processes generated and sustained by interaction. In this sense it served as something of a catalyst for approaches that were more explicitly and avowedly phenomenological. Silverman's *Theory of Organisations* (1970) stands as a significant example.

Silverman confidently urges, with a nod in Kuhn's direction, the embracing of a new paradigm — the social action paradigm — to replace the systems orthodoxy. In formulating his alternative he draws on sources such as Weber, Berger and Luckmann, Shutz, Goffman and Cicourel. What emerges is an emphasis on the centrality of understanding action; the constellations of meaning they produce and the ways in which through interaction they are sustained, modified or changed. Silverman contrasts this approach to explanation with 'positivism'. '. . . explanations of human action must take account of the meanings which those concerned assign to their acts; the manner in which the everyday world is socially constructed yet perceived as real and routine becomes the crucial concern of sociological analysis. Positivistic explanations, which assert that action is determined by external and constraining social or non-social forces, are inadmissable' (op. cit., p. 127).

Silverman does indeed see his work as phenomenological and this affects his treatment of the role of causality in social explanation. His comments on Goldthorpe *et al.* help to illuminate this. He argues for example, that in treating 'orientations to work' it is not enough to consider the meanings which people bring to the work situation, the meanings specific to the organisation also have to be considered. It is how these types of meaning come together in the actor's experience which affects the type of involvement or attachment he will have to that organisation. There is at least a difference of emphasis in Silverman's position from that of Goldthorpe *et al.* More weight is given to the following point: 'By arguing that work orientations are determined by a combination of internal and external factors, one may miss the way in which people's view of themselves and of their situation is the outcome of an on-going process, i.e., never fully determined by one or another set of structural constraints but always in the act of 'becoming' as successive experiences shape and re-shape a subjective definition of self and society' (op. cit., pp. 184-5). Now this perspective is explicitly linked with the work of the Chicago school and its approach to the study of occupations, and Goffman's congruent interest in 'moral careers'. In writing of the Chicago school Silverman says: 'Their sociology of work has stressed the concept of "career", the typical series of opportunities and dangers, rewards and disappointments, that confront the new entrant into an occupation. It has further sought to emphasise the subjective experience of various kinds of career-passage, for instance the nature and extent of particular types of commitment to an occupation and/or to an organisation and the characteristic forms of occupational cultures. But always in their works one is encouraged to view subjective experience *in process*' (op. cit., p. 185).

It is precisely the interest in subjective experience in process that deepens Silverman's appreciation of what it is to study the meaning of social action (with methodological implications that participant observation is more appropriate than interviewing or survey work). It is particularly instructive to see that in developing this theme he refers to Becker's paper, 'Becoming a Marijuana User', as a classic working through of the relationship between definition of the situation and the way it is changed through successive experiences to constitute an ongoing social process. The link here with parallel developments in the sociology of deviance is very explicit.

The engagement with industrial relations

When Flanders and Clegg first wrote *The System of Industrial Relations in Great Britain* in 1954 they could admit to the lack of any specifically sociological input on the grounds that not much was available and that what was published was not very good. And, it might be added, the term 'system' there employed only denoted the set of formal institutions in the area of industrial relations. Industrial relations in so far as it had any disciplinary association was linked with labour economics (itself an underprivileged member of the academic economic enterprise). Looking back over two decades, one can see a growing engagement of sociology with industrial relations and there are several salient features which are worthy of note.

First there were industrial relations writers who while sometimes making anti-sociology noises were markedly sociologists in their own work. The best example I can think of is H.A. Turner who, in *Trade Union Growth, Structure and Policy* (1963), combined historical analysis with heuristic typologies of union organisation in a stimulating manner. Later with colleagues he produced a study of the car industry (Turner *et al.*, 1967). This was notable not only for its institutional analysis but also for his resort to the comparative method, both within Britain and with reference to other countries. And his interpretation of strike statistics sought to relate movements in the employment cycle with an account of strikers' reasons for industrial action.

Secondly, industrial relations scholars became a little self-conscious about the need for theory. Dunlop's *Industrial Relations Systems* (1958) obviously served a purpose. This was itself derived from a consideration of Parsonian systems theory. In Britain Allan Flanders took it up with enthusiasm (see Flanders 1970 for a good over-view of his position). The debate took the utility of this approach still continues in the industrial relations journals.

Thirdly, sociologists in the late 1950s and early 1960s began to move into the industrial relations field — notably the Liverpool industrial sociology group and the Cambridge-based affluent-worker study discussed elsewhere. My own book *Industrial Disputes* (1968) I think reflects some of the interchange between industrial relations and sociology — indeed it was subtitled 'Essays in the Sociology of Industrial Relations'. Use was made of the Dunlop systems model, whilst seeking to detach it from its functionalist implications and expressing doubts on its treatment of power. The position taken was that the sources of conflict and co-operation, order and instability have equally valid claims to problem status. The adequacy of the 'technological implications' position as it relates to industrial conflict was considered and the possibilities of a 'social action perspective' explored. This latter led to a view that competing rationalities might co-exist in the industrial relations arena. This did not rule out the possibility of irrationality but was an implicit critique of some contemporary polemics on industrial relations which blamed workers for 'stupid' and 'irrational' strikes (usually unofficial). The recognition of the centrality of conflicts of interest in industrial relations was also a reason for examining with some scepticism the 'withering away of the strike' thesis. In retrospect one can see even more clearly that that was part of the 'end of ideology' argument.

Fourthly, there was a movement of industrial relations scholars into industrial sociology. The most notable case was Alan Fox. His research paper for the Donovan Commission *Industrial Sociology and Industrial Relations* (1966) had an academic and public impact somewhat parallel to that of Woodward's *Management and Technology* a decade earlier.

The question of worker rationality again comes up and is treated in terms of the now widely disseminated distinction between unitary and pluralist focus of reference: 'Like conflict, restrictive practices and resistance to change have to be interpreted by the unitary frame of reference as being due to stupidity, wrong-headedness or out of date class rancour. Only a pluralistic view can see them for what they are: rational responses by sectional interests to protect employment, stabilise earnings, maintain job status, defend group bargaining power or preserve class boundaries. The unitary view must condemn them as morally indefensible: the pluralistic view can understand them and by understanding is in a position to change them.' (op. cit., p. 12). Again as with Woodward it is a twin-pronged approach to fellow academics and to management with real problems to solve. It bears of course directly upon the question of the relationship between theory and practice. I want now to explore some of the issues which arise when attempts are made to be 'relevant' and to adopt a pragmatic stance in confronting 'the real world' as an academic. The field of industrial relations is I think a particularly instructive example.

On pragmatism

Since pragmatism would appear to direct our attention to the real world where we may locate men engaged in common-sense solutions to everyday problems, it is a little disconcerting to find that this world has something of a will-o'-the-wisp character. There are I think a number of reasons for this.

1. On the simplest rendering pragmatism is defined as the matter-of-fact treatment of things. This no-nonsense view is reflected in the notion that the facts speak for themselves. Inferences on this rendition are irresistible and one is scarcely conscious of making prescriptions for there can be no argument about what has to be done 'in the light of all the facts'. Certainly people can come to believe this and they might also be heard to add that if you have all the facts you don't need theories. A reply is not difficult to come by and should perhaps be offered since such views allegedly rooted in common sense can be treated among practitioners and academics in industrial relations.

(a) Facts do not speak for themselves, you speak for them. This means that you decide what facts you are going to select. Some facts may remain unspoken either because you choose to remain silent or do not know of their existence.

(b) Although you may wish to claim that you are not theorising (since in this context this is thought of as abstract or irrelevant) the method you employ to build fact upon fact to draw a logical conclusion is indeed inductive reasoning. It is theorising at least in the Baconian mode.

(c) Facts are frequently disputable, even those which to you are self-evident. This can sometimes be at a very primitive level — matters of counting or calculating say in relation to accidents, strikes, absenteeism, labour turnover, manning or wages. Sometimes it is because of the interpretation placed on the facts. The history of work measurement, job evaluation and collective bargaining bears eloquent testimony to that.

(d) Language in use is not simply a catalogue of facts. In industrial relations as in any other sphere of social life there are what Baldamus has aptly called pragmatic concepts. In conversation about industrial relations we employ everyday concepts like 'productivity', 'differentials', 'demarcation', 'incentive', 'effort', 'responsibility', 'parity'. But all these terms may be subject to conflicting meanings as to what they signify and what the use of such concepts is intended to accomplish in practical activity. They are subject to definition and redefinition and as concepts their meaning can only be appreciated in context. When we put the concepts in context we find that they are arranged and linked with other pragmatic concepts in implicit or explicit ways. I think myself that the examination of this vocabulary, which one discovers to be part technical, part moral, can be rewarding in the sense that it tells us how the men in the action define, see and conceptualise the world of industrial relations. It suggests too that we might observe changes in the vocabulary — either in the way that terms are employed or in the invention of new terms like 'productivity bargaining' and 'efficiency bargaining'. It is worth noting here incidentally that pragmatic concepts are also employed by students of industrial relations and they may be the progenitors of such terms which enter into everyday industrial relations conversation — one thinks of 'bargaining agent', 'participative management' and the like. What remains a question is whether the student of industrial relations as a theorist has to or does move beyond pragmatic conceptualisations in offering explanations of what is going on. But here we may note that the theorist who uses analytical concepts like socio-technical systems or social action is using another language from the participant and this difference in language may be what is meant when comment is made about the gap between theory and practice. Again, however, we have to note that the two worlds are not separate. The theorist almost inevitably uses pragmatic concepts direct from the industrial relations world; the participants may come to use and deploy the language of the theorist so that it is not impossible to have factory managers talking about Theory *X* and Theory *Y* or trade unionists talking about formal and informal systems. This interchange and mutual extension of vocabularies has not been examined systematically nor its significance evaluated for the theory and practice of industrial relations.

2. Pragmatic solutions to industrial relations problems are commonly identified by their exponents as *realistic*. They are contrasted with

notions of *myth* and *ideology*. By labelling in this way and, by implication, contrasting reality with ideology to the latter's disadvantage, one is certainly making a pre-emptive strike when it comes to prescriptions for industrial relations. But again I should like to illustrate the kinds of difficulties and conundrums we encounter.

Usually exponents of this position are interested in changing some of the existing arrangements of industrial relations. The fact that something comes to be defined as a problem suggests that change of one sort or another is called for. Hence the notion of myth often comes to be associated with a critique of traditionalism. Things are supposed or believed to operate in a certain way to produce certain results but in reality they don't. A good summary of how this appeared in the Donovan report is found in W.E.J. McCarthy's paper *Changing Bargaining Structures*:

> Having made this contrast between myths of the industry-wide system and the realities of shop-floor life Donovan sought to show that the defects of the present system could not be solved by seeking to force reality to conform to myth. Industry-wide dispute procedures could not hope to cope with the rising tide of shop floor demands, in different kinds of firms with different sorts of production systems operating in varied labour markets. Increases in shop floor demands, given such a system, were bound to result in a rise in strikes. Industry-wide wage agreements could not hope to prevent wage-drift, or cope with the effects of defective piece work systems subjected to work group pressure. As for labour restrictive practices . . . they largely derived from management inefficiency and work groups 'reacting to concrete situations and defending and promoting their job interests as they saw them'. It followed that they too could not be improved by action taken at the remote level of the industry-wide agreements . . . The heart of the Donovan message was that in each instance the initiative rested with management — especially top management.
>
> (In Kersler and Weekes (ed.), *Conflict at Work*, BBC Publications, 1971, pp. 84-5)

In the generic sense what is being attacked here is 'custom and practice'. If these are to be changed then they may well be resisted by those who feel they have something to lose and don't share the analyst's view of what is realistic. Since we are dealing here with areas of control over work and wages and since in a number of instances the participants may express a good measure of satisfaction with existing arrangements, matters are not always straightforward. The analyst's response has to be that in principle he knows better and can demonstrate that he is right. A working consensus is manufactured through a process of enlightenment. In the context of British industrial relations this was clearly formulated by Hugh Clegg: 'The job to be done, therefore, was educational, beginning with the Donovan report itself and subsequently to be carried on by the new Commission. When managers and trade unionists saw that current ideas about industrial relations were out of touch with reality and had become a prop for outrun institutions, they would be ready to carry out the reforms that were needed' (Clegg, *The System of Industrial Relations in Great Britain*, 1972, p. 454).

In other words, once people can be enabled to see things as they really are through the clear eyes of enlightened self-interest, they may be induced, encouraged and persuaded to change. Now setting aside the important consideration that there were widespread disagreements among and between academics, politicians, employers and employees both as to diagnosis and prescriptions, what is clear is that this particular pragmatic solution did have an ideological content. If we are to give a lable to it, then it is Fabian pragmatism. Commenting on the Royal Commission's reports for example H.A. Turner summed them up in this way: 'The "Oxford Line" might be described as combining an industrious extension of established avenues of enquiry (and particularly in meticulous pursuit of institutional detail), in preference for the short term rule of thumb over the broader generalisation . . . and in variety of propagandist's mini-reformism which consists getting leading people boldly in the direction they appear to be going anyway. This approach was clearly influential on the Commission' (The Royal Commission Research Papers, *BJIR*, vol. vi, no. 3, November 1968, p. 359).

The comment is not quite fair since they did not manage to lead successive governments in that direction at all. However, what is at issue here can be illustrated in another way. In his essay *What Are Trade Unions For?* Allan Flanders proceeded by rejecting two answers to the question put forward by Marxists and Tories respectively. Putting on one side the detailed objections, his general complaint is that 'those who hold them believe they know more about what trade unions are for than the unions and their members know themselves' (Flanders, Allan, in *Management and Unions*, 1970, p. 38). The corollary would appear to be that to answer the question one must do so in terms of members' own definitions, whether you happen to approve or not. But that is not what Flanders actually does. He proceeds to commend an incomes policy to the trade union movement even though he acknowledges that many trade unionists do not share his view. Only by sharing his view, however, will unions remain true to their purpose of participation in job regulation. So the pragmatic solution does not consist in finding out what participants are actually doing and then letting them get on with their problem-solving, it consists of a particular kind of solution within the context of political debate.

The kind of pragmatism involved here, with its critique of traditionalism, is an appeal to experience, which is really in terms of the proof of the pudding being the in the eating, is similarly reflected in Flander's essay Trade Unions and the Force of Tradition where he maintains: 'Argument may be needed to induce trade unions to embark on new and uncharted courses of behaviour, as in the early days of incomes policy, but experience in the end is the main lever of permanent change' (ibid,. p. 294).

What this particular example also illustrates is that the pragmatic solution is conceived in terms of a middle of the road compromise — in this case social democracy (with an explicit reference to the Swedish example) in between Marxism and Toryism. It is the middle way which is propounded as a hard-headed realistic method of proceeding as opposed to 'extremist' ideological solutions. This view of industrial relations is in essence similar to that of Clark Kerr who wrote of the need to seek practical and constant adjustments around the golden mean. Although at times Kerr sees the industrial relations order as vulnerable, at other times he sees such solutions as an inevitable result of accumulated experience:

> The age of ideology fades. When men first entered the irreversible journey into industrialisation, there were innumerable views about the best way to organise society. Some of them have largely disappeared from the scene: anarchism, syndicalism, communalism, co-operativism. Others of them have been blunted and revised from their original form, particularly capitalism and socialism. The age of utopias is past. An age of realism has taken its place — an age in which there is little expectation of either utter perfection or complete doom. One of the results of the past century is the accumulation of experience about the realistic alternatives . . . Men learn from experience how better to do things, and the rough edges are evened off.
>
> (Industrialism and World Society, (1961), in *Labor's Management in Industrial Society*, 1964, p. 363.

We see from this a view of the end of ideology as resulting in pragmatic problem-solving. It is arguable that this in itself is a form of ideology and that part of its power derives from the fact that other solutions are labelled in a pejorative way as ideological — that is dogmatic and impractical — and consequently the terms in which debate actually takes place are reduced to adjustments around the mean. I should like, however, to make two further points here:

Firstly, despite the emphasis on practical solutions to pressing and identifiable problems which at first conveys the impression of piecemeal 'non-theoretical' responses, the pragmatists in emphasising the need for realistic solutions often carry a good deal of conceptual and theoretical baggage around with them. So, for example, instead of asking how can we solve our manpower problem, our strike problem or our productivity problem, we ask what is wrong with the industrial relations system. Now this can lead to an analysis in which the writer reminds his readers of the facts of life as he sees them and the tensions and conflicts within the system which individuals and groups will have to live with. But he then goes on to assure them that the system can cope. John Dunlop, for example, in a paper on *Future Trends in Industrial Relations in the United States* maintained:

> The American industrial relations system, or that of any country, will continue to live with a number of inner tensions: the conflicts between local unions and their members: the different interests of local and national unions: the balance between union democracy or responsiveness to members and the need for responsibility and efficiency in management and the economy: the difficulties of reconciling diffused private collective bargaining and a degree of national economic planning, the conflicts among the objectives of high employment, price stability, labour management peace, and international goals etc. But the industrial relations system does accommodate and adjust to these conflicts and tensions . . . The constructive direction of future industrial relations policy lies in expanding tripartite discussion — pragmatic problem-solving.
>
> (IIRA. , 3rd World Congress, September 1973, pp. 13-14)

The point to notice about this is that it does not pronounce on ends, only on methods. The only end is the maintenance of the system in some sort of working order. It is not difficult to see that even within the system outcomes as well as methods matter to the participants. And with the coalescence towards middle-of-the-road solutions it is plain that questions surrounding the distribution of power in the system tend to be rather constrained.

This concern with method rather than ends is I think reflected in much of the current discussion on joint regulation. This method is set against unilateral forms of control: it is seen as a method of collaboration between management and labour and is preferred to the coercive activity of one group against another. Leaving on one side the question of whether it is realistic in terms of their interests for groups to give up the power they possess, one observes that the appeal to adopt the methods is also an appeal to interests. But how you make the appeal depends on whom you are speaking to. If it is to management you point out that: 'Under modern conditions, when the motives for coercion become increasingly doubtful it is upon the promotion of this joint "problem-solving" that management's freedom to innovate largely rests. We thus reach the paradox that only by fully recognising and accepting the constraints imposed by the aspirations of its subordinates, and working through these constraints towards a new synthesis, can management now enjoy any creative role in its handling of the social organisation' (Fox, Alan, *The Sociology of Work and Industry*, 1971, pp. 172-3). If, on the other hand, it is to workers who take an anti-capitalist stance and are suspicious that integrative bargaining is yet another technique for management domination you say: 'The correct response . . . is not flatly to oppose the new capitalist strategies but to use them as a vehicle for mounting an offensive campaign for "workers' control" — i.e. for fundamental changes in procedural norms' (ibid., p. 175). This may or may not be sound political advice but I cannot help thinking that someone somewhere is going to be disappointed when he finds that the method does not deliver the goods he assumed it would when he first adopted it for impeccably pragmatic reasons.

The second observation I want to make is that the answer to the question, what is to be done, can be defined as a matter of urgency if the industrial relations system is diagnosed as being in a state of acute disorder. In this respect we are familiar with the Fox and Flanders' use of the anomie concept and the programme for the reform of industrial relations which is then promulgated (in Flanders, op. cit., pp. 241-76). Leaving aside academic doubts as to whether or not the analysis of anomie is based on a correct reading of Durkheim, what we do notice is that this is an attempt to unite theory and practice. What needs to be stressed, however, is that all this takes place within a functionalist and pluralist framework with a good number of assumptions built in. No one has pointed this out recently more forcefully than Fox himself (in Child, John (ed.), *Man and Organisation*, 1973, pp. 185-231). And it is here that we appear to come full circle in the discussion of pragmatism as differentiating between myths and reality: 'Unquestionably', he says, 'the pluralistic perspective has vital uses as a working instrument when we involve ourselves in public policy. In such contexts pluralism might be said to serve as something in the nature of a Platonic "noble myth". But it is a further implication of the reasoning of this essay that pluralism may also operate as an ignoble social myth by offering a misleading picture of the realities of social power, thereby serving those who, by the test of "cui bono" have an interest in the propogation of a comforting and re-assuring message' (ibid., p. 231).

It ought now to be added, at least by way of remembrance, that the unity of theory and practice is sometimes attempted on quite other bases and the Marxist concept of *praxis* bears witness to this. I say this not to assert the superiority of Marxist method over Durkheimian method but to recall the existence of competing orientations and to point out that if we are to accept one method of analysis as more realistic than another we should know what theoretical (and epistemological) assumptions we are making and have some criterion of judgement for choosing between them. It may however be that we have Humean logical objections to both of these approaches, which seek to lead us from the 'is' to the 'ought'.

Thirdly, what I have attempted to disentangle so far in the discussion of pragmatism is the curious mixture of facts and concepts, of theory and anti-theory, or ideology and anti-ideology, of a pre-occupation with method rather than ends in formal terms whilst in substantive terms arguing for a middle-of-the-road consensus. (The road is already built so to speak and one doesn't ask too many questions as to where it is going, rather one looks to the steering.)

There is, however, one more aspect of pragmatism that I want to take into account. It is to recall that pragmatism has also been defined as a philosophical doctrine that estimates any assertion solely by its practical bearing upon human interests. What is useful therefore depends on what purpose it serves and purposes are related to specific interests of definite individuals and groups. It was on these kinds of ground that pragmatism as a style of thought opposed absolutist views of truth, but by the same token it rather splinters a common-sense view of what should be done in particular situations because common sense is related to interests and utility. A plurality of interests represents a plurality of utilities. Now although particular interest groups may well have moral scruples about what they should or should not do in pursuing their purposes, it is the case that a pragmatic approach can come to be defined in terms of what is expedient or opportunist. Such pragmatism may have a somewhat amoral even ruthless character. It points to the world of sanctions, threats, broken promises and corruption. More prosaically ideologies may be deployed for expedient reasons: rhetoric and myth known to be such but utilised to achieve other ends. This is brought out in Delamotte and Walker's observations on the humanisation of work movement:

> Humanising innovations in work organisation are undoubtedly made by managements for serious practical reasons. In some cases the objective is to obtain a more flexible work organisation in order to cope more effectively with a variable economic environment. In others the aims are to resolve certain perennial problems such as absenteeism, labour turnover, difficulties in recruitment, unsatisfactory standard of work, etc. To the extent that such problems persist or become more serious management will continue to be driven to search for solutions. Unless jobs become scarce once more, humanising innovations in work organisations are likely to be among the possible expedients tried. Only experience will show to what extent they provide 'solutions' to the practical problems involved. There are some indications that the improvements achieved through such innovations are not always maintained over a long period.
>
> (*Humanisation of Work and the Reality of Working Life — Trends and Issues*, IILS Bulletin, Vol. 11, p. 13)

The possibility for counter-attack exists of course as soon as opposing interest groups come to suspect what is going on — when they see the rhetoric for what it is and say 'we know what your game is'. It is the kind of issue which is well-illustrated in L.E. Karlsson's discussion of industrial democracy in Sweden ('Industrial Democracy in Sweden', in G. Hunnins *et al.* (eds), *Workers' Control*, 1973, pp. 176-92). The general point, however, is this: that the simple distinction between myth and reality cannot easily be sustained since powerful myths can be put to work and can be very real in their consequences. This is so whether one is talking of myths surrounding work-ins, sit-ins, strikes or using the concept of the national interest to sustain and justify policy decisions. The creation of myths as powerful symbols or the contest to use them as between conflicting parties is part of the warp and woof of industrial relations. Sociologists and others may, so to speak, try to demythologise but myths can never be eradicated and may serve many purposes and interests. The academic task is surely to identify myths in use with a view to understanding their function and purpose in industrial relations.

I would argue that any analysis of industrial relations — certainly at a macro-level — cannot be adequate if it examines conduct in the industrial sphere, and the institutional arrangements located there, in isolation from the rest of the social structure. That is why John Goldthorpe's paper on social inequality and social integration seems to me to carry more weight when it comments on prospects and possibilities for British industrial relations, than those analyses that simply ask what is wrong with the industrial relations system and then promulgate procedural reforms in system terms. The point of Goldthorpe's analysis is not that one has to accept the goal of social equality or give it high priority, but that structured social inequality which has no moral legitimacy in the society at large does seem to suggest certain concomitants:

> What *can* be argued sociologically is that those who are prepared to accept social inequality more or less as it presently exists must *also* be prepared to accept 'disorderly' industrial relations, the 'wages jungle' and general economic 'free for all' more or less as *they* now exist — or, as the one remaining possibility, to support attempts at entirely authoritarian solutions to these problems. This last course of action, however, would be perhaps the most effective way of breaking down the insulation of the British political system from issues and grievances stemming from inequality — the insulation which the national political culture has hitherto provided. In other words, it would carry the very real threat of extending economic into political instability.
>
> (in Wedderburn, Dorothy (ed.), *Poverty, Inequality and Class Structure*, 1974, p. 233)

It is interesting to notice that the significance of this approach has not altogether been lost on students of industrial relations within the Oxford school. I would refer here not only to Fox's more recent writings, but also to the concluding section (p. 198) of McCarthy and Ellis's book *Management by Agreement* [1973]:

> The ideas of social planning and industrial democracy that inform and underlie the notion of management by agreement, are related to more general aims and aspirations that extend beyond the workplace . . . What government must do is to demonstrate that they are at least aware of the connection between industrial relations reform and their other policies. They should not appear resentful or even surprised, when told that what they felt they must do to safeguard the currency, reduce taxation, fulful their treaty obligations, or secure votes, has set back the source of industrial relations reform. At least they should look as if they were aware that this might happen and that they have counted the cost of their actions.

Industrial relations and industrial capitalism

I want now to explore two central themes in the sociology of industrial relations: the cash-nexus relationship and the incorporation thesis. This serves as a way of prising open a good deal of the literature on industrial relations in capitalist societies. It has been argued that a good deal of this literature is 'static' in that it only serves to supply an academic rationalisation to the existing structure of industrial relations (Allen, 1971). This is allegedly because it is dominated by systems analysis which stresses value consensus in industrial relations and in the wider society. It is certainly possible to find accounts of industrial relations which do appear to have a view of industrial relations systems as containing self-correcting mechanisms making for the stability of the whole (Dunlop, 1958).

Despite the demolition job on writers who adhere to systems analysis, one discovers that Allen's 'dynamic' analysis, which he identifies as historical materialism, stipulates among other things that 'a part cannot be understood without reference to the whole, that segments of systems cannot be analysed in isolation from each other or their environments' (Allen, 1971, p. 9). As a programmatic statement this seems reasonable enough, since it leaves open the question of the stability or instability of the systems being analysed. As it happens, the issues surrounding the instability of systems have not been entirely ignored to which the recent debate on the degree of anomie in British industrial relations bears witness (Flanders, 1970; Eldridge, 1971; Goldthorpe, 1974; Fox, 1974).

As always the difficulty lies in putting flesh on the bones of programmatic statements. What concepts are to be employed, what theories formulated? Some of the problems encountered in the struggle to do this are reflected in the discussion that follows. How does one ground the surface phenomenon of industrial relations to give a coherent explanation of what is observed? How does one set 'events' in 'context'? The two themes which I have chosen to look at represent a range of attempts to account for the form, character and changes of industrial relations in capitalist societies. A good deal of the literature constitutes a debate with Marx but the divisions of judgement are by no means to be classified as Marxist versus non-Marxist as we shall see.

Industrial relations and the cash nexus

In this section I want to discuss the concept of the cash nexus and what relevance it may have to questions of control and conflict in industrial relations. The point of departure is located in Marx's writings. In the *Communist Manifesto* (Marx, 1973) Marx analyses the breakdown of the feudal order and its guild system and seeks to account for the advent of capitalist society with its factory organisation. He comments (p. 70) explicitly on the revolutionary part which the bourgeoisie played in this transforming process:

> The bourgeoisie, wherever it has got the upper hand, has put an end to all feudal, patriarchal, idyllic relations. It has pitilessly torn asunder the motley feudal ties that bound men to 'his natural superiors', and has left remaining no other nexus between man and man than naked self-interest, than callous 'cash payment'. It has drowned the most heavenly ecstasies of religious fervour, of chivalrous enthusiasm, of philistine sentimentalism, in the icy waters of capitalistic calculation. It has resolved personal worth into exchange value.

One paradox that is much discussed in Marx's writing is this. The bourgeoisie in capitalist society are immensely powerful. With single-minded energy they control the state and the economy and hence the industrial proletariat. Yet (pp. 70-1) the system they seek to control is inherently unstable, so much so that ultimately they will be unable to control it:

> The bourgeoisie cannot exist without constantly revolutionising the instruments of production, and thereby the relations of production, and with them the whole relations of society. Conservation of the old modes of production in unaltered form, was, on the contrary, the first condition of existence for all earlier industrial classes. Constant revolutionising of production, uninterrupted disturbance of all social conditions, everlasting uncertainty and agitation distinguish the

> bourgeois epoch from all earlier ones . . . All that is solid melts into the air, all that is holy is profaned, and man is at last compelled to face with sober senses, his real conditions of life and his relations with his kind.

Marx's *Capital* is, in an important sense, a detailed exposition and analysis of the sources of instability entailed in a system of wage labour (Marx, 1957). There is, for example, a critical distinction drawn between the social division of labour and the division of labour in the workshop. The first is characterised by anarchy because it rests inexorably upon competition and is reflected in the fluctuation of market prices. The division of labour in the workshop is affected by this wider process and contributes to it. If then one looks at the first capitalist society, Britain, the intricate and considered discussion of such matters as the length of the working day, shift and relay systems, child labour, methods of wage payment, industrial legislation and the effects of machinery upon workers, one can see that Marx is actually attempting to chart out the dimensions of a struggle which is, in essence, over the buying and selling of labour power.

The underlying rationale for the buying of labour power is expressed in the idea that 'the value of labour-power, and the value which labour power creates in the labour process, are two entirely different magnitudes; and this difference of the two values was what the capitalist had in mind when he was purchasing labour-power' (p. 174). But can the capitalist live indefinitely on this basis of control through the appropriation of this surplus value created by labour? For Marx the despotism of the workplace could be a desperate reality to those exposed to its oppression. Indeed, part of his commentary is designed to depict the misery of living under a regimented factory system, subject to the overlooker's book of penalties and working like an automaton, as an appendage to a machine. As he contemplates the worst abuses of employer power over factory labour moral indignation is interwoven into his sober economic and social analysis. The heat, the dust, the noise, the lack of light, air and personal safety in workshops overcrowded with machinery combine to assault the senses of the worker. Yet this powerlessness of labour in relation to the conditions of its existence was not the last word. Proletarian consciousness — the awareness of the nature of its own exploitation — would develop with revolutionary economic and political consequences. An understanding that the real relationship of the bourgeoisie with the wage labourer was embodied in the cash-nexus was a critical factor in developing such consciousness. This prediction was, in Marx's view, bound up with the immanent laws of capitalist development relating to the social division of labour: the growth in the scale of capitalist undertakings involving, through competition, the expropriation of many capitalists by the few. It is this very process which creates a disciplined, united and organised proletariat, a revolutionary class: 'The monopoly of capital becomes a fetter upon the mode of production, which has sprung up and flourished along with, and under it. Centralisation of the means of production and socialisation of labour at last reach a point where they become incompatible with their capitalist integument. This integument is burst asunder. The knell of capitalist private property sounds. The expropriators are expropriated' (p. 789).

What is of significance for our purposes is that industrial relations comes to be viewed as an arena in which the struggle for control over labour power is played out. At the same time industrial relations may be reckoned as shifting in character with structural changes that occur in the social division of labour. A Marxist perspective might appear to suggest therefore that one should take readings of the industrial relations temperature to measure the degree of revolutionary class consciousness. One might reformulate this to ask how exposed is the cash-nexus relationship in a given situation, since Marx implies that a growing awareness of this relationship between capital and labour reveals a truth, the knowledge of which is a prelude to revolutionary change.

The problem I want to consider is this: what kind of temperature gauge is the cash-nexus relationship? In what sense does it or might it contain Marxist implications? For example, a number of studies of industrialisation refer to the development of calculative economic behaviour among workers. Much of the comment on and interpretative analysis of machine-breaking and resistance to technological change during the industrial revolution hinges around the question as to how far this behaviour was related to the perceived economic interests of the participants (including employers who were often ambivalent in their attitudes to change). Whether these activities were successful in accomplishing their aims is essentially a matter for historical enquiry. In any event, so far as the participants were concerned, such activities could affect the pace and timing of technological change and give them, as it were, some breathing space in their struggle for survival in the labour market (Hobsbawm, 1964; Thomis, 1974). There were, in addition, less dramatic forms of resistance that strongly suggested an economic motivation. The attempts made by factory owners and their overseers to control the work-force entailed the struggle to impose a time-discipline and to get the required amount of work out of the employees once they entered the factory. This struggle is reflected in the array of sanctions and rewards deployed by employers and the forms of resistance generated by workers against speed-ups, tight piece rates, unsatisfactory working hours and conditions. Some of this resistance might well have been undertaken on grounds of tradition. The attempt may have been made to maintain the status quo so far as possible, irrespective of possible future economic benefits accruing from adapting to change. But some behaviour was more calculative as E.P. Thompson points out: 'The first generation were taught by their masters the importance of time. The second generation founded their short-time committees in the ten-hour movement; the third generation struck for overtime or time and a half. They had captured the categories of their employers and learned to fight back within them. They had learned their lesson that time is money only too well' (Thompson, 1967, p.86).

The time struggle is inextricably intermeshed with what has come to be termed the effort bargain (Behrend, 1957). What constitutes a fair day's work for a fair day's pay? To ask the question seriously leads to a probe into the nature of the employment contract. Whether people are paid for the expenditure of physical or mental effort, to carry out instructions or to exercise responsibility, a principle of compensation is involved for the time spent in the employment of another and for the energy deployed in work. Some of the shop-floor studies undertaken by sociologists reveal the ways in which workers may operate the effort bargain in an endeavour to improve their terms of trade (e.g. Lupton, 1963).

I am suggesting that the cash-nexus proposition has close affinities with the effort-bargain concept. Certainly the awareness of the effort bargain serves to reveal the essentially economic nature of the employment contract. One way in which this awareness can develop has been traced out in Gouldner's fascinating studies *Wildcat Strike* and *Patterns of Industrial Bureaucracy* (Gouldner 1955 and 1959). There we see the communal relations of an American gypsum mine corroded and subordinated to economic goals, as a result of the way in which management responded to the increasing competitiveness of the product market. The 'indulgency' pattern, whereby certain work practices and habits were tolerated as an expression of good will between management and men (and were supported by local community values) was replaced by a 'stringency' pattern in which the attempt was made to bring about worker compliance to imposed bureaucratic rules. The various worker responses to this new code included strikes, absenteeism and work-to-rules. The general point which emerged was that, while some workers hoped by their actions to bring about a return to the traditional situation, the dominant worker adjustment was in terms of a market orientation. If management focuses on costs, then labour will more consciously come to do so. As the language of the market is more explicitly spoken so the employment contract comes to be more closely geared to a consideration of market power by the bargainers.

Market power is a concept which can apply and be seen to operate at various levels: the individual worker, the work group, the factory work force, the skilled craftsman, the occupational group, the trade union and the professional association. In a diversity of ways the attempt may be made to discover, exercise, defend or improve market power by these various categories. Thus one observes attempts to control the supply of labour, resistance to technical changes and work practices held to be disadvantageous, output control and the withholding of labour. The accounts of trade union history witness to the ways and circumstances in which these and other practices have taken place, sometimes as a substitute for negotiation and sometimes as a context-setting activity for bargaining. Likewise, the weapons of the employers are also recorded including hiring and firing practices and lock-outs in the struggle to determine the market price of labour (Webb, 1894; Turner, 1962; Lane, 1974). However, the realisation of market power does not necessarily have anything to do with a generalised or universal proletarian consciousness. Indeed, at the level of what the Americans call 'business unionism' this pre-occupation with the market price for labour has been labelled as 'economism' by socialists echoing Lenin because it does not generate any political activity devoted to revolutionary change. It may rather inhibit such action (Lenin, 1961).

Market power is differentially distributed as between groups of employees. It is precisely this reality which undergirds discussions of wage and salary differentials. For example, recent British experience of the militancy of low-paid workers (especially in the public sector) and of professional groups such as teachers and doctors represent attempts to realise effective market power. The language deployed typically relates to arguments over parity, comparability and to restoring or improving one's place in the earnings league table. What is of particular interest in recent British experience is the way in which white-collar workers and middle-class professional groupings have become more contract conscious (Bain, 1972). This has meant that 'vocational' attitudes which have stressed the ethic of service have become subordinated to a more stringent scrutiny of the terms and conditions of work. So, for example, doctors in the National Health Service have come to treat hours of work as something that needs to be calculated and consciously related to remuneration. Rather than a fixed salary with a flexible interpretation of work load and working hours, the language of piece rates, time rates and overtime payments now comes into the reckoning. This concern with the economics of the employment contract can lead, not to greater egalitarianism within an occupation but to the stretching out of differentials. In teaching and in medicine the concept of career structure is applied in negotiations.

Once the cash-nexus becomes of central concern the character of employer-employee relations is affected, whether or not Marx was correct in the inferences he drew from this fact. One more recent analysis of the matter that has certain affinities with Marx's treatment is found in Baldamus's *Efficiency and Effort* (1961). In a closely argued study, he considers the factors which serve to institutionalise effort values (and which are reflected in the terms of the effort bargain) and the sources of instability that may disrupt them. An increase in the available supply of labour and tougher competition in the product market, for example, will, Baldamus suggests, tend to lead to an attempt on the part of management to intensify effort controls. The converse of these conditions may lead to a more favourable effort bargain being struck by employees. For heuristic purposes Baldamus utilises the notion of wage parity, as a hypothetical equilibrium between effort and pay on a given level of expectations. He then considers the likely consequences of shifts from that position in terms of the concept of wage disparity. The existence of wage disparity is treated by Baldamus as a central explanatory factor to account for industrial conflict in its range of manifestations.

The parties to the conflict may or may not be aware that wage disparity is the heart of the problem. Historically in industrial societies, Baldamus suggests, some wage disparity in favour of employers has been condoned by employees because of certain moral expectations attached to the idea of work as a duty. Where such work obligations are firmly institutionalised they are not experienced as a contradiction to the principle of effort compensation. However, it is further suggested that the growth of large-scale organisation is accompanied by processes that reveal the basis of the employment contract:

> For the very methods that are the main administrative instrument of effort intensification, such as payment by results, make the process of effort compensation and particularly, the relation of effort to earnings, more and more transparent. The growing pre-occupation with the administration of effort values may thus possibly reach a point where the normative aspects of industrial work are less concealed or taken for granted than at present. This would amount to a general drift in the institutional basis of employment from status to performance criteria. Unless a new pattern of social supports emerges the disruptive effects of industrial conflict can then no longer be absorbed, as they have been hitherto, by the employees' tacit acceptance of work obligations (p. 112).

It is precisely the shift from status to performance criteria that the comments made above concerning the new-found militancy of teachers and doctors serve to illustrate. It is a particularly significant example, however, because whereas the moral commitment to some industrial occupations may be somewhat limited in the first place, here we are dealing with the erosion of moral obligations which are traditionally embedded in the idea of vocation. What follows from this contract consciousness is that general goals such as 'the welfare of the patient' or 'the education of the young' become much more contingent commitments.

What this discussion of the role of the cash-nexus suggests is that an awareness of this relationship clarifies the basis of the employment contract. This contributes to the instability of social relationships and reflects other changes taking place in the industrial and occupational systems. It is possible now to indicate how Weber's discussion of class and status relations can throw further light on the matter (Weber, 1961). Weber, like Marx, treats class as an economic category. Ultimately class situation is defined as market situation: 'We may speak of a "class" when (1) a number of people have in common a specific causal component of their life chances, in so far as (2) this component is represented exclusively by economic interests in the possession of goods and opportunities for income, and (3) is represented under the conditions of the community or labour markets' (p. 181).

Class situation is contrasted with status situation — the formation of socially ranked groups, embodying distinctive life styles. Such groups are described by Weber as 'communities' and are able to control mechanisms admitting or excluding people into membership and seek to regulate behaviour according to the values it cherishes. The question Weber confronts is under what conditions the class relations become exposed to reveal basic structural antagonisms that lead to class-conscious action. His answer is explicit: 'Every technological repercussion and economic transformation threatens stratification by status and pushes the class situation into the foreground. Epochs and countries in which the naked class situation is of predominant significance are regularly the periods of technical and economic transformations' (p. 194). It is precisely at such times that a given distribution of property or structure of an economic order is no longer taken for granted. The 'life chances' of class groups which stem from these formations may be challenged. It is then, for example, that 'rational associations' established to prosecute class interests are likely to emerge and trade unions are a classic case in point. But if class situations are strictly economic and are seen by Weber as related to the labour market, the commodities market and the capitalist enterprise in industrial societies, it is clear that the variations which may occur here will not necessarily line up with a portrayal of generalised proletarian action of a universal and revolutionary nature. Essentially it becomes an empirical question to discover how far, for example, the evolution of the industrial proletariat moves in the direction of increasing uniformity of heterogeneity. The occupational structure (not only factory work), the scale of industrial organisation and the process of bureaucratisation are all of relevance in that they affect the contours of the market situation and therefore the shape of class antagonism.

The Weberian perspective does I think present something of a dilemma to Marxist analyses of the cash-nexus. In Marxist terms, where there are internal variations in the market situation for different groups of wage labour, 'rational associations' organised to protect and represent specific interest groups may be labelled sectionalist. The activities they pursue and the interest groups so constructed may even be cited as examples of 'false consciousness'. This indeed is one of the reasons why Marxists have frequently had ambivalent attitudes to such phenomena as craft unions and, moreover, the general doubt that trade union activity expresses an approach of mere economism, that may inhibit revolutionary consciousness is also expressed. The problem for the Marxist may be illustrated by reference to one or two recent studies and commentaries.

In his excellent study, *The First Shop Stewards' Movement*, Hinton (1973) traces the pattern of growth and decline of the workers' committees and shop stewards' organisations in various parts of the UK from 1910 to the early 1920s. This was a time of highly class conscious activity, he argues, with explicit revolutionary intentions built into the movement. The key to success and failure was in an important sense located in the same phenomenon: craft consciousness. 'Craft work induced a pride and an independence which manifested itself in a tenacious resistance both to managerial encroachments in the work-place, and to the logic of bureaucratisation both in industry and in the trade unions . . . To the extent that the shop stewards' movement succeeded in taking the craftsmen beyond exclusiveness, it was able to release these traditions of craft control and of local autonomy from the narrow embrace of a defensive craft consciousness, to transform them into weapons of an ambitious class offensive' (p. 15). It was in areas such as Glasgow, Sheffield and Manchester, where the craft traditions were most developed and, at the same time threatened by dilution, that the movement was strongest. The conflict between the anti-bureaucratic craft-control system and the pressures of capitalist rationality intensified as a result of the war was combined with revolutionary syndicalist doctrines. The ambiguity resided in the fact that the labour aristocracy was a vehicle for a revolutionary potential subversive to the capitalist order, but also held on to its sense of craft exclusiveness. Hinton concluded: 'Faced with the prospect of making a decisive challenge to the Government, the craftsmen's elan shrivelled into a conservative militancy, the defence of vested interest. But however subordinate the revolutionary possibilities, they had been there, and had been seen by the revolutionary movement to be there' (p. 337). The study then is partly a reflection on what might have been, but even more the way in which such movements provide a glimpse of what is possible in some revolutionary future when capitalist rationality is transcended. In a way this pays unconscious tribute to the strength of the Weberian perspective.

This last point can be further illustrated by Westergaard's instructive commentary on the cash-nexus proposition (Westergaard, 1970, 1972). Westergaard suggests that a number of recent studies of British industrial relations that emphasise the instrumental behaviour of workers and reflected in strike activities and work attitudes are actually pointing to the exposure of the cash-nexus (Turner, 1967; Eldridge, 1968; Lane and Roberts, 1971). This is most developed, he argues, in industries such as motor manufacture where variations in earnings and job security go hand in hand with high monetary expectations. 'If the wage packet is the only link that ties the worker to a grudging commitment to his work, to his bosses, and to society at large, that is a brittle strand, liable to wear thin or to snap when the dependability of earnings is threatened or pay rises fail to keep pace with rising demands' (Westergaard, 1972, p. 162). Moreover, in these circumstances, 'even industrial disputes formally confined to wages and immediately related questions seem likely to bring wider issues of control, authority and economic policy recurrently into focus' (p. 162).

Westergaard is interested in the ways in which industrial conflict has been extended and deepened as class conflict in British society and in some respects he sees the breaking down of local community ties and of some occupational boundaries as a means of transcending particularistic and sectional solidarities. The possibility of a socialist transformation is thereby placed on the agenda but for all that the future remains open. Westergaard remains cautious about drawing any revolutionary conclusions as a necessary consequence of his analysis. Rather he seeks to underline the potential for social protest which changes in the economic and social structure of British society have made possible.

One final example of the continued relevance of Weber's approach to class analysis must suffice. I would refer here to Hyman's paper, 'Industrial Conflict and the Political Economy', which is a considered evaluation of contemporary British industrial relations from a Marxist standpoint (Hyman, 1974). Recent experience of industrial militancy in Britain has, in his view, (p. 125), been sectional in character:

> While the size of wage demands in the last few years seems, by previous standards, remarkably ambitious, they appear far more modest when set against such factors as the rise in the cost of living (and in particular food prices), the effects of 'fiscal drag', and the 'poverty trap' . . . Moreover, the focus in wage disputes is still the relative pay of different sections of workers — rather than the process of exploitation which affects all workers. Or again, many of the major struggles of recent years may be seen as a response to the initiatives of employers in seeking to curb public sector pay rather than as a reflection of an autonomous eruption of worker militancy. And even the recent developments in the *methods* of industrial conflict — the wave of sit-ins, flying pickets, occasional mass solidarity actions — need by no means imply that the traditionally restricted aims of trade unionists in conflict have been significantly transcended.

While Hyman treats such collective action as a response to economic exploitation and the deprivation of control — which he sees as inherent in the institution of wage labour, he does not regard it as signifying or even by itself generating 'an explosion of consciousness' in the working class. From a Marxist standpoint he concludes (p. 130) that political education is required to be able to shift industrial conflict from its sectional basis to that of the working class as a whole.

> Effective intervention in the current industrial struggle necessitates an adequate general theory of capitalism and the transition to socialism; a theoretical analysis of the present disposition of the class struggle — the objectives of the ruling class, the role of the unions, and the state of working class consciousness; and a set of strategies and tactics, of immediate and transitional demands, which are internally coherent and are explicitly related to the first two elements. In addition organisational recourses and ability are essential for the integration of theory and practice.

As with Westergaard's discussion of the cash-nexus, the question, what does the future hold, is hedged with uncertainty and unpredictability. The relevance of the cash-nexus in helping us to appreciate some salient features of industrial relations and industrial conflict can scarcely be doubted, but the linkage with the immanent laws of capitalist development is, to say the least, not a straightforward matter.

Containment or encroachment? Some frayed edges of the incorporation thesis

There are many variations on the theme of incorporation and a range of judgements as to the desirability of the processes discerned. What does seem to be implied with greater or lesser degrees of firmness is the proposition that wage labour in Western societies has been contained by the capitalist system. This thesis does typically present itself as an alternative to the polarisation thesis of class conflict. Indeed, it partly addresses itself to the question of why such revolutionary conflicts have not occurred. Commentators examine the ways in which civil and political rights are extended to all classes of the population in the nation-state; the bureaucratisation of trade unions and the political parties; the institutionalisation of collective bargaining; and the role of parliamentary government in canalising political conflict. Strong and weak versions of this thesis exist among Marxists and non-Marxists and I want in this section to indicate some of the rough edges and ambiguities that need to be considered as they bear upon industrial relations.

Take first the issue of union bureaucratisation. The consequences of this process since the writings of the Webbs and Michels have been associated with 'the iron law of oligarchy' (Webbs, 1911; Michels, 1962). This has pointed to the great difficulties which rank-and-file union members may encounter in seeking to exercise democratic control over their leaders. Michels developed this 'law' as a way of drawing attention to the fact that the democratic rhetoric associated with trade union and socialist party organisation might not, for various structural and psychological reasons, accord with reality. He recognised that democratic ideals could and did challenge oligarchical rule and himself advocated the spread of education to reduce the power and information gap between leaders and led. A well-documented 'exception' to the law is a study of the International Typographical Association (Lipset *et al.*, 1956). Other writers, notably Gouldner, have suggested that one can go further than this exception to the rule argument. He maintains that the iron law of oligarchy is not based on an irresistible argument. Rather it is a product of 'the pathos of pessimism': 'It is only in the light of such a pessimistic pathos that the defeat of democratic values can be assumed probable, while their victory is seen as a slender thing, delicately constituted and precariously balanced' (Gouldner, 1966, p. 507).

The relation of leaders to led is manifestly a critical factor in any discussion of union democracy and it is not difficult to see that education of union members can heighten an awareness of the significance of union rule books, of organisation structure and of the mechanisms of policy implementation. There is also the question of what union leaders do, in particular how they behave in their dealings with business leaders and the state. The incorporation thesis sometimes seems to stress the corruptibility of union leaders and to suggest that this has facilitated the integration of the trade unions to the state. This formed part of Michel's own account. The matter cannot be reduced to psychological instances. That this is so may be illustrated in a number of ways.

Take, for example, Wright Mills's discussion of labour leaders in the USA. As he surveyed the complex interaction between union leaders, business corporations and the state, he concluded that the role of union leaders was not one of 'transcending' the existing capitalist and elitist social structure, but rather one of 'maximum accommodation'. Accordingly, union leaders are locked into a structural drift towards an elitist dominated mass society. They are not fighting it but seeking to join it albeit on the most favourable terms for themselves and the union they represent. Consequently:

> These unions are less levers for change of that general framework [of political economy] than they are instruments for more advantageous integration with it. The drift their actions implement in terms of the largest projections is a kind of 'procapitalist syndicalism from the top'. They seek, in the first instance, greater integration at the upper levels of the corporate economy rather than greater power at the lower levels of the work hierarchy, for, in brief, it is the unexpressed desire of American labour leaders to join with owners and managers in running the corporate enterprise system and influencing decisively

the political economy as a whole.

(Mills, 1963, pp. 108-9)

What is implied by this kind of analysis is that industrial relations must be understood in context and at the societal level this means considering them within the framework of political economy. What trade union leaders do cannot simply be accounted for by reference to their personal ambitions or corruptibility. This treatment of incorporation in terms of structural drift finds some echo in Marcuse's work, notably *One Dimensional Man* (1964). More important in this connection is Miliband's *State in Capital Society* (Miliband, 1968). In the latter study we have a more explicit and worked out extension of the Mill's thesis from American to other advanced capitalist societies. Miliband maintains that American trade union leaders accept the capitalist order in theory and in practice. To that extent business unionism is scarcely a surprising phenomenon. In West European societies, on the other hand, trade union leaders may be ideologically committed to a socialist order but in practice their behaviour is similar to their American counterparts. Assessing the nature of the collaboration between business, government and the trade unions, Miliband argues: 'Trade union leaders have found it easy to believe that because they have been recognised as a necessary element in the operation of capitalism, they have also achieved parity with business in the determination of policy. In fact their incorporation into the official life of these countries has mainly served to saddle them with responsibilities which have further weakened their bargaining position, and which has helped to reduce their effectiveness' (p. 161).

It is fair to add that Miliband does, elsewhere in his study, express the view that there are profoundly destabilising forces at work in capitalist society and that ultimately the working class will no longer be incorporated but will acquire the faculty of ruling the nation. Nevertheless between then and now is a gap which he does not see easily bridged. Moreover, given the realities of state power and the divisions in the labour movement and the socialist parties, he envisages a movement towards more authoritarian forms of state control as a not unlikely outcome in liberal democratic societies.

The structural-drift argument has been referred to as an alternative to over-psychologistic explanations of union leadership. It is, however, not the only kind of structural explanation available and it will be helpful to set it against other perspectives. One well-known version of the incorporation thesis is located in Dahrendorf's *Class and Class Conflict in an Industrial Society* (1959). There, great emphasis is placed on the institutionalisation of collective bargaining in 'post-capitalist' societies and in the separation of political from industrial conflict, which has served to insulate industrial conflict within the industrial system. The stability of industrial societies is thereby enhanced.

This borrows a good deal in conception from the liberal pluralist analyses of Clark Kerr and his colleagues and in consequence has certain affinities with the 'end of ideology' interpretation of conflict in industrial societies (Kerr *et al.*, 1962; Kerr, 1964). There is, however, one important difference. Whereas in the systems analysis of the liberal-pluralist industrial conflict is seen as contained and controllable, for Dahrendorf (p. 278-9) the bureaucratisation of trade unions is a process which may contain and pattern certain forms of conflict, but also may generate conflict, especially of an inter-union type: 'The fact that industrial conflict has become less violent and intense in the last century does not justify the inference that it will continue to do so. On the contrary, experience shows that in the history of specific conflicts more and less violent, more and less intense periods follow each other in unpredictable rythms. It is certainly conceivable that the future has more intense and violent conflicts in store.'

There are, in addition, other dimensions to the issue of containing industrial conflict. The impact of inflation is a particularly important case in point. If one looks at Galbraith's study, *American Capitalism* (1963) one of the salient features of it is that the thesis of 'countervailing power' is put forward partly as a tendency statement and partly as a policy prescription for managing capitalism. Galbraith sees countervailing power as a curb on economic power and sees the labour market as an important exemplar of this mechanism. He notes that in the USA industries which are dominated by large corporations, such as steel, automobiles and farm machinery, have been the breeding ground of strong unions. Where countervailing power is not, as it were, self-generating, Galbraith concludes that the state must assist. Such an intervention will serve to defuse more violent conflicts that otherwise might have played out into the political sphere. It is the existence and promotion of countervailing power that forms the keynote of Galbraith's response to the Marxist critique of monopoly capitalism: '. . . the Marxian attack has not been on capitalism but upon monopoly capitalism. The fact that the power of the genus of monopoly is ubiquitous has not been difficult to show. So long as competition remains the conservative's defence, the left is bound to have a near monopoly of the evidence and the logic' (pp. 182-3).

A more recent study by Giddens, whilst different in many significant respects, comes up against the same obstacle (1973). Giddens argues that state socialism, as an alternative variant to liberal capitalism, has its best chance of coming into being when a society is at a relatively low level of economic development moving from feudalism to capitalism. If the revolutionary outcome does not occur at that stage then working class protest is likely to be incorporated and institutionalised through the extension of political, industrial and legal rights to the whole population. For him, therefore, it is the presence of revolutionary class consciousness, rather than its absence, that requires explanation.

Nevertheless, Giddens recognises the contradictions that can occur in a managed mixed economy, especially in periods of growing inflation. The stability of liberal democratic societies which the process of incorporation brought about can become threatened and even fragile. This is because even if union leaders may seek with the government of the day and with employers to agree on the regulation of the economy (and that is not unconditional) it will be no easy coalition. Attempts to regulate wages and long-term contracts may well meet with rank-and-file resistance. The ability to carry their members with them can become an issue and, in consequence affect the credibility of their leadership. In such circumstances the likelihood of class conflict spilling over into the political arena is strong. This is directly contrary to a major tenet in the incorporation thesis, namely the institutional separation of industrial from political conflict. With continuing attempts to control incomes through statutory or voluntary incomes policies in capitalist societies has lent a certain artificiality to this notion for many years now. Further, if as a result of inflationary pressures liberal capitalist societies are unable to generate real wage increases, then movements for workers' control may be translated into political and economic action that has the effect of transcending capitalism (see also, Hunnius (ed.), 1973; Glyn and Sutcliffe, 1972). This is, to say the least, a strong caveat to the incorporation thesis.

The incorporation thesis has always provided a challenge if not a threat to Marxist theories of class consciousness. A good summary of many of the Marxist and neo-Marxist responses to the thesis is found in Hyman (1973). It is not necessary to re-capitulate all the lines of the argument. Clearly, from a Marxist standpoint, incorporation has to be treated as a transient phenomenon. Certainly, Marx and Engels may be said to have revised their theory of class conflict. The polarisation of classes based upon the increasing poverty and misery of the working class had to reckon with a British working class, which in their view was becoming more bourgeois. This, however, they anticipated would only be the case while Britain maintained a dominant position in the world economy. A commonly held derivative view is that at a later stage of capitalist development crises will occur leading to breakdown and the ultimate triumph of the proletarian revolution. Since the 1930s this view has not had much immediate evidence to feed upon. In the 1970s it has re-emerged in the wake of more general doubts as to the continuing validity of the Keynesian economic methods to serve as a basis for managing capitalist or neo-capitalist societies. This indeed serves as a basis for Glyn and Sutcliffe's critique, referred to above.

This dramatic prospect is not the only one which Marxists are able to call upon. In the event that capitalism does not break down as a result of recurring and intensifying crises, there remains what may be called the 'prosperity is not enough' motif. This really suggests that when all there is to be said about the economic and cultural subordination of the working class, the hegemony of the state, the benefits of economic growth albeit within a structure of social inequality, it will not be the last word. The relevant text here is Marx's *Grundrisse* (Marx, 1973; see also Nicolaus, 1972). The argument is that it is possible to portray capitalism in its most advanced forms, with the payment of 'surplus wages' to workers with the application of science to industry and the growth of automation, with even the decline of working class occupation compared to middle class occupation, and yet to envisage the transcendence of capitalist society. It is not proletarian revolution which must needs bring this about.The system, with all its incorporating tendencies, provides an arena in which the material forms of production come into conflict with the existing relations of production. The reason is that the system of production based upon the concept of exchange-value becomes thoroughly undermined. Through advanced technology, and automation, man stands at the side of the production process instead of being its chief actor and by the same token he comes to realise that this mastery over nature is not dependent upon the theft of labour-time (that is exploitation). What had been perceived by the capitalist as technological innovation brought into being in the service of profit has unintended consequences. 'Productive forms and social relations . . . appear. Forces of production and social relations — two different sides of the development of the social individual — appear to capital as mere means, and are merely means for it to produce on its limited foundations. In fact, however, they are the material conditions to blow this foundation sky-high' (Marx, 1973, p. 706).

All this of course opens up questions concerned with the nature of class consciousness in advanced capitalist societies (sometimes labelled post-industrial) on which discussions of the 'new working class' and the 'new middle class' have focused, (Mann, 1973). In particular it raises questions as to what kind of collective control of such economies is possible and realistic. How far any encroachment begun that tames the arbitrary power of capital and makes it more accountable to the community and to the producer? How far has the 'revolution' recurred behind the backs of those who proclaim the need for it? Or is it at least in progress?

It is possible to have a wooden, static view of the incorporation thesis, which is rather odd when one recalls that it is process that is being described not the end of history. Naturally it can lead to pessimism among those commentators who do not like what they see but cannot envisage any effective political change taking place. For example one of the problems encountered by those who see the work place as a battleground between labour and capital is can the resistance to managerial prerogatives that one observes be transformed into anything other than guerilla warfare? This is something of a key question for those who look for political transformation as opposed to adjustments within the present system. It is posed by Beynon in his notable study *Working for Fords* (1973). He is impressed with the amount of time and energy spent by shop stewards in representing the interests of their members. Yet, as it seems to him they necessarily become absorbed in the day to day minutae of negotiations. This leads to an *ad hoc* approach to the challenges of the day rather than a systematically developed policy of encroaching on managerial prerogatives. They have found themselves pushed into a position of trying to control the assembly line but have not set out to control the plant. Hence even 'factory consciousness' is a rather tender plant and talk of workers' control is little more than rhetoric.

This kind of argument involves a built in scepticism of union bureaucracy, of collective bargaining and of political activity within the Labour Party. It is of interest to compare it with the approaches that have a somewhat different emphasis, not least because they put the incorporation thesis in a somewhat ambiguous light.

There are approaches which, while recognising the problem of bureaucratisation for union and industrial democracy also point at the inroads that unions and union leaders can make on the running of capitalist society, which if not revolutionary certainly change its character in some important respects. Perhaps the most developed recent work on these lines is Banks's *Marxist Sociology in Action* (1970). Looking at the British industrial scene in historical perspective Banks points to the role that union leaders played in advocating and working for the public ownership of industry. The role of the union leadership in the case of both the mining and the iron and steel industries serve as examples and insofaras capitalist owners were removed from the ownership of strategic areas of industry, this can be defined as no small change. That state ownership can create other problems and certainly cannot be regarded as a recipe for industrial peace is not the point. The opposition to private ownership, although sometimes grounded in economic and technical considerations of efficiency, was typically rooted in moral objections. In an enquiry into the coal industry at the beginning of the century (the Foster Report) a representative of the Northumberland coal owners' association cross-examined a leader of the Northumberland miners. What possible difference could it make to the miner, he wondered, whether the profits of the industry were collected by the few or many, or by a neutral body like the State, so long as he got his fair share? 'Because he is now realising that he is a citizen of the State', replied Straker for the miners (Carter Goodrich, 1920).

Banks's argument, in the British context, puts a rather different slant on the incorporation thesis as compared to the approaches of Mills and Miliband discussed earlier. He stresses the idea of organisation consciousness among trade union leaders as a phenomenon that was in fact revolutionary in its consequences. The organisations which they lead have not so much been incorporated by capitalist society but have acted to change its texture in an anti-capitalist direction: 'The whole history of trade union participation in British politics, both before 1926 and afterwards, is a history of the acceptance of the constitutional machinery with the express purpose of using it legally to improve the situation of the working class. In so far as deliberately, or willy-nilly, this has actually resulted in the piece-meal erosion of the capitalist system of exploitation, such participation is, of course, revolutionary in the present context' (p. 111). With this interpretation Banks takes over Lenin's concept of the vanguard of the proletariat and applies it to trade union leaders, rather than to trained professional revolutionaries. Incidentally, on this reading it is the rank-and-file union member who is more open to Lenin's charge of economism and not the trade union leader who has operated on an economic and a political front.

The pessimism of writers such as Beynon and to some extent Hyman can in part be explained by their scepticism if not cynicism with official union structures and the operation of collective bargaining. Consequently they see the rank and file as hemmed in and encapsulated even by their own union organisations. Banks' approach suggests a different perspective. So too does the approach of writers such as Hughes (1970) who advocate the development of strategic collective bargaining. This is a view which seeks to link together a concern to articulate economic and social policies that not only recognise the realities of the concentration of capital and the role of multi-internationals in the economy, but also to contain if not tame their power by making them accountable to the work-force and to the community. This is an approach which does not operate in either/or terms (either political action or industrial action; either rank-and-file action or collective bargaining) but is multi-faceted and is well summed up (p. 72) in the following statement: 'It has to be a strategic objective of collective bargaining to enhance the elements of workers' control within the domain of the giant firm; at the same time pressure has to be directed through political channels and through the T.U.C., to ensure that statutory powers can also be directed at strengthening workers' rights in the giant combine, and to strengthen the community's right to ensure efficient operation and the minimisation of market expoitation through monopoly power.' It is precisely this kind of approach which Hughes sees as building a bridge between the day to day needs of trade union bargaining and socialist demands of community control over the centres of industrial power.

Conclusion

Are there any general lessons which may be learned in the light of the above discussion from the standpoint of the sociology of industrial relations?

1. In order to understand and evaluate what is being said, it is continually necessary to examine the assumptions that are made, the evidence they are based on, the concepts formulated to account for the underlying 'reality'. It is also important to try and see how these explanations are linked to policy recommendations or prescriptions as to what should be done.

2. It is instructive to see when ideological closures operate. This may occur in some version of the 'end of ideology' thesis when it is tied to complacent notions of a system able to maintain itself and resolve tensions within it. Or it may occur in some Marxist accounts which favour mechanistic engineering metaphors of social change — for example, the transmission belts through which revolutionary consciousness is inevitably generated.

3. Some ideological closures are more apparent than real (whether Marxist or non-Marxist) and this comes from a recognition of the complexities of analysis and consequent uncertainties as to what the future may hold. This does not lead to empty-minded speculation but to a disciplined awareness of alternative possibilities. For those who want to be involved in the action as well as to observe and explain it, it leads very naturally to discussions and proposals for strategy and tactics in industrial relations. In their judgment the future may not be wholly open, but it is open enough, containing within it a range of alternative possibilities, and is worth fighting for. A sociology of industrial relations need not therefore generate political somnolence (cf. Hyman, 1972, Ch. 6).

4. Analytically it would appear that a good deal of purchase can be obtained from considering industrial relations in relation to the notion of control. This is because it is a question that can be pursued at various levels (work group, factory bureaucracy, union, society) and the connection between these levels considered. If one seriously pursues the questions, who or what is being controlled to what purpose, to whose benefit and with what degree of effectiveness, then one can approach the study of industrial relations in a way that tries to confront the realities of power.

7 A NEW CRIMINOLOGY: SOMEWHERE OVER THE RAINBOW

It is not easy to summarise the issues surrounding the study of deviancy in their particular manifestations in British sociology. Geoffrey Pearson has coined the term 'misfit sociology', and as an epithet it has a pleasing ambiguity (G. Pearson, 'Misfit Sociology — the Politics of Socialisation', in Taylor, I., Walton, P. and Young, J. (eds.), *Critical Criminology*, 1974, and *The Deviant Imagination*, 1975). The following quotation gives the sense of his meaning and at the same time might suggest why adequate summary is difficult to accomplish:

> This area of scholarship is an odd theoretical cocktail, constructed out of sociology, psychiatry, criminology, social administration, media studies, law, social work, political science, cultural criticism, social psychology and even some strands of popular culture and music. This inter-disciplinary misfit finds its focus in the study of deviants but it is more than an inter-disciplinary exercise . . . Schur has lumped many of the strands together as 'the labelling perspective', although the sociology of labelling is only one of its elements. Within the same domain one finds what passes for 'phenomenology' and also a sort of 'Marxism'. Anti-psychiatry has left its mark and Schur, again, points to the affinities with existential psychology. To add to this mix one of the central contributions in this area owes a considerable debt to Durkheim. Here, clearly, is an area of high theoretical dispersion, a *zeitgeist* of sorts which allows for an apparent harmony between some widely differing perspectives. It is also rightly or wrongly a theoretical jig-saw which has earned the reputation of being 'radical'.
>
> (Pearson, 1975, p. 51)

One way of pursuing the subject is to take as a point of departure Taylor, Walton and Young's study *The New Criminology: For a Social Theory of Deviance* (1973). This is a book which has been widely reviewed and generally celebrated by 'radical' sociologists. The first thing one notices is that it bears a foreword, full of unstinting praise from Gouldner who regards it as a comprehensive critique of the totality of European and American studies of crime and deviance. Part of Gouldner's cause for rejoicing was that he saw *The New Criminology* as seeking to relate the substance of a particular area of study to the concerns of a general social theory to the mutual enrichment of both levels. And this illustrates again an issue which I have discussed elsewhere in this review. Gouldner (pp. xi-xii) says:

> There is . . . a certain generalised tension between the theoretical centre and the specialised peripheries. Cut off from the theoretical centre, the technical specialisations inevitably become the dwelling place of routinised technicians who prattle about their 'autonomy', even as they become the paid auxiliaries of the 'Welfare State'. Yet totally assimilated into the theoretical centre and reduced to a merely exemplary significance — exemplary, that is, of a higher theoretical rationality — specialisations easily lose the kind of *intrinsic* worth that might ensure them continued development. In short, instead of simply seeing the relation between theoretical centre and peripheral specialisations as one of a mutual 'dependence' of theory and practice or application, as a kind of wedding in which the bride and groom live happily ever after, it is also necessary to see this relation between centre and periphery dialectically as having its own *contradictions* — even if these are not antagonistic contradictions.

Gouldner makes two points which illustrate this two-way relationship and tension. On the one hand a general Marxist social theory (of which *The New Criminology* is an exponent) which relegates crime and deviance to the dustbin of history and as irrelevant to the study of class conflict is too mechanistic unless the empirical work has been examined: it assumes what it should properly seek to establish. On the other hand a Marxist social theory, can engage critically with work such as that of the Chicago school of criminologists. Their appreciative (as opposed to depreciative) stance to crime and deviance was essentially non-moralistic. This relativistic stance can lead to the tracing out and documentation of a variety of forms of life whether conventionally regarded as 'respectable' or 'unrespectable'. But this reading could be located in a wider understanding of social structure which does not take the status quo for granted and the future as without hopes for those whom deviance, however 'authentic' is also a result of oppression: 'What becomes increasingly necessary is a theoretical position that accepts the reality of deviance that has a capacity to explore its *Lebenswelt*, without becoming the technician of the 'Welfare' State and its zoo-keepers of deviance' (op. cit., p. xiv). Given its attempt to do this *The New Criminology* gets Gouldner's seal of approval.

It is because *The New Criminology* has an end in view, whilst being a comprehensive review of the subject, that it can serve a useful purpose here. *The New Criminology* is a robust book. In its critical review of the literature the authors have an instinct for the jugular. This is necessary in that their own purposes are ambitious, namely to set up a programmatic alternative to what has gone before or is currently available. In that respect it reminds me of Durkheim's way of dealing with opponents — the argument by elimination — in order to strengthen the claims of his own proposed alternative.

To sharpen the focus I want to bring into the centre of the stage the authors' own standpoint, with its pre-suppositions and claims.

1. There is an ontological assumption about the nature of man derived from a particular reading of Marx. This assumption has to be set against others (implicit or explicit) and a judgement of some kind made 'In part, Marxism stands or falls on the basis of certain assumptions it makes about the nature of man. Where other social theories (cf. as described by Durkheim and Weber) operate with implicit assumptions about man's nature, Marx made his starting point a quite explicit philosophical anthropology of man' (op. cit., p. 219).

The reference is to Marx's *Economic and Philosophical Manuscripts of 1844*, where man is defined as a *species-being*, whose true nature is to find freedom in relationship with others in community. The authors continue:

> The bulk of Marx's later work is concerned with the demonstration of the ways in which man's social nature and consciousness have been distorted, imprisoned or diverted by the social arrangements developed over time. These social arrangements are the product of man's struggle to master the conditions of scarcity and material under-development. These social arrangements, developed as a response to man's domination by poverty, imprison man tightly in social relationships of an exploitative nature and alienate men from men, and thus from the objects of their labour. Man is struggling to be free, but cannot realise freedom (or himself as a fully-conscious, sensuous species being) until such time as he is free of the exploitive relationships which are outmoded and unnecessary.
>
> (op. cit. pp. 219-20)

The significance of this assumption and its implications are made very plain by the authors:

> To be a satisfactory explanation a Marxist theory would proceed with a notion of man which would distinguish it quite clearly from classical, positivist or interactional 'images' of man. It would assume, that is, a degree of consciousness, bound up with man's location in a social structure of production, exchange and domination, which of itself would influence the ways in which man defined as criminal or deviant would attempt to live with their outsiders' status. . . . One consequence of such an approach . . . would be the possibility of building links between the insights of interactionist theory, and other

> approaches sensitive to man's subjective world, and theories of social structure implicit in orthodox Marxism. More crucially, such a linkage would enable us to escape from the straitjacket of an economic determinism and the relativism of some subjectivist approaches to a theory of contradiction in social structure which recognises in 'deviance' the acts of men in the process of actively making, rather than passively taking, the external world.
>
> (op. cit. pp. 220-1)

2. The message of *The New Criminology* is encoded in the above paragraphs. Consider how it unfolds:

(a) Social construct theories — varieties of utilitarianism — did not take into full account the unequal distribution of property. Crime among the propertyless is seen as irrational. But we should not assume that such acts were irrational.

(b) Positivism with its premise that human activity (like activity in the physical world) is law governed, is too deterministic and takes away responsibility from the agent. It rests on the assumption that there is a prevalent consensus in a society about the nature of morality. Positivism, while it may deny human freedom, seeks to understand in order to eliminate crime and deviance. So it may be postulated by positivists that if scientists come to understand the mechanisms by which behaviour is determined they may develop appropriate ways of changing it. This is rejected as spurious, and dangerous scientism a form of social control based on correction to dominant values through therapy. The general position is rejected on grounds of logic and morality and epistemology: 'The epistemology of social science is of a different order to that of natural science: a social theory must have reference to man's teleology — their purposes, their beliefs and the contexts in which they set out these purposes and beliefs' (op. cit., p. 61). The authors make frequent reference not simply to Marx but to symbolic interactionist writers to reinforce their point.

(c) Durkheim transcends the control theorists and the positivists. Furthermore he is far more radical than many interpreters have appreciated. This is revealed in his analysis of the forced division of labour and his view that laws of inheritance created unfair inequalities and unjust contracts. But, it is contended, his image of man's nature is incorrect and hence his view of the ideal society. This society would not remove inequitable structures as the division of labour but would seek to match a man's aptitudes and abilities with his work and reward him according to his merits. Furthermore whilst some deviancy is seen by Durkheim as rational (the product of reason) some is 'meaningless'. The category of meaningless behaviour must at all times be questioned.

(d) Merton's anomie theory builds on Durkheim, but what begins as a formidable-looking critique of American society ends up by taking the existing society more or less for granted. The deviant's behaviour may be construed as rational (in terms of the typology of individual adaptation) but basically he is constrained. His choices are constrained. Merton's approach and that of colleagues like Cloward and Ohlin is reformist: seek for ways of widening and opening up the opportunity structure — through such means as poverty programmes and community action. The American Dream is supported rather than challenged. But it is the logical and methodological difficulties of the anomie paradigm that are criticised above all.

(e) The Chicago ecologists and those who follow in their footsteps such as Sutherland on differential association, Lewis on the culture of poverty and other subcultural theorists are essentially approaches which have a positivistic view of the relationship between man and his environment. The emphasis is on environmental constraints with an ambiguous free will thrown in: 'There is no sense of men struggling against social arrangements as such: no sense of a social structure riven by inequalities and contradictions, and no sense of men acting to change the range of options' (op. cit., p. 114). Essentially they omit the notion of human purpose and therefore have a defective concept of human nature.

(f) Varieties of 'labelling theories' associated with writers such as Becker, Lemert, Erikson and Schur are seen as important advances, not least because in Meadian fashion they see the self responding to social control agencies, defining and redefining its own self concept. The authors of *The New Criminology* argue in contradiction to labelling theorists that deviant behaviour is usually a quality of the act — not just of the label. More generally labelling is to be seen as a one-sided approach to deviance study (and hence in need of supplementing). The explanatory weakness is built in so as to query whether what is called labelling theory is a theory at all. Lemert is, as it were, cited against himself: 'Interaction is not a theory or explanation at all. It does little more than set down a condition of inquiry, telling us that dynamic analysis must supplement structural analysis, and is best understood as a necessary reaction to the metaphysical explanations of human behaviour among nineteenth century writers' (quoted p. 159). In short, the sources of rule breaking are not examined. Where will they be located? 'Ultimately in the larger social inequalities of power and authority' (op. cit., p. 154). The emphasis on process laudable in itself needs a reference back to structure. If Merton *et al.* are structure without process, Becker *et al.* are process without structure.

(g) Essentially the same critique stands for the phenomenological work of Matza. His treatment of motivation, particularly the discussion of neutralisation techniques is stimulating, yet for all his subtlety he tends to deny the possibility of self-conscious oppositional meaning to deviant acts. The notion of drift by the same token minimises the actor's consciousness. The alternative perspective of the new criminologists is offered: 'If . . . Matza had been operating with a rather more explicit view of the relationships of men to structures of power and authority he might have become aware that the cultural options available to the majority of citizens in an inequitable capitalist society are designed to make opposition look like neutralisation rather than the critique of the frustrated and the deprived' (op. cit., p. 185).

(h) The ethnomethodologist's stance gets short shrift not surprisingly for its solipsism, its atomistic reductionism, its denial of a social totality, and its failure to recognise that while men create society they do not do so in circumstances of their choosing.

(i) There are available structural analyses of crime. They have built in assumptions which have to be transcended. There is the treatment of crime as false consciousness, which scarcely allows any place for oppositional striving to deviants and criminals. This is a Marxism which, it is held, contradicts Marx's own philosophical anthropology. Other forms of conflict theory such as those of Turk and Quinney are seen as being derivative upon the pluralistic conflict theories of Dahrendorf and the American political science pluralists respectively. While conflict theories are a step in the right direction away from consensual theories it is held that they are overdetermining, understressing the role of men as purposive creators and innovators of action.

What emerges from all this is a critique that sees various developments in the study of deviance as themselves critical responses to existing theories. None of these however are seen as constituting a fully social theory of deviance. Criticisms of these range from logical, methodological, ontological and ideological considerations. In their programmatic conclusion the authors argue for a general theory which will seek to explain: the wider origins of the deviant act, the immediate origins of the deviant social reaction, the wider origins of deviant reaction, the outcome of the social reaction on deviants' further action and the nature of the deviant process as a whole. The theory is not as general as it might be in the sense that it says very little about non-capitalist societies (for example feudal societies or socialist societies). What it does do is stress the possibilities for re-interpretation such that 'meaningless acts' may be recognised as 'rational' (i.e. having a purpose), that deviance may sometimes be seen as an element of opposition to existing orders and hence 'political' and in general opposes the notion of actors as 'cultural dopes'.

It is clear that the authors of *The New Criminology* want to assert the superiority of their position over available alternatives. Hence some positions are rejected (e.g. positivism) and others are modified to facilitate incorporation (e.g. interactionism). But the claims for superiority in part at least rest on an image of man. Whether such an ontological assumption is itself open to empirical scrutiny is a question of some interest. A 'scientific socialist' position might claim that it is; a humanistic socialist like Goldman would see such matters as in the end based on faith. In any event it is this ontological claim that leads the authors of *The New Criminology* to insist that their theory is a normative one: 'It should be clear that a criminology which is not normatively committed to the abolition of inequalities of wealth and power, and in particular of inequalities in property and life chances, is inevitably bound to fall into correctionalism' (p. 281). And again: 'The new criminology must be a normative theory' (p. 280). And the aim of this normative theory is to lead in theory and practice to a society in which the domination of men by men is abolished, where consensus is 'genuine' rather than imposed by the powerful (see p. 252).

The New Criminology stands as a significant expression of an approach to deviancy studies developing in the late 1960s and early 1970s in Britain. Its authors were prominent members of the National Deviancy Conference. Accounts of the emergence and growth of this organisation have been given (see Stanley Cohen, 'Criminology and the Sociology of Deviance in Britain', in Rock and McIntosh (1974); and Stanley Cohen and Laurie Taylor, 'From Psychopaths to Outsiders: British Criminology and the National Deviancy Conference, in Bianchi, Simondi and Taylor, 1975). The accounts focus on the reaction of some young sociologically minded criminologists and students of deviant behaviour from the 'establishment' as represented by the Cambridge Institute of Criminology, while at the same time not sensing much support from 'establishment' sociology in Britain. Hence they were, on this definition, outsiders on two counts. But they were articulate outsiders. In quick succession publications were forthcoming. *Images of Deviance* (Cohen (ed.), 1971) displayed a stance which opened or re-opened topics such as industrial sabotage, football hooliganism, gangs, drugtakers, vandals and blackmailers. A great deal of the inspiration (whether or not the idols were later felt to have feet of clay) came from the naturalism of the Chicago school. This was represented by the proclaimed need of sociology to be faithful to the phenomenon studied. It encouraged a strong appreciation (sometimes an explicit sympathy) with the actors' viewpoint. I would say that the kinds of influence that helped to condition the climate of thought were mediated in the writings of Becker, ('Becoming a Marijuana User' having legendary status), Matza, Goffman and more generally H. Blumer, Wright Mills, Peter Berger, Jack Douglas and A. Cicourel. *The Social Construction of Reality*, *The Social Meaning of Suicide* and *Method and Measurement in Sociology* provided important inputs into the sociology of deviance (amongst others). Naturalism could co-exist alongside other phenomenological approaches. So in Cohen and Taylor's *Psychological Survival: the Experience of Long Term Imprisonment* (1972) it was the experience of the prisoners that constituted the focal point with much of the theoretical reflection prompted by Sartre and Goffman. This represented a very different approach to the psychological testing that such prisoners might be subjected to by prison psychologists.

One of the pre-eminent things which is incorporated into this general methodological stance is the awareness of multiple meanings and motives behind actions that might be conventionally dismissed or 'explained' as motiveless, meaningless or irrational. The interest in a sociology of motivation was developed not only from the obvious Weberian source but more directly from C. Wright Mills. This informs such contributions as Taylor and Walton on 'Industrial Sabotage: Motives and Meanings' (in Cohen, 1971); Taylor on 'The Significance and Interpretation of Replies to Motivational Questions: The Case of Sex Offenders' (1972); Cohen on 'Property Destruction: Motives and Meanings' (in Ward, 1972). It is also the case of course that a sociology of motivation as with Wright Mills can be located back to structural considerations and hence incorporated into causal process models. That is what one notices in the approach to deviancy amplification as a theme in subcultural theory. This has most notably been worked upon by Young (1971) in his study *The Drugtakers: the Social Meaning of Drug Use*, together with a development in his paper 'New Directions in Sub-Cultural Theory (in Rex (ed.) 1974) and also by Cohen (1972) in *Folk Devils and Moral Panics*. The interest is in how the police and/or the media 'amplify' deviant acts or practices so far as public consciousness is concerned, giving rise to an actual increase in the acts defined as deviant as attempts are made to control them. This kind of analysis incidentally has its strong parallels in Myrdal's principle of cumulative causation and notably his analysis of the way in which race prejudice can create discrimination and give rise to greater amounts of prejudice (in *An American Dilemma*). It is also reminiscent of Merton's treatment of 'vicious circles' and 'virtuous circles' and his discussion of how bureaucratic controls can have dysfunctional effects (in *Social Theory and Social Structure*). In the deviancy field the work of Wilkins (1964) on social deviance pre-dates the new deviancy theorists but in Young's opinion Wilkin's model of deviancy amplification is mechanistic in that it doesn't grant the actor consciousness and purpose. Nonetheless the affinities are noteworthy and the interest in amplification is clearly causal in character and not a descriptive phenomenology. What the work of Young and Cohen contains, however, is the sense of irony of unintended consequences as those with the power to define deviance, in their attempts to control it, find they have created unanticipated problems. Deviance is in this sense of their making. The reference to the media as amplifiers of deviance draws attention to media studies themselves. Examples of this linkage are located in Young, 'Mass Media, Drugs and Deviance' (Rock and McIntosh, 1974); S. Hall, 'Deviance, Politics and the Media' (Rock and McIntosh, 1974); and J. Halloran *et al.*, *Demonstrations and Communication* (1970). What is notable is that such studies suggest alternative causal models to those appealed to in conventional wisdom. Therein lies their sociological novelty and, since they handle topics of general public interest, represent an implicit political challenge if only because 'official' or 'dominant' definitions of the situation are shown not to exhaust the reality to which they are addressed.

There is I think an instructive tension here between the strictly phenomenological approach and the attempt to introduce causal analysis. In the former the injunction to be faithful to the phenomenon is rendered as a call to description. The radical imprint resides in the making available of a range of descriptions 'popular' and 'unpopular', 'official' and 'unofficial', and so on. These descriptions will commonly include actors' 'explanations' and 'interpretations' but they are placed, as we have learned to say, in phenomenological brackets. It is the sociologist, by making available a range of accounts, who provides disturbing information to those who did not know, or preferred not to consider alternative accounts (or who had techniques for down-grading those they were aware of). But the move to a causal account (which may incorporate 'reasons'/'motives'/'purposes' into the causal nexus) is in principle to claim the superiority of one explanation over another. What the sociologist then has to do is to provide evidential grounds to sustain a causal account. Apart from the issues of corroboration that this raises it may be noted that logically the phenomenological models which various groups of actors hold may have differing degrees of accuracy. That is, one account is empirically more 'correct' than another and not simply an alternative view. Which group this might be (dominant or subordinate), which version of how it is (official or unofficial) is a matter for empirical investigation. And ironical though it may be in relation to a researcher's personal sympathies, the 'underdog' model may be less accurate than the 'overdog'. One cannot know in advance. Furthermore, if the sociologist's causal model is different from available accounts of the actors, one has to allow for the possibility that this new explanation, when it becomes publicly available, may be differentially received by those who come to hear of it. A good recent example of the amplification spiral is found in 'Some Notes on the Relationship between the Societal Control Culture and the News Media, and the Construction of a Law and Order Campaign' (in S. Hall *et al.*, 1976). This is represented in a 3 stage formulation.

1. The control culture as primary definers: media as reproducers. Thus:

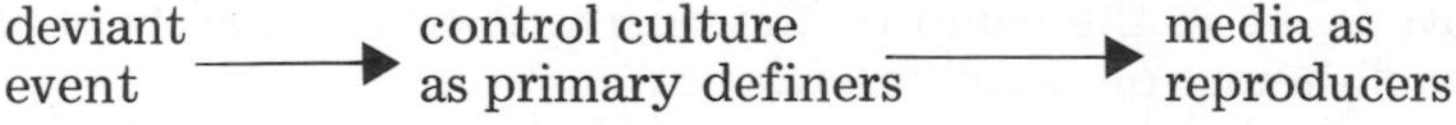

e.g. a case of mugging is reported via representations of the control culture (police, judiciary, Home Office).

2. The media as producers: transformation, objectification and the 'public voice'. Thus:

deviant event → control culture as primary definers → media as producers (assumed audience)

It is suggested that once primary definitions occur, the media transform them by translating them into their own public language.

3. The closure of the circle.

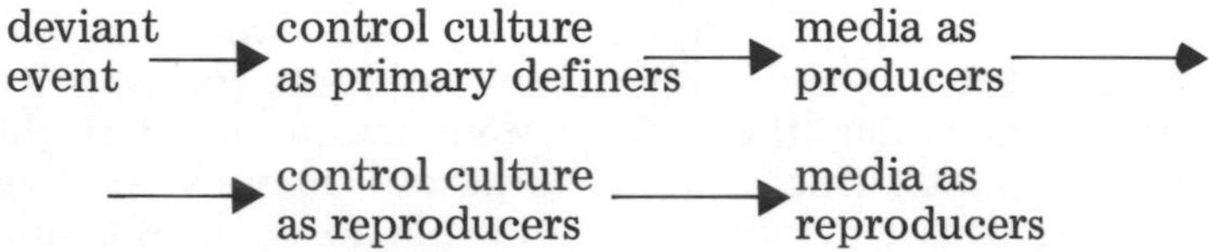

This leads to a complex statement of causal relations: 'Once the media have spoken in their voice, on behalf of the inaudible public the primary definers can then use the media's statements and claims as legitimations (magically, without any visible connection) for their actions and statements, by claiming press — and via the press, public support. In turn, the ever attentive media reproduce the Control Culture statements, thus completing the magical circle, with such effect that it is no longer possible to tell who first began the process: each legitimates the other in turn' (op. cit., p. 76).

Establishing adequate causal accounts is a difficult matter and no sociologist would be inclined to think otherwise. Indeed, there is clearly something of a divide between those who think it is possible and those who do not. This difference can be played out in various critiques and counter-critiques. By way of illustration I want to comment on two recent reflections on 'the new criminology' because they reflect this division. They also, as it happens, differ in tone. Paul Rock's essay, 'The Sociology of Crime, Symbolic Interactionism and Some Problematic Qualities of Radical Criminology' (in Downes and Rock (eds.), *Deviant Interpretations* (1979)) is in my view an over-dramatised version of the failings of the new criminologies, anti-causal in its methodological thrust. Jason Ditton's *Controlology: Beyond the New Criminology* (1979) is a brisk and cheerful monograph, which suggests that one does not have to be in the camp of the positivist criminologists to argue for the establishment of causal models.

Rock attacks the pretentiousness of the new criminologists. They make absolutist claims to truth. They have a fantasy conception of social totality, which runs alongside their equally spurious claim to understand social reality. They think they can distinguish between true and false consciousness and they are both mistaken and elitist to suppose that they can. They think they can detect essences under the surface of mundane appearance and they cannot. They substitute political criteria of judgement for sociological when evaluating competing theories. They are accused of having no principled adherence to empiricism, ethnography, science, rationality and facts, substituting for these *a priori* reasoning. Their criminology becomes a form of secular theology and they appear not to notice that in everyday life people are frightened and hurt. And where does all this lead, these spurious claims to truth and superior knowledge? 'Truth so recognised lays a road to totalitarianism. It encourages the forcible rescue of 'fully human' men from the trappings and deceits of the empirical world. It speaks in the name of a noumenal humanity, whatever the actual protestations of people may be. It leads to a stance which urges the forcing of man to be free. None but the sociological elite can know the real condition of man and the real nature of liberation. Such a sociology and a politics are obedient only to the intuition of a group which resists almost every intellectual discipline. They can ward off all criticism because they have become detached from rationality and sublunary realities' (op. cit., p. 81).

That just criticisms can be made of the new criminologists I do not doubt (indeed it would be a strange inversion of critical sociology if it were not itself open to criticism). I have already indicated some reservations. I think there is an over-politicised view of crime, a relative neglect of the crimes of the powerful and a somewhat romantic view of 'the deviant'. There is undeniably a utopian strain in a book which can imagine a society in which crime can be abolished, a difficult though scarcely ignoble thought. But Rock's criticism, in the guise of advocating a non-absolutist position is intemperate and dogmatic. The exuberance of the new criminologists does sometimes lead them into methodological indiscretions and over-stated theoretical claims. But Rock turns these, as it were, into a crime against humanity and effectively accuses them of intellectual Stalinism. It is conceded that these same criminologists can do 'diligent' and 'intriguing' empirical research. One can only hope this will knock a few years off the secular purgatory for which they are surely destined. There must after all be some good in them even if it consists in the fact that, on this reading, they are subverting their own vision.

But how does Rock come by such knowledge of his adversaries? He does, after all, offer explanations of the intentions of the new criminologists and their role in the development of criminology and draws inferences concerning the social consequences of this kind of thinking. Rock argues that all knowledge is uncertain and that it is impossible to establish a systematic theory of society. No axiomatic schemes, no Aristotlean logic can be used in sociology. But what is real for men is real for all practical purposes. The implication is that one must abandon the architectonic schemes of high sociology and settle for ethnography and in this way build a 'scientific mosaic': 'The construction of a mosaic is neither an ambitious nor a massively satisfying enterprise. Interactionism provided little re-assurance that every significant problem can be subdued, that sociology represents an especially powerful or privileged medium of thought, or that the sociologist can hope to accomplish much. Sociology is translated into a relatively humble undertaking which is pursued without any prospect of palpable success. It can progress only when the sociologist acknowledge uncertainty' (op. cit., p. 66).

One is inclined to ask — why bother? To suggest that all knowledge is provisional does not in itself mean that more ambitious theories than Rock suggests cannot be usefully constructed. Not to put too fine a point on it, Rock's position challenges the whole nature of historical and comparative sociology. Moreover, Rock's advocacy of ethnography alone leaves him with one method, or at least it is the only one he refers to, participant observation. One is then entitled to ask what status the knowledge thus propagated has. It is provisional, privileged and, presumably, untestable. Meaning, according to Rock, must be creatively discovered: it is neither invented or self-evident. But if it is not self-evident, the interactionist must surely give grounds for showing why things are not as they seem. Yet Rock appears to believe that the problems of participant observation go away if you do not think about them: 'The actual experience of field work makes perfectly manageable what appears to be methodologically impossible. The contrary states of participation and observation are intolerable only when they are brought to consciousness. They need present no practical impediment to the business of research' (op. cit., p. 68).

This all starts to look suspiciously like a privileged position, because the sociologist, by virtue of his analysis, actually knows more than the actor (precisely what he attacks in the new criminology and macro-sociology). But in this instance we are offered no way in which rules of evidence can be held to operate. To suggest that there are grounds on which one interpretation of social life may be granted more validity than another, in Rock's curious vocabulary is translated into a form of absolutism. Where he actually leaves us is in the swamp of inter-subjective processes with no suggested criteria for judging between alternative accounts. If all knowledge is reduced to such a relativistic state, why should we believe Rock's stories — even his story of the new criminology? It may sound plausible, but it is of course provisional and uncertain knowledge with no privileged status. Perhaps it is true but then again perhaps it is just an ugly rumour.

Jason Ditton's monograph *Controlology* is an altogether more challenging and constructive response to the new criminology. As earlier observed, much of the impetus for developing a new criminology was the love-hate relationship with the labelling approach to deviance. The main outcome was an attempt to appreciate but nevertheless refute the labelling perspective by a critical criminology. Ditton suggests that, for various reasons, both the labelling and the critical approach have tended to leave the conventional positivist criminologists still in control of research money, resources and policy-related studies.

The labelling perspective tended to focus on deviant groups like strippers, teddy boys and drug users but not look at issues of murder, violence and theft, which topics tend to constitute the staple diet of conventional criminologists responding to perceived social problems of law and order. Like the critical criminologists, Ditton thinks the phenomenological approach of the 'labellers' to be inadequate. But unlike them he does not want to move on to theories of the state and thereby abandon, as he sees it, a central concern with crime as the main subject of study. Rather he wishes to reconstitute the labelling approach so that it is more soundly based as a theory and not just to be treated as a perspective. He wants on the basis of this strategy to take the positivist criminologists on in their own territory as it were.

An important bridging device used to accomplish this object is a reworking and a refinement of Wilkin's deviancy amplification model. The crucial element in the strategy is to establish that the issue of control can be shown to be operating independently of crime. To demonstrate this in logical terms will clear the ground for a repaired (non-phenomenological) labelling theory.

Wilkin's causal model had postulated the sequence:

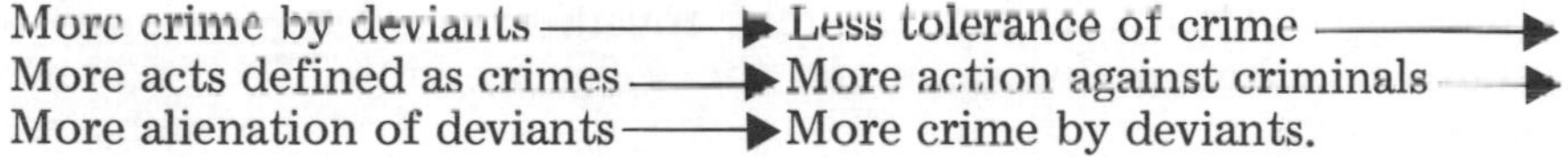
More crime by deviants ——▶ Less tolerance of crime ——▶
More acts defined as crimes ——▶ More action against criminals ——▶
More alienation of deviants ——▶ More crime by deviants.

This spiral formed the amplification of crime. Ditton points out that to speak of a crime rise may mean five different things:

1. More originally non-deviant acts are *defined* as deviant (*Constructed* crime rise).
2. More of these acts originally committed are *discovered* (*fantasy* crime rise).
3. More (subsequently or originally) discovered deviant acts are officially *collated* (*book-keeping* crime rise).
4. More mass media *coverage* of deviant acts (*reporting* crime rise).
5. More originally defined acts are *committed* (*real* crime rise).

Once these different categories are recognised and illustrated this makes it impossible to demonstrate that an increase in the crime rate is evidence of a real crime rise. In particular, one should have no truck with a position that imagines (whether from a positivist or labelling perspective) that one can somehow make allowances for the 'dark figure' of crime to reach approximations of how many deviant acts are committed. The point about the 'dark figure' is that you, or more importantly those in positions of power, can make of it anything. It is infinitely elastic. Ditton's key contention is indeed that it remains useful to look at crime rates, not because the above-mentioned difficulties can ever be solved in positivist terms, using notions of best approximations and so on, but because changing rates give evidence of control waves.

This also serves to remind us that reported crime rates do rise *and* fall and therefore creates a problem for any simple notion of cumulative amplification, or for that matter, attenuation. Control becomes *the* causative issue: 'the size of the "criminal" population is wholly determined by the exercise and experience of control, with particular members being periodically extended into or included from the "normal" population. That is the logical parameter of the control model: in fact, its pragmatic operation is guaranteed by forms of temporary banishment (deportation, or incarceration) which are critical because they contribute to the "wave effect of control" ' (op. cit., pp. 34-5). Ditton's argument is concisely put and more subtle than I have indicated, but it is clear that he is concerned both in logic and theory to explain the significance of control in terms of its impact on crime rates. In particular, this informs and provides the justification of his ethnography — a very different matter from purveying endless stories for jaded sociologists. It further provides a logically necessary role for historical inquiry. Under what conditions are forms of control exercised, with what degree of intensity, for what purpose and in whose interests? This suggests that one has to hold together in creative tension the situational ethnographic work and the wider accounts of social control expressed in societal terms. Thus the details of ethnography may suggest something about the processes of control which have a wider application at the macro-level.

If Ditton is correct in the thrust of his argument, the implications are considerable. Not only is new life breathed into labelling theory, but his approach does provide a challenge to positivist criminology. By focusing on the control impulse one can point to the controllers rather than the controlled and directly consider their plans and purposes. 'Official' criminology tends to look at the criminal and the criminal impulses as a problem to be studied and can be absorbed into the control system, as well as reflected in policy recommendations. It is in this respect that the 'common sense' of positivist criminologists and, more generally, public opinion, may be radically questioned by Ditton's analysis. It advocates ethnographic and historical work to elucidate crime waves. It does not resort to a phenomenological approach which cannot be validated or even effectively undertaken in the historical dimension. But because in principle it appeals to logical relationships and causal models it retains a toughness that can challenge 'conventional' criminology on its own ground. Watch this space!

8 AN EDUCATIONAL BABEL?

> The problem of the sociology of education is . . . centrally one of what it is that is being explained.
>
> (Ioan Davies, 'The Management of Knowledge — a Critique of the Use of Typologies in the Sociology of Education', in Young (ed.), 1971, p. 273)

Supposing one argued that the problem to which Davies alludes is solved in British sociology by saying that what is being explained is the relationship between education and social inequality. This would echo the view of Archer (1970), who claims that in both England and France over the post-war period the sociology of education has had researchers who shared a common view of what the problems to be investigated were. In England during the 1950s, she maintains, two types of investigation tended to predominate: 'the first confirmed the influence of social class origins upon various levels and types of educational achievement, while the second indicated that a variety of factors related to attainment were also associated with social background. This stress upon inter-class differences led to a complementary neglect of intra-class variations' (op. cit., p. 120). She draws a number of conclusions from this state of affairs. First she appears to have reservations on the utility of class (as employed by educational sociologists) in models of explanation, supporting the view that it is 'a gutless variable'. Second, she labels those who pursue such studies as 'levellers', suggesting that they have often been advocates in political debate. In particular they have endorsed educational expansion as a means of diminishing inequalities of access: 'It seems a clear consequence of factors other than equality being forgotten that expansionism can be advocated *solely from a consideration of input* without consideration of its effects on education and society' (op. cit., p. 122). Third, she suggests that research problems that focus on educational opportunity and social stratification actually encourage a trend towards psychological reductionism. Thus the problem of differential occupational life chances is related back to secondary selection procedures, then back to achievement in the primary sector, into the child's environment, including the role of pre-school education and finally into the mire of the nature/nurture debate. An incidental consequence of this is that research is deflected away from higher education and the topic remains relatively under-studied.

I think that Archer overstates her case. It is true that class as a variable can be and has been used as a catch-all concept that has little explanatory power. On the other hand, there are those who have initial suspicions about the importance of the class concept who find that in one way or another they have to reckon with it. A good example of what I have in mind is found in the work of the Newsons (1968). Their paper 'Parental Roles and Social Contexts' (in Shipman, M. (ed.) 1976) is particularly illuminating in this respect. Commenting on their findings in which the influence of social class on child rearing problems is shown to be pervasive almost from birth they say (p. 30):

> In our discussions of child-rearing, from minutiae to the total schemata, we have given the class factor the attention which, without pre-judging the issue it seemed to deserve: and it is only in response to the inescapable salience of the social class patterns into which our data has fallen that we have presented class as the major isolatable influence in the ways people feel and act in bringing up their children. Thus our work is now regarded as having a strong sociological flavour as opposed to a psychological one . . . this is not because we had at the outset some theoretical pre-occupation with social status, but because we have been compelled to speculate in terms of socio-economic factors and social reference groups in trying to make some sense of divisions in our data which were unpectedly clear-cut.

The Newsons state that they were indeed surprised at the significance of the class variable. This may have been because their disciplinary allegiance was psychology, hence some sociological work on class differences may have escaped them. But, as they themselves observe, when they began fieldwork in 1958 Douglas', *The Home and the School* (1964), Davie, Butler and Goldstein's *From Birth to Seven* (1972) and Bernstein's forays into the relationship between language and social class had yet to be published.

I think too that Archer overstates her reductionist argument. It is of course true that the nature/nurture debate continues to bubble notably in the contexts of race and education. Contrasting views are found in Eysenck's, *Race, Intelligence and Education* (1971) and Richardson and Spears (eds.), *Race, Culture and Intelligence* (1972). At the same time one should not play down the amount of research that has been done at the level of secondary education — see for example Hargreaves (1967) and Banks and Finlayson (1973) on the secondary school; Lacey (1970) on the grammar school, Ford (1969) on the comprehensive school, Lambert *et al.* (1966 and 1969) and Wakeford (1969) on public schools, And in any event, notwithstanding the search for 'ultimate' explanation, patterns of structured inequality could be revealed to suggest other things about the nature of British society. A good example of this is Guttsman's study *The British Political Elite* (1968 revised) which examines the educational and class background (noting the link between the two) of politicians, cabinet ministers and civil servants. I would also refer to the collection of papers edited by Stanworth and Giddens *Elites and Power in British Society* (1974). This includes a further contribution by Guttsman, a study by Kelsall of recruitment to the higher civil service and F. and J. Wakefords' discussion of the universities in relation to the study of elites. Such studies point to the effects of structural inequalities in educational opportunities in terms of who it is that comes to exercise political, administrative and economic power. That is their focus and that is what they want to explain (usually on the basis of statistical information and trend studies).

Despite the caveats entered on Archer's analysis it can scarcely be disputed that the main axis on which the sociology of education has operated in Britain for many years is that of stratification and educational opportunity. One can even document pre-war research such as Kenneth Lindsay's *Social Progress and Educational Waste* (1926), in which the inadequacies of previous government attempts to improve the access of working-class children to secondary education are documented. The work of David Glass and his colleagues are reported in *Social Mobility in Britain* (1954) does serve as something of a bench mark. On the one hand, looking back on the expansion of secondary education from the beginning of the century till the 1940s, Jean Floud in her paper 'The Educational Experience of the Adult Population of England and Wales as at July 1949', concluded that the middle rather than the working classes had been the beneficiaries. On the other hand, there were expectations that the 1944 Education Act would provide for a great expansion of educational opportunity. Subsequent studies could consider the consequences and how far intentions were realised.

I want now to refer to Olive Banks's Leicester inaugural lecture 'Sociology and Education: Some Reflections on the Sociologist's Role'. Writing within the stratification/mobility tradition she suggests that 'the study of the unanticipated consequences of social action, as Max Weber has put it, must indeed not only be a central concern of sociology as an academic discipline but also, perhaps, its major contribution to the making of social policy.' This perhaps is the role of the sociologist as coroner. As the reference to Weber suggests, this is no new role — historical sociology may inquire 'why did capitalism not develop in China and India?' and that is an inquest on a large scale. But the sociologist, when identifying a gap between intentions and consequences, policies and practice, goals and accomplishments, is put in the position of social coroner since the discrepancy calls for explanation. It may be of course that the sociologist is more aware than most of the possibility of unanticipated consequences of planned human action. The research question, however, is how are such eventualities to be analysed and accounted for? The implication is further that whatever one's political or moral predilections the evidence must be sifted and evaluated as rigorously as possible. Weber's analysis of the growth of rational/legal forms of administration and policy, despite his personal dislike of the trend, still serves as a model of this approach.

In the sociology of education a number of studies have something of this character. Olive Banks herself in *Parity and Prestige in English Secondary Education* (1955) concluded that the doctrine of 'parity of esteem', when applied to different kinds of secondary schools, simply did not stand up. Of course in retrospect it is difficult to see how such a doctrine could have been seriously held. If you did not pass the 11+ you failed it and you went to the secondary modern school along with the other failures. It was not a question of separate and equal but separate and ranked. Floud, Halsey and Martin in their well-known study *Social Class and Educational Opportunity* (1956) revealed a gap between policy and practice on educational opportunity. This did turn attention to material factors in a child's environment such as parental income and housing conditions, which were seen as related to performance in the 11+. Success was class related as also were differences in parental aspiration, which was seen as affecting children's progress and performance: with children of middle-class parents tending to stay on at school longer. This general position finds further support and elaboration in Douglas (1964 and 1968) and in the Plowden Report *Children and their Primary Schools*. The fact remains that children from working-class backgrounds, although their position has improved through the expansion of educational facilities at secondary and tertiary levels, still do less well and make less use of the system than their middle-class peers. Recently Westergaard and Resler (1975) have summarised evidence which suggests that 'even when all manual workers' children are taken together — those from skilled families as well as those from poorer homes — these were still, in the early 1970s, less likely to enter a university than children of "professional and technical" fathers by a factor of nearly nine times' (op. cit., p. 323).

In the wake of such research activity, questions of what to do in terms of policy changes do arise. What about positive discrimination in educationally deprived areas? What about compensatory education for those who are socially disadvantaged? Here one enters what might fairly be called difficult territory. This I think is because policy and advocacy, theory and ideology clash in various combinations. Consider for example Bernstein's essay 'A Critique of the Concept of "compensatory education" ' in Wedderburn (ed.) (1974). First he reflects a common dichotomy in the deprivation debate — is it the child's environment or is it the school? He claims (pp. 110-11):

The concept 'compensatory education' serves to direct attention

> away from the internal organisation and the educational context of the school, and focus it upon the families and children. The concept 'compensatory education' implies that something is lacking in the family, and so in the child. As a result the children are unable to benefit from schools. It follows then that the school has to 'compensate' for something which is missing in the family and the children become little deficit systems. If only the parents were interested in the goodies offered. if only they were like middle-class parents, then we could do our job. Once the problem is even implicitly seen in this way, it becomes appropriate to coin the terms 'cultural deprivation', 'linguistic deprivation' and so on. And then these labels do their own sad work.

There is, I think, an inconsistency in the statement. If compensatory education means that the school has to make up for some lack in the child's family environment then such changes must impinge upon the internal organisation of the school. Certainly, in advocating 'positive discrimination' in deprived areas, the Plowden Report argued that this must be reflected in school building improvements, improved staffing, auxiliary help and supplemented salaries.

Bernstein proceeds to express his worries about labelling children as culturally or linguistically deprived. To describe them as culturally deprived is to cast unwarranted aspersions on the adequacy of parents and creates a sense of conflict between the school and the family instead of making them mutually supportive. The 'culture' of which the family is a part is devalued. What one has here is a form of cultural relativism which, like the anthropologist defending the way of life of his tribe, is based on the principle of no change. It is not only the possibility of personal parental inadequacy that is discounted but the existence of material disadvantages transmuted into an argument about the symbolic representations and images of culture. In doing this, real material inequalities are ignored — it becomes a disembodied assertion about the equal value of different 'cultures'. Even a walk round some of the 'deprived areas' might give cause for reflection before accepting such a contention.

One can understand Bernstein's unhappiness that his own theory of linguistic codes has been used to assert the linguistic deficiency of working-class children. In the paper cited Bernstein takes the position that those children who tend more frequently to use a restricted code are not linguistically deprived since they possess the same tacit understanding of the linguistic rule system as any other child. Hence: 'because the sub-culture or culture through its forms of social integration generates a restricted code, it does not mean that the resultant speech and meaning system is linguistically or culturally deprived, that the children have nothing to offer the school, that their imaginings are not significant' (op. cit., p. 120). Yet Bernstein in his paper becomes very convoluted in so far as he accepts the apparently necessary existence of an elaborate code in schools. Given that position, the working-class child who suffers from a technical linguistic deficiency may be at a disadvantage compared to more habitual users of the elaborated code. Bernstein is, to say the least, ambiguous in his formulations and inferences. As Rosen in his paper *Language and Social Class* (1972) reminds us: 'You cannot protest very convincingly against the harm done by the label 'linguistic deprivation', when your own theory points to a deficit, indeed when you have actually stated elsewhere that 'the normal linguistic environmeng of the working class is one of relative deprivation', (Bernstein, 1971, p. 66) and that codes 'are highly resistant to change'. (op. cit., p. 91). The labels 'restricted' and 'elaborated' also 'do their own sad work' (op. cit., p. 15). More generally Rosen's paper has put a sizable explosive charge under Bernstein's work not least because it sharply reminds us of the totally inadequate treatment of class in a theory which purports to tell us how the class sytem acts upon the deep structure of communication in the process of socialisation.

In the sociology of education in Britain it is A.H. Halsey who has responded most affirmatively (although I think without illusions) to the possibilities of action research compensatory education programmes (see 'Government against Poverty in School and Community', in Wedderburn, 1974, and 'Educational Priority', *EPA Problems and Policies*, vol. I, 1972). Halsey really operates on a premise grounded in Plowden that equality of opportunity without equality of condition becomes a bogus notion. So far as the EPA project is concerned he makes clear that it was within the context of approaching the poverty problem he linked cultural deprivation and educational deprivation together. Hence the interest in the community school. But there is a more general implication namely that 'the EPA school is impotent except in the context of a comprehensive organisation of social services in the community' (Halsey, 1972, p. 18).

Halsey, however, makes plain that if compensatory education programmes are expected by themselves to break the poverty cycle then they will never be judged successful. This is because quite other things affect the opportunity structure in society. Indeed, such American programmes as 'Head Start' are criticised by Halsey for setting themselves unrealistic objectives. At the same time he offers a more supportive judgement of the programme than is usual in the UK by suggesting that such programmes may have an impact on the political consciousness of the poor. This is precisely because it may come to be recognised that a purely educational response to breaking the poverty cycle is insufficient.

Halsey's general position on the question of compensatory education is that in principle something is better than nothing but that one should not put too much weight on the educational system as an agent of social change: 'Too much has been claimed for the power of educational systems as instruments for the wholesale reforms of societies which are characteristically hierarchical in their distribution of chances in life as between races, classes, the sexes and as between metropolitan/suburban and provincial/rural populations' (op. cit., p. 7). The argument between those who want to see opportunities widened and the poverty cycle broken is whether indeed compensatory education schemes serve as catalysts for further action in other spheres of society or whether they result in new frustrations and fatalisms if the structure of opportunities in the labour market, to name a most crucial area, (and which are affected by racial, familial and social origins) remain untouched.

The compensatory education programmes in favour of the 'disadvantaged' (itself a term covering a heterogeneous population) is of course in part an argument about resource allocation. But Byrne and Williamson (1972) have suggested that Plowden anyway was not nearly enough about resource allocation. Indeed they argue that 'cultural compensation' can become a substitute for the redistribution of resources. By looking at intra-regional variations in educational provision and their bearing on educational attainment they seek to show 'that the provision of educational resources in an area may be a significant factor in explaining variations in school attainment of different social groups. Factors which can be associated with the socio-cultural learning environment of the child and the material situation of the family — social class factors — can be traced in their influence on educational policy and educational provision' (op. cit., p. 72). It is suggested, following a study of educational provision in the North East of England that the determinant of the policy set and pursued by a local education authority is the social-class composition of the area it covers. From an analysis of education expenditure, at primary and secondary level, against areas with different social class mixes it is concluded that 'those authorities with a high proportion in low social classes resident within their area both devote a higher proportion of their income to education than do authorities with higher social class constituences, and spend their money on primary education rather than on secondary education, the reverse being true of the "high social class" authorities' (op. cit., pp. 81-2). Hence opportunities for children are mediated at the LEA level in a class-related way. This does indeed shift the nature of the argument about unequal opportunities centrally into questions of resource allocation as reflected in differential patterns of expenditure at the LEA level. This seems to me to be a pre-eminent example of the way in which the argument about inequality of opportunity is opened up in a fresh and illuminating way. At the same time it serves as a non-trivial example of the application of official data and quantified techniques.

The educational Babel so far would seem to be about ways of explaining and responding to continuing inequalities in access to and use of educational provision. Although, as we have seen, the focus of the study and the explanations offered may differ, there are probably many sociologists who would agree with the view expressed by Olive Banks in her inaugural lecture that 'proposals for reform, such as comprehensive secondary education, and compensatory education, judging by the studies we have to hand, appear to affect the situation only in a small way, leaving the general pattern of inequalities largely unchanged'.

But apart from the arguments already noted there is another troubling of the waters. This is reflected in the growing interest in how knowledge is selected, organised and stratified in the educational system. How is it categorized and transmitted in curricula? Even to put the questions is to recognise the affinities that such an endeavour would have with the sociology of knowledge. The most generally available treatment pursuing these matters is Young (ed.), *Knowledge and Control, New Directions for the Sociology of Education* (1971). A good deal of the sound and fury which has erupted in the clash between 'old' and 'new' is not simply because of the change in focus (from Who is educated? to What counts as education?) but because of new approaches. These are a mixture of symbolic interactionism, phenomenology and ethnomethodology with perhaps a special debt to Berger and Luckman's *Social Construction of Reality*. Without doubt there are parallels and convergences with the sociology of deviance. This we see explicitly in Hargreaves's use of labelling theory in his studies of social interaction and deviant behaviour in secondary schools (1967 and 1975). Similarly in commenting on the notion of educational failure Keddie in her paper 'Classroom Knowledge' (in Young, 1971) says that the recent studies on the defining process recurring within the school 'suggest that the processes by which pupils are categorized are not self-evident and point to an overlooked consequence of a differential curriculum: that is part of the process by which educational deviants are created and their deviant identities maintained' (op. cit., p. 133).

To enter the world of the new sociology of education is to be invited to consider Schutzian typifications, the desirability of 'grounded theory', the virtues of classroom ethnography. All of this may be linked to methods of data collection emphasising observation techniques and extended interviews plus the hardware of tape recorders, film and videotaping. What remains a highly contentious matter is what constitutes reliable knowledge which can be made publicly available and subjected to critical scrutiny. What does the researcher count as evidence in the course of ethnographic explorations? What is discarded and on what criteria in writing up the research? Philip Robinson, for example, in his paper 'An Ethnography of Classrooms (in Eggleston, 1974), maintains that Keddie in her work does not give enough information about the process used in selecting evidence. But neither does he really tell us how to solve the problem. Research, he says, should be more relevant and means by this that we should understand classrooms as they are to children, teachers and parents. Persistent observation and shared analysis of 'events' as they happen are needed. But the nature of analysis and explanation, other than implying that we should think the actors thoughts after (indeed with) them, is not revealed. It is the nagging worry of the doubters of the 'new' sociology of education that one might be left with endless description and a sequence of plausible stories. To say that one wants more long-term studies of classrooms and schools and that if this is done 'possibly we will be in a position to generate theoretical statements having wider applicability than the local classroom' (Robinson, op. cit., p. 263) could well be construed, I suppose, as bringing Bacon in by the backdoor. Of course not everyone is as convinced about the status of theorising as that. So Julienne Ford, reflecting on reactions to her book *Social Class and the Comprehensive School* (1974), seems to conclude that research findings only operate at the level of rumour and counter-rumour anyway (see her contribution in Shipman, 1976). Despite caveats on Bernstein noted above I do have much sympathy with his comment that 'whilst we are told of the aims of empiricism, of the abstracted fictions created by observers' categories and arithmetic, of the importance of close ethnographic study of situated activities, we are not told precisely what are the new criteria by means of which we can both create and judge the accounts of others' (in Rex (ed.), 1974, p. 154). And he goes on to maintain, and again I am in strong agreement, that 'it is a matter of some importance that we develop forms of analysis that can provide a dynamic relationship between "situated activities of negotiated meanings" and the "structural" relationships which the former presuppose. Indeed, it is precisely what is taken as given in social action approaches which allows the analysis to proceed in the first place' (op. cit., p. 155).

If Bernstein's injunction is pursued, one might well find again that questions of power and control re-emerge and how they are reflected in patterns of inequality. I think at times the enthusiasm for 'new approaches' blurs the issue but it has not gone unrecognised. Young (1971) accepts that interactional analysis, without taking into account the socio-historical contexts in which particular realities become available, is deficient. Keddie (in Young, 1971) also states that there is a need to examine linkage between schools and other institutions: 'In particular, there is a need to understand the nature of the relationship between the social distribution of power and the distribution of knowledge in order to understand the generation of categorisation of pupil, and categories of organisation of curriculum knowledge in the school situations (op. cit., p. 156) Ethnography it seems its not enough. The actor's view of the world will not be sufficient either, if such linkages are to be examined and established. Having brought people back in, perhaps the sociologist as privileged observer, commentator *and* theorist should be brought back in as well.

9 RELIGION: WHERE THE ACTION ISN'T?

> Once anonymity and impersonality became the dominant experience of man in western society, so Christianity, like any institutionalised religion, lost its grip on culture. No religion can solemnise electronic controls, parking meters and computers.
>
> (Bryan Wilson, *Contemporary Transformations of Religion* (1976), p. 103)

Religion as a form of social control; as a source of moral order; as a collective re-presentation of society or community; as a basis of social conflict; as a factor in social and economic change: these are all possibilities for sociological exploration. Sociologists in Britain have responded in various ways.

Perhaps the first post-war debate of significance for the sociology of religion was the Young and Shils-Birnbaum debate on the meaning of the coronation (Young, M. and Shils, E., 'The Meaning of the Coronation', *SR*, 1 February 1953; Birnbaum, N., 'Monarchs and Sociologists', *SR*, 3 January 1955). What this did was to focus attention on a Durkheimian interpretation of religion as re-affirming the traditional values of society, an interpretation then subjected to a Marxian-style critique by Birnbaum. This exchange I think left its mark even though the topic itself was not much pursued. It was a sharp reminder that interpretations of religious activities were no simple matter, particularly in pluralist societies.

A much more sustained research activity has however been in the field of sect analysis. Most of the credit for this must surely belong to Bryan Wilson. The first fruits of his work were described in *Sects and Society* (1961). This was a very well documented study of three sects: Elim Foursquare Gospel Church, Christian Science, and the Christadelphians. In each case Wilson deals with the doctrines, the history, the organisation, the social teaching and the social composition of the movements. The documentation was combined with participant observation and interviewing in a Midland city. Although it is not often remarked on, this work does offer very interesting suggestions and possibilities for the sociology of organisations. There is, for example, a very interesting account of the leadership struggle in the Elim movement in which the charismatic founder, George Jeffreys, was ousted by the bureaucratic administrators.

One sees in Wilson's work the influence of Weber, not only in the topic but also in his attempt to argue against any strict economic determinism of religious belief and practice. 'The diversity of our social structure, the complexity of and segmentation of modern life, the rapidity of social change, and the rapidly accelerating rate of such change, offer some reason to expect a wider range of sectarian expression than could be allowed for on a strict relation of religious belief to economic and social position' (op. cit., p. 5). He argues that sects as such (*pace* Niebuhr) are not necessarily one generation affairs, nor are they always the religions of the disinherited in an economic sense. However, he argues, sects like Elim may recruit from the culturally disinherited and the socially isolated.

Wilson's work in this area has extended in a number of ways. Others have taken up the analysing of sects in Britain. As a result of Wilson's edited collection, *Patterns of Sectarianism* (1967), we now have very good accounts of such groups as the Salvation Army, the British Israelites and the Brethren. Alongside this one can place Beckford's study of Jehovah's Witnesses (1975) and Wallis on Scientologists (1975). Wilson himself went on to develop a typology of sects and in modified forms this has guided his later work *Religious Sects* (1970) and *Magic and the Milennium* (1973). The first of these ranges widely across the world but still mainly with reference to the Christian religion in its multifarious forms. The second is concerned to look comparatively at religious movements and makes extensive use of anthropological studies and protest movements in the Third World. Whilst he applies a sect model, not all the groups relate to Christianity, although many do. It is a very ambitious essay in comparative sociology.

In essence what Wilson suggests (pp. 72-3) is that in less-developed societies most religious movements manifest one or other of two responses to the world: thaumaturgical or revolutionist.

> Thaumaturgical movements seek to cope with evils that exist in the social system or the prevailing environment, supernatural, natural or social. These evils are personal and particular, and the afflicted individual needs protection, therapy or propitiation . . . The ills recognised in a revolutionist movement are ills which affect men commonly and collectively as part of their social situation . . . The response is collective belief (and may ultimately give rise to collective action); the arena of response is the total social situation; and the expected consequence of belief, prayer, and of the soon-expected supernatural action, is to affect the whole prevailing dispensation.

Much of this work has implications for the analysis of adventist and millennial movements which tend to occur in periods of social distraction and clearly has important connecting links with studies such as

Cohn's *The Pursuit of the Millennium* (1952) and Worsley's *The Trumpet Shall Sound* (1957). Wilson for example discusses how far millennial movements may be treated as 'rational' or 'political' in character: why some movements have involved armed insurrection and others have looked in a more quietist or non-violent way for supernatural deliverance from perceived injustice and oppression.

In the English context, such questions have been raised by historians of the Civil War period and of those who have looked at religion in the process and wake of industrial revolution. One sees this developed a little in sociological writings. For example Martin's study *Pacificism* (1965) discusses the myth of the apocalypse and its relationship to pacifism in the Civil War period. Under what conditions did religious sects then flourishing become political and secularised and what promoted withdrawal from the world into religious communities or individual mysticism? Martin's book is also of interest for its attempt to apply sect analysis to the British Labour Party in the period before World War II. This was of course related to the strong pacifist tendencies in the movement that Martin wished to analyse. A second study to mention here is Moore's *Pitmen, Preachers and Politics: The Effects of Methodism in a Durham Mining Community* (1974). This very fine study combines documentary analysis of the relationship between economy, polity and religion on the Deerness valley community with the technique of oral history. It takes up the Weberian theme of protesttantism and capitalism in a new context and adds new dimensions to the discussions of the role of Methodism in political activity already contributed to by Halevy, Hobsbawm and E.P. Thompson.

Since a good deal of this discussion has to do with the relationship between belief and action (including political and economic action) one might have expected more of the debate or social imagery and consciousness to have shown more attention to the topic. In the main, however, with exceptions such as Moore's paper in Bulmer (ed.), *Working Class Images of Society* this does not happen. A clue to possible developing connections is provided by Lockwood's comment, which while cryptic is suggestive: 'While the concepts of "theodicy" and "soteriology" may appear inappropriate concepts for the analysis of secular ideologies and full understanding of the humbler, everyday solutions of the problems of suffering and injustice is probably only to be arrived at in such terms. In this respect the original essay, by treating images of society simply as ideal cognitive replications of the social mileux, leaves much to be desired' (in Bulmer, op. cit., p. 250). The other main debate in the study of religion has of course been over the question of secularisation. This takes up a topic which one can find raised in various ways by Durkheim, Marx, Engels and Weber. In Britain more recent dispute has taken place on the nature and character of the phenomenon and indications of the conceptual and empirical elements may be found in Wilson's *Religion in Secular Society* (1966), Martin's *The Religious and*

Figure 9.1: A theory of Secularisation: basic patterns

	American	*English*	*Scandinavian*	*Mixed*	*Latin*	*Statist (Right)*	*Statist (Left)*	*Nationalist*
Religious pluralism	High	Medium	Low	High (Duopoly)	Very low	Very low	Very low	Very low
Anti-clericalism	Low	Fairly low	Fairly low/medium	Fairly low	Very high	Very high	Very high	Very low
Clerical status	Low/varied	Medium	Fairly high	Fairly high	High/low	High/low	Low	High
Cultic participation	High	Fairly low	Very low	High	High/low	High/low	Low	High
Internal religious conservatism	Varied	Fairly high	Fairly high	High/low	High/low	High	High	High
Intellectualism in religion	Low/varied	Medium	High	High in the elite	High	Low	Low	High and low
Stability of democracy	High	High	High	High	Low	Low	N.A.	Varied
Communist influence	Low	Low	Low/Medium	Low	High	High	High	Low
Catholic political orientation	Centre-left	Centre-left	N.A.	Centre-left	Right then centre	Right then centre	Opposi-tional	Mostly right
Civil religion	Religiously toned	Religiously toned	Mostly secular	Religiously toned	Tension with religion	Absorbs religion	Anti-religious	Pro-religious
Church-State nexus	Broken	Retained	Retained	Retained	Strained or broken	Retained	Broken selectively	Intimate
School system	Secular	Religious then semi-secular	Secular with religious fringe	Mixed	Increas-ingly secular	Religious	Secular	Strong religious influence
Intelligentsia	Fairly religious less than status equivalents	More and less religious than status equivalents	Secular and less so than status equivalents	Fairly religious but less so than status equivalents	Less religious than status equivalents	Less religious than status equivalents	Secular	Strong religious influence
Religious parties	Non-existent	Non-existent	Very minor	Influential	Extensive	N.A.	N.A.	Influential

the Secular (1969) and MacIntyre's *Secularization and Moral Change* (1967). Without getting involved in the semantics of the problem, which has led some to suggest abandoning the term secularization I think it worthwhile to observe that sociological debate of this kind encourages both historical and comparative work. At its best it also has to link the sociology of religion with other branches of the subject in order to deal with such matters as urbanisation, science and technology, bureaucratisation and industrialisation. Such studies probably also shift the perspectives within which sociological studies commonly take place. It is necessary to work with generous time scales when taking secularisation as a theme. This is a welcome antidote to studies that are more compressed, taking their bench marks for measurement as a decade or two at the most.

That David Martin should title his recent contribution to the subject *A General Theory of Secularisation* (1978) might occasion some surprise given his earlier conceptual critique of the concept. It quickly emerges that what he intends is not a full-blown general theory but a specification of some of its components. Martin nominates a number of tendencies, in industrial societies that bear upon the secularisation process: religious institutions are weakened by the presence, of heavy industry, especially where the area is homogeneously proletarian; this is intensified with the increasing size of towns and cities. Increasing rates of geographical and social mobility, especially when they lend to a relativisation of perspectives on the world also have an adverse effect. These general tendencies, Martin notes, relate to the growth of class relations breaking down 'vertical bonds' between master and men and to the weakening of 'horizontal' bonds with the growing anonymity and depersonalisation of relationships in industrial societies, expecially in an era of electronic technology and media.

While Martin sees these as general empirical tendencies and terms them 'universal processes' he does not claim they are inevitable. But he does think they are sufficiently well established to justify relating them to a typology of cultural contexts in order to show the kind of variability that may be discovered. The range of typologies and the sensitising elements that Martin deploys are well encapsulated in Figure 9.1.

The general weakening of religious institutions, allowing for variation and even exceptions to the rule, is, in Martin's view, reflected in church life and organisation:

> The Church itself must reflect these varied pressures: the bureaucratisation and impersonality, and the reaction in the form either of a familistic suburban religion or else in radical celebrations of personal authenticity or community. The rationalisation of church organisation and liturgy runs *pari passu* with cults of encounter, authenticity and charismatic excitement, all of which leap over the constricting limits of the contemporary organisation of roles. Authenticity at

> upper status levels expresses one reaction to privatisation and bureaucratic limitation which is complemented by Pentecostalism at lower and more provincial status levels. At the same time the fragmented detritus of contemporary social organisation is partly picked up by close intimate sects like Witnesses and Mormons, offering substitutes for the experience of the family. At the upper levels of Church organisation the bureaucratic form is constantly at war both with the charismatic impulse and also with the staid familistic constituency on which contemporary active religion largely relies.
>
> (op. cit., pp. 89-90)

Contradiction thus abounds. In an important sense secularisation for Martin constitutes a form of social disintegration. It constitutes a reconsideration of Durkheim's question — how can the moral order be maintained in industrial societies when the traditional sources of moral order, religious belief and practice, are being eroded? Martin poses the question of social control, so far as the West is concerned, in terms of how much anarchy can be born without complete disintegration and, if I read him aright, subsequent totalitarian re-integration. The question is also put — what alternative secular metaphysics are available? In Eastern Europe, as against the incipient anarchy of Western industrial societies, Martin sees social control exercised in terms of a communist metaphysic allied with force.

It is then the problem of order that arises for Martin in the wake of the secularisation process. Although he and Bryan Wilson are often seen (and correctly so) as disputants concerning the nature and significance of secularisation, in this they are at one. Nowhere is this more sharply revealed than in Wilson's lecture 'The Social Meaning of Religious Change' (Ch. 3 of *Contemporary Transformations of Religion*, 1976) where he does, I think, run into something of a difficulty.

Secularisation is treated as the major contemporary transformation of religion in Western society and the co-existing contemporary cults are dismissed as 'no more than transient and volatile gestures of defiance' (op. cit., p. 112). His comments on what can loosely be called 'counter culture' turn into a comprehensive indictment, even though on his reading they are to be seen as marginal to society in general. Whether religious or political in impetus, active or passive in their stance to the world, pleasure-seeking or ascetic, they all stand condemned. Why is this?

In part, the reason is to be found in Wilson's cultural critique of the manipulative character of commercial exploitation. Thus, it is argued, that even those groups that protest against the prevalent commercial values are themselves compromised by the cultural power of the mass media which informs their perception. The cults then are seen as part of the problem not the remedy. The problem is the problem of social order engendered by the absence of reliable authority and secure knowledge: 'The communications explosion of our times has itself contributed powerfully to the process of secularisation by the diffusion of widely diverse and relatively disordered knowledge. Just what people should know, and in what order they should acquire knowledge, is something that our contemporary society has lost the power to assert. Modern man lives in a random supermarket of knowledge that is in fact a maze' (op. cit., p. 106).

The cults (all of them it would seem) represent a false search for authentic knowledge. They do not solve the problem of the legitimation of society which has been created by the collapse of a shared conception of social order. They do not serve society because they do not generate conceptions of self-restraint or the co-ordination of individuals within the wider society. Yet this is what all 'on-going social systems' require, argues Wilson. He maintains that, like it or not, modern advanced society has to depend on scientific and bureaucratic routines and that, at the same time, belief and commitment are necessary for the continuance of social order and the well-being of individuals. But belief and commitment to what? Like Durkheim he suggests that we now know no moral order that will give meaning to our social order. Yet any and every alternative is rejected as a self-indulgent attempt to achieve personal fulfilment — whether through pleasure or discipline, withdrawal or radical action. He writes: 'If a transformation of the individual's consciousness is achieved, it must not be supposed that this, in contexts such as these, will lead to a transformation of the social order, upon which the consciousness of the mass of mankind will always depend' (op. cit., p. 115).

This is to reject any dissentient activity as irrelevant, or disorderly, or exotic, or elitist, or with whatever other pejorative action may suit the polemical purpose. Wilson in his cultural pessimism appears to be weeping for a lost world, albeit, as he must very well know, one in which there was plenty of dissent which in its time played its part in shaping the social world we now inhabit. To dismiss all contemporary movements as irrelevant, both in practical terms, and as providing clues for an understanding of social consciousness, is an astonishing thing to do. Neither are we offered any solution to the problems posed by Wilson. If the alternative solutions are rejected *in toto*, then it is reasonable to ask what a proper solution would look like. Either Wilson does not think there is a solution or he is keeping his counsel on the matter. Stones instead of bread is cold comfort.

An interpretation of secularisation which results in the conservative nihilism promulgated by Bryan Wilson, is not the only one available. For an approach to the topic that has a greater sense of the ambiguities and ambivalent aspects of the process, the writings of the American sociologist Peter Berger can be consulted with profit. *The Social Reality of Religion* (1969) and *The Heretical Imperative* (1979) both give a different weight to the relation between the past and the present. The connection between secularisation and modernisation is again affirmed. The effect of modernisation is to 'pluralise both institutions and plausibility structures'. This does lead to crises of legitimation and also of belief. At the same time the change represents a movement from fate to choice and that carries with it promises as well as threats. The notion that men and women may now pick and choose in the light of available alternatives in modern societies is central to our understanding of social consciousness. This is what Berger means by his contention that heresy has become universalised.

> Today, as modernisation has become a world-wide phenomenon no longer restricted to its Western matrix, the confrontation with the heretical imperative has also become world-wide. It can be observed in the most sophisticated discussions at, say, Buddhist centres of learning or at centuries-old Muslim universities — but also in the homespun advice being given to illiterate villagers by religious functionaries barely able to read their holy scriptures. If nothing else, this has given all the religions in the world a commonality of condition that must have an effect on their self-understanding — and should have an effect on their relations with each other.
>
> (*The Heretical Imperative*, p. 31)

The future may be uncertain and full of contradictory possibilities as Berger recognises, but that is far removed from Wilson's negative and bleak perspective.

10 COMMUNICATION: A BRIEF EXCURSUS

In a recent study commissioned by the BBC, Elihu Katz gave, among other things, a thumbnail sketch of the ebb and flow of communications research *Social Research on Broadcasting: Proposals for Further Development*, BBC, 1977. 'The history of communications research is very erratic — we have witnessed periods of drastic narrowings of concerns and of dramatic re-awakenings. At this moment in history, however, I think it is correct to say that communications research is experiencing a major revival. Conceptually, the revival is based on a renewed commitment to the idea that the mass media are powerful after all in ways which older traditions of work are said to have ignored' (p. 21).

Since he is writing mainly about broadcasting, Katz refers back to the American studies of Lazarsfeld and his colleagues focusing on media effects and gratifications. The work of Robert Park of Chicago on journalism is also noted, although this is much more fully explored in Gouldner's *The Dialectics of Ideology and Technology* (Macmillan, 1976). Katz argues that effects studies tended to lose their impetus in the 1950s and that the revival of interest in communications studies in the 1960s was associated with the black revolt, the youth revolt, women's liberation, the Vietnam War and Watergate.

> Television was a convenient scapegoat for politicians, in thwarting criticism directed at themselves (Agnew), and in explaining the eruptions of all of the demographic variables: age, sex, class and race. Serious attention was directed to the violent and sensational content of American television — and a number of researchers began to look again . . . At the behest of a Committee of the US Senate, there was established Surgeon-General's Research Committee on Television and Violence. A scientific committee, including representatives of Government, academics and the media, invited research proposals and commissioned some 25 studies at a cost of $1 million.
>
> (op. cit., p. 26)

It is not just a response to changing times, but a coming together of a range of disciplines and theoretical approaches that has broken the log-jam of communications research: students of popular culture, literary critics as well as social psychologists and sociologists. Empirical research techniques are combined with more sensitive qualitative approaches. Thus semiotics may lead to innovating forms of content analysis, socio-linguistics may provide fresh stimulus to the exploration of media talk. Approaches may be found which point to the possibilities of 'distorted communication' (deriving from the Frankfurt school), conversational analysis (as in Harvey Sach's work), flow analysis (as in Raymond Williams). All of these contribute to our heightened understanding of communication as a process of encoding and decoding.

There are three comments I wish to make about research in this area. First, there is a long history of difficult, often hostile relationships between academic researchers and media professionals. This incidentally can be traced back to the Lazarsfeld days as Burns has recently reminded us in *The BBC: Public Institution and Private World*: 'If there is any one institutional disease to which the media of mass communications seems particularly subject, it is a nervous reaction to criticism. As a student of mass media I have been continually struck and occasionally puzzled by this reaction, for it is the media themselves which so vigorously defend principles guaranteeing the right to criticize' (p. xv). Burns's own experience of the BBC's veto on publishing his research is a classic illustration of the same disease. The range of symptoms can be noted in the edited collection of papers *Broadcaster/Researcher Co-operation in Mass Communication Research* (1971) with contributions from media professionals and researchers. Variations on this conflict can be seen in Halloran *et al.*, *Demonstrations and Communication* (1970) and in Glasgow University Media Group's study *Bad News* (1976). The long standing nature of this conflict is probably itself worthy of study. It is, however, particularly interesting to see that Katz concludes that there is a high degree of overlap between the interests of broadcasters and research. But this, he recognises does not dispense with the need for critical research and seems to accept that both sides may at times have to live with acrimony. This is because of the value he places on independent research into broadcasting institutions and activities as opposed to in-house studies designed to be of immediate use to programme makers.

Second, if one wishes to relate communications activities to the wider society it may be appropriate to consider how the picture of the work therein portrayed matches other available versions of what the world is like. This may be done at a factual and interpretive level. Hence in the *Bad News* study statistical comparisons were made with television news coverage of industrial disputes as against Department of Employment figures throughout the period. But case studies of particular stories were also undertaken to consider whether any dominant framework of interpretation was present. This provided a way of considering the topic of news values and also offered a basis for a critique of the concepts of balance, objectivity, neutrality and impartiality in news output. Katz argues that comparing output with external indices of reality is a research activity that could usefully be extended.

Third, there are those sociologists who wish to insist that studies of the cultural sphere need to be rooted in an understanding of economy. A good illustration of this view is found in Murdock and Golding's paper 'Capitalism, Communication and Class Relations' (in James Curran *et al.* (eds.), *Mass Communication and Society*, Arnold, 1977). The authors note (p. 17) that a number of cultural theorists are Marxists but argue that they inconsistently (from a Marxist perspective) put cultural criticism rather than economic analysis at the centre of things: 'Instead of starting from a concrete analysis of economic relations — the ways in which they structure both the processes and results of cultural production, they start by analysing the form and content of cultural artefacts and then working backwards to describe their economic base. The characteristic outcome is a top-heavy analysis in which an elaborate anatomy of cultural form balances insecurely on a schematic account of economic forces shaping their production.'

This clearly touches on a substantial problem of method, but Murdock and Golding at the same time recognise the complexity of the issue, because to understand the ways in which the media mediate reality is no small matter. If in a Marxist sense they wish to claim priority for economic factors, even on their reading the relationship between economy and culture is not one way. Still it does call into play again such matters as the ownership of media institutions, their relationship to the state and to prevailing systems of social stratification. The first two of these receive some treatment in the literature but, as they correctly point out, the last of these is generally ignored.

In concluding this short chapter I should mention that issues concerning the role of the mass media are also discussed in chapters 7 and 11.

11 TOWNS AND CITIES: CONFLICTS IN PROCESS

Community studies are not, I think, much in fashion in Britain at the moment, but there is something quite modish claiming to be a new urban sociology. I want to consider what we have learned about society through community studies in Britain — in terms of cultural changes, class and ethnic relations. And I want in conclusion to consider briefly some of the issues raised by the new urban sociology.

There is, of course, a social anthropological tradition of community studies in Britain and much of this is well summarised in Frankenberg's text *Communities in Britain* (1966). The anthropologists tended to choose small villages in rural Britain. These were small-scale groupings and could be studied intensively by an investigator. The studies are well researched using a combination of methods: participant observation, documentary materials, together with some historical and demographic analysis. Such small communities are perhaps a natural choice for anthropologists to make and, not surprisingly, a great deal of attention is given to kinship structures. The outside world is not ignored. In Littlejohn's study of Westrigg this is notably so as the breakdown of the rural community is charted. But in some instances it seems only to serve as a remote point of reference as the anthropologist becomes fascinated with the minutiae of conflict resolution at village meetings.

I want to turn now, however, to a number of studies which in one way or another have 'the working class' as their focus. Some of these have become very well known well beyond the bounds of a professional sociological readership — and deservedly so.

Consider first that remarkable study *The Uses of Literacy* (1958). Grounded in personal experience of an upbringing in urban Leeds, Hoggart seeks to clarify ways of life which can be summarised as working-class culture. The intention is to describe habits, rituals, expressed attitudes — reflected in the sense of the local, the personal and the concrete and lived out in particular neighbourhoods. While for shorthand purposes it might be called a portrayal of the traditional working class, many of its members in the first part of this century had an oral family history that linked them with the countryside. The 'tradition' expressed ways of surviving in a difficult, hostile environment-men who had to 'put up with' unpleasant and uninteresting work, women who had to 'make do with' low wages to feed and clothe their families. It was embodied in working men's clubs, friendly societies, the pub, music hall, singing and dancing and family life. It could breed a sense of fatalism — there was little the individual could do about the main elements of his situation. Life must be accepted as hard — taking life as it comes, learning to 'live and let live'.

Although Hoggart doesn't go in for an elaborate structural analysis (indeed he rather consciously eschews it) what he does do is remind us of the constraints which objectively limited the chances of working-class people changing their life situation and the material conditions of their home and working lives:

> The prevalent grime, the closeness and the difficulties of home life I have sufficiently described: we have to remember as well that the physical conditions of the working-lives of men, and of some women, are often noisy, dirty and smelly. We all know this in our heads, but realise it freshly only if we have to pass through some of those deep caverns in Leeds where the engines clang and hammer ceaselessly and the sparks fly out of huge doorways and men can be seen, black to the shoulders, heaving and straining at hot pieces of metal: or through the huge area in Hull which has a permanent pall of cooking fish-meal over it, seeping through the packed houses. The heavy, rough and beast-of-burden work is still there to be done and working class people do it. These are not conditions which produce measured tones or the more padded conversational allowances.
>
> (p. 67)

If the picture of the traditional working-class community is used as a bench mark against which to describe the impact of cultural change, Hoggart attempts to evaluate its limitations as well as its strengths. But throughout he is describing and as a cultural critic evaluating. Hence, as he proceeds to consider what changes in working-class attitudes are taking place, he recognises that

> To concentrate on the probable effects of certain developments in publications and entertainments is, of course, to isolate only one segment in a vastly complicated interplay of social, political and economic changes. All are helping to alter attitudes, some of them for the better. I shall be especially concerned with regrettable aspects of change, since these seem the more evident and important in the field I am examining.
>
> (pp. 137-8)

What follows is a judgement that, with the growth of mass media, the working class has been subjected to cultural robbery. Reading mattter in mass circulation publications is unimaginative, narrow, conservative, with a low level of taste. The attack Hoggart mounts is sustained and uncompromising, not least because he thinks cultural subordination imposed by competitive commerce is more insidious and dangerous than economic subordination. The subordinated is less aware of what is happening to him because his values are undermined and ways of thinking and feeling contaminated. There is no doubt that Hoggart saw his book as a tract for the times. In his concluding pages he dwells on the paradox of a society which in the name of freedom and tolerance 'allows cultural developments as dangerous in their own way as those we are shocked at in totalitarian societies'. And he goes on:

> the problem is acute and pressing — how that freedom may be kept as in any sense a meaningful thing whilst the processes of centralisation and technological development continue. This is a particularly intricate challenge because, even if substantial inner freedom were lost, the great new classless class would be unlikely to know it: its members would still regard themselves as free and be told that they were free.
>
> (p. 287)

Cultural change is then seen and related to the growth of 'mass society'. Critical judgements are not based on the dichotomy traditional (good)/modern(bad) but on the sense that the opportunities for enlarging democratic values of freedom and tolerance are being lost. And accordingly it is upon the cultural instruments of mass society, the mass media, that the attack is made.

Although I doubt that Hoggart ever puts it so formally, the explanatory problem is that of the relationship between culture and structure. Structure here may refer to the organisation of working-class communities. But it may also refer to the wider society and in his case with special reference to the structure of mass communications. And the under-pinning value is a commitment to a 'democratic culture'. Against this he sets the advent of a 'consumers' culture' which inadequately replaces or by-passes 'high culture' and 'popular culture'. Not only so, the mass media, he holds, severely restricts the effective and open-ended discussion of public issues:

> The Establishments, however well-intentioned they may be and whatever their forms (the State, the Church, voluntary agencies, political parties), have a vested interest in ensuring that the public boat is not violently rocked, and would like so to affect those who work within the mass media that they will be led insensibly towards forms of production which, though they go through the motions of dispute and inquiry, do not break through to the point where such inquiries hurt. They tend to move, when exposing problems, well within the accepted cliche-ridden assumptions of democratic society and neither radically question those cliches nor apply these

disturbingly to features of contemporary life; they stress the 'stimulation' the programmes give, but this soon becomes an agitation of problems for the sake of the interestingness of that agitation in itself: they will therefore, again, assist a form of acceptance of the *status quo*. There are exceptions to this tendency but they are un-characteristic.

'Mass Communications in Britain', in *Speaking to Each Other*, (1973), p. 144

In the work of Raymond Williams we find parallel concerns to those of Hoggart and also from the standpoint of what we may lightly label a left-Leavisite. It is the literary critic who can in concluding *Culture and Society 1780-1950* write: 'There are ideas, and ways of thinking, with the seeds of life in them, and there are others, perhaps deep in our minds, with the seeds of a general death. Our measure of success in recognising these kinds, and in naming them, making possible their common recognition, may be literally the measure of our future' (Penguin, 1961, p. 324). It is the social critic who writes about the need for an educated democracy that can experience and share in a genuinely common culture, based on the value of equality of being. And Williams like Hoggart is drawn to the idea of cultural robbery through the growth of mass communications and the depersonalising conception of 'mass society'. Processes or urbanisation and industrialism have led in a period of social transition not to a more open society and availability of 'the great tradition' but to a disinheritance from it:

> In the worst cultural products of our time, we find little genuinely popular, developed from the life of actual communities. We find instead a synthetic culture, or anti-culture, which is alien to almost everybody, persistently hostile to art and intellectual activity, which spends much of its time in misrepresenting, and given over to exploiting indifference, lack of feeling, frustration and hatred. It finds such common human interests as sex, and turns them into crude caricatures or glossy facsimiles. It plays repeatedly around hatred and aggression, which it never discharges but continually feeds. This is not the culture of 'the ordinary man': it is the culture of the disinherited.
>
> (*Communications*, 1976, p. 115, first published 1962)

For Williams the linguistic affinity between community and communication is seen as a clue to cultural analysis and judgement of societies. Indeed he explicitly argues that any real theory of communication is a theory of community (see *Culture and Society*, p. 301). It is necessary to add that his theory of community is normative and that this, as one would expect, leads to a normative theory of communication. On both fronts he poses the question how can we get genuinely democratic communities and democratic communication. Hence he writes, 'It is very difficult to think clearly about communication, because the pattern of our thinking about community is normally dominative. We tend in consequence, if not to be attracted, at least to be pre-occupied by dominative techniques. Communication becomes a science of penetrating the mass mind and of registering an impact here. It is not easy to think along different lines' (ibid., p. 301).

This might lead one to ask to what extent are actual communities systems of domination. In Williams's case however the more typical move is to examine the political and economic context in which communication takes place — its institutional embodiments and cultural forms. This indeed is in line with his approach to a theory of culture whiich studies the relationships between elements in a whole way of life' 'The analysis of culture is the attempt to discover the nature of the organisation which is the complex of these relationships. Analysis of particular works or institutions is, in this context, analysis of their essential kind of organisation, the relationship which works or institutions embody as parts of the organisation as a whole' (*The Long Revolution*, Pelican, 1975 p. 63, first published 1961).

Williams in his work has always been sensitive to the importance of class analysis but it has never been mechanical in its application. This is characteristically expressed in his discussion of 'bourgeois culture' and 'working class culture'. Hence while working with a Marxist-derived notion of dominant class which in a society can control the transmission and distribution of the common inheritance he explicitly recognises that 'even within a society in which a particular class is dominant, it is evidently possible both for members of other classes to contribute to the common stock and for such contributions to be unaffected by or in opposition to the ideas and values of the dominant class' (*Culture and Society*, p. 308). And he goes on to note that in a society where the working class becomes the dominant class, the nature of the inheritance would be such that the patterns of culture would not be class-linked in any simple and direct way.

Even, therefore, if it is felt necessary to maintain some kind of base/superstructure model the inter-relations are such as to justify close examination of what in Marxist terms might usually be regarded as pertaining to superstructure. Williams conveys no sense that he is examining the shadow rather than the substance of society. It is the very opposite as the conclusion to the latest edition of *Communications* makes clear: 'The intervening years (i.e. since 1960) with their different kinds of development, have shown that communications is, in modern societies, a central social, cultural and political issue. Looking forward from 1975 I believe that this will be shown to be even more true' (p. 189).

For Hoggart and for Williams there has been this inter-related interest in the growth in communications, in its forms, structure and content.

The cultural critique at its best goes alongside the structural and organisational critique. For example, Hoggart in 'Television as the Archetype of Mass Communications' distinguishes between state-controlled, commercially impelled and democratic structures of broadcasting (see *Speaking to Each Other*, pp. 161-72). The last named is his preference and leads him into discussion of the relationship between broadcasters, governments and the public and explores the issues of autonomy and accountability of professional broadcasters in a pluralist society. Williams, for his part, offers a fourfold classification of communication systems: authoritarian, paternal, commercial, democratic (see *Communications*, pp. 129-37). Again it is the last-named that is preferred and seen as potential rather than actual. The democratic system of communication 'shares with the early commercial system a definition of communication which insists that all men have the right to offer what they choose and to receive what they choose. It is firmly against authoritarian control of what can be said, and against paternal control of what ought to be said. But it is also against commercial control of what can profitably be said, because this also can be a tyranny' (ibid., p. 133). These kinds of normative arguments ultimately involve a consideration of what communication systems have existed. They lead one back to the implications of existing structures for the control of and access to the systems. They add to the classic communications formula that research in this area is about 'who says what, how, to whom, with what effect' the phrase'with what purpose?: They lead one on to consider alternative structures and indeed technologies of communication. And by the use of the critical method — with its mix of qualitative, empirical and normative elements — they provide a substantial response to the question' what is the relationship between research and policy?

There are other significant studies of 'traditional' working-class communities. The most frequently quoted example is probably Dennis, Henriques and Slaughter, *Coal is Our Life* (1956). In this example the authors are dealing with a one-industry (mining) village. It is also to all intents and purposes a one-class community. The authors (unlike the authors of the rural village studies) might be described as Marxist anthropologists, which at the time of writing was somewhat unusual on the British scene. There is certainly an awareness that while Ashton may share characteristics with other mining villages, in terms of its work situation, leisure and cultural activities, sexual divisions and family organisation, it was not a microcosm of British society — only of one section of the working class. Other traditional working-class communities studied are rather differently placed. They are part of larger populations in urban areas. Hoggart's partly autobiographical account discussed above was published at about the same time as *Coal is Our Life* and tends to be conjoined in discussions of the (northern) working class. But there is considerable awareness in Hoggart of the internal social differentiation in the urban working class, based on such things as occupation (or lack of it), type of housing and degrees of 'respectability'. This is paralleled in Robert Roberts's *The Classic Slum* (1973). This Salford study of life in the first quarter of the twentieth century is of the same high calibre as *The Uses of Literacy*. The complexity of social differences within the class is carefully teased out. The picture drawn (p. 28) is of a class divided against itself in the 'battle of life'. 'All in all it was a struggle against the fates, and each family fought it out as best it could. Marxist 'ranters' from the Hall who paid fleeting visits to our street and insisted that we, the proletariat stood locked in titanic struggle with some wicked master class . . . Most people passed by; a few stood to listen, but not for long: the problems of the "proletariat" they felt, had little to do with them.'

Such working-class areas are seen as places where people struggle to survive against the odds with a sense of fatalism as to outcomes. The struggle is to resist being overwhelmed, not a revolutionary struggle. Indeed Roberts (p. 168) observes that in his district the vote was usually solid Conservative: 'Apathy, docility, deference: our village as a whole displayed just those qualities which, sixty years before, Karl Marx had noted, stamped the poor industrial workers — qualities which convinced him that the English proletarian would never revolt of his own accord.' This did not mean that members of the class did not participate in strikes and lock-outs. They did and could be the victims of police violence. But Roberts emphasises both the ways in which internal social differentiation mitigated against class solidarity and writes also of the industrial 'undermass' as being ignorant, ill-organised with neither the wit nor the will to revolt. However one sums up this picture with its prestige hierarchies, its respectable and disreputable, its unionists and its lumpen proletariat, it is considerably different from the one-industry, one-class situation of Ashton.

The Bethnal Green working-class community studied by Young and Willmott takes us south and moves us forward to the early 1950s. As is well known the great emphasis was on a community that was bound together by close kinship ties, and one that had shaken down over a period of time. Central importance is given to the interaction between length of residence and kinship. This not only evidenced the close mother/daughter relationship but also the importance of family links in the local labour market: the docks, printing, the markets and the shops.

The Bethnal Green studies contain an affirmative view of the community. They also retain the anthropological interest in kinship noted in the village studies. It can without difficulty I think be seen why the subsequent work of Elizabeth Bott on *Family and Social Network* (1957) should have been regarded as of general theoretical relevance to community studies. 'Network' becomes an important metaphor to encapsulate the notion of community and indeed of community breakdown. What is more, in principle, networks (although sometimes very complex) are subject to measurement. It is perhaps true to say that in the British context network analysis as such has remained undeveloped — although the implications for social anthropology were enthusiastically taken up by Max Gluckmann in his preface to the revised edition of Bott's book (1971) and have been notably taken up by Clyde Mitchell (see his edited book *Social Networks in Urban Situations*, 1969). It also informs the organisation of Frankenberg's account of community studies.

Although network analysis as such may have been relatively neglected in Britain, one can see how it provides an instructive way of re-interpreting social structure. In particular it can lie behind interpretations of the impact of ecological change on community life. Hence life on new housing estates (private and public) provides grounds for theses on 'privatisation'. The new situations are seen as leading to a decline in family and social contexts and withdrawal into the nuclear family with little outside support and a decline in community (especially working-class) values of solidarity.

What the network approach did, both in re-interpreting older studies and informing those which post-date her, was, as Bott suggests, to enlarge our conceptual repertoire. However studies of working-class communities in the Young and Willmott mould were not just academic voyeurism. They saw their work as relating research findings to social policy. Their assumption was that policy-makers were 'insufficiently aware of the needs and views of the working class people who form the bulk of the users of the social services, and we hoped that social research might help to provide a more realistic basis for policy' (M. Young and P. Willmott, *Research Report No. 3*, Institute of Community Studies: Bethnal Green, *Sociological Review*, July 1961, p. 2).

Given their own value standpoint, Young and Willmott could (and did) give an unequivocal answer to the now modish question 'Whose side are you on?' How far does one have to break down communities like Bethnal Green they ask, as opposed to saving houses that are structurally sound and modernising them. 'The problem was formidable, but if the purpose of re-housing is to meet human needs, not as they are judged by others but as people themselves assess their own, it is doubtful whether anything short of such a programme will suffice' (*Family and Kinship*, p. 198). And in so far as some movement proved inevitable in the process of urban renewal then thought should be given to the manner of re-housing. 'Movement of street and kinship groupings as a whole, members being transferred together to a new setting, would enable the city to be re-built without squandering the fruits of social cohesion' (ibid., p. 198).

It is the planners who Young and Willmott have in their sights. It is they who have to be both attacked and persuaded:

> Yet even when the town planners have set themselves to create communities anew as well as houses, they have still put their faith in buildings, sometimes speaking as though all that was necessary for neighbourliness was a neighbourhood unit, for community spirit a community centre . . . But there is surely more to a community than that. The sense of loyalty to each other amongst the inhabitants of a place like Bethnal Green is not due to buildings. It is due far more to ties of kinship and friendship which connect the *people* of one household to the *people* of another. In such a district community spirit does not have to be fostered, it is already there. If the authorities regard that spirit as a social asset worth preserving, they will not uproot more people, but build the new houses around the social groups to which they already belong.
>
> (ibid., pp. 198-9)

So here the threat to community is not, as in Hoggart, the growth of mass communications but the planners, whose approach to social change is inadequate because not based on a 'proper' understanding of community.

Who will plan the planners? Karl Mannheim's question continues to be asked in one way or another by sociologists (among others). This often has a particular focus on plans that affect working-class areas. In addition to the work of the Institute for Community Studies the work of Dennis (1970, 1972) in Sunderland and Davies (1972) in Newcastle serve as leading examples. If one reads the sceptical and at times hostile way in which planners are viewed by Dennis and Davies one will understand better the very bitter attack launched on sociologists and most of their works by Eversley (pp. 739-40) in *The Planner in Society*, (1973). Apparently it is no good planners looking to sociologists for guidance:

> British sociologists have, collectively and individually, roundly condemned just about everything that has been done since the war to provide a new environment for almost half the population of the British Isles (8 million new houses and at least a million converted, improved or entirely rehabilitated). They do not like new towns, they do not like peripheral estates, they like neither segregation of social classes nor mixtures, they condemn the monotony of terraces as they do the tower blocks, they have judged privacy to be unnecessary, and open plan housing to be anti-social. The planner looks in vain for any ray of light.

This is too sweeping a statement to admit of much evaluation other than of the author's anger. But unless the sociologist is defined as (or perhaps paid to be) the planner's friend, which puts him in the equivalent position of a managerial sociologist in the industrial context, then one must expect work which will not leave the planner untouched.

One of the sociologists who gets a clean bill of health from Eversley is Pahl. Yet in his essay 'Whose City' (1969) one can see how the sociologist may typically offer a more radical analysis of urban poverty. This is because the spatial and physical arrangements of cities are seen as an expression of the distribution of power in society and the outcome of competition between interest groups. Planners may operate at the level of symptoms and not causes of urban problems. He comments:

> Making physical changes without parallel changes in the social structure may serve to add to the problem by drawing sections of the population further apart. Clearly no one wants British cities to be centres of poverty and social intolerance. However, there may be some danger that if British planners feel that their main task is to concentrate on the future and to spend their time worrying about the provision of motorways and yachting marinas in 1991, they may take attention away from present problems and so, indirectly, help to make them worse.
>
> ('Whose City?', op. cit., p. 191)

Here again one comes up against the question of what is defined as a problem, the nature of the explanation and the proposed solution. To shift it back to a problem of power, as opposed to a technical or social engineering problem is in itself to alter the frame of reference. Solutions which start with the distribution of power as the problem are likely to proceed in terms of redistributing power to achieve a more acceptable outcome. These may be of a reformist liberal-democratic kind or some variant of Marxism as represented in the currently fashionable Castells, or, and in my view more instructively, by David Harvey in his stimulating book of essays *Social Justice and the City* (1973). When this shift in the frame of reference takes place the discussion of working-class community moves away from kinship and social cohesion to problems of political economy. Whether one is reporting close-knit communities exhibiting a high degree of social solidarity and a developed culture, or a ghetto of an ill-organised anomic underclass, explanations of their character and formation are traced back to the market: the competition for space and resources in the city and the political context in and through which change takes place. It is after all not only the community network of Bethnal Green that forms part of the working-class literature on cities, but the 'dreadful enclosures' so starkly described by Damer in his Wine Alley case study (in Wiles, P. (ed.), *The Sociology of Crime and Delinquency in Britain*, 1976, pp. 175-206).

Mention should also be made of small-town community studies. The obvious example in the British literature is the work of Stacey and her colleagues in two studies of Banbury in *Tradition and Change* (1960) and *Power, Persistence and Change* (1975). These studies are worthy of note, apart from any other virtues they may possess, for the simple reason that follow-up studies of this kind are rare. In the introduction to the second study Stacey records the challenges and the difficulties that this presented in terms of data collection, choice of methodology and conceptualisation. It is not only communities that change but sociologists' ideas as to how they may best be studied.

In the first study the heart of the analysis was to show how Banbury was bisected in two ways.

	Middle class	Working class
Traditional	1	2
Non-traditional	3	4

The traditional order, with its class divisions referred to those groupings with a long-standing network of relationships between functions and friends. The values of social stability and support for existing institutions predominated. The extent and significance of this was worked out in the descriptions of religious adherence, political affiliation, membership of voluntary associations and place of work. Between the two most polarised groups, of traditional middle-class Conservatives and non-traditional working-class Labour, were groups that were more blurred in their differences with one another by virtue of cross-cutting membership.

We can see that the concept of traditional here has a different content from that of traditional working class in, say, Bethnal Green. The traditional working class in Banbury were likely to vote Conservative, thus in effect signifying a supportive attitude to the presiding local system of stratification. As Stacey recognises, if one shifted to Swansea, one would probably have a mirror-image picture. The traditionalists there in supporting the local status quo would be the Labour working-class voters. Banbury was not regarded by Stacey as a microcosm by British society. What *Tradition and Change* could do, however, was show the impact of externally induced change in the industrial sphere (the advent of Alcan) on social relationships and community activities. In this her work has much in common with the small-town studies in the USA of the Lynds, Warner *et al.* and Vidich and Bensman.

Even in the first study it is clear that Stacey does not hold a closed concept of community; she relates what can be ascertained about a locality to the wider society — notably changes in manufacture and economy. This is reflected in her subsequent article 'The Myth of Community Studies' (1969). What remains of interest to her is the extent to which local social systems do exist and what they look like. This is connected with an interest in social stratification: the testing and if necessary modifying of statements about social stratification made at a national level. In *Power, Persistence and Change* (p. 4) these interests are exemplified in a number of ways and serve as a modest justification of the cumulative possibilities of social science knowledge. 'In the event we have found that outside the political arena there is no local social system any longer definable. The demarcation between the locality and the outside world has indeed decreased such that identifiable local social relations are not discernible in any local holistic sense.'

The picture that emerges is of a multi-faceted pluralist society. Outside Banbury it is argued, taking the Banbury expansion plan as an example, there are a number of elites and influential groups: administrative groups from ministries and local authorities by no means in agreement, a variety of industrial interests. Following Aron it is argued that there is a 'differentiation of ruling hierarchies' and a 'dissociation of powers'. Within the town complex and cross-cutting, patterns of stratification are discerned related to production systems, position in the consumption market, the housing market, family membership, age and sex categories.

> Thus the society is complex, linked through many social relations with other parts of Britain and beyond, and pluralist in the sense of being composed of a kaleidoscope of interlocking groups and networks. Associated with these were many sets of values, often inconsistent with each other, which people appeared to espouse depending on the situation they were in. This gave individuals at least some sense of a freedom of choice between various courses of action and some chance to manipulate affairs among groups. The kaleidoscope of groups is not without meaning or explanation: it depends upon the interests which are seen being pursued or are seen to be threatened at any one time.
>
> (ibid., pp. 134-5)

This has implications for how people see society, their position in relation to others, what they think they can or cannot accomplish. It has implications for class theory and for judgements about social imagery: no small matter.

Race, ethnicity and the urban scene

Studies of race relations in Britain have a longer history than is popularly recognised I suspect. Among studies in the early post-war period one can cite Kenneth Little's *Negroes in Britain* (1947)., Michael

Banton's *The Coloured Quarter* (1955), Sydney Collin's *Coloured Minorities in Britain* (1957) and Anthony Richmond's *Colour Prejudice in Britain* (1954). Some brief comments might be made about these early studies. At one level there is an expressed dissatisfaction with existing theories. Thus Banton (p. 15) says: 'The study of race relations is one of the least systematised spheres of social science and existing theories help the research worker very little.' In fact one observes that Little, Banton and Collins all make use of a social ecological approach explicitly derived from the Chicago school or uban sociologists such as Park, Thomas and Wirth. This involves studying 'connections' in spatial as well as functional terms and of the patterns of social relationships thus engendered. This was typically combined with a research technique of participant observation: Little in Cardiff and Banton in Stepney, for example.

The significance of this ecological approach is reflected in such comments as the following by Collins writing of ethnic 'communities' in Britain:

> Ecologically these communities tend to follow a defined pattern. A core of immigrants form a nucleus of settlement composed mostly of newly arrived and other persons least adjusted to British society. The settlement is formed in the least desirable area, usually near the docks or some slum elements of the town. Here the cluster of immigrants is usually densest, dispersing as the settlement fans out into the better type of residential area. The further from the nucleus, the higher the social status and the better adjusted to British society the immigrant tends to be.
>
> (op. cit., p. 14)

The notion of adjustment here assumes what may now be thought to be a simplistic idea of integration but the ecological perspective remains of interest. And Collins later suggests that the time dimension is important in the study of race relations because we are dealing with dynamic not static relationships: 'In the process of social adjustment there occurs oppositions, conflicts, compromises . . . there are varying degrees of acceptance or rejection, acceptance and integration. . . . The changing economic and social conditions of the host society directly affect the immigrant situation' (op. cit., p. 32). What one has in essence here is an ecological perspective, the patterning of which shifts in relation to social and economic change and applied to 'the immigrant'. Whatever its weaknesses in detail or conceptualisation it is recognisably sociological in character. Little too, as I have noted, used an ecological approach. In that context, however, in his attempt to account for English attitudes towards coloured immigrants he offers a 'cultural' explanation namely, 'the complicated background of overseas exploration, slave ownership, colonial expansion and their rationalisations and incorporation in the cultural heritage' (op. cit., p. 218). Prejudice he saw as further re-inforced by a general ignorance of the background of coloured immigrants, due to faulty formal education on the subject in schools and the effect of films which were based upon and produced stereotyped racial attitudes.

I want to indicate some of the ways in which the debate and work on race relations and immigration has moved on, first in the British context and second in a more comparative context. I think it likely that the most widely read book on race relations within a British context is Rex and Moore's *Race, Community and Conflict* (1967). This may in part have been because by the late 1960s race relations were a much more widely discussed phenomenon in the public and political arena and here was a study that addressed itself to how things were in Birmingham. It would have been surprising if some press attention was not devoted to it. And without doubt it did address itself to the problems of race and immigration (although not in the way that had characterised much media and political comment). At the same time the study was concerned with offering an analysis of race relations in sociological terms. The attempt to do this, and the issues raised, in many ways place the study alongside the *Affluent Worker* study of which I have written elsewhere. I say this notwithstanding the methodological problems of getting an adequate sampling frame and the difficulty of interpreting a good number of the statistical tables in the book. Indeed one is almost tempted to conclude that the image of British sociological research in the 1960s is encapsulated for many sociologists by these two studies — plus Bernstein on language codes.

Why did *Race, Community and Conflict* prove so stimulating? Among the reasons I would list the following:

1. There is a professional reason in that the case for a sociological as distinct from historical or psychological explanation of race relations is propounded. The attack on the adequacy of psychological explanations (more prominent in the USA but widely discussed) was of particular interest. Just as Goldthorpe *et al.* had denied the validity of psychological studies of job satisfaction as an adequate basis for analysing work behaviour and attitudes so do Rex and Moore (pp. 2-3) reject another kind of psychological 'universal'. Whatever ultimate utility such explanations might have, methodologically it was not the right place to start:

> It may be that amongst the people of Birmingham whom we studied some discriminatory behaviour was due to innate and universal tendencies. And it may be that some of it was the product of personality disturbance. But it is also the case that a great deal of it was sufficiently explained, once we knew something of Birmingham's social structure and conflicts and the constellation of interests and

roles which was built into Birmingham society. At the very least it must be said that the universal factors and those having their roots in the individual personality could only be known if the factor arising from the social economic and cultural system were first sorted out.

This sort of methodological point incidentally underlies much of what is at issue in the debate on intelligence which in the fields of education and race offers a classic spectacle of scholars talking past each other to general public confusion. It is not only what is to be explained that is partly at issue but where the most fruitful point of departure for explaining social phenomena is to be located.

2. Within the realm of sociology there is also an attempt to shift the character of some prevailing modes of explanation. This involves a criticism of functional explanations which do not allow enough scope for considering the actor as agent. This did not, however, involve rejecting the notion of a social system. It was accepted that, while there may be many conflicts of interest (and the purpose of the research was to trace out many of these), organisational means could exist as mechanisms of tension-management. However, to analyse seriously conflicts of interest meant in Rex and Moore's view breaking with some of the received race-relations vocabulary of 'assimilation', 'integration' and 'accommodation'. This bears explicitly upon previous work referred to:

> Such vocabularies assume a host-immigrant framework in which the culture and values of the host society are taken to be non-contradictory and static and in which the immigrant is seen as altering his own patterns of behaviour until they finally conform to those of the host society. The frame of reference is a cultural one and culture is seen as an independent variable which may change regardless of a man's position in the structure of social action and relations and regardless of the degree to which he possesses property and power.
>
> (op. cit., pp. 13-14)

In passing one may note that just as the social action perspective in industrial sociology is embedded in Fox's *A Sociology of Work in Industry* so does this conceptual reformulation in race relations become incorporated in Sheila Allen's text *New Minorities, Old Conflicts: Asian and West Indian Immigrants in Britain* (1972).

The explicit shift to property and power as key concepts in a theory of conflict of which race conflict is an example is a crucial strategic change. Thus, although like Collins, Rex and Moore make use of the Chicago ecologists they link what they say with a theory of competition for scarce resources such as land and housing back to groups who are differentially placed in the competitive struggle. This enables them to build upon Weber's theory of class and groups of people in a similar market situation with similar life chances and apply it to the housing market. Again, instead of assuming that the 'zone of transition' where most immigrants were located was an internally integrated community in the sense in which some middle-class or working-class residential areas are they say: 'It is a transitional life only and the communal institutions which it evolves are to be regarded as a means of fighting discrimination and providing temporary security until some kind of outward move can be made' (op. cit., p. 9). Within the area a mixed population exists, with varying degrees of permanence and conflicts of interest.

Setting the study of race relations within the context of urban sociology also meant that the question of citizenship rights could be explored, in relation to immigrants. This allowed a further examination of T.H. Marshall's thesis on citizenship and social class. Whilst it was one approach to the view that the working class has been incorporated into British society through the extension of political, legal and social rights, its application to immigrants was a matter for empirical inquiry. Although perhaps this was not a central theme in the study it did bear upon the more general contention that ethnic conflicts were not identical with class conflicts. And it may be recalled that in the eclectic study co-ordinated by Rose and Deakin in *Colour and Citizenship* (1969) the citizenship theme is taken up very fully (see especially Chs. 2 and 3) and set alongside the analysis of social integration in British society which had taken class as a major source of differentiation — notably Runciman's *Relative Deprivation and Social Justice* (1966).

3. The third source of stimulus which *Race, Community and Conflict* offered was a sense of the inter-connectedness of social life. This meant that the urban setting also provided the opportunity to examine aspects of life and experience in the city which impinged on the immigrant: the churches, the schools, the political parties and the immigrant associations. Not only so but the ideologies of interest groups in the situation are outlined, particularly in the area of housing allocation in a differentiated market. And in true Weberian style the paradox of unintended consequences of human action is revealed. The two dominant political ideologies in considering housing emphasised respectively the property-owning democracy and housing as a social service. Yet neither of these outlooks were fulfilling housing needs in Birmingham. It is the parish group of landlords who fill the gap in the twilight zone of areas such as Sparkbrook and are condemned by left wing and right wing. Are they not exploitative landlords to be condemned by the left? Are they not failing to provide satisfactory accommodation to be condemned by the right as unhealthy dwelling places?

> So the city having failed to deal with its own housing problem, turns on those upon whom it relies to make alternative provision, and

> punishes them for its failure. Punishment, however, cannot go too far. For the consequence of driving the lodging-house landlords out of business would be to leave large numbers of the population to sleep in the parks and on the railway tracks. What has to be done, therefore, is to tolerate the lodging-houses within loosely defined limits in certain areas and 'to stop the evil from spreading' to other areas where the property-owning democracy and the welfare state may be preserved intact.
>
> (op. cit., p. 41)

And as the authors go on to point out this is the recipe for the creation of urban ghettos inhabited by immigrants and the dispossessed of the host society.

In addition to the above points there is another element in the study to which I wish to draw attention. It is simply that at the end a number of policy recommendations are made. They have to do with ways of reversing the trend to ghettos and racial hostility which they chart in the book. They include suggestions such as reviewing existing local authority policies of housing allocation, considering plans for urban renewal and more educational investment in deteriorating urban areas. Indeed I think this needs to be remembered when one reads Rex's later and somewhat angry essay 'Policy-Oriented Research and the Sociology of Race Relations' (in Rex, 1973). There we find him calling a plague on all the houses of the race relations writers. Rose *et al.*'s *Colour and Citizenship* is portrayed as a tangled mixture of theory, ideology and empirical work, which does not examine the realities of political power in Britain. Even more sociological work is treated as unrealistic and somewhat supportive of the ideology supporting *Colour and Citizenship*. In considering the contribution of writers such as Halsey, Banton and Lambert he concludes that they seem to be premised on assumptions which rule out the real possibility of social disintegration and the acceleration of race conflict. He is pre-occupied with the worry that sociology will become ideology — whether conservative or revolutionary. He is equally concerned (p. 177) with Marxist dogma. 'What I wish to see, and to see developed urgently, is a framework for the analysis of all race relations problems which is both realistic and undogmatic.'

Hence, in his plea for objectivity on a perplexing social problem, Rex concludes his essay (pp. 181-2) in this way: 'I believe that it is possible for sociologists to turn their eyes away from the immediate problem of advising the Home Office or the Black Causes and to begin to argue about a typology of colonial situations, a typology of advanced capitalist industrial societies and a typology of the sorts of process which are generated by the migration of individuals from colonial situations to metropolitan capitalist countries.'

It is possible that Rex was a little unfair to his sociological colleagues but they are quite capable of framing their own responses and from time to time do so. It may sometimes seem that Rex regards himself as an Elijah figure — the one left who has not bowed the knee to Baal. But it must be said that for him what is at issue is crucial to the task of sociology as being something other than propaganda for causes with whick one may sympathise. It is a Weberian sociology in which ethical neutrality is advocated but not moral indifference. Nowhere is this better illustrated I think than in the opening sentences of *Race Relations in Sociological Theory* (1970).

> The problem of race and racism challenges the conscience of the sociologist in the same way as the problem of nuclear weapons challenges that of the nuclear physicist. This is not to say that sociology can dictate to men and nations how they should behave towards one another any more than that the nuclear physicist had some special competence to advise the American President whether or not he should drop the atom bomb on the Japanese. But it is to say that in so far as whole populations have been systematically discriminated against, exploited and even exterminated, the sociologist might legitimately be asked to lay the causes of these events bare.

With that kind of concern the likelihood of sociology becoming a trivial occupation is surely reduced.

One of the questions that causal analysis quickly confronts is the relationship between race and class. Can race conflict be subsumed under class conflict or does it have a dynamic of its own as implied for example in Segal's *The Race War* (1966)? This leads Rex into a theoretical discussion of stratification and race — Parsonian, Marxist and the pluralist treatments of Furnivall and M.G. Smith. For his own part the attempt is based upon seeking to relate belief systems, which enter into social relations and make them racial, to underlying social structures: '. . . given that a true race relations situation exists where men have beliefs of a certain kind, it is also the case that such beliefs are associated only with a limited range of structures. One of the tasks of the sociology of race relations therefore will be that of discovering and listing what these structures are' (op. cit., pp. 9-10).

The study accordingly proceeds to consider a range of colonial situations, followed by a discussion of minorities in metropolitan societies, with the clear recognition that what emerges in the latter has to be seen with reference to the former at this period of human history. As I see it this illustrative typological discussion of Rex is an attempt to direct and refocus the strategy of race relations research, rescuing it from being simply responsive to *ad hoc* issues or to becoming ideologically committed.

One student of race relations who needs no such encouragement is

Philip Mason. I refer particularly to his very fine book *Patterns of Dominance* (1970). It is a quite remarkable tour de force as a comparative and historical account of race relations in almost a world context, as emerging from the process of European expansion and conquest in Latin America, the Caribbean, Africa and India.

It seems to me quite a startling example of what a historically informed sociology can accomplish. 'It is a main purpose of this book to look at the general development of human society towards patterns of dominance and subordination and then to consider the revolt against them. Against this background, are described in more detail, but in relation to this main franework, some of these patterns — the systems and myths that have been used to make inequality permanent in different parts' (op. cit., p. 4). The intention thus clearly outlined is with continuing lucidity pursued. At the same time Mason has to deal with the complexity of patterns of contact between ethnic groups. His true metaphor of the growth and inter-twining of branches to illustrate the range of situations is illuminating. It starts from the basic distinction of those who migrate as dominant conquering groups and those who migrate as subordinate to a dominant host society. This allows for a careful teasing out of similarities and differences and permits an approach that can take account of the uniqueness of particular cultures whilst locating them within a range of others with partial resemblances (See his figure from p. 82 reproduced here).

What Mason also does is to argue that patterns of domination and subordination are not just colour (or social) phenomena: 'Colour gives it a special sharpness. . . . But Russian serfs were not much better off than negro slaves and the reaction of the oppressed against the dominant is surely part of a world-wide phenomena and stage in the development of human populations from simple food-gathering groups to far more complex and highly organised societies' (op. cit., p. 3).

If one takes the examples of groups migrating to subordinate positions, then historically much of this has been linked with slavery. But once one moves into the realm of wage labour then the relationship between the immigrants and the indigenous working class invites examination. One example of a Marxist perspective on this is Castles and Kosack's *Immigrant Workers and Class Structure in Western Europe* (1973). This comparative study, by focusing on the immigrants' position in the socio-economic structure, sought to argue that the question of colour as such is not the major consideration. Hence race or racialism was not to be seen as determining the individual's social position but rather his immigrant status.

Castles and Kosack, in a well-documented study, report that on the labour market (which they see as the key determinant of class position) immigrant workers are markedly over-represented in the lowest occupational categories — the overwhelming majority being semi-skilled or unskilled manual workers. But it is argued they should not be regarded

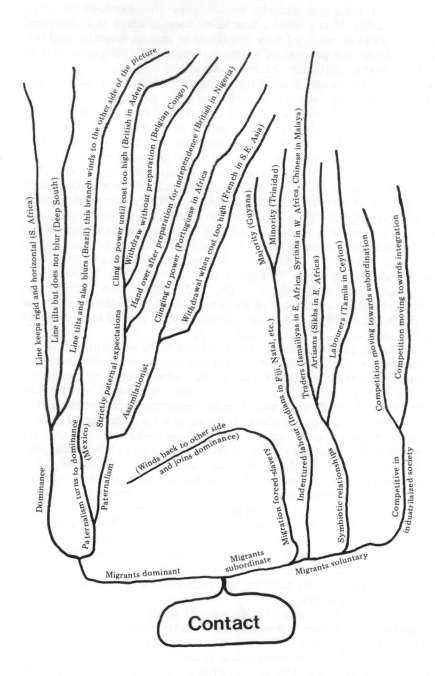

Figure 11.1 Relationships which arise from European expansion.

as a 'new proletariat', 'sub-proletariat' or 'lumpen proletariat'.

> Immigrant workers and indigenous workers together form the working class in contemporary Western Europe, but it is a divided class. The immigrants have become concentrated in the unskilled occupations and the indigenous workers have tended to leave such jobs. Immigrants have lower incomes and inferior housing and social conditions. The two groups are more or less isolated from each other through differing positions and short-term interests. This objective split is reproduced in the subjective sphere: a large proportion of indigenous workers have prejudiced and hostile attitudes towards immigrants. They lack solidarity with their immigrant colleagues and favour discriminatory practices. Often immigrants find themselves isolated and unsupported when they take collective action to improve their conditions. We may therefore speak of two strata within the working class: the indigenous workers, with generally better conditions and the feeling of no longer being right at the bottom of society, form the higher stratum. The immigrants, who are the most under-privileged and exploited group of society form the lower stratum.
>
> (op. cit., pp. 476-7)

This leads the authors to conclude that this divided working class with this immigrant/indigenous-worker split serves in practice to stabilise the capitalist societies of Western Europe both politically and economically. And given their Marxist perspective, one is not surprised to see them labelling the indigenous workers who acquiesce in the exploitation of immigrants as victims of false consciousness. This analysis should be compared to that of Moore's in his paper 'Migrants and the Class Structure of Western Europe' (in Richard Scase (ed.) *Industrial Society: Class, Cleavage and Control*, 1977). Moore, with a Weberian view of class as determined by 'life chances' in market situations argues that immigrant workers in Western Europe are indeed a new class and that in extreme cases, where they lack citizenship rights, they are a new helotry. Indeed he argues that Castles and Kosack's work provides information of a diversity of differentiating factors between immigrants and indigenous workers which makes their own conclusions rather forced to fit pre-ordained categories of analysis. There are differences of interest and some of these are real, not a product of false consciousness: 'Migrants are both part of aand separate from the European labour force. They have both the same and different interests. This paradox is resolved by treating the migrant as belonging to two overlapping (and connected) systems of conflict: European class conflicts and colonial conflicts. There is an ambiguity in the migrant's situation which provides a real basis for political confusion amongst and between migrant and indigenous workers' (op. cit., p. 148).

I think it worth pointing out that this kind of debate is not a matter

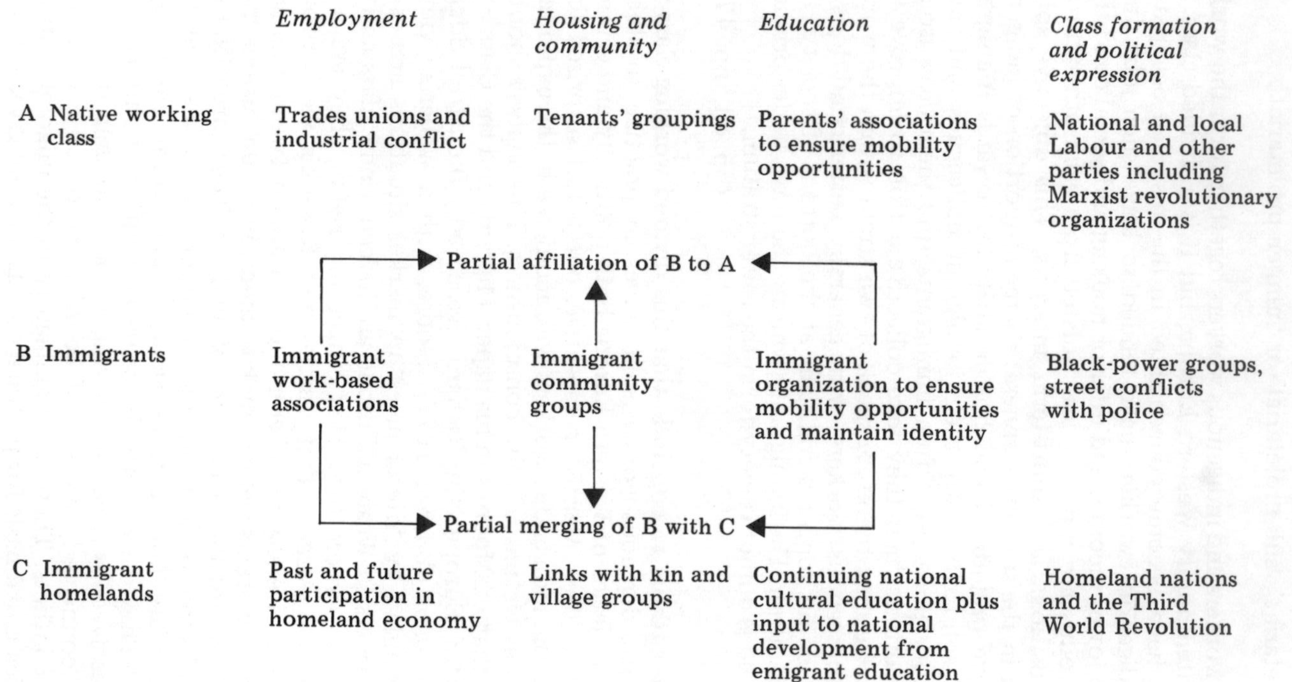

Employment
Housing and community
Education
Class formation and political expression
A Native working class
Trades unions and industrial conflict
Tenants' groupings
Parents' associations to ensure mobility opportunities
National and local Labour and other parties including Marxist revolutionary organizations
Partial affiliation of B to A
B Immigrants
Immigrant work-based associations
Immigrant community groups
Immigrant organization to ensure mobility opportunities and maintain identity
Black-power groups, street conflicts with police
Partial merging of B with C
C Immigrant homelands
Past and future participation in homeland economy
Links with kin and village groups
Continuing national cultural education plus input to national development from emigrant education
Homeland nations and the Third World Revolution

Figure 11.2 *Social and political orientations of immigrant communities*

of conceptual heads or tails. In the end one will be shown to be more consistent with what is observed and provide a more satisfactory explanation of the phenomenon to be explained. I would back the second version as likely to prove more fruitful than the first.

This issue has been further explored in Rex and Tomlinson's recently published study of Handsworth, *Colonial Immigrants in a British City* (1979). One of the central questions considered is how far group consciousness and sense of identity is organised on an ethnic basis and how far individual members have transferred their attachments to class- and status-based groups. The alternative orientations are spelt out in diagrammatic form (see Figure 11.2). The tendency of immigrants and their children to link with ethnically based groups in the sphere of education, housing and employment is noted. It is suggested that the growth of black consciousness movements is linked with the tendency to look to the Third World struggles to liberate themselves from neo-colonial forms of domination. The success of those struggles in the Third World is seen as a key to dimishing social and economic inequalities based on ethnic divisions that continue to persist in Britain. The book (p. 274) is more pessimistic than the Sparkbrook study in its prognosis for ethnic conflict:

> there is evidence of growing racism in the white community matched by a growing lack of confidence in white good will and increasing militancy amongst immigrants. We do not see that this line of development will be arrested unless or until decisive action is taken with the support of all major political parties to stop racial incitement, to attack racial discrimination and to give West Indian and Asian descended men and women a secure sense of citizenship. . . . The main problem lies in British party politics and in the fact that it now looks as though the electoral advantage to be gained from 'opposing immigration' and thereby appearing to be against the black population is overwhelming.

The White Paper on immigration put forward by the new Conservative administration only confirms that judgement. Indeed even a former Conservative minister Lord Boyle, now Vice-Chancellor of the University of Leeds, was moved to describe its provisions as blatantly sex and race discriminatory.

The implications of all this for class and stratification theory are still unclear. Parkin has correctly observed that contemporary social theory has difficulties explaining the emergence of ethnic identity in advanced industrial societies — yet conflicts based on these groupings are now normal rather than deviant (see F. Parkin *Marxism and Class Theory*, 1979). He suggests that when the political character of collective action is shaped by the social and cultural make-up of different ethnic groups, a class model derived from the categories of the division of labour, property ownership and the productive system is inadequate.

Rex and Tomlinson, whilst acknowledging the different possibilities for class formation engendered by ethnic groupings, remain in some respects agnostic. Thus, when discussing the concept of housing classes they write: 'We do not wish to dispute here the possibility of the ultimate demonstration in terms of Marxist political economy of the dependence of the housing system upon the needs of capitalism and the industrial class struggle' (op. cit., pp. 128-9).

Whatever the outcome of these debates there is one book that concentrates on the subjective experience of migrant work in Europe and which sociologists and politicians would do well to ponder — Berger and Mohr's *A Seventh Man* (1975). This is described as a book of images and words. Jean Mohr's photographs are intended in themselves to 'make a statement'. They record individual faces, arrivals, departures, reception centres, the medical examination which decides whether a migrant is fit to work and stay in the metropolis, the housing and barracks where the migrants live and aspects of the work they undertake. John Berger's text, as one might expect from a novelist of his stature, is spare and precise. The account of migrant work in Geneva, for example, tells of the installation of a new and extensive drainage system under the city with 100 per cent migrant labour. The difficulties and the dangers of the work are described, unsuccessful attempts of the workers to improve their working conditions and the failure of the trade union organisation to support them. After work it is back to the barracks — cramped, over-crowded with inadequate washing and lavatory facilities. The motif of the study (p. 7) is this: 'To outline the experience of the migrant worker and to relate this to what surrounds him — both physically and historically — is to grasp more surely the political reality of the world at this moment. The subject is European, its meaning global. Its theme is unfreedom. This unfreedom can only be fully recognised if an objective economic system is related to the subjective experience of those trapped within it. Indeed, finally, the unfreedom is that relationship.'

The effect of reading such a book is to be reminded of 'the other Europe' and which too often falls outside the debates concerning the 'new working class' in Europe, let alone more 'advanced' topics such as industrial democracy. In that sense the migrants are marginalised — treated as outside the mainstream of industrial and political activity — and yet it is they who build the tunnels, the motorways, the office blocks and the air terminals. In that sense the marginals are central to the economic activity of European societies.

Returning finally to the British situation, one detailed ethnographic study by the West Indian sociologist Ken Pryce deserves special mention. *Endless Pressure* (1979) is based on field work among West Indians in Bristol during the period 1969-74. It is based primarily on participant observation methods and is rich and detailed in its ethnography. The

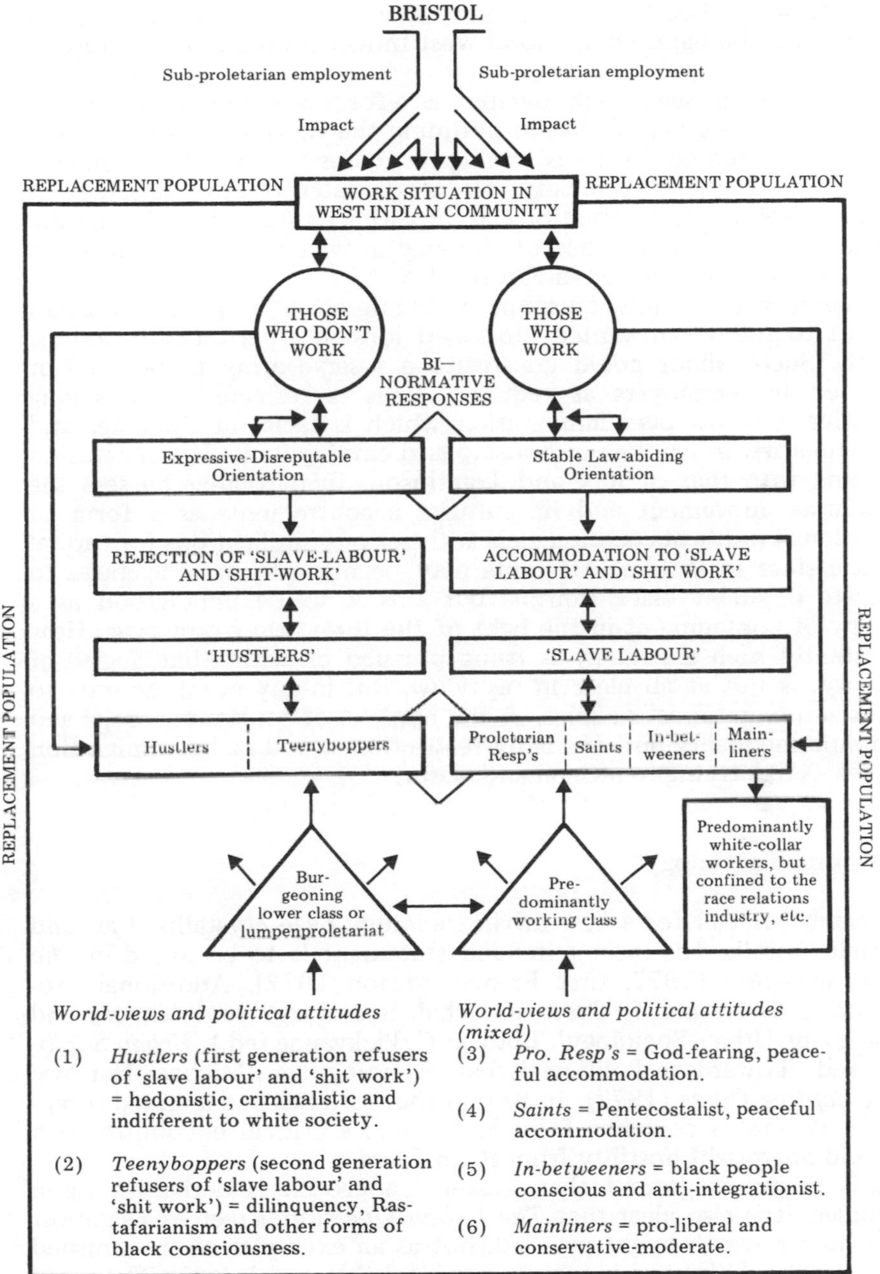

Figure 11.3 Life-style map showing the impact of 'slave-labour' and 'shit-work' on the life styles of West Indians in Bristol.

appendix on method is of more than usual interest — not least Pryce's agreement to be baptised in a local West Indian church that he chose to study.

Pryce does not see his ethnography as a form of empiricist phenomenology. Rather he claims that in outlining the varying life styles of the West Indian community he is tracing responses to their disadvantaged position in a capitalist society. He treats interpretative analyses of motives, feelings and intentions as linked to these wider structural considerations. A good sense of the way in which this is organised in Pryce's work is summarised in Figure 11.3.

Pryce sees the whole question of immigration into the UK as an attempt to fill the unwanted, unskilled jobs in a period of economic growth. Such labour could constitute a reserve army to be used or discarded by employers as required. This is reflected in changing legislative controls over immigration which is racist in character and discriminatory in practice in housing and employment. His conclusion is in line with that of Rex and Tomlinson. In particular he sees the Rastafarian movement and its cultural accoutrements as a form of anti-colonial political consciousness with serious implications for capital and the state in Britain. Attempts may be made by state agencies to integrate dissident black youths, but this is to be understood as a strategy of containment in the light of the threat they now pose. How consistently such a strategy is being pursued or with what degree of intensity, is not at all clear in my view. But in any event, to seek to combine integrationist policies, in the context of continuing social and economic inequality and of highly restrictionist and racist immigration policies, is like trying to mix oil and water.

A new urban sociology?

The claims or call for a new urban sociology have crystallised around Manuell Castells. His most extended statement is to be found in *The Urban Question* (1977, first French edition 1972). Additional programmatic essays are 'Is There an Urban Sociology?' and 'Theory and Ideology in Urban Sociology', both in C. Pickvance (ed.), *Urban Sociology* and 'Towards a Political Urban Sociology', in Michael Harlowe (ed.), *Captive Cities* (1977). In Britain the work has had a mixed reception — general acceptance from Pickvance, a critical encounter with Pahl and downright hostility from Ruth Glass.

It is common ground that Castells' approach is derivative upon Althusser. It is also clear that *The Urban Question* is seen as a signpost as to how research might proceed, not as an exemplar of the finished product. The Althusserian tone is unmistakable and is fairly illustrated (p. 5) in the Epistemological Introduction to the book:

> Thus this is indeed, then, a properly theoretical work, that is to say, one bearing on the production of tools of knowledge, and not on the production of knowledge relative to concrete situations. But the way of expressing the mediation necessary in order to arrive at the theoretical experience proposed has consisted in examining this or that historical situation while trying to transform our understanding of it with the help of advanced theoretical instruments or, too, in showing the contradiction between the observations at one's disposal and the ideological discourses that were juxtaposed with them.

Castells says the book was born out of astonishment. Some readers will share the feeling. Perhaps the best place to start the book is with the Afterword written in 1975, where we are told that the theoretical principles were merely stammerings and that some of the conceptions are quite useless. There is also, we are informed, too rapid a jump from a theoretical critique to an extremely formalised theoretical system. He comes to acknowledge (p. 438) that a little more respect for history would have been in order. Indeed, it is suddenly indispensable:

> In fact the 'urban system' with its elements and relations is a formal construction the essence of which, that is to say, the dynamism of its articulations, is produced by laws of historical development and social organisation of which this 'theory of the urban' does not take account. The most important task, from the point of view of the present place of theoretical work, is not, therefore, to define elements and to formalise their structure. but to detect historical laws at work, in the so-called 'urban' contradictions and practices. It is primitive at the moment to try to reach the level of structural formalisation proposed, for historical laws determine the forms of the structure rather than the reverse.

So what kind of theory was it in the first place? Despite all its attacks on the ideologies of other theorists and its concern with scientific analysis the truth is there is no theory at all: nothing that was systematically formulated or capable of empirical investigation and testing. It was simply an example of conceptual constipation in the Althusserian mode. Ruth Glass, with an impressive record of urban research behind her, makes the above comment sound mild. In a review of *The Urban Question* and *Captive Cities*, headed 'Verbal Pollution' (*New Society*, 29 September 77) she attacks Castells's work in a direct and uncompromising way. She accuses him of an utter disregard for the rules of evidence, factual errors and obscurantism. His postulates acquire the status of facts and his whole approach is described as a prioristic, opportunistic and mechanistic. When he deals with particular matters like the growth of the Greater London new towns, on which Glass is a recognised authority, he gets it wrong. The whole approach should be dismissed as a load of humbug in Glass's view. She does not dispute that it is a new approach: 'I do not know of anything else that is a similarly slovenly, fatty, pretentious concoction.' Why then has it attracted a following? Not despite but because of its slushiness, she suggests (p. 669):

> In a field which lacks criteria of craftsmanship and in which the use of jargon has blunted critical abilities, here is an exceptionally pretentious enterprise in obfuscation that is economical all round. The 'new urban sociology' has a special line in 'double-speak': non questions are put forward in the name of a new 'problematic'; fogginess is called 'precision'; gibberish is presented as profundity; obtuse phraseology is called theory. The title of a Marxist approach is used to promote anti-Marxist tendencies. Under the flag of allegiance to the class struggle, the Castells school does its best to obstruct social and class consciousness.

Now this kind of attack may, I suppose, generate some solidarity among the Castells group and it did prompt some correspondence in *New Society*. At the same time, just as Castells appears to be trying to create some space between himself and Althusser, so some of his sympathisers are distancing themselves from him. I think this comes through clearly enough in *Captive Cities*. Elizabeth Leba's paper, 'Regional Policy Research: Some Theoretical and Methodological Problems', serves as a good example. Commenting on *The Urban Question* and Castells and Godard's *Monopolville* (1974), she accepts the usefulness and legitimacy of this Marxist theorisation. Yet she emphatically criticises the ahistorical approach as weakening the explanatory effectiveness of the work. Categorisation of fractions of capital and fractions of classes without an account of what is entailed does not, she suggests, promote an adequate analysis of class conflict. R. Pahl, as a non-Marxist urban sociologist, always has maintained his distance. In an instructive paper, 'Managers, Technical Experts and the State Forms of Mediation, Manipulation and Dominance in Urban and Regional Development' (in *Captive Cities*), he suggests that there have been fruitful shifts of interest in the focus of urban sociology. Attention is now given to the sphere of consumption, the distribution and scale of urban infrastructural investment and to the role of the state. He welcomes the attempt to remedy the relative neglect of such topics in sociology. Moreover, he claims (p. 57) that Marxist and non-Marxist urban sociologists would be in broad agreement over the following propositions:

(a) That territorial injustice is inevitable.
(b) That uneven development takes place in all advanced societies.
(c) That some form of exploitation takes place in all societies, with

the possible exception of certain hunting and gathering societies.

(d) That the state is growing both in importance and in relative autonomy in capitalist societies.

(e) That Marxist theories of the capitalist state have hitherto proved inadequate.

(f) That there are wide differences between capitalist societies in economic structure, political organisation and the power and autonomy of the state.

(g) That Marxist attempts to analyse and explain these differences have not proved very successful — this failure applies equally to bourgeois theories too.

(h) That, in particular, the lack of Marxist analysis of the state in Eastern European societies is a serious weakness.

In consequence Pahl offers a way forward that has to do with translating programmatic statements of Marxists and non-Marxists into concrete research with an emphasis on comparative analysis. But the Castells approach leaves unsolved problems for Pahl. In practice he suspects its formalism of becoming in practice a version of functionalism. But what about the analysis of collective consumption? To explore the role the state plays in regulating collective consumption sounds as though it should be an important task but yet again one is brought up short with ambiguities and confusing definitions. In his paper, 'Collective Consumption and the State in Capitalist and State Capitalist Societies' (in R. Scase (ed.), *Industrial Society: Class, Cleavage and Control*, 1977) Pahl makes this point very strongly. If the study of collective consumption underlines the rationale for comparative work we need to know how states — capitalist and socialist — actually intervene in the process of consumption and to what effect. If material production is increased does this involve the increasing socialisation of the means of production in capitalist societies? Can the means of collective consumption be defined in relation to a specific mode of production such as advanced capitalism. Pahl does not think so. Not only are there problems of operationalising such a contention, but the work has not been done that could begin to establish its validity. Pahl considers that when Marxist urban analysis defines its object of research as 'the urban' considered as a unit of collective consumption it is either unclear in its specifications or tautological in the sense that all modes of production must reproduce labour power.

The main value of new approaches to urban sociology seem to me to lie in the ways in which problems of urban life have come to be more explicitly related to the role of the state. Pahl is surely justified in calling for comparative research. James O'Connor's *The Fiscal Crisis of the State* (1973) is beginning to serve as something of a talisman, especially for Marxists. But, as Daniel Bell has observed in *The Cultural Contradictions of Capitalism* (1976), the call for a fiscal sociology can be traced back explicitly to Joseph Schumpeter.

Schumpeter thought that the modern tax state could, under certain conditions, collapse. If more and more public expenditure was demanded then this would not fit easily with the motives of self-interest which brought capitalist society into being. The built-in contradiction is that finances, through taxation, created the modern state and the state then utilises finance to make inroads on private enterprise. It thus transforms the economy out of which it sprang. Social needs come to be redefined in welfare terms and shifts are made in the allocation of resources. There may be distributive conflicts and conflicts between private wants and public needs in times of economic growth. But it is in times of inflation, especially when coupled with diminishing, zero or negative economic growth that the contradictions become sharper. The fiscal crisis centres on the gap between state expenditure and revenues and the attendant increasingly difficult political problem of how to deal with this. These are intense and contemporary problems and deserve the closest attention. For those who claim the solution to the crisis is 'socialism' then the flesh and bones of what that would mean in practice needs to be provided. In any event a new urban sociology that can analyse and appraise these tendencies and possibilities in an empirical way would be of the greatest practical, theoretical and political relevance.

12 A NEW SOCIOLOGY OF DEVELOPMENT: PANACEA OR PROGRAMME?

Rich and poor societies connect together in the world economy. The main pre-occupation of the sociology of development as commonly understood is to recognise the linkage and then focus on its implications for the poor countries. Various approaches have co-existed, and still do, although there have been shifts in emphasis.

As a point of departure I refer to A.G. Frank's paper 'Sociology of Development and Underdevelopment of Sociology' (in *Latin America: Under-development or Revolution?*, 1969). This is an explicit attempt to reject some available theories of development in order to clear the ground for an alternative formulation. This new sociology of development has itself become the subject of fresh debates. I will try to give some indication of how far British sociological work has become encompassed by these debates.

An examination of Frank's essay shows that it is primarily geared to the sociology of development as pursued in the United States. The main targets are Hoselitz's *Sociological Factors in Economic Development* (1960), Rostow's *Stages of Economic Growth* (1960) and McClelland's *The Achieving Society* (1961). Each of these constitute approaches to modernisation and are negatively evaluated in terms of their empirical validity, theoretical adequacy and policy effectiveness. The substance of the critique naturally varies in relation to differently organised studies. In general terms, however, Frank regards the distinction between traditional and modern societies inadequate, a tendency to neglect the history of underdeveloped societies which itself leads to a failure to understand them, and no serious analysis of the relationships existing between the developed and underdeveloped societies in the context of the world economy.

The alternative formulation, to which Frank only alludes in the essay cited, is to move away from the assumption that the history of under-developed societies resembles the earlier history of the developed. The developed societies may once have been undeveloped but not under-developed. In 'The Development of Underdevelopment', Frank writes (p. 9): 'underdevelopment is not due to the survival of archaic institutions — the existence of capital shortage in regions that have remained isolated from the stream of world history. On the contrary, under-development was and still is generated by the very same historical process which also generated economic development: the development of capitalism itself.'

Frank makes great play of the distinction between metropolitan (capitalist) societies and satellite societies, arguing that the satellites achieve their greatest periods of economic growth when they are only loosely linked to the metropolis. The metropolis — satellite distinction is then repeated within the colony so that inequalities between town and country are manifested as part of the system of unequal exchange. Associated with this kind of analysis is a call to develop a new political economy of growth and a revolutionary strategy of socialism: 'Though science and truth know no national boundaries, it is probably new generations of scientists from the underdeveloped countries themselves who most need to, and best can, devote the necessary attention to these problems and clarify the process of underdevelopment and development. It is these people who in the last analysis face the task of changing this no longer acceptable process and eliminating this miserable reality' (op. cit., p. 15). There remains therefore a role for the revolutionary intelligentsia.

Although Frank is in principle concerned with the world capitalist economy and its imperialist ramifications, it is Latin America that constitutes the substantive focus of his interest — notably Chile, Brazil and Mexico. And it is American imperialism that is his dominant preoccupation although of course the role of European powers in the history of Latin America does not escape his attention. But in castigating the proponents of the sociology of development it is American writers that he attacks, seeing their work as an ideological expression of imperialism. The bitterness of his dismissal of Rostow is especially marked, not least because of Rostow's advisory role in the Johnson Administration.

How has this impinged upon British sociology? By and large the objects of Frank's scorn have not been widely accepted as academic exemplars in Britain. Rostow perhaps has been the most well known of those mentioned, but has primarily been discussed among economic historians. A useful collection of essays to mention here is Tom Burns and S.B. Saul (eds.), *Social Theory and Economic Change* (1967). This includes an essay by Hagen, 'British Personality and the Industrial Revolution: The Historical Evidence', which is an extended coda to his book. However, Burns and Saul conclude that the approach has fundamental difficulties — it is too vague to be falsifiable and the distinction between traditional and industrial societies is too strongly made. It does not take sufficient account of changes in so-called traditional societies. Neither are the editors convinced of the validity of applying Freudian psycho-analytic theory, given the paucity of evidence on the one hand and the scale of the application on the other. The degree to which evidence can be obtained on child-rearing practices and the reliability of the inferences to be drawn lead Burns and Saul to doubt the scientific content of the theory. Flinn, in his essay in the same book, 'Social Theory and the Industrial Revolution', refers to the work of Rostow, Hoselitz and McClelland. What comes through strongly is a scepticism of the kind of general theories they espouse to explain economic growth. While therefore it may be useful to consider the industrial revolution in Britain and what made for economic growth at that time and in that place, it was unique if for no other reason than the fact that it was first. Although Flinn is more sympathetic to some of the approaches he reviews than Frank, he is unconvinced as to their generalisability and is emphatic that they must be subjected to the historian's detailed scrutiny of particular situations.

The same volume also contains an essay by the American sociologist Reinhard Bendix 'The Comparative Analysis of Historical Change'. This includes a discussion of nationalism and concludes (p. 84): 'there is no precedent in our experience for the emergence of "nations" in the context of three competing world systems which can quickly transform every tension of a social structure into an issue of international relations under the threat of nuclear war.'

Bendix's approach to social change is not discussed by Frank. But then neither is there any systematic treatment of writers as varied as Joseph Schumpeter, Gunnar Myrdal, Colin Clark, W. Arthur Lewis or Peter Worsley. To claim as he does in 'The Sociology of Development and the Underdevelopment of Sociology' that he has summarised available theories and analyses of economic development and cultural change is to overstate his accomplishment.

Frank's work has been subjected to reappraisals by British scholars involved in the sociology of development. In the two main edited collections de Kadt and Williams, *Sociology and Development* and Oxaal, Barnett and Booth, *Beyond the Sociology of Development*, Frank is the focus of much discussion and in the second of the two volumes is the central figure in two of the essays. In a generally sympathetic appreciation of Frank, David Booth argues that the mechanisms by which capitalism generates international and inter-regional uneven development are never really spelled out, certainly not in his discussion of the Chilean economy. Although Frank's exposition of 'the chain of exploitation' is Marxist in intention and bears similarities to the work of Baran and Sweezey, its theoretical status has been questioned by other Marxists. Ernesto Laclau's paper 'Feudalism and Capitalism in Latin America (*New Left Review* 67, May-June 1971) is a case in point. For example, Laclau maintains that Frank does not define capitalism and feudalism as modes of production and this makes impossible an adequate account of the transition from one mode to another. There is an accompanying confusion because two distinct concepts the 'capitalist mode of production' and 'participation in a world capitalist economic system' are not separated out. It is Laclau's view that the existence of a variety of modes of production within the world capitalist system provides the basis for an important set of explanatory hypotheses relating to the specifically capitalist epoch of European expansion. Booth supports this critique and argues (p. 73) that Frank is in his analysis of underdevelopment 'singularly insensitive to the variations to be observed as between the major epochs of world history'. This view is shared by the Marxist economist Michael Barratt-Brown in *The Economics of Imperialism* (1974). Booth suggests that Frank's own purposes have to be seen as a reaction to the economic theories of the UN Economic Commission for Latin America. Even granted the applicability of his explanations for Latin America (which Laclau and other Marxists have questioned) they cannot be generalised into a global theory of the development of underdevelopment.

One can sense that a theory is running into trouble when its concepts have to be elaborated and neologisms invented to deal with empirical difficulties. So, for example, in *Lumpenbourgeoisie: Lumpendevelopment* (1972) Frank deploys the term 'ultra-underdevelopment' to describe regions like north-east Brazil, which once had a flourishing primary-export economy that went into decline, leaving a wasteland of social degradation and extreme poverty. But, as Booth points out,

> Frank has insisted all along that, rather than a merely quantitative state of affairs, under-development is a structural ailment created simultaneously with the *development* of the metropolitan economies by the *incorporation* of the satellites into the process of world capitalist expansion. It follows that 'ultra-underdevelopment' must be the product of 'ultra-incorporation' of a satellite into the metropolitan sphere. To this it has been objected that, by this criterion, the most untra-underdeveloped part of today's Latin America is not the north-east of Brazil, but rather 'booming' oil-exporting Venezuela, 'where contemporary rather than past colonialism assumes its most extreme forms.' The objection is valid in Frank's terms. Consequently he has agreed 'very provisionally' to designate the Venezuelan oil boom as an example of the 'active' development of ultra-underdevelopment in the exporting regions of earlier periods in the development of world capitalism.
>
> (p. 76)

The Parsonian pattern-variables have an easy linguistic elegance when compared with that run around.

The failure to spell out the precise relations of dependency forms the main plank of O'Brien's critique of the Latin American-focused theories (in *Beyond the Sociology of Development*). As with functionalism, everything is related to everything else in the system but how and why is less clear. This can lead, in O'Brien's view, to a circularity of argument. Dependent countries are those which lack the capacity for autonomous growth. Why do they lack it? Because their structures are dependent ones. And just as Frank had criticised the policy inadequacies of the modernisation theorists so he in his turn is criticised by O'Brien for the vagueness of his policy implications. What is left is a reminder that internal social structures are interrelated with international structures. This is the beginning, not the end, of inquiry.

One can see therefore that objections to dependency theory can be raised at the level of empirical validity, theoretical adequacy and policy effectiveness. Slogans, polemics and neologisms are dubious foundations for a new theory. As Cohen, Shanin and Sorj put it: 'Key phrases and terms like "the development of underdevelopment" or "metropole-satellite" were invoked as simple master keys to unlock the universe without sweat. Such a move has often promoted a semantic rather than a substantive solution to the lacunae in sociological theory as it pertained to developing societies' ('The Sociology of Developing Societies: Problems of Teaching and Definition, *Sociological Review*, 1977, p. 256). These are quite fundamental doubts but Cohen and his colleagues still think that interest in dependency theories can encourage scholars to explore a more general Marxist tradition. They might go on to explore early Marxist writings on imperialism, forms of Marxist historiography, theories of unequal exchange within the global capitalist economy and to examine overlapping modes of production.

The possibility also arises that some explorations may be more fruitful than others. This is the burden of Aidan Foster-Carter's paper, 'Marxism versus Dependency Theory? A Polemic', (1979) which contains the plea that dependency theory be not taken over by Althusserianism. Given the aggressive ahistorical stance of the latter this would constitute an about-face for the former. This contrast illustrates well enough the fact that in the Marxian house there are many mansions — indeed dependency theory, in the view of some of the authors already cited, might only form an outhouse. But, as Roxborough observes in an extremely perceptive article, 'new paradigms do not always turn out to be panaceas' ('Dependency Theory in the Sociology of Development: Some Theoretical Problems', 1976, p. 132).

Roxborough maintains that, whilst Frank's intention is to treat colonial analysis and class analysis as complementary, this is not in practice done with clarity or precision. For example the peasantry tend to be absorbed into the proletariat in a theory of change that is closer to populism than Marxism. Hence the neologisms already referred to which can be further amplified by such amorphous categories as 'marginalised masses' and 'underclasses'. But to move into other Marxist terrain is to confront new problems. For example, to reorientate analysis so that modes of production become the pivotal point, as Laclau had insisted should be done, leads one back to unresolved debates concerning base and superstructure, and into the problems of identifying and specifying modes of production. Whether the nation state is always the appropriate level of analysis and unit of comparison is itself problematical. Roxborough, in drawing attention to such problems, does not lack conviction in the fruitfulness of the Marxist project but insists (pp. 131-2) that theories and concepts must be historically informed and tested:

> Purely theoretical attempts to construct an exhaustive list of all possible pre-capitalist modes of production *a priori* are not likely to long survive the rigours of empirical historical research. Granted that the concept of a mode of production is a highly analytic one, and that the analysis of specific social formations is unlikely to provide us with examples of the working of 'pure types' of modes of production, the question of how one goes about constructing a list of modes of production is still an unresolved one, and one whose epistemological implications need to be considered very carefully. This is not to suggest that the attempt should be abandoned, it is merely a recognition of the immense amount of work still to be done. Nor is it a plea for theoretical empiricism: theory and research have to go hand in hand.

This suffices to remind us that whether one is referring to the dependency theory perspective or to some variant within Marxism, there is much more that is programmatic than has actually been accomplished. I suspect this calls for international co-operation in scholarly activity to a greater extent than in any other branch of sociology. One such recent attempt to bring together research findings, often considerably detailed, within a broadly conceived approach to class analysis, is Cohen, Gutkind and Brazier's edited collection, *Peasants and Proletarians* (1979). They argue that the approach is rooted in the study of modes of production, the analysis of productive forces, the figuration of relations of production, the analysis of antagonistic relations. But the complexity of internal systems of stratification and the varieties of experience which may be located are clearly recognised. The selection not only draws on Third World experience, dealing with issues of class categorisation, the role of the peasantry, the urban working class, ethnic groups and kindred matters, but also utilises work on the experiences of Third World workers in the metropolitan countries. This makes the connection between the sociology of development and the study of race and ethnic relations and which I discuss elsewhere in this volume. Cohen and his colleagues (p. 22) pose two questions to which they do not feel able to offer clear-cut answers: 'Are we to witness the collapse of proletarian internationalism upon the shoals of racism, as we once, in 1914, witnessed its collapse to the ideologies of jingoism and nationalism? Or are metropolitan workers going to establish bonds of solidarity with migrants at home and their brothers abroad, so as to match the flexibility and adaptability of trans-national capital?'

It would I think be misleading to conclude this discussion without making reference to Peter Worsley's path-breaking study, *The Third World* (1963). It was of course written before the debates concerning Frank and dependency theory. The strength of Worsley's work is that it constitutes a wide-ranging discussion of European colonialism and the subsequent process of decolonisation. In doing so he pays great attention to the diversity of political responses, including themes sometimes neglected by Marxists: nationalism, populism and the relation of elite leaders to mass parties. He recognises that in certain circumstances, as for example in a number of African countries, ethnicity can be a more important bond between people than class. And nationalism, which although from a Marxist perspective is sometimes defined as a form of false consciousness, is still real in its consequences. The ways in which countries of the Third World actually respond to their situations varies considerably, both in terms of internal political organisation and external relations with industrial societies. Thus we have some new states which take on the character of revolutionary socialism, others which in various pragmatic ways accept their client status with the West or with Eastern Europe. Some may talk the language of socialism, whilst at the same time building up a capitalist economy based on entrepreneurial peasants or local industrialists.

Whilst Worsley focuses on the Third World, he is explicitly aware of the ambiguities of usage and their ramifications for international relations. Thus the Third World may be seen in contradistinction to the First and Second Worlds — the capitalist and communist political groupings. It may be seen as referring to those countries with a colonial past and a neocolonial present. It may include China in the Third World. Or it may refer to the notion of a non-aligned, non-capitalist, non-communist grouping. Worsley tends to emphasise the neocolonial shared experience and to argue that although classes in the Western industrial societies sense may not exist, or if so only embryonically, that class relations have to be understood in the context of international capitalism. It is in this respect that he agrees with Fanon that Marxist categories have to be slightly stretched when applied to colonial societies.

Worsley echoes Myrdal in pointing to the need for a massive redistribution of world resources that is required if an adequate response is to be made to poverty in the Third World. He is clear that present trends show a widening gap between rich and poor nations and sees this as something that the industrial nations — capitalist and communist — must seek to reverse. Although such trends give grounds for perssimism, Worsley emphasises the moral character of the choice. In the spirit of Tawney he argues that short-run material interests should not be the basis for calculating whether or not to assist underdeveloped societies, rather an equalisation of the wealth is justified primarily in moral terms. In taking this position Worsley (p. 274) also embraces a view of the role of social science:

> We emphasise choice instead of positivistically enunciating 'laws' and 'prediction' because social science cannot tell us 'what will happen'. It can enable us to understand what forces are at work, to assess the significance of the values according to which we act and the likely practical implications of our choices. It enables us to choose rationally and not blindly or dogmatically. What we lose in dropping the spurious certainty of deterministic dogmas, we compensate for in other ways, for this width of uncertainty and relativity also carries with it a corresponding share of hope and freedom, an enhancement of human choice and values, whatever the constraining conditions which sane men have to take account of.

What this expresses so well, and is evident in much British sociology, whether formally labelled neo-Marxist or neo-Weberian is the scepticism of systems, however powerful, having the inevitability of the last word. Ideas and ideals may not rule the world in the Hegelian sense, but they are not to be relegated to the shadows of history. Creative moral responses can be made to desperate situations.

13 SOCIAL STRATIFICATION: THE UNCONCLUDED ARGUMENT

How is social stratification to be defined, described and analysed? How do patterns of stratification change and in what directions? How can change be measured? What, if any, is the relationship between one's view of the world and one's position in a system of stratification? What, if any, is the relationship between class 'imagery' and collective action? What shapes and develops class consciousness and with what consequences? These questions have already been touched on in preceding pages. In British sociology the debates and the empirical work have often been of a high level, giving evidence of rigour and conceptual sophistication. I want to further illustrate that in what follows.

First I would cite the debate on the 'new' working class and the question of embourgeoisement. Goldthorpe and Lockwood's article, 'Affluence and the British Class Structure' (*SR*, 2, 63) was an important conceptual elaboration that not only guided their own research efforts but provided a basis for critical discussion, particularly through the differentiation of normative, relational and economic aspects of stratification.

The *Affluent Worker* study, especially in the third volume, seeks to place the Marxist and non-Marxist accounts of embourgeoisement (with the more general ramifications this may have for the convergence thesis) in the light of its own reported research findings. Bearing in mind the base-superstructure issue in Marxism it is of interest to note what Goldthorpe *et al.* regard as a curious paradox:

> While . . . anti-Marxist adherents of the thesis of embourgeoisement stress the importance of changes in the 'material basis' of modern society, the defenders of the Marxian standpoint are led in the end to underline the importance of 'superstructural' factors in rejecting the idea that the political potential of the working class is no longer of major significance. In the latter view, what now emerges as necessary for the emergence of radical political action on a mass scale is that the *subjective* conditions for this should be brought about; and this in turn means the left-wing vanguard gaining victory in the crucial struggle for hegemonic power.
>
> (op. cit., pp. 17-18)

The conclusion of the affluent worker study itself places great importance on political leadership in shaping the character of social change. A system of 'classless inegalitarianism' offering no basis for, or response to, radical initiatives would not be satisfactorily accounted for by some inner logic of industrialism or by mass social and psychological manipulation in neo-capitalist society. This emphasises the 'voluntaristic' stance to social change underpinning the author's work.

So far as the 'new working class' is concerned, the search continues: it is growing to be as long and tortuous as the quest for the Holy Grail. One quite well-worn path is in the direction of the advanced technologies of continuous-process industries. Two notable travellers have been Serge Mallet and Robert Blauner, whose very different accounts are found in *La Nouvelle Class Ouvriere* (1969) and *Alienation and Freedom* (1964) respectively. While both claim to have located a new working class they are at almost total variance concerning the significance of the find.

Do these new forms of automated industry create a work force that is more securely integrated into the enterprise with management and, by extension, into capitalist society? In the light of Duncan Gallie's recent research a number of interesting points are made. This is reported in his book *In Search of the New Working Class* (1978). While he applauds the way in which both Mallet and Blauner have raised central questions about the dynamics of social structure, it soon becomes clear that he has doubts about the methodological and empirical adequacy of both men's work. Indeed, he comes to the conclusion that the theories of both are 'irredeemably flawed'.

Gallie's own study focused on four oil refineries owned by BP, two in France and two in Britain. In each case a survey of manual workers was undertaken, documentary material relevant to industrial relations collected and lengthy interviews conducted with key management and union representatives. There were differences between the French and British responses, despite the similar technology. For example, in the French plants, but not the British, salaries and standard of living were judged to be the greatest source of tension. To that extent the conclusion reached by both Blauner and Mallet that automation leads to the disappearance of major grievances about salaries was clearly questionable. Again the scope for different payment systems (including what appeared to be a rather pernicious merit bonus scheme in France) within similar technologies is well illustrated. On further inspection this was seen to reflect a difference in workers' attitudes to managerial authority. The French workers were subject to much more unilateral forms of managerial decision-making which, in Britain, were accepted by management as negotiable and subject to joint regulation. British workers generally accepted the legitimacy of the formal power structure. The French workers did not: they had an exploitative image of their work situation. They appeared to be deeply suspicious of managerial authority in the enterprise. 'They felt that they were confronted by a highly centralised form of management that remained sovereign over the entire field of decision-making. They regarded the institutions of participation provided by the law as largely a facade, and they tended to reject the idea that the discussions that did take place between management and their representatives even amounted to consultation. The predominant feeling was one of powerlessness' (op. cit., p. 145). Hence within the same technological conditions a 'co-operative' model of management-worker relations in the British case and an exploitative one in the French case could be found. Not only is this one more nail in the coffin of technological determinism but the importance of cultural differences in explaining worker-management relations is indicated. Hence the new working class is not readily identified after all. Gallie suggests that the differences between the French and British samples reflects more general differences between the working classes of the two societies. One cannot conclude that these industries, which are treated as 'prototypical' of advanced industrial societies, point the way to a process of incorporation within capitalist society or, on the other hand, to increasing class awareness and class conflict. Both possibilities are there but they are dependent on other cultural, political and economic factors. The 'new working class' in this sector of industry is therefore neither inevitably revolutionary or incurably conservative.

A closely affiliated debate relates to the ways in which stratification systems are legitimated. Take, for example, the opening sentence of Runciman's *Relative Deprivation and Social Justice* (1966): 'All societies are inegalitarian. But what is the relation between the inequalities in a society and the feelings of acquiescence or resentment to which they give rise? Peoples attitudes to social inequalities seldom correlate strictly with the facts of their own position.' What then follows is an imaginative methodological mix — involving historical method and a survey investigation. This is melded into reference group theory and an analysis of values via Rawl's treatment of 'justice as fairness'. Part of Runciman's argument had to do with the tendency of people to choose groups close to themselves in the social order when judging the fairness of their rewards and opportunities. This is used to buttress the view that through such reference group attachments, social stability has been maintained notwithstanding 'objective' class differences in the distribution of power, income and status.

Similar kinds of considerations, albeit by different routes, appear in Parkin's *Class Inequality and Political Order* (1971) and Mann's *Consciousness and Action among the Western Working Class* (1973). Parkin's treatment of value systems tends to suggest that dominant value systems in advanced capitalist societies can prevail over subordinate (working class) value systems and that the scope for radical collective action outside of compromised Labour Party politics is very limited. Working-class people may not share or endorse the dominant value system but they accept it in a pragmatic sense and are not likely to turn to revolutionary action to overturn it. From an explicit Marxist standpoint, Westergaard and Resler provide a very full and detailed analysis of British society: *Class in a Capitalist Society* (1975). The comprehensive discussion of forms of inequality marks a return of Marxist empirical work. One observes that, while the authors are in disagreement with the interpretations offered by writers such as Runciman and Parkin, the acquiescence of the working class, whether in moral or pragmatic terms, is recognised. What is disputed is the extent to which expressions of 'radicalism', 'militancy' or dissent to capitalist ideology can be organised into successful revolutionary opposition. It is to the structural difficulties inherent in capitalism that they look for the conditions that would make such an outcome more probable.

Intertwined in discussions about the legitimation of stratification systems are arguments about the forms and significance of social imagery. Goldthorpe and Lockwood's paper, 'Affluence and the British Class Structure', referred to above, draws together some prevailing notions of working-class and middle-class perspectives, but it is Lockwood's later paper 'Sources of Variation in Working Class Images of Society' (*SR*, 14 March 1966) that has served to focus much discussion. This was especially seen at the Durham conference organised by the SSRC in 1972, where the paper was the basis of proceedings, being subjected to conceptual elaboration and scrutinised in the light of empirical work. The main papers are now available in Bulmer (ed.), *Working Class Images of Society* (1975). As Bulmer points out (p. 14) the papers 'form part of a larger concern to inter-relate both structure and meaning in sociological explanation, and to establish links between occupational, community and family characteristics and images of class structure'. Part of the ensuing argument related to how far the Lockwood typology had foreclosed on the possibility of radical, oppositional and collectivised working-class consciousness and notably reflected in the contributions of Westergaard and Lockwood respectively. The arguments are extremely interesting and I have in fact discussed Westergaard's general position and approach earlier in this review. Here I would remark that I find Lockwood's comments on the problematical relationship between 'images of society' and 'consciousness' instructive. In asking under what conditions does adhesion to a 'radical meaning system' become extensive among the working class he maintains (p. 258):

> this problem resolves itself first and foremost into the question: under what conditions does socialist ideology articulate with workers' images of society? For the emergence of a radical class consciousness has its pre-condition in the affinity between the theoretical consciousness of socialist soteriology and the practical consciousness of working class life. The problematic nature of the relationship

> between these two levels of consciousness must be the starting point of any analysis of working class radicalism . . . The question is surely how the political connotation of holding one or another kind of belief about the structure of social inequality affects the worker's receptivity to ideologies which seek to present an alternative vision of society.

A good deal of the substantive discussion revolved around the finer details of how to combine work situation and community situation in developing an appreciation of social imagery. In view of my earlier comment on the hiatus between communications research and social stratification it is noteworthy that Willener, in his paper, notes that the conference papers rarely refer to television as a potent source of social imagery. (I suspect that Willener's paper could very profitably be studied for hints as to how to approach the study of social imagery in ways quite other than British sociologists have so far attempted.)

Goldthorpe and Bevan (1975) have suggested that work in this area is very inconclusive. This may be due to inadequacies on the part of sociologists. There may be conceptual confusions as to what is to count as ideology and perhaps a failure to distinguish between basic social imagery and attitudes and opinions related to specific socio-political issues. Again, differences in research design and methods of data collection may give rise to differences in research findings that tell us more about the sociologists than the population studied. At the same time, part of the problem may be its complexity: if the experience of social reality is full of contradictions — affluence and redundancy, conflict and co-operation — then interpretation of these experiences may be ambiguous and shifting. Further conflicting interpretations of that reality may be offered by politicians, journalists and even academics and add to the confusion and inconsistency of social imagery.

One can discover studies that emphasise overlapping class models and images of society, which do not tie in neatly with social action, as in the work of Richard Brown and his colleagues on ship-building workers. Other studies stress variation in images of society within an occupational category, as in Howard Newby's study of agricultural workers. Here again, the relationship between social imagery and actual relations based on a tradition and ritual of deference is not consistent. Or other studies may suggest, beyond the admitted ambiguities, the possibility that workers across a range of occupations may come to articulate attitudes to property rights that do now accord with the dominant value system. This is represented in papers by H.F. Moorhouse and C.W. Chamberlain (see, for example, 'Lower Class Attitudes to Property', *Sociology*, 8, 1974). Further, not only the topic, say property rights, may affect the salience and degree of variability of attitudes and ideology, but also the sphere in which the study is carried out. For example, studies of working-class attitudes to the Labour Party, such as

B. Hindess's *The Decline of Working Class Politics* (1971) reveal apathy and disaffection, whereas studies focused upon shop floor militancy in industry may yield more active and positive aspirations.

One recent British study which has attempted to come to terms with variations in social imagery is Howard H. Davis, *Beyond Class Images* (1979). The empirical data he uses comes from interviews with three occupational groups all located in different parts of Scotland — maintenance fitters at a Grangemouth petro-chemical plant (also in the Gallie study mentioned earlier), clerical workers in an Edinburgh life assurance company and first-hand melters in a West of Scotland steel plant. Among the steel workers, for example, Davis found a strong occupational consciousness supported, he suggests, by community relationships — but no sign of class or 'proletarian' consciousness. Indeed, in this context he found no aggregate of attitudes or perspectives indicating an image of society as a whole. He points out that this conclusion differs from other studies of workers in 'traditional' communities. Whereas, Brown *et al.* and Newby drew attention to the variation and ambivalence of workers' images of society 'they cling to the expectation that workers will have and on occasion will need to use a "totalising" approach. Indeed, they perpetuate Lockwood's assumption that the solidarity of traditional occupational communities — if not destroyed by internal conflicts — is particularly conducive to the emergence of a class image of society. There is no evidence from our own study to justify this assumption' (op. cit., p. 142). How far Davis's position here is distinctive I am not quite sure. It is not suggested that revolutionary class consciousness is latently available in these traditional communities. Rather what Lockwood and certainly Brown seem to share with Davis is the recognition that external changes in market situation may impinge on a community and lead to technological and organisational changes in work that, in turn, may lead to the possibility of developing oppositional views to society.

Beyond his own data, however, Davis points to two trends which may have contradictory effects on class and social consciousness: on the one hand, the trend to greater social and cultural diversity; on the other, the tendency for organised opinion, especially in the mass media, to emphasise the commonality of social and political interests. The first trend emphasised the fragmentation of consciousness, the second, uniformity. Davis suggests that varieties of social consciousness may be expressions of these conflicting tendencies. The methodological problems entailed in showing this are I think formidable, although not perhaps insurmountable.

Davis argues (p. 193):

> If social consciousness is itself a complex set of reactions with a variety of objects, it is reasonable to expect a certain degree of flexibility and even inconsistency in the relation of consciousness to

such multi-faceted objects as 'class' and 'society'. The problem of analysis is to trace these objects and their paths of influence as well as their place in consciousness. It appears that, depending on the questions asked and the context in which they are asked, the majority of members in the surveyed groups are capable of articulating both views which use class and views which deny class as the basis of social differentiation. This is not necessarily because of any fatal flaws of method or interpretation.

Davis's approach is rooted in the work of Touraine and Popitz. From Touraine he derives the threefold analytical distinction of identity, opposition and totality. The first refers to a consciousness of self which provides a rationale for particular demands. The second represents consciousness of the adversary. The third defines the field of social conflict. Whether these principles in experience represent class identity and consciousness in Marxist terms is a matter for inquiry. Social consciousness may come to be seen as something else beyond class images. So what begins in Touraine as a neo-Marxist approach to workers' consciousness may become a generalised method of analysing social movements, which may, for example, have ethnic, religious or nationalist orientations. And, of course, since manual workers are not the only category to have images of society, the method may be generalised to other groups.

From Popitz, Davis takes the suggestion that images constitute 'a bricolage of symbols, concepts and expressions which may be governed by personal experience, hearsay, knowledge, an ideology or (as is most likely) by a combination of all four' (op. cit., p. 31). The implication is that individual responses, which may be variable and eccentric, will point to social consciousness. Hence concrete statements emerging from interviews may provide clues which indicate what rules and regularities of discourse are shared by defined groups of people. Just as some linguists make it their task to look for generative rules in grammar and interpret variety and creativity in relation to them, so sociologists can seek for the rules people respond to in defining and reflecting on their social experience. Just as there are, in principle, identifiable speech communities, so there may be groups with shared social consciousness. The problem then is not only to identify the relevant rules but to appreciate that different, even contradictory rules may co-exist. Further, the rules themselves may be subject to change as a result of economic, cultural and technological developments. The attempt is thus made to mesh a phenomenological method with an objective account of cultural and economic structure.

The discussions on stratification seem to me to be on a different basis from the elaborated American arguments on the efficacy of functionalist theories. It is more adequately seen as an attempt to trace through the significance of Marxist and Weberian contributions, but I do not intend by that to convey the notion of two camps. The give and take in discussion is too open-ended for that to be the case as is the general respect for empirical evidence. This is well illustrated in Bottomore's paper 'Class Structure and Social Consciousness' (in Mezaros (ed.) *Aspects of History and Class Consciousness*, Routledge, 1971 pp. 49-64). This is written from the standpoint of a Marxist sociology. It can be usefully compared with Goldthorpe's paper 'Class, Status and Party in Modern Britain: Some Recent Interpretations. Marxist and Marxisant' (*EJS*, 13, 1972). Bottomore accepts that the understanding of political consciousness and the factors which shape it is fraught with a good deal of uncertainty and obviously thinks this should be frankly acknowledged. That there are tensions for Marxism as an ideology in exposing itself to empirical research cannot be denied — this would be so in principle for any ideology which made claims to a special, true knowledge of reality, and then put those claims to the test. Whether Marxism as a system with empirical content and critical historicist elements can maintain its coherence in continuing dialogue with empirical sociology is something Goldthorpe questions. But in any event what he does accept is that the 'debate with Marx' has been a very productive one in the social sciences precisely because it has involved issues of fact in relation to issues of theory.

Issues of fact in relation to issues of theory arise nowhere more sharply, one might suppose, than in the analysis of social mobility. The main empirical reference for Britain for so long now has been the work of Glass and his colleagues *Social Mobility in Britain* (1954). It is important in conclusion to draw attention to the work of Goldthorpe and his colleagues at Oxford and Payne and his colleagues at Aberdeen, who are in the process of giving us a much more up-to-date picture of processes and trends (see Goldthorpe and Llewellyn 'Class Mobility in Modern Britain, *Sociology*, 11 February 1977, pp. 257-87; and 'Class Mobility', *BJS*, vol. XVIII, no. 3, 1977, pp. 269-302; Payne, Ford and Robertson 'A Re-appraisal of Social Mobility in Britain', *Sociology*, 11 February 1977, pp. 289-310). Payne *et al.* offer a methodological critique of the Glass study and conclude that (apart from errors of methodology they impute to the study) the changes in social and occupational structure since 1957 are enough to counsel great caution in treating it as relevant for a sociology of modern Britain. Goldthorpe and Llewellyn, with the aid of their own data, question how far going theories of class mobility can be confirmed. I will not here attempt to unravel the questions at issue — to do so would require very detailed comment. But the potential significance of the work may be gleaned by the following illustrative quotation:

> the possibility must be raised that in drawing on the results of previous mobility research, as part of the empirical grounding of their analyses of class structure, the writers with whom we are

concerned have in one respect misconstrued the significance of these results. They have tended, one may suggest, to take the evidence of wide and persisting inequalities of opportunity, which has been very generally produced, as if it were at the same time evidence of relatively secure and unchanging constraints on the extent of mobility. To make this equation may well be seriously misleading; for . . . . it is perfectly possible for a high degree of inequality of opportunity, which must refer to relative mobility chances, to be observed *together with* levels and trends of absolute mobility rates which mean that closure, buffer-zone and counter-balance theses cannot readily be borne out. Moreover, we would wish to argue that a situation of this general kind is in fact that which has been most typically revealed by, at all events, the more recent mobility inquiries undertaken in other advanced western societies.

('Class Mobility in Modern Britain', p. 277)

The Glass social mobility study provided something of a spearhead for sociological research in Britain in the immediate post-war situation. In later years it did tend to be labelled as empirical in the pejorative sense of being non-theoretical. After all the twists and developments of sociology in Britain in the past quarter of a century it is somewhat ironical that social mobility shouod become the site of a central debate that is clearly empirical and theoretical. Perhaps this is what is meant by a revolution in sociology?

PART III FORMS OF RELEVANCE

Mr. Shandy, . . . would see nothing in the light in which others placed it; — he placed things in his own light; — he would weigh nothing in common scales; — no, — he was too refined a researcher to lay open to so gross an imposition. — To come at the exact weight of things in the scientific steel yard, the fulcrum, he would say, should be almost invisible, to avoid all friction from popular tenets; — without this the minutae of philosophy, which should always turn the balance, will have no weight at all . . . He would often lament that it was for want of considering this properly and of applying it skilfully to civil matters as well as to speculative truths, that so many things in this world were out of joint; — that the political arch was giving way; — and that the very foundations of our excellent constitution in church and state, were so sapped as estimators had reported it.

Laurence Sterne, *The Life and Opinions of Tristram Shandy*

14 THE RELEVANCE OF HISTORY

'Sociology at present faces two opposite dangers. The first is the danger of losing itself in abstract and meaningless generalisations about society in general. The other danger is that foreseen by Karl Mannheim almost a generation ago, and much present today, of a sociology split into a series of discrete technical problems of social adjustment'. Sociology is concerned with historical societies every one of which is unique and moulded by specific historical antecedents and conditions. But the attempt to avoid generalisation and interpretation by confining oneself to se-called 'technical' problems of enumeration and analysis is merely to become the unconscious apologist of a static society. Sociology, if it is to become a fruitful field of study, must, like history, concern itself with the relation between the unique and the general. For the rest, I would only say that the more sociological history becomes, and the more historical sociology becomes, the better for both.

(E.H. Carr, 'What is History?', *The Listener*, 4 July 1961, p. 771)

Sociology does from time to time succumb to the dangers mentioned by E.H. Carr. Indeed, an anti-historical approach to sociological analysis seems to be engraved on some theoretical banners, notably those of the structuralists. There are, nonetheless, signs of a continuing dialogue between sociology and history in recent British sociology. This I will illustrate, albeit briefly. My own view is that a sociology that does not cultivate an historical awareness cripples itself, since it cannot begin to encounter some of the central problems of explanation and interpretation.

I begin with E.P. Thompson: historian of nineteenth-century and now eighteenth-century England, unrepentant socialist humanist and a polemical essayist of formidable power. *The Making of the English Working Class* (1963) figures on the reading lists of many sociology courses and rightly so. As the title indicates, the emphasis of the study is on process. Thompson treats class as an historical phenomenon 'unifying a number of disparate and seemingly unconnected events, both in the raw material of experience and in consciousness' (op. cit., p. 9). His insistence that history involves looking at real men in real contexts involves him in lively argument — with other historians, with Marxists and with sociologists. In each case there are particular targets

The argument with sociologists is of two kinds. He rejects the kind of functionalist role analysis of social change as exemplified in Neil Smelser's *Social Change in the Industrial Revolution* (1959) on the grounds that it is too static in treatment. How and why did some people come to occupy some social roles, say that of employees, whilst others occupied the employer role? Thompson says that Smelser does not relate his role analysis firmly enough to a wider appreciation of the structure of authority in society. Such structures themselves have to be historically analysed. So Thompson objects to the kind of sociology that is too pre-occupied with methodology to the exclusion of historical study, citing Dahrendorf's *Class and Class Conflict in Industrial Society* (1959) as a case in point. For Thompson 'class is defined by men as they live their own history, and in the end, this is its only definition' (op. cit., p. II).

His argument with fellow historians is, at least in part, to draw attention to contrasts in styles and purposes. Historians may show, for example, how trade union organisation developed, how the standard of living changed, although such matters are by no means beyond controversy. But the selectivity involved in considering a particular theme or statistical trend is not the only way of handling the historical narrative. Thompson is an exponent of 'history from below' in which specific experiences of working people are documented and the voices of the losers as well as the winners are heard again. His intention is clearly stated, and in my own view impressively executed: 'I am seeking to rescue the poor stockinger, the Luddite cropper, the 'obsolete' handloom weaver, the 'utopian' artisan, and even the deluded followers of Joanna Southcott, from the enormous condescension of posterity. Their crafts and traditions may have been dying. Their hostility to the new industrialism may have been backward-looking. Their communitarian ideals may have been fantasies. Their insurrectionary conspiracies may have been foolhardy. But they lived through these times of acute social disturbance, and we did not. Their aspirations were valid in terms of their own experience' (op. cit., pp. 12-13).

This 'history from below' also characterises Thompson's more recent *Whigs and Hunters* (1975). In his assessment of the significance of the Black Act of 1723, which among other things permitted capital punishment for more than fifty different offences, Thompson takes as his starting point 'the experience of humble foresters'. So, instead of looking at social control 'from above' and examining the Walpole administration, he deliberately starts at the other end. This approach will surely commend itself to any sociologist who sees social analysis as involving an examination of social processes. This must always go beyond examining the intentions of the powerful to consider the ways in which they impinge on the experience of the powerless.

Thompson is not a voice in the wilderness so far as this emphasis in historical writing is concerned. Christopher Hill's work on an earlier historical period — the English Revolution — is a notable example. In *The World Turned Upside Down* (1972) the Levellers, the Ranters, the Seekers and the Quakers live again. The mood of his work is well caught in the following comment: 'We may find that the obscure men and women who figure in this book, together with some not so obscure, speak more directly to us than Charles I or Pym or General Monck' (p. 18).

As with Thompson, there is an interest in the neglected and the often unsuccessful subversive. This is done without patronising and, indeed, with the thought that through it all there may be insights and voices which can speak to our condition — to be precise, egalitarian voices that may have some cautionary words for our inegalitarian democracies.

Alongside Thompson, and often concerned with similar times and places, is Eric Hobsbawm, whose essays in *Primitive Rebels* (1959) and *Labouring Men* (1964) are extremely fine examples of the genre. Hobsbawm, with George Rudé, is also the author of *Captain Swing* (1969) a path-breaking study of rural incendiarism in England in the 1830s. Taking inspiration from writers such as Thompson, Hill and Hobsbawm (and, one may note in passing, the important parallels with an approach to French history as represented by writers such as George Lefebvre, Louis Chevalier and Emmanuel Le Roy Ladurie) there has been a growing interest in micro-history, institutionalised in the History Workshop and co-ordinated by Ralph Samuel at Ruskin College, Oxford. This has produced a number of stimulating essays in which the writers have utilised their personal experiences and the method of oral history as well as documentary sources. They have encompassed a whole series of topics including work relations, sex roles and family life, popular culture and education. The rationale of this development is not that micro-history becomes another specialist enclave but that it might provide material which can be related to more general considerations. The contributors themselves would describe their own convictions as socialist, which perhaps explains both the choice of topics and the motivation. As Ralph Samuel puts it' 'The socialist historian has the privilege of keeping the record of resistance to oppression, but also the duty of analysing the enemy's campaign, and showing how men and women become accomplices in their own subjection. Of every event one should be able to ask, what meaning did this have in people's lives, how did it affect them; of every movement, who were the rank and file' (in *Village Life and Labour*, 1975 p. xix).

From the work of such historians the sociologist can learn much. Knowledge about social control is a prime example. The attempts to impose political, industrial, religious or legal control — the array of sanctions deployed and the forms of resistance — are impressively documented. The analysis of social stratification is immensely enriched — for example, in detailed exposition of class and intra-class relations, such as we get in John Foster's *Class Struggle in the Industrial Revolution* (1974); in the treatment of 'deference' and its significance such as we find in Hobsbawm and Rudé; and in the well-worn but unresolved topic of the labour aristocracy which has now spawned a considerable literature in its own right.

What about Thompson's argument with other Marxists? This turns out to be a multi-faceted affair. If it be the case that class is a social and cultural formation which, to be understood, has to be examined as a process in history, then the particular ways in which those processes work through will lead to considerable variations. So clear is Thompson on this that he recognises the cultural formation of Welsh and Scottish classes to be different from England and therefore concentrates only on the English working class (for a useful collection of essays on Scotland see A. Allan Maclaren (ed.), *Social Class in Scotland*). Thompson's respect for the discipline of historical inquiry and the status of what he terms historical logic leads him to reject those (including Marxists) who attempt to impose 'models' or 'theories' on the historical record without due care. Trimming history to fit the model is, for Thompson, a cardinal sin against truth. His essay 'The Peculiarities of the English' (1965) (reprinted in *The Poverty of Theory*, 1978) is primarily an attack on erstwhile colleagues on the *New Left Review*, Perry Anderson and Tom Nairn, for what he regards as their misleading and cavalier treatment of British history and social structure. He is of course fighting on home ground and his attack is devastating. He rebukes them with the remark that real history 'only discloses itself after much hard research; it will not appear at the snap of schematic fingers' (op. cit., p. 66).

It is not only a failure of execution, however, that comes under scrutiny but what he regards as an imperfect model. Given Thompson's position on the role of experience and of cultural formations in historical analysis, it is not surprising to see the Anderson-Nairn base-superstructure model criticised. The metaphor does not convey the flexibility needed for looking at change and conflict in society. It is reductionist in tendency and it leads to assertions about relationships between base and superstructure rather than explanations. The heart of Thompson's critique is this:

> First, in the actual course of historical or sociological (as well as political) analysis it is of great importance to remember that social and cultural phenomena do not trail after the economic at some remote remove; they are at their source, immersed in the same nexus of relationship. Second, while one form which opposition to capitalism takes is in direct economic antagonism — resistance to exploitation whether as producer or consumer — another form is, exactly, resistance to capitalism's innate tendency to render all

> human relationships to economic definitions. The two are interrelated of course; but it is by no means certain which may prove to be in the end more revolutionary.
>
> (op. cit., p. 84)

This alone is enough to remind us that Thompson is not some mindless empiricist who has no use for models at all. Rather he objects to the mechanical application of models at the expense of historical accuracy. The adequacy of the Anderson-Nairn model is queried on general grounds. Neither does it work well in a substantive sense, suggests Thompson, because although concerned with English history it takes the French Revolution rather than the English Revolution as its exemplar. The effect is to compound the mistake. To have taken the English Revolution seriously, Thompson insists, would have led to more emphasis on cumulative developments and a series of critical transitions rather than a single dramatic one. Thompson's suspicion of models is not total. If it was there would be greater force in Richard Johnson's criticism that Thompson's stress on 'experience' in historical studies leads to an underdevelopment of theory and a tendency to reject analytical distinctions as a matter of principle (Richard Johnson, 'Three Problematics: Elements of a Theory of Working-Class Culture', in John Clarke, Charles Critcher and Richard Johnson, *Working-Class Culture*, 1979) Thompson calls rather for a more subtle and sensitive use of models:

> Must we dispense with any model? If we do so we cease to be historians, or we become slaves of some model scarcely known to ourselves. The question is rather how is it proper to employ a model. There is no simple answer. Even in the moment of employing it the historian must be able to regard his model with a radical scepticism, and to maintain an openness of response to evidence for which it has no categories. At the best . . . we must expect a delicate equilibrium between the synthesising and empiric modes, a quarrel between the model and actuality. This is the creative quarrel at the heart of cognition. Without this dialectic intellectual growth cannot take place.
>
> (op. cit., p. 78)

In other words this approach does more and claims to do more than reproduce an unproblematic raw experience. It does not, as Johnson suggests, leave its findings locked up in specific historical contingencies. But an appreciation of these contingencies and the variety of social structures that they express is essential. Otherwise concepts like culture and ideology will be clumsily manipulated into spurious explanations of, say, the nature of class relations. And the concept of the state will come to be used in a one-dimensional way.

What Thompson understands by historical logic is spelt out with great clarity in *The Poverty of Theory*. This is a remarkable essay. There is I suppose a touch of St George and the dragon about it as our hero, a humble Marxist historian, deals death blows to the mighty Marxist philosopher Althusser. The essay itself moves from high seriousness to pantomime. Those who read the essay should be warned that they might find it difficult to read Althusser afterwards with a straight face, assuming they think it is any longer worth the effort.

The attack on structuralism is forthright and comprehensive. It is epistemologically suspect, claiming privileges for its position that it cannot justify other than by fiat. It is self-confirming. It emphasises synchronic procedures to the almost total exclusion of diachronic procedures and in doing so denies the possibility of obtaining knowledge through the methods of historical inquiry. It generates a Marxist theology rather than a critical approach to the historical record. Most of all it evicts the human agency from history. In effect it says that process is fate. The attack spills over on to other Althusserians including the leading British exponents:

> it might be argued that Althusser, in his generosity, has presented to historians not one concept, but several volumes of concepts and hypotheses, which should now be tested in historical laboratories. But this will never be possible, unless in such factories as those of Messrs Hindess and Hirst, who have discovered the secret of manufacturing synthetic history and synthetic sociology out of conceptual air. For Althusser's categories have already been de-socialised and de-historicised before we start.
>
> (op. cit., p. 287)

No doubt Hindess and Hirst will make their own rejoinders but the challenge to a certain style of Marxist sociological theorising could not be more plainly made. Thompson's attack, be it noted, is not on the concept of structure — he is not a subjectivist simply because he wants to give due weight to 'experience' — it is on structuralism. His proper concern with the role of structure in social explanation leads him simultaneously to attack the methodological individualism of Karl Popper (for whom he has a healthy regard) because he does not think it makes sense to dismiss all notions of collectivity as abstractions imposed by the observer. Armies, as well as individual soldiers, exist in the real world. But structuralism reifies process: it operates a system of closure which leads to an unjustified arrogance about its own (privileged) theoretical standing and by an unconvincing sleight of hand settles the problem of the relation between subject and object.

One can see why alongside the non-Marxist functionalism of Parsons and Smelser, the Marxist functionalism of Althusser and Poulantzas comes under judgement. Indeed, because they are all forms of self-confirming conceptualisations — empty because unhistorical boxes — they are in the pejorative sense of the word ideological: not susceptible to rational argument and inquiry: 'For the project of Grand Theory — to find a total systematised conceptualisation of all history and human occasions — is the original heresy of metaphysics against knowledge' (op. cit., p. 303). I think that Thompson's essay summarises much of the tension within contemporary Marxist scholarship, but also within sociology, certainly in Britain, at the present time. Hence charges of dogmatism and sterility are exchanged for accusations of empiricism and positivism.

The emphasis in Thompson, as has been stressed, is on the analysis of social processes over extended periods of time. Much of his criticism of some forms of Marxism and sociology is that this activity has been supplanted by too great a pre-occupation with the synchronic. I will now, however, refer to two examples of a concern with social process over extended time spans. One is Marxist and the other not. Each display differing styles and approaches.

The first example is Perry Anderson's two-volume study, *Passages from Antiquity to Feudalism* (1974) and *Lineages of the Absolute State* (1974). It is of course the same Anderson whose essay with Nairn on British social history was so roundly criticised by Thompson. The broad comparative and historical scope of the above works is something else. Anderson works, as does Thompson, within the perspective of historical materialism. He is modest in his claims and does not restrict himself to Marxist historians in his scholarship as he examines the transition of the ancient world into European feudalism and the emergence of absolutist states. I want here simply to comment on the rationale of this kind of study. Anderson aims to bring together the general and the particular in historical analysis:

> The premise of this work is that there is no plumb-line between necessity and contingency in historical explanation, dividing separate types of inquiry — 'long-run' versus 'short-run', or 'abstract' versus 'concrete' — from each other. There is merely that which is known — established by historical research — and that which is not known: the latter may be either the mechanisms of single events or the laws of motion of whole structures. Both are equally amenable, in principle, to adequate knowledge of their causality.
>
> (*Lineages*, p. 8)

Anderson's strategy, therefore, is to develop typologies of absolutist states by surveying the different developments in Western and Eastern Europe.

The variability of the changes documented moves away from any simplistic picture of one society evolving out of another in a wholly determined sequence or indeed from the notion of an economic base determining the superstructure in pre-capitalist social formations. This leads Anderson to recognise the significance of legal, political and religious elements as having decisive effects, as it were in their own right, in affecting the direction of social change. The result is that it becomes difficult in practice to see how this approach differs from a Weberian comparative sociology. Perhaps the key to the matter is that within the category 'mode of production', which is taken as an analytic device by Anderson, the whole of society is subsumed. This conflation allows him to follow his historical inquiries where he will, including incidentally a very worthwhile discussion of the Asiatic mode of production.

Anderson states: 'The precise forms of juridical independence, property and sovereignty that characterises a pre-capitalist social formation, far from being merely accessory or contingent epiphenomena, comprise on the contrary the central issues of the determinate modes of production dominant within it' (*Lineages*, p. 404). An economic base model as determining the superstructure is then rejected in this study, although Anderson appears to reserve his position on the capitalist mode of production. The consequence of this is that mode of production comes to represent a social totality and then the actual work of disentangling and establishing actual inter-relations in particular societies begins. Mode of production on this reading does not explain anything. All it does is to provide a context for explanation: for the variability that is found for example in different feudal societies. Historical inquiry then proceeds without a straitjacket but arguably at the expense of conflating the category mode of production so that it includes everything. Is this anything other than a ritualistic nod to Marx before the serious business of historical inquiry begins? But perhaps the relevance of this form of historical inquiry is that the more restricted view of mode of production can be shown to be inadequate as a way of explaining social change. At least it cannot bear the weight that has sometimes been put on it. One consequence of this is that it becomes very difficult to draw an intelligible dividing line between Marxist and non-Marxist accounts of social change.

My second example is *The Civilising Process* (1978) by Norbert Elias. The original German version of this book was published in Switzerland in 1939, but only recently has the study received the attention and acclaim it deserves. Elias contends that it is of great importance to study long-term transformations of social structures in an empirical way and that this will, by the same token, tell us about long-term changes in personality structures.

Elias looks at the history of manners in Western Europe from the late Middle Ages into the modern bourgeois period. At first sight this might seem to be a subject which is unusual and certainly entertaining, but no more than an exercise in careful description. Thus we are instructed about medieval books on etiquette and we glean information from paintings and other documents as to what is considered socially acceptable behaviour and to whom the standards are applied. But it is the specific changes in a range of behaviour and the attitudes towards them that fascinates Elias. He discusses shifts in what he terms shame standards to which the documents and records bear witness. He analyses shifts towards more restraint and the establishment of taboos and prescriptions on conduct. These may affect what is regarded as socially permissible behaviour at table or in the bedroom. They also mark out with increasing precision the situations and places in which various bodily activities — pissing, shitting, farting, spitting and nose-blowing — are forbidden. The shift in the shame standard and the associated embarrassment to oneself or others when the standard is infringed is what Elias understands by the civilising process. The emergence of these controls was a very slow development but today is compressed into controls over children who, as Elias puts it, have in the space of a few years to attain the advanced level of shame and revulsion that has developed over many centuries. He draws a general inference:

> A child that does not attain the level of control of emotions demanded by society is regarded in varying gradations as 'ill', 'abnormal', 'criminal' or just 'impossible' from the point of view of a particular caste or class, and is accordingly excluded from the life of that class. Indeed from the psychological point of view, the terms 'sick', 'abnormal', 'criminal' and 'impossible' have, within certain limits, no other meaning; how they are understood varies with the historical mutable models of affect formation.
>
> (op. cit., p. 141)

This is an historically grounded approach to sociology which emphasises that in tracing social processes we can understand social order. The particular example, that is so skilfully done, illustrates Elias's approach to sociological analysis in which the concept of figuration is central. What this entails is well brought out in the metaphor of the dance:

> The image of the mobile figurations of interdependent people on a dance floor perhaps makes it easier to imagine states, cities, families, and also capitalist, communist and feudal systems as figurations. By using this concept we can eliminate the antithesis resting finally on different values and ideals, immanent today in the use of the words 'individual' and 'society'. One can certainly speak of a dance in general, but no one will imagine a dance as a structure outside the individual or as a mere abstraction. The same dance figurations can certainly be danced by different people; but without a plurality of reciprocally oriented and dependent individuals there is no dance. Like every other social figuration a dance figuration is relatively

independent of the specific individuals forming it here and now, but not of individuals as such. It would be absurd to say that dances are mental constructions abstracted from the observations of individuals considered separately. The same applies to all other figurations.

(op. cit., p. 262)

The above quotation is from a later 1968 essay appended to the English translation. It is a powerful metaphor and it expresses his view that sociology can be re-orientated not only to make use of historical materials in an empirical way but to dissolve the false dichotomies between individual and society, freewill and determinism. He points to a way of doing comparative sociology that is rooted in the long-term analysis of specific social transformations. In doing so, he proposes an approach to the study of social development that does not share the ideological pre-occupations of a Comte or a Hobhouse, but does offer a way of appreciating the unintended consequences of social action. Whether he thinks that anything, other than appreciation of the nature of social change and its ironies, is possible I am not sure. Is it possible to catch the owl of Minerva before it flies away? Or, to put it more prosaically, is it possible to understand in order to control in a world where unintended consequences may be catastrophic in their effects? This, I suspect, remains an unresolved problem for Elias as it does for most of us (see also, *What is Sociology?*, 1978).

14 THE RELEVANCE OF 'PURE' THEORY

There are a number of social theorists in Britain whose writings characteristically cut across the boundaries of sociology, social philosophy, the philosophy of science and the methodology of the social sciences. As far as the practice of sociology is concerned their influence is diffuse and yet the issues they raise are I think of continuing importance. The authors I have particularly in mind are Karl Popper, Ernest Gellner, Alasdair MacIntyre, Peter Winch and Steven Lukes. My interest here is to suggest some of the ways in which their reflections on the nature of sociological knowledge have impinged on the practice of sociological work in Britain. Those who wish to explore in a wider context the ramifications of the debates to which such writers contribute may refer with profit to such texts as Alan Ryan's *The Philosophy of the Social Sciences* (1970), Richard J. Bernstein's *The Restructuring of Social and Political Theory*, (1976) and Anthony Giddens, *New Rules of Sociological Method* (1976). A collection of helpful expository essays on a diversity of topics is Anthony Giddens's *Studies in Social and Political Theory* (1977). Two of those essays, 'Positivism and its Critics', and 'Hermeneutics, Ethnomethodology and Problems of Interpretative Analysis', have relevance to some of the issues I shall discuss below. However, my aim is different, namely to locate some of these general debates within the context of the development of British sociology.

Karl Popper cannot be avoided. His is the voice of critical rationalism. the distrust of all authority making absolutist claims to knowledge. As the seeker after a never wholly obtainable truth his epistemology finds political expression in liberalism and is testified to in his conception of the open society. Although his writings in the philosophy of science were formidably expressed in the German version of *The Logic of Scientific Discovery* (1959) as early as 1934, it was I think *The Open Society and its Enemies* (1943) and *The Poverty of Historicism* (1957) that first penetrated the world of social science. There we have the attack on deterministic accounts of social change, whether idealist or materialist, evolutionary or revolutionary. This is centred on the proposition that since human history is strongly influenced by the growth of human knowledge and since it is impossible to predict in any logical way the future growth of scientific knowledge, it is therefore logically impossible to predict the future course of human history.

Those who claim otherwise are making indefensible assertions and indeed the political extension of such claims may lead to tyranny and totalitarianism.

As is well known, Popper lays great stress on the testability of scientific theories and their necessary exposure to the criterion of falsifiability (which criterion has itself become the subject of intense debate with notable contributions from Kuhn and Lakatos). In the strictest sense Popper does not think that the natural and social sciences are comparable in respect of the applicability of this criterion. This is one reason which supports his claim not to be a positivist. But the social sciences do share with the natural sciences what Popper famously calls the searchlight theory of science — that is the use of facts that are highly selective, and which depend on an interest or a point of view. However, the hypothetico-deductive method which, according to Popper, undergirds the scientific enterprise, is more difficult to carry out in the social sciences, especially history, because the available facts to investigate a problem may be limited or difficult to uncover and because history cannot be re-enacted. Nevertheless, granted the imperfections, Popper argues that rival interpretations of historical events can be examined and some at least can be shown to be inconsistent with known facts and to that extent not all interpretations are equal. Unless one embarks on this critical task, albeit one that is never finally completed, the field is left open in social explanation to historicism, which in Popper's view is logically impossible as an explanatory model, but dangerous and beguiling for all that.

Platonism, Hegelianism and Marxism are all scrutinised by Popper for their historicist elements and judged accordingly. Indeed there is strength in the suggestion that the Popper critique kept academic Marxism at bay in Britain and that its re-emergence in the 1960s necessitated a counter-attack on Popper. And when it did reappear deterministic theories of Marxism were very little in evidence, much more typically the emphasis was on voluntaristic theories and on the role of human agencies in affecting change. Bearing this in mind it is worth re-recalling that in *The Open Society*, Popper was very generous in his judgement of Marx's moral stature, properly noting (p. 211) his humanist concern for freedom, equality and justice:

> Marx showed that a social system can as such be unjust; that if the system is bad then all the righteousness of the individuals who profit from it is a mere sham righteousness, is mere hypocrisy. For our responsibility extends to the system, to the institutions which we allow to persist. It is this moral radicalism of Marx which explains his influence and that is a hopeful fact in itself. This moral radicalism is still alive. It is our task to keep it alive, to prevent it from going the way which his political radicalism will have to go. 'Scientific' Marxism is dead. Its feeling of social responsibility and its love of

freedom must survive.

Again, it is well known that Popper rejects holistic explanations of behaviour in favour of methodological individualism. In this he parallels Weber (whom he occasionally cites) and more particularly in his denial that methodological individualism is to be equated with psychological reductionism. Those who argue that Popper intends to undermine the sociological enterprise have perhaps looked at his critique of the sociology of knowledge without appreciating what he has to say about the autonomy of sociology. There he argues explicitly — even identifying with Marx on the point — that the analysis of social situations, such as market situations, is not reducible to explanations in terms of motives or general laws of human nature. In his discussion of the logic of the situation he is recognising that there is a sociological level of explanation, but at the same time that it has indeterminate qualities in that unintended consequences of intended human actions are part of the web of social life.

Popper makes what is for him a crucial distinction between utopianism and piecemeal social engineering. His opposition to utopianism is on various grounds: it is irrational (a cardinal Popperian sin); it is rarely thoroughly worked out and therefore, despite idealistic intentions, might have highly unpleasant (even if unintentional) consequences of a coercive and totalitarian kind; it confuses means and ends and devalues the role of experience. Piecemeal social engineering proceeds by trial and error, it is provisional and open to correction in the light of experience, it allows for difference and debate. Popper's declared preference for piecemeal social engineering is widely regarded as an anti-revolution stance and one that favours the existing social order. Yet it does need to be remembered that, with Kant, he sees philosophy as having a revolutionary character. We can learn 'that the role of thought is to carry out revolutions by means of critical debates rather than by means of violence and warfare; that it is the great tradition of Western rationalism to fight our battles with words rather than with swords. That is why our Western civilisation is an essentially pluralistic one, and why monolithic social ends would mean the death of freedom: of freedom of thought, of the free search for truth, and with it, of the rationality and dignity of man' (op. cit., p. 396).

Popper's anti-utopianism, his use of the fact-value distinction, his methodological individualism and his recognition that scientific activity is grounded in notions of problem-relevance, are all features that may be located in Weber's writing, who also shares with him an admiration for Kantian philosophy. Given the undoubted interest in Weber in recent British sociology and the continuing debate with Marx it is not surprising to see the way in which Popper is pressed into service by neo-Weberians and/or neo-Kantians. Two notable examples I have in mind are Ralph Dahrendorf and John Goldthorpe.

Dahrendorf in his academic life has straddled the German, North American and British scene. But much of his work bears the imprint of his postgraduate days at the London School of Economics. The influence of Popper is plain to see and even in more recent writing continues to be evident.

In *Class and Class Conflict in an Industrial Society* (1959), Dahrendorf identifies with Popper's position as to what constitutes a scientific theory and draws attention to two of his characteristic metaphors. Theory is a 'net' cast to catch 'the world' and explain some feature of it. Theory is a 'searchlight' illuminating a sector of reality. In both instances the selectivity of facts is emphasised in relation to the problem under investigation, the provisional nature of the explanation recognised and the criterion of testability seen as central to scientific activity.

Dahrendorf claims that the elements in Marx's theory of class that are amenable to testing have been refuted and that those elements which cannot be tested are by definition unscientific. When it comes to formulating his own alternative theory, clearly it is intended to supersede Marx, whilst being itself subject to refutation. This he does in part be redefining class to refer to authority relations in imperatively coordinated associations, and to loosen the concept in consequence from its dependence on property relations. In addition he proposes in a formal (albeit tentative) way a theory that seeks to account for variations in the violence and intensity of class conflicts. (The propositions are spelt out on pp. 236-40). There is in the study a good deal of reference to Weber, especially on the theme of bureaucratisation. More generally he shares with Weber and Popper a reluctance to predict on the basis of trends: 'Whatever trends toward reduction of violence and intensity of conflict there may be in the industry of post-capitalist society, there are counter-trends also and it is hard, if not impossible, to derive predictions in that sphere' (op. cit., p. 279).

Again there is a view shared with Popper of the relevance of the distinction between free societies and totalitarian societies. Whereas a totalitarian society seeks to suppress social conflict and impose a homogeneous political and social order on its subjects, a free society recognises 'the justice and the creativity of diversity, difference and conflict' (op. cit., p. 318). And, like Popper, he advocates a 'free society' writing as a political liberal in which piecemeal rather than radical changes emerge through orderly conflict. It is not my purpose here to offer a critique of Dahrendorf's study. But since the scientific gauntlet of testability is thrown down I commend Hugh Stretton's somewhat neglected book *The Political Sciences* (1969), where the challenge is taken up in style. One point I do want to make however, is that it is not only observations that are theory impregnated, as Popper suggests, but concepts too. It is not therefore a matter of indifference that the central concept of class is redefined by Dahrendorf, because upon that linguistic decision much else also depends.

In Dahrendorf's *Essays in the Theory of Society* (1968) a sense of the value-impregnated character of concepts comes through in his comments on pre-theory and in his remarks that behind concepts such as liberty different usages may reflect different concepts of human nature. (The parallel with Gouldner's discussion of domain assumptions in *The Coming Crisis of Western Sociology* may be noted in passing.) The implications of this position are not altogether worked through from a Popperian standpoint. In general the adherence to Popperian social science remains and is well illustrated in the essays, notably 'Values and Social Science', and 'Uncertainty, Science and Democracy'. The first makes particular use of the distinction between the logic and psychology of scientific inquiry in theory formation. The second draws explicitly on Popper's paper, 'On the Sources of Knowledge and of Ignorance', to discuss linkages between epistemological theories of knowledge, the ethics of social research and political life. The argument rests on the principle of uncertainty which characterises the human condition and scientific activity. Given this, the context of representative democracy, it is held, provides the best foundation for the growth of knowledge and the realisation of human freedom, since it is non-absolutist and recognises the legitimacy of conflicts of interest in competition.

If one holds a view about the connections between epistemology and the political and social implications then this is likely to colour one's approach to the value question in sociology. Whether the distinction between facts and values is as clear cut as Popper's general position would seem to entail is itself open to question. I think this issue becomes visible in Dahrendorf's Reith Lectures, *The New Liberty* (1975). There the debt to Popper is again explicit. The distinction between utopian and piecemeal social engineering is drawn and a preference for the second declared. At the same time it is argued that a policy based upon piecemeal social engineering is not to be equated with pragmatism, it must have a sense of direction guided by a concern for liberty. Hence in this respect the separation between fact and value is not total and the relationship should be duly noted. The tone is nicely captured (pp. 98-9) in the concluding lecture as Dahrendorf names and follows his 'demon' liberty:

> I have never tried to join the ranks of those *simplistes* who are so suspiciously certain of their explanation of current evils: that they are a question of the amount of money printed for example, or of the loss of parliamentary sovereignty, of a hidden conspiracy, or even of the contradiction of capitalist societies. There is no one explanation of a complex reality nor is there one answer to its problems. Analysis and design cannot be simple therefore: but the attitudes with which we approach them are. What matters most in the world is

> liberty, that is, human life chances. They are threatened today by the consequence of our own actions: they are also capable of great new development. To meet the threat and to realise the potential, we do not need a doctrine of salvation. We have the weapons we need, our minds. Reasoned analysis, imaginative designing and an experimental approach to action form a rational, or at any rate reasonable triptych which has always served men well. This is the method of liberty: its substance is defined by the new conditions in which we live today.

In this way the attempt is made to bridge the gap between is and ought, which a radical distinction between facts and values, ends and means would seem to require. Whether liberty is the necessary primary value given Dahrendorf's epistemological position, or whether it is choice set against other possible candidates, say equality or fraternity, is not clear to me and perhaps not to Dahrendorf. Presumably to start with another such value would be to put the 'reasonable triptych' to different work.

I turn now to a number of seminal essays by John Goldthorpe, which provide some clear connecting links with Popper and are, I think, illuminating. They represent not simply more of the debate with Marx but discussions of neo-evolutionary sociology and also reflections on the epistemological status of ethnomethodology. The debate with Marx is best illustrated in his paper 'Class, Status and Party in Modern Britain: Some Recent Interpretations Marxist and Marxisant' (*EJS*, 1972). One of the key elements in the paper is the reference to the loss of confidence in Marxist historicism. While in itself this is welcomed, Goldthorpe suggests that this has been associated with approaches that have diminished the empirical status of Marxist theory. This has entailed a relative neglect of a central question posed by Marxism, namely the implications for class relationships of the structural problems of the economy. Further, Marxism tends to be treated as a general sociological orientation in Merton's sense of the term, rather than as the basis for formulating specific testable hypotheses. Here, of course, we are back to Popper. Against what he regards as fragmentation in Marxism and a pre-occupation with the meta-theoretical, Goldthorpe urges (p. 372) the return to empirical propositions and a critical testing of them: 'That these propositions have frequently proved false has doubtless been damaging to Marxism, understood as a political doctrine. But in quest for such refutations, much social research of a focussed, systematic and often highly revealing kind has been accomplished, and successive revisions of Marxism have been fertile in new hypotheses of social scientific interest as well as in mere 'saving' clauses. In other words, the 'debate with Marx' *because* it has regularly involved issues of fact in relation to issues of theory, has been a remarkably productive one for social science.'

Goldthorpe's critique of neo-evolutionism and its application to industrial societies first appeared in the essay 'Social Stratification in Industrial Society' (in P. Halmos (ed.), *The Development of Industrial Societies*, 1964) but it is extended and amplified with explicit reference to *The Poverty of Historicism* in 'Theories of Industrial Society: Reflections on the Recrudescence of Historicism and the Future of Futurology' (1971). The object of Goldthorpe's scrutiny is the cluster of mainly American theorists of industrial society - Clark Kerr and his colleagues, Talcott Parsons and W.W. Rostow. Whereas Raymond Aron had analysed industrial societies as a considered critical reply to Marxist determinism, as he saw it, in the hands of the American writers non-Marxist determinist theories stressing 'the logic of industrialism' or 'stages of economic growth' carried their own historicist baggage. Emanating from them are versions of the convergence thesis and the idea of the post-industrial society. Predictions are made about the future of industrial societies and in the light of these, evaluations of current situations and social movements are made.

What provides a new twist to the critique is that the new form of historicism embraces a liberalism which Popper himself generally supports:

> It can . . . scarcely be questioned that the new technocratic historicism is little less politically committed than were the historicist doctrines of the nineteenth century. The most significant difference is that while the latter aimed for the most part to provide legitimation for 'extremist' positions, whether of a *laissez-faire* or revolutionary character, the politics of technocratic historicism are those of the centre - of 'moderation', 'gradualism' and 'piecemeal social reform': ironically, very much the politics advocated by Popper and those who followed him, as an extension of their critique of historicism in its earlier, more dramatic forms.

What Goldthorpe rejects is the kind of forecasting and trend extrapolations typically based on immanentist theories of history that squeeze out human choice and the range of possibilities for the future. That is, for him, a real failure of imagination. The corollary is that piecemeal social policies do not have privileged status as they do in Popper: 'The viability of designs for the future based on piecemeal methods is to be as critically considered as that of designs of a more sweeping character. For the question must always be raised of whether a projected change in the *status quo* can be effected piecemeal or only as part of some wider transformation. Examples of the ineffectiveness of piecemeal social engineering are not, after all, very hard to find' (op. cit., p. 287-8). We have then a modification of the Popperian position which breaks down the rigid dichotomy between piecemeal and utopian change. But this shift is done in the name of another

Popperian principle — the importance of formulating conjectures that can be critically examined. If the future is open with real choices available then it is to the possibilities and their implications that attention must be turned. Not to do so is a methodological failure and betrays a poverty of imagination.

I have so far made little reference to Popper's theory of knowledge. The corpus of his work reveals not only a measure of optimism regarding the growth of knowledge but also a rejection of ordinary language philosophy and subjectivist theories of knowledge as fruitful ways forward. For our present purposes we may recall that the ethnomethodological approach to sociology does draw sustenance from just such sources. When, therefore, Goldthorpe in a much-cited review article 'A Revolution in Sociology?' (*Sociology*, 1973) contested the ethnomethodologists' claims to provide a new paradigm for social inquiry, it is not surprising to see Popper enlisted in a supporting role.

Is the social world to be apprehended solely in terms of inter-subjectivity? Not if the force of Popper's argument on what he terms 'the third world' is taken into the reckoning. This matter is dealt with in *Objective Knowledge* (1972) and especially in the essays 'Epistemology Without a Knowing Subject' and 'On the Theory of Objective Mind'. The first and second worlds refer to physical and mental states respectively and the third world to "the world of intelligibles", or of *ideas in the objective sense* it is the world of possible objects of thought; the world of theories in themselves, and their logical relations; of arguments in themselves; and of problem situations in themselves' (*Objective Knowledge*, p. 154). The three worlds constitute the basis of a philosophical pluralism which offers a solution to the subjective/objective dispute in sociology and philosophy. Popper argues for the objective reality of all three worlds and suggests that the second world mediates between the first and third worlds. Whilst the third world can be seen as originating from the products of human activity, once in existence it has an autonomy and reality independent of its originators. Language is an important case in point.

Goldthorpe deploys this argument to challenge the view that sociology is nothing other than the interpretation of social action. This may seem surprising coming from a sociologist who is himself associated with an emphasis on the action frame of reference in sociological analysis. But even to put social action at the centre of social inquiry is not to treat it as exhausting the field or as subjective in the ethnomethodological sense. Recognising that 'non-meaningful' phenomena can surround and condition action is, it may be added, consistent with Weber's sociology of action also.

As the argument is pursued the inference is drawn that processes of interaction between the different 'worlds' will be typically complex and will not necessarily be understood by the actors in their everyday lives. In certain circumstances the accounts of sociologists of, say, inflation or occupational mobility, may have a corrective or revelatory function in relation to lay members' understanding. It is through the exercise of sociological imagination that a growth in real knowledge of the actors themselves might be accomplished. The point that Goldthrope emphasises in consequence of all this is that sociology is not just another folk account on a par with other folk accounts, but is, or can be, a form of knowledge that is publicly available and open to critical scrutiny and improvement. On this reckoning sociology is more than a series of more or less plausible stories and does not fall into the infinite regress of solipsism. The attack on 'conventional' sociology which is the ethnomethodological equivalent of the Marxist attack on 'bourgeois' sociology, is shown to operate from a not very secure base. The counter-attack is strong and the reverberations of the battle are still with us.

Debates about the role of language in social explanation and the problem of objectivity have, of course, a long history. Kant, it may be re-called, held the view that if a dispute continued for a long time in philosophy then this suggested the existence of a problem not about 'mere words' but a genuine problem about things. This is also Popper's view. 'Never let yourself be goaded into taking seriously problems about words and their meanings. What must be taken seriously are questions of fact, and assertions about facts; theories and hypotheses; the problems they solve and the problems they share' (*Unended Quest*, p. 19). That is boldly put and it is easy to see how from such a standpoint he was bound to quarrel with Wittgenstein — an amusing account of an encounter at a Cambridge seminar to which Popper had been invited to speak is to be found in *Unended Quest*. One sociologist who shares a respect for Kant and something approaching scorn for Wittgenstein and the ordinary language philosophers is Ernest Gellner.

Words and Things (1959) was a forthright and bitter attack on Wittgenstein (early and late) and the linguistic philosophers, notably Austin. The book (which twenty years later has just been reprinted with a new introduction by Gellner) had a double advantage when it appeared. It carried an approving preface by Bertrand Russell and also received the seal of disapproval from Gilbert Ryle who would not permit a review in *Mind*. Gellner objects to Wittgenstein because, he says, explanation is ruled out as impossible and the practice of philosophy is reduced to description. It is the endless description of language in use. Philosophical problems about the world are abandoned in favour of puzzling about language. In a way ordinary language philosophy was something of a revolution, as its proponents claimed it was (see, for example G, Ryle (ed.), *The Revolution in Philosophy*, 1956). But what kind of revolution was it? In Gellner's view, one which put triviality in place of serious thought, which abandoned epistemology and took the world for granted and which was therefore an ideologically very conservative doctrine: 'Linguistic philosophers, and in particular Wittgenstein have done what has so often been done before: the carrying out of a revolution which inverts everything and installs appearance as true reality, and condemns the 'reality' as previously conceived and sought, as a chimaera, a snare and a disease. Once again — only, this time, with special reference to language — the Real is to be proclaimed to be the Rational. And, as usual, the ultimate justification of this apotheosis of the actual is the absence of anything outside it which could be its yardstick' (op. cit., p. 97).

Hence we are left with a set of claims that cannot be authenticated since they are not capable of testing against a world which they subsume and take for granted. It is the relationship between language in use, concept formation and critical reasoning about the nature of the world that Gellner wishes to re-state as problematic and not solved by the linguistic philosophy enterprise. The idiographic study of particular expressions becomes for Gellner utterly self-defeating if it is not connected to some more general philosophical or, indeed, sociological problem. To attempt such an exercise actually entails smuggling in one's own view of reality anyway, but pretending all the while not to do so: 'Philosophy is indeed partly a matter of making explicit our concepts *and*, in so doing, evaluating them. This activity is but very seldom so abstract that substantive considerations are irrelevant. This activity proceeds as most thinking does by the formulation of general ideas and by checking them by argument or in the light or particular cases. It is neither desirable nor even possible to do it at the latter level only (i.e. particular cases *without* ideas): those who think they are doing so are deceiving themselves. Their second-order concepts, like their values, are not absent but smuggled in' (op. cit., p. 268).

So Gellner stands outside Plato's cave, as it were, protesting about those who, in the name of philosophy walk back into it in an irrational affirmation that the world is as it is after all. The exercise of critical thought and systematic doubt is thereby abandoned. It is not metaphysics but thought itself which is the casualty.

In the light of such an attack on Wittgenstein one would expect Gellner to have critical reservations about Peter Winch's *The Idea of a Social Science* (1958) which was an attempt to relate Wittgenstein's philosophy to the task of gaining knowledge of the social world. This is the case. But it is worth recalling that in *Words and Things* Gellner indicated that he could see some point in looking at language in its social context and had chided the linguistic philosophers for the artificiality of their examples. Of course, to do this seriously would entail learning something about the world and its activities instead of assuming such knowledge. Unlike Popper, who, as I observed above, seems not to be interested in words and their meaning but only in propositional statements, Gellner argues for the importance of analysing concepts and the way they are employed in particular societies.

It is possible to see how functionalist accounts of belief systems and Wittgensteinian treatments of 'forms of life' can converge by emphasising not only cultural diversity but the necessity for understanding how the participants see themselves. Methodologically, especially in the second case, this will be associated with a denial of the possibility of causal explanations. And it may be held that the recognition of a diversity of cultures and belief systems is a bulwark against ethnocentric thinking. Yet Gellner wants to contend that analysing societies involves more than reproducing a range of cultural contexts. The possibility that some beliefs are absurd or inconsistent and can be subjected to logical scrutiny linked to empirical investigation is proposed. To rule such a possibility out *a priori* is a methodological decision. To take 'meaning' or the hermeneutic task seriously is the beginning but not the end of inquiry: 'I for one do not feel that, in the realm of concepts and doctrines, we may say that *tout comprendre c'est tout pardonner*. On the contrary, in the social sciences at any rate if we forgive too much we understand nothing. The attitude of *credo quia absurdum* is *also* a social phenomenon, and we miss its point and its social role if we water it down by interpretation to make it just one further form of non-absurdity, sensible simply in virtue of being visible' ('Concepts and Society', in *Cause and Meaning in the Social Sciences*, p. 43).

In his essay 'The New Idealism — Cause and Meaning in the Social Sciences' (in *Cause and Meaning*) Gellner argues that Winch's work reveals its inadequacies through an in-built solipsism which had similarly plagued Wittgenstein. 'Forms of life' are not insulated from each other: they impinge, conflict and compete. Some of them don't even claim ultimate validation for themselves either. There are those who are aware of conceptual and moral alternatives and therefore not imprisoned in some deterministic way by language. The relativism that Winch postulates concerning the diversity of cultures and morals is not a solution to questions of judgement and evaluation, it simply poses the problem. Winch is commended for seeking to relate Wittgenstein's abstract model of 'form of life' to reality but he is criticised for not revising the model when applying it to the real world. For example, cultures are unequal in cognitive power' 'Some possess concepts and methods which enable them to attain some degree of understanding of their environment, and some possess such understanding only to a minimal degree. To deny this cognitive inequality is an affectation, which can at most be sustained in the study, but not in real life' (op. cit., p. 68).

This argument and the particular example is central to Gellner's position. The asymmetrical distribution of knowledge as between different societies is an organising principle in *Thought and Change* (1964). His contention is that to recognise such differences is part of the social scientist's task. This may or may not coincide with a particular actor's context-bound knowledge in specific societies. But if there is a growth in real knowledge then this is significant data for the social scientist and cannot be ignored. In some respects Gellner's confidence in the actuality of the growth of knowledge outstrips Popper's approximations but he recognises that moral choices about the use of knowledge still remain. To recognise the real basis of knowledge will, however, make for a greater understanding of the possibilities as well as the dangers of industrial societies based on scientific knowledge.

When one considers Gellner's later book, *Legitimation of Belief*, (1974) it is to discover him confronting the paradox of the simultaneous collapse and unprecedented growth of knowledge. His book is a defence of critical monism: 'the attempt to restore intellectual order by the sustained application of simple, delimited, lucid principles designed to isolate and use the marks of genuine knowledge, an attempt which is mandatory in conditions of intellectual chaos such as in fact often obtain — such monism is absolutely essential for our life (p. 22). It is to Kant and Weber that he looks as significant discussants of rationality. Whereas Kant concentrated on the inner logic of rationality and connected it with the universal structure of the human mind. Weber located the emergence of 'rational man' in the modern world and in a particular historical setting. It is the double-edged account of rationality and disenchantment. It is knowledge at a price — not the self-authenticating faiths or ideologies, however comforting or challenging, whether of old religions, Marxism or Wittensteinism — but the price of serious thought applied to the question: given the new productive, organisational and cognitive bases of society, what are their limits and consequences?

The use of this knowledge is set against the irrationality of self-justifying ideologies. Publicly available knowledge may be tested against experience and used to consider the alternative implications and limitations of specific proposals. Gellner propounds (p. 202) a case for what he terms 'truncated evolutionism': 'if the conceptual megalomanic of the nineteenth century versions is avoided, the suitably cut-down-to-size pre-occupation with social development must be one of our central concerns. Only it can give us a concrete understanding of the options we face. In other words, we cannot dispense with sociology.' This does not lead to inevitable moral prescriptions. What it does do is to make it possible for certain choices when checked against available knowledge to be shown as inconsistent, or irrational or based on ignorance.

The debate about *The Idea of a Social Science* has been a source of stimulating argument. Two notable contributors have been Alasdair MacIntyre and Steven Lukes. MacIntyre accepts that it is relevant to study the agent's intentions, motives and reasons for action and also that the social scientist must understand the concepts and beliefs of the people studied before establishing other for explanatory purposes. But this does not eradicate the role of causal explanations. Indeed reasons for action may be part of the causal nexus and social scientists may legitimately deal with causal relations in social analysis which are not about actors following rules. MacIntyre points out that there are a variety of systematic regularities discoverable in society. Some of these relate to rules that agents profess to follow, others to rules they do follow, some which are causal but not rule-governed. The task of social science is to recognise this variety and to explain the inter-relationship that may occur between them. Winch's view, he thinks, is myopic and cramped by contrast. If the force of his argument is conceded, then MacIntyre suggests that concepts like false consciousness and ideology can still come into play even if the actors don's use the concepts themselves. This in turn implies that to use an imposed concept recaptures the possibility that criteria other than those available in the society may be established to judge its rationality (see, 'The Idea of a Social Science', in *Against the Self-Images of the Age* (1971)).

Steven Lukes claims that there are criteria of truth and validity that are not context-bound or theory dependent. What is at stake in denying cognitive relativism?

> Only such a denial makes it possible to examine and indeed acknowledge the possibility of false consciousness, where men's beliefs about their own and other societies can be characterised as mistaken or distorted or empirically inadequate, and, in virtue of these features, have significant social and political consequences. Only by assuming that one has access to a reliable, non-relative means of identifying a disjunction between social consciousness on the one hand, and social realities on the other, is it possible even to raise questions about the ways in which misperceptions and misunderstandings of all kinds arise and play their part in preventing, or promoting, social change. . . . Similarly, only the application of non-context or non-system dependent rules of logic allow one to investigate the social role of absurdity. Finally, only a denial of cognitive relativism allows one to raise questions about the differential cognitive success of different societies in different domains, and seek to explain these.
>
> ('Relativism: Cognitive and Moral',
> in *Essays in Social Theory*, 1972, p. 160)

It is upon the response to just such issues that the conduct of sociological research depends and its claims and assumptions are to be evaluated. The unreflective cultural relativism of the functional anthropologists, the linguistic relativism of Wittgenstein and Winch, the subjective solipsism of the ethnomethodologists and the self-insulating character of incommensurate paradigm promulgators has created a heady mixture. It is only a rigorous logical response that will get sociologists out of the self-imposed paralysis which prevents critical and rational social research from proceeding. The cognitive anti-relativism of Lukes does not prevent him from adopting a position of moral relativism. This is because he recognises some concepts in social use and analysis as 'essentially contested'. The way they are used — and the examples he cites are strategic ones such as justice and power — may reflect the interests and purposes of particular groups. What the sociologist can do however, is to recognise that such concepts are contested. The nature of the contest represents part of the task of elucidation. The sociologist may come to represent a particular moral standpoint in the way he or she uses a strategic concept — anomie and alienation are specific examples given by Lukes — but part of the work of social analysis remains: the clarification of the roles such concepts play in theorising and checking them empirically against alternative views of social reality. We are back then to the rules of logic and the perennially difficult task of sifting and evaluating evidence — in other words back to sociological enquiry, warts and all.

PART IV RECENT BRITISH SOCIOLOGY: A BIBLIOGRAPHY

Cast thy bread upon the waters:
for thou shalt find it after many
days.

Ecclesiastes

RECENT BRITISH SOCIOLOGY: A BIBLIOGRAPHY

The following bibliography of recent British sociology spans the period 1960-79. The bibliography is organised in the following way. There are sixteen sub-sections:

Art, music and literature
Cities, towns, communities and planning
Contemporary sociological theory
Crime, law and deviance
Education, language
History of sociology and classical theorists
Knowledge/Science
Leisure and sport
Mass media
Method, and problems of research
Military
Organisations, industrial relations, professions and economic life
Race, ethnicity and nationalism
Religion, morals
Sex, gender, generation
Social change, transition, development, underdevelopment
Social stratification: class, status, party

These are fairly conventional divisions. I have placed references directly in only one sub-section. There is a measure of arbitrariness about placement which can scarcely be avoided.

The sections are divided into four categories: Textbooks, Readers and edited collections, Specific studies and monographs, Review papers and critiques. The first three categories are book references, the fourth is done from journal articles or specified contributions to books. The book references are extensive. Although no claim for completeness is made they do give a good indication of the kind of work undertaken within the orbit of British sociology. The papers and articles in the fourth category are much more selective. I have listed contributions which either constitute an overview of a particular sub-section or a significant area or topic within it. Hence they will be characterised by a critical appraisal of a concept, a theoretical perspective or a research strategy. They represent working examples of the internal dialogues which are engendered by sociological thought and work in particular areas.

By British sociology I have chiefly in mind work accomplished within the UK context. In some instances scholars whose academic origins rather than present employment are in the UK have been referenced.

List of journals and occasional papers cited
(Abbreviations indicated where used)

Annual Review of Sociology
British Journal of Criminology
British Journal of Industrial Relations *BJIR*
British Journal of Sociology *BJS*
Capital and Class
Contemporary Crisis
Cultural Studies *CS*
Current Sociology
Economy and Society
Ethnic and Racial Studies
European Journal of Sociology *EJS*
Forum
Industrial Relations Journal *IRJ*
International Journal of Health Services
Journal of Biosocial Science
Journal of Communication
Journal of Health and Social Behaviour
Journal of Management Studies *JMS*
Journal of Peasant Studies
New Left Review *NLR*
Radical Education
Scottish Journal of Sociology
Social Compass
Social History
Socialist Register
Social Science and Medicine
Social Science Information
Sociological Review *SR*
Sociological Review Monograph
Sociology
University of Durham Working Papers in Sociology
University of Glasgow Discussion Papers in Social and Economic Research

University of Leeds Occasional Papers in Sociology
West African Journal of Sociology and Political Science

Art, music and literature

Texts

Hall, John, *The Sociology of Literature*, Longman, 1979.
Laurenson, D. and Swingewood, Alan, *The Sociology of Literature*, MacGibbon & Kee, 1972.

Readers and edited collections

Barker, F. *et al.*, *1848: The Sociology of Literature*, University of Essex, 1978.
Barrett, M. *et al.* (eds.), *Ideology and Cultural Production*, Croom Helm. 1979.
Burns, E. and T. (eds.), *Sociology of Literature and Drama*, Penguin, 1973.

Specific studies and monographs

Carroll, John, *Puritan, Paranoid, Remissive: A Sociology of Modern Culture*, Routledge & Kegan Paul, 1977.
Frith, Simon, *The Sociology of Rock*, Constable, 1978.
Madge, Charles and Weinberger, Barbara, *Art Students Observed*, Faber, 1973.
Orr, John, *Tragic Realism and Modern Society: Studies in the Sociology of the Novel*, Macmillan, 1978.
Raynor, H., *Music and Society Since 1815*, Barrie & Jenkins, 1976.
Rust, Frances, *Dances in Society: An Analysis of the Relationship between the Social Dance and Society in England from the Middle Ages to the Present Day*, Routledge & Kegan Paul, 1969.
Shepherd, J., Virden, P., Vulliamy, G. and Wishart, T., *Whose Music? A Sociology of Musical Languages*, Latimer New Dimensions, 1977.
Swingewood, Alan, *The Novel and Revolution*, Macmillan, 1975.
Swingewood, Alan, *The Myth of Mass Culture*, Macmillan, 1977.
Tudor, Andrew, *Image and Influence. Studies in the Sociology of the Film*, Allen & Unwin, 1974.
Weber, W., *Music and the Middle Classes*, Croom Helm, 1975.
Williams, R., *The Country and the City*, Paladin, 1975.
Williams, R., *Marxism and Literature*, Oxford University Press, 1977.
Wolff, Janet, *Hermeneutic Philosophy and the Sociology of Art*, Routledge & Kegan Paul, 1975.

Review papers and critiques

Craig, Ian, 'Sociological Literature and Literary Sociology: Some Notes on G by John Berger', *SR*, vol. 22, no. 2, 1974, pp. 321-33.

Filmer, Paul, 'The Literary Imagination and the Explanation of Socio-Cultural Change in Modern Britain', *EJS*, no. 10, 1969, pp. 271-91.

Forster, Peter and Kenneford, Celia, 'Sociological Theory and the Sociology of Literature', *BJS*, vol. XXIV, no. 3, 1973, pp. 353-64.

Frye, N., 'The Social Context of Literary Criticism', in Burns, E. and T. (eds.), *The Sociology of Literature and Drama*, 1973.

Gluckman, M., 'A Hard Look at Lucien Goldmann', *New Left Review*, no. 56, 1969.

Green, Michael, 'Raymond Williams and Cultural Studies', *Cultural Studies*, no. 6, 1974, pp. 31-48.

Mellors, A., 'The Hidden Method', *Working Papers in Cultural Studies No. 4*.

Pincott, Roger, 'The Sociology of Literature', *EJS*, vol. II, 1970, pp. 77-195.

Ruff, Ivan, 'Can there be a Sociology of Literature?', *BJS*, vol. XXV, no. 3, 1974, pp. 367-72.

Williams, Raymond, 'Developments in the Sociology of Culture', *Sociology*, vol. 10, no. 3, 1976, pp. 499-506.

Wolff, Janet, 'The Sociology of Art versus Aesthetics', *University of Leeds Occasional Papers in Sociology*, no. 1, 1975.

Wright, Derek F., 'Musical Meaning and its Social Determinants', *Sociology*, vol. 9, no. 3, 1975, pp. 419-35.

Cities, towns, communities and planning

Texts

Bell, C. and Newby, H., *Community Studies*, Allen & Unwin, 1971.

Frankenberg, Ronald, *Communities in Britain*, Penguin, 1966.

Mann, P., *An Approach to Urban Sociology*, Routledge & Kegan Paul, 1965.

Mellors, J.R., *Urban Sociology in an Urbanised World*, Routledge & Kegan Paul, 1978.

Morris, R.N., *Urban Sociology*, Allen & Unwin, 1968.

Pahl, R.E., *Patterns of Urban Life*, Longman, 1970.

Thorns, David C., *Suburbia*, MacGibbon & Kee, 1972.

Readers and edited collections

Bell, C. and Newby, H. (eds.), *The Sociology of Community: A Selection of Readings*, Cass, 1974.

Lambert, Camilla and Weir, David (eds.), *Cities in Modern Britain*, Fontana, 1975.

Pahl, R.E. (ed.), *Readings in Urban Sociology*, Pergamon, 1968.

Pickvance, C.G., *Urban Sociology — Critical Essays*, Tavistock, 1976.

Specific studies and monographs

Abrams, Philip and McCulloch, Andrew, *Communes, Sociology and Society*, Cambridge University Press, 1976.

Cockburn, Cynthia, *The Local State: Management of Cities and People*, Pluto Press, 1977.

Davies, John Gower, *The Evangelistic Bureaucrats: A Study of a Planning Exercise in Newcastle-upon-Tyne*, Tavistock, 1972.

Dennis, Norman, *People and Planning. The Sociology of Housing in Sunderland*, Faber, 1970.

Dennis, Norman, *Planning and Public Participation*, Faber, 1972.

Dennis Norman, *Public Participation and Planners' Blight*, Faber, 1972.

Elias, N. and Scotson, J., *The Established and the Outsiders*, Cass, 1965.

Gill, Owen, *Luke Street*, Macmillan, 1977.

Hall, Peter *et al.*, *The Containment of Urban England*, Allen & Unwin, 1973.

Jackson, Brian, *Working Class Community*, Routledge & Kegan Paul, 1968.

Lambert, John, *Housing Policies and the State Allocation, Access and Control*, Macmillan, 1978.

Littlejohn, J., *Westrigg: The Sociology of a Cheviot Parish*, Routledge & Kegan Paul, 1963.

Moser, C.A. and Scott, W., *British Towns*, Oliver & Boyd, 1961.

Newton, K., *Second City Politics*, Oxford University Press, 1976.

Pahl, R.E., *Whose City? And Other Essays on Sociology and Planning*, Longman, 1970.

Ravetz, Alison, *Model Housing and Planned Housing at Quarry Hill, Leeds*, Croom Helm, 1974.

Roberts, R., *The Classic Slum*, Manchester University Press, 1971.

Robson, B.T., *Urban Analysis: A Study of City Structure with Special Reference to Sunderland*, Cambridge University Press, 1969.

Rose, Hilary, *The Housing Problem*, Heinemann, 1968.

Seabrook, J., *City Close-Up*, Allen Lane, 1971.

Stacey, Margaret, *Tradition and Change: A Study of Banbury*, Oxford University Press, 1960.

Stacey, Margaret, Batstone, Eric, Bell, Colin and Murcott, Anne, *Power, Persistence and Change. A Second Study of Banbury*, Routledge & Kegan Paul, 1975.

Timms, D.W.G., *The Urban Mosaic*, Cambridge University Press, 1971.

Williams, W.M., *A West Country Village: Ashworthy*, Routledge & Kegan Paul, 1963.

Review papers and critiques

Abrams, Philip, 'Towns and Economic Growth: Some Theories and Problems', in Abrams, P. and Wrigley, E.A. (eds.), *Towns in Society*,

Cambridge University Press, 1978, pp. 1-33.
Brook, Eve and Finn, Dan, 'Working Class Images of Society and Community Studies', *Cultural Studies*, no. 10, 1977, pp. 127-45.
Bulmer, M., 'Sociological Models of the Mining Community', *SR*. vol. 23, no. 1, 1975, pp. 61-92.
Clark, David B., 'The Concept of Community — A Re-examination', *SR*, vol. 21, no. 3, 1973, pp. 397-416.
Critcher, Charles, 'Sociology, Cultural Studies and the Post-War Working Class', in Clarke, John, Critcher, Charles and Johnson, Richard (eds.), *Working Class Culture*, Hutchinson, 1979, pp. 13-40.
Day, Graham and Fitton, Martin, 'Religion and Social Status in Rural Wales' "Buchedd" and its Lessons for Concepts of Stratification in Community Studies', *SR*, vol. 23, no. 4, 1975, pp. 867-91.
Damer, S., 'Wine Alley: The Sociology of a Dreadful Enclosure', *SR*, vol. 22, no. 2, 1974, pp. 221-48.
Elliott, Brian, 'Social Change in the City: Structure and Process', in Abrams, P. (ed.), *Work, Urbanism and Inequality*, Weidenfeld & Nicolson, 1978, pp. 17-54.
Pickvance, C.G., 'On a Materialist Critique of Urban Sociology', *SR*, vol. 22, no. 2, 1974, pp. 203-20.
Plowman, D., Minchinton, W. and Stacey, M., 'Local Social Status in England and Wales', *SR*, vol. 10, no. 2, 1962, pp. 161-201.
Stacey, Margaret, 'The Myth of Community Studies', *BJS*, vol. XX, no. 2, 1969, pp. 134-47.
Taylor, Brian K., 'The Absence of a Sociological and Structural Focus in Community Studies', *EJS*, vol. XVI, 1975, pp. 296-309.

Contemporary sociological theory

Texts

Cohen, Percy., *Modern Social Theory*, Heinemann, 1968.
Filmer, Paul, Phillipson, Michael, Silverman, David and Walsh, David, *New Directions in Sociological Theory*, Collier-Macmillan, 1972.
Mennell, Stephen, *Sociological Theory: Uses and Unities*, Nelson, 1974.

Readers and edited collections

Connerton, Paul (ed), *Critical Sociology*, Penguin, 1976.
Thorns, David C. (ed.), *New Directions in Sociology*, David & Charles, 1976.

Specific studies and monographs

Atkinson, Dick, *Orthodox Consensus and Radical Alternative: A Study in Sociological Theory*, Heinemann, 1971.

Badcock, C., *Levi-Strauss, Structuralism and Sociological Theory*, Hutchinson, 1975.

Bauman, Z., *Culture as Praxis*, Routledge & Kegan Paul, 1973.

Bauman, Z., *Towards a Critical Sociology: An Essay on Common Sense and Emancipation*, Routledge & Kegan Paul, 1976.

Bauman, Z., *Hermeneutics and Social Science*, Hutchinson, 1978.

Benton, Ted, *Philosophical Foundations of the Three Sociologies*, Routledge & Kegan Paul, 1977.

Binns, David, *Beyond the Sociology of Conflict*, Macmillan, 1977.

Bottomore, Tom, *Sociology as Social Criticism*, Allen & Unwin, 1975.

Brittan, Arthur, *Meanings and Situations*, Routledge & Kegan Paul, 1973.

Brittan, Arthur, *The Privatised World*, Routledge & Kegan Paul, 1978.

Coulter, Jeff, *The Social Construction of the Mind: Studies in Ethnomethodology*, Macmillan, 1979.

Craib, Ian, *Existentialism and Sociology: A Study of Jean-Paul Sartre*, Cambridge University Press, 1976.

Dixon, Keith, *Sociological Theory: Pretence and Possibility*, Routledge & Kegan Paul, 1973.

Fay, Brian, *Social Theory and Political Practice*, Allen & Unwin, 1975.

Fletcher, Colin, *The Person in the Sight of Sociology*, Routledge & Kegan Paul, 1975.

Gellner, Ernest, *Contemporary Thought and Politics*, Routledge & Kegan Paul, 1974.

Giddens, Anthony, *Studies in Social and Political Theory*, Hutchinson, 1977.

Giddens, Anthony, *Central Problems in Social Theory*, Macmillan, 1979.

Gluckmann, Miriam, *Structural Analysis in Contemporary Social Thought; A Comparison of the Thought of Claude Levi-Strauss and Louis Althusser*, Routledge & Kegan Paul, 1974.

Jenkins, A., *The Social Theory of Claude Levi-Strauss*, Macmillan, 1979.

Jessop, Bob, *Social Order. Reform and Revolution*, Macmillan, 1972.

Kilminster, Richard, *Praxis and Method*, Routledge & Kegan Paul, 1979.

Lukes, Steven, *Essays in Social Theory*, Macmillan, 1977.

Lukes, Steven, *Power, A Radical View*, Macmillan, 1974.

MacIntyre, A., *Against the Self-Images of the Age*, Duckworth, 1971.

MacIntyre, A., *Marcuse*, Fontana, 1970.

Menzies, Ken, *Talcott Parsons and the Social Image of Man*, Routledge & Kegan Paul, 1977.

O'Neill, John, *Sociology as a Skin Trade*, Heinemann, 1972.

O'Neill, John, *Making Sense Together: an Introduction to Wild*

Sociology, Heinemann, 1975.
Rex, John, *Sociology and the Demystification of the Modern World*, Routledge & Kegan Paul, 1974.
Roche, M., *Phenomenology, Language and Social Science*, Routledge & Kegan Paul, 1973.
Rock, Paul, *The Making of Symbolic Interaction*, Macmillan, 1979.
Savage, Stephen P , *The Theories of Talcott Parsons*, Macmillan, 1979.
Slater, P., *Origins and Significance of the Frankfurt School. A Marxist Perspective*, Routledge & Kegan Paul, 1979.
Smart, Barry, *Sociology, Phenomenology and Marxian Analysis*, Routledge & Kegan Paul, 1976.
Swingewood, Alan, *Marx and Modern Social Theory*, Macmillan, 1975.
Thompson, E.P., *The Poverty of Theory*, Merlin Press, 1978.

Review papers and critiques
Albrow, Martin, 'Dialectical and Categorical Paradigms of a Science of Society', *SR*, vol. 22, no. 2, 1974, pp. 183-201.
Bauman, Z., 'The Structuralist Promise', *BJS*, vol. XXIV, no. 1, 1973, pp. 67-83.
Benton, Ted, 'How Many Sociologies?', *SR*, vol. 26, no. 2, 1978, pp. 217-36.
Best, R.E., 'New Directions in Sociological Theory? A Critical Note on Phenomenological Sociology and its Antecedents', *BJS*, vol. XXVI, no. 2, 1975, pp. 133-43.
Bottomore, Tom, 'Competing Paradigms in Macro-Sociology', *Annual Review of Sociology*, 1975, pp. 191-202.
Brown, George, 'Some Thoughts on Grounded Theory', *Sociology*, vol. 7, no. 1, 1973, pp. 1-16.
Bryant, Christopher G.A., 'Kuhn, Paradigms and Sociology', *BJS*. vol. XXVI, no. 3, 1975, pp. 354-9.
Chambers, Iain, 'Roland Barthes' Structuralism/Semiotics', *Cultural Studies*, no. 6, 1974, pp. 49-68.
Corrigan, Philip, 'Dichotomy is Contradiction: On "Society" as Constraint and Construction. Remarks on the Doctrine of the "Two Sociologies" ', *SR*, vol. 23, no. 2, 1975, pp. 211-43.
Dawe, Alan, 'The Underworld View of Erving Goffman', *BJS*, vol. XXIV, no. 2, 1973, pp. 246-53.
Dawe, Alan, 'The Two Sociologies', *BJS*, vol. XXI, no. 2, 1970, pp. 207-18.
Dawe, Alan, 'The Role of Experience in the Construction of Social Theory: An Essay in Reflexive Sociology', *SR*, vol. 21, no. 1, 1973, pp. 25-55.
Freeman, Michael, 'Sociology and Utopia: Some Reflections on the Social Philosophy of Karl Popper', *BJS*, vol. XXVI, no. 1, 1975, pp. 20-35.
Frisby, David, 'The Frankfurt School' Critical Theory and Positivism' in

Rex, J. (ed.), *Approaches to Sociology*, 1974, pp. 205-29.
Giddens, Anthony, 'Recent Works on the Position and Prospects of Contemporary Sociology', *EJS*, vol. II, 1970, pp. 143-54.
Giddens, Anthony, 'The Prospects for Social Theory Today', *Berkeley Journal of Sociology*, vol. XXIII, pp. 78-9, 201-23.
Glucksmann, Miriam, 'Structuralism', *BJS*, vol. XXII, no. 2, 1971, pp. 209-13.
Inglis, Fred, 'Good and Bad Habitus: Bourdieu, Habermas and the Condition of England', *SR*, vol. 22, no. 2, 1979, pp. 353-69.
Kilminster, Richard, 'On the Structure of Critical Thinking', University of Leeds Occasional Papers in Sociology, no. 2, 1975.
Lassman, Peter, 'Phenomenological Perspectives in Sociology', in Rex, J. (ed.), *Approaches to Sociology*, 1974, pp. 125-44.
Mann, Michael, 'Idealism and Materialism in Sociological Theory', in Bertaux, D. and Freiberg, T. (eds.), *Current Trends in European Critical Theory*, Heath, 1977.
Martins, Herminio, 'Time and Theory in Sociology', in Rex, J. (ed.), *Approaches to Sociology*, 1974, pp. 246-94.
Morgan, David, 'British Social Theory', *Sociology*, vol. 9, no. 1, 1975, pp. 119-24.
Runciman, W.G., 'What is Structuralism?', *BJS*, vol. XX, no. 3, 1969, pp. 253-65.
Rusher, Robin, 'What is it he's done? The Ideology of Althusser', *Cultural Studies*, no. 6, 1974, pp. 70-96.
Scott, John P., 'Critical Social Theory: An Introduction and a Critique', *BJS*, vol XXIX, no. 1, 1978, pp. 1-20.
Sklair, Leslie, 'Ideology and the Sociological Utopia', *SR*, vol 25, no. 1, 1977, pp. 51-72.
Wolff, Janet, 'Hermeneutics and the Critique of Ideology', *SR*, vol. 23, no. 4, 1975, pp. 811-28.
Worsley, Peter, 'The State of Theory and the Status of Theory', *Sociology* vol. 8, no. 1, 1974, pp. 1-17.

Crime, law and deviance

Box, S., *Deviance, Reality and Society*, Holt, Rinehart & Winston, 1971.
Hood, Roger and Sparks, Richard, *Key Issues in Criminology*, Weidenfeld & Nicolson, 1970.
Morris, Terence, *Deviance and Control. The Secular Heresy*, Hutchinson, 1976.
Taylor, I., Walton, P., and Young, J., *The New Criminology: For a Social Theory of Deviance*, Routledge & Kegan Paul, 1973.
Taylor, Laurie, *Deviance and Society*, Michael Joseph, 1971.

Readers and edited collections

Campbell, Colin and Wiles, Paul (eds.), *Law and Society. Readings in*

the Sociology of Law, Martin Robertson, 1979.
Carlen, P. (ed.), *The Sociology of Law*, Sociological Review Monograph, 1976.
Carson, W.G. and Wiles, Paul (eds.), *Crime and Delinquency in Britain*, Martin Robertson, 1970.
Cohen, S. (ed.), *Images of Deviance*, Penguin, 1971.
Downes, David and Rock, Paul (eds.), *Deviant Interpretations*, Martin Robertson, 1979.
Giddens, A. (ed.), *The Sociology of Suicide*, Cass, 1971.
Holdaway, Simon (ed.), *The British Police*, Edward Arnold, 1979.
Rock, P. and McIntosh, M. (eds.), *Deviance and Social Control*, Tavistock, 1974.
Taylor, I. and Taylor, L. (eds.), *Politics and Deviance*, Penguin, 1973.
Taylor, I., Walton, P. and Young, J. (eds.), *Critical Criminology*, Routledge & Kegan Paul, 1975.
Ward, C. (ed.), *Vandalism*, Architectural Press, 1973.
Wiles, Paul (ed.), *The Sociology of Crime and Delinquency in Britain: the New Criminologies*, Martin Robertson, 1976.

Specific studies and monographs

Atkinson, J. Maxwell, *Discovering Suicide. Studies in the Social Organisation of Sudden Death*, Macmillan, 1978.
Baldwin, John and Bottoms, A.E., *The Urban Criminal: a Study in Sheffield*, Tavistock, 1976.
Bankowski, Zenon and Mungham, Geoff., *Images of Law*, Routledge & Kegan Paul, 1976.
Bean, Philip, *The Social Control of Drugs*, Martin Robertson, 1974.
Bean, Philip, *Rehabilitation and Deviance*, Routledge & Kegan Paul, 1976.
Bottomley, A. Keith, *Decisions in the Penal Process*, Martin Robertson, 1973.
Bottoms, A.E. and McClintock, F.H., *Criminals Coming of Age*, Heinemann, 1973.
Cain, Maureen, *Society and the Policeman's Role*, Routledge & Kegan Paul, 1973.
Carlen, Pat, *Magistrate's Justice*, Martin Robertson, 1976.
Chapman, D., *Society and the Stereotype of the Criminal*, Tavistock, 1968.
Chibnall, Steve, *Law and Order News*, Tavistock, 1977.
Cohen, S., *Folk Devils and Moral Panics*, Paladin, 1973.
Cohen, Stanley and Taylor, Laurie., *Long-Term Imprisonment*, Penguin, 1972.
Cohen, Stanley and Taylor, Laurie, *Resistance to Everyday Life*, Allen Lane, 1976.
Ditton, Jason, *Part-time Crime: An Ethnography of Fiddling and*

Pilferage, Macmillan, 1977.
Ditton, Jason, *Controlology — Beyond the New Criminology*, Macmillan, 1979.
Downes, David, *The Delinquent Solution: A Study in Sub-Cultural Theory*, Routledge & Kegan Paul, 1966.
Downes, David *et al.*, *Gambling, Work and Leisure: A Study Across Three Areas*, Routledge & Kegan Paul, 1976.
Grace, Clive and Wilkinson, Philip, *Sociological Inquiry and Legal Phenomena*, Macmillan, 1978.
Hall, Stuart and Jefferson, Tony, *Resistance Through Rituals. Youth Sub-Culture in Great Britain*, Hutchinson, 1976.
Hall, Stuart *et al.*, *Policing the Crisis: Mugging, the State and Law and Order*, Macmillan, 1978.
Henry, Stuart, *The Hidden Economy; Context and Control of Borderline Crime*, Martin Robertson, 1978.
Hepworth, Mike, *Blackmail*, Routledge & Kegan Paul, 1975.
Hirst, Paul, *On the Law and Ideology*, Macmillan, 1979.
Hood, Roger, *Sentencing the Motoring Offender*, Heinemann, 1972.
Hunt, Alan, *The Sociological Movement in Law*, Macmillan, 1978.
McClintock, F.H. and Avison, N. Howard, *Crime in England and Wales*, Heinemann, 1969.
McIntosh, Mary, *The Organisation of Crime*, Macmillan, 1975.
Mack, John A. and Kerner, Hans Jurgen, *The Crime Industry*, Saxon House, 1975.
Marsh, Peter, Rosser, Elizabeth and Harre, Rom, *The Rules of Disorder*, Routledge & Kegan Paul, 1978.
Martin, J.P. and Wilson, Gail, *The Police: A Study in Manpower*, Heinemann, 1969.
Morris, Pauline, *Put Away*, Routledge & Kegan Paul, 1969.
Patrick, James (pseud.), *A Glasgow Gang Observed*, Eyre Methuen, 1973.
Pearce, Frank, *Crimes of the Powerful*, Pluto Press, 1976.
Pearson, Geoffrey, *The Deviant Imagination*, Macmillan, 1975.
Plummer, Kenneth, *Sexual Stigma: an Interactionist Account*, Routledge & Kegan Paul, 1975.
Plant, Martin A., *Drugtakers in an English Town*, Tavistock, 1975.
Punch, Maurice, *Policing the Inner City. A Study of Amsterdam's Warmvet Straat*, Macmillan, 1979.
Robertson, Roland and Taylor, Laurie, *Deviance, Crime and Socio-Legal Control: Comparative Perspectives*, Martin Robertson, 1973.
Rock, Paul, *Making People Pay*, Routledge & Kegan Paul, 1973.
Tobias, J.J., *Crime and Industrial Society in the Nineteenth Century*, Penguin, 1967.
Walsh, I.P., *Shoplifting. Controlling a Major Crime*, Macmillan, 1978.
Wilkins, Leslie T., *Social Policy, Action and Research: Studies in*

Social Deviance, Tavistock, 1967.
Willett, T.C., *Drivers after Sentence*, Heinemann, 1973.
Willis, Paul, *Profane Culture*, Routledge & Kegan Paul, 1978.
Young, Jock, *The Drugtakers: The Social Meaning of Drug Use*, MacGibbon & Kee, 1970.

Review papers and critiques

Atkinson, J. Maxwell, 'Versions of Deviance', *SR*, vol. 22, no. 4, 1974, pp. 616-25.
Bankowski, Zenon, Mungham, Geoff and Young, Peter, 'Radical Criminology or Radical Criminologist?', *Contemporary Crisis*, vol. 1, 1977, pp. 37-52.
Clarke, Michael, 'On the Concept of "Sub-Culture" ', *BJS*, vol. XXV, no. 4, 1974, pp. 428-41.
Clarke, Michael, 'Social Problem Ideologies', *BJS*, vol XXVI, no. 4, 1975, pp. 406-16.
Cohen, Stanley, 'Criminology and the Sociology of Deviance', in Rock and McIntosh (eds.), op. cit., 1974, pp. 1-40.
Cohen, Stanley, 'Guilt, Justice and Tolerance: Some Old Concepts for a New Criminology', in Downes and Rock (eds.), op. cit., 1979, pp. 17-51.
Cohen, Stanley, 'Breaking Out, Smashing Up and the Social Context of Aspiration', *Cultural Studies*, no. 5, 1974, pp. 37-63.
Cohen, Stanley and Taylor, Laurie, 'From Psychopaths to Outsiders: British Criminology and the National Deviancy Conference', in Bianchi, H., Simondi, M. and Taylor, I. (eds.), *Deviance and Control in Europe*, Wiley, 1975.
Coulter, Jeff, 'What's Wrong with the New Criminology?', *SR*, vol. 22, no. 1, 1974, pp. 119-35.
Downes, David, 'Promise and Performance in British Criminology', *BJS*, vol. XXIX, no. 4, 1978, pp. 483-502.
Downes, David, 'Praxis makes Perfect: a Critique of Critical Criminology', In Downes and Rock (eds.), op. cit., 1979, pp. 1-16.
Fine, Bob, 'Labelling Theory: An Investigation into the Sociological Critique of Deviance' *Economy and Society*, vol. 6, no. 2, 1977, pp. 166-93.
Manning, Peter K., 'Deviance and Dogma: Some Comments on the Labelling Perspective', *British Journal of Criminology*, vol. 15, no. 1, 1975, pp. 1-20.
Plummer, K., 'Misunderstanding Labelling Perspectives', in Downes and Rock (eds.), op. cit., 1979, pp. 85-121.
Rock, Paul, 'The Sociology of Deviance and Conceptions of the Moral Order', *British Journal of Criminology*, vol. 14, no. 2, 1974, pp. 139-49.
Rock, Paul, 'Phenomenalism and Essentialism in the Sociology of Deviance', *Sociology*, vol. 7, no. 1, 1973, pp. 17-29.

Rock, Paul, 'The Sociology of Crime, Symbolic Interactionism and Some Problematic Qualities of Radical Criminology', in Downes and Rock (eds.), op. cit., 1979, pp. 52-84.
Roshier, Bob, 'Corrective Criminology', *University of Durham, Working Papers in Sociology*, no. 10, 1976.
Taylor, Ian and Walton, Paul, 'Values in Deviance Theory and Society', *BJS*, vol. XVI, 1975, pp. 296-309.
Young, J., 'New Directions in Subcultural Theory', in Rex, J. (ed.), *Approaches to Sociology*, Routledge & Kegan Paul, 1974, pp. 160-86.
Young, J., 'Working-Class Criminology', in Taylor, Young and Walton (eds.), op cit., 1975, pp. 63-94.

Education/language

Texts

Banks, Olive, *The Sociology of Education*, Batsford, 1968.
Demain, Jack, *Contemporary Theories in the Sociology of Education*, Macmillan, 1978.
Evetts, Julia, *The Sociology of Educational Ideas*, Routledge & Kegan Paul, 1973.
Mackinnon, D., *Language and Social Class*, Open University, 1977.
Musgrave, Peter, *The Sociology of Education*, Methuen, rev. edn., 1979.
Musgrove, Frank, *School and the Social Order*, Wiley, 1979.

Readers and edited collections

Archer, M.S. (ed.), *Students, University and Society. A Comparative Sociological Review*, Heinemann, 1972.
Bernbaum, Gerald (ed.), *Schooling in Decline*, Macmillan, 1979.
Brown, R.K., (ed.), *Knowledge, Education and Cultural Change*, Tavistock, 1973.
Cosin, B. (ed.), *Education: Structure and Society*, Penguin, 1972.
Craft, Maurice (ed.), *Family, Class and Education: A Reader*, Longman, 1970.
Dale, R. *et al.* (eds.), *School and Society*, Open University Press, 1971.
Dale, R. *et al.* (eds.), *Schooling and Society: A Sociological Reader*, Open University Press, 1976.
Eggleston, John (ed.), *Contemporary Research in the Sociology of Education*, Methuen, 1974.
Flude, M. and Ahier, J. (eds.), *Educability, Schools and Ideology*, Croom Helm, 1974.
Holly, D. (ed.), *Education and Domination*, Hutchinson, 1974.
Hopper, E. (ed.), *Readings in the Theory of Educational Systems*, Hutchinson, 1971.

Jenks, Cris. (ed.), *Rationality, Education and the Social Organisation of Knowledge*, Routledge & Kegan Paul, 1978.
Karabel, J. and Halsey, A.H. (eds.) *Power and Ideology in Education*, Oxford University Press, 1977.
Keddie, Nell (ed.), *Tinker, Tailor . . . The Myth of Cultural Deprivation*, Penguin, 1973.
Lister, I. (ed.), *Deschooling*, Cambridge University Press, 1974.
Musgrave, P.W. (ed.), *Sociology, History and Education: A Reader*, Methuen, 1970.
Raynor, J. and Harden, J. (eds.), *Equality and City Schools*, Routledge & Kegan Paul, 1973.
Silver, H. (ed.), *Equal Opportunity in Education: A Review in Social Class and Education*, Methuen, 1972.
Wilson, B. (ed.), *Education, Equality and Society*, Allen & Unwin, 1975.
Young, M.D.F. (ed.), *Knowledge and Control. New Directions in the Sociology of Education*, Collier-Macmillan, 1970.
Young, Michael and Whitty, Geoff, *Society, State and Schooling*, Falmer Press, 1977.

Specific studies and monographs

Abbott, Joan, *Student Life in a Class Society*, Pergamon, 1971.
Adlam, Diana S., *Code in Context*, Routledge & Kegan Paul, 1977.
Archer, M., *Social Origins of Education Systems*, Sage, 1974.
Banks, Olive and Finlayson, Douglas, *Success and Failure in the Secondary Schools*, Methuen, 1973.
Bellaby, Paul, *The Sociology of the Comprehensive School*, Methuen, 1976.
Bernbaum, Gerald, *Social Change and the Schools, 1918-1944*, Routledge & Kegan Paul, 1967.
Bernbaum, Gerald, *Knowledge and Ideology in the Sociology of Education*, Macmillan, 1977.
Bernstein, Basil (ed.), *Class, Codes and Control*, 3 vols, Routledge & Kegan Paul, 1971, 1973.
Bernstein, Basil and Brandis, Walter, *Primary Socialisation, Language and Education*, Routledge & Kegan Paul, 1970.
Blackstone, Tessa, *A Fair Start: The Provision of Pre-School Education*, Penguin, 1971.
Blackstone, Tessa, Giles, Kathleen, Hedley, Roger and Lewis, Wyn, *The Poverty of Education: A Study in the Politics of Opportunity*, Martin Robertson, 1975.
Byrne, Eileen, *Women and Education*, Tavistock, 1978.
Coard, B., *How the West Indian Child is Made Educationally Sub-Normal in British Schools*, New Beacon Books, 1971.

Corrigan, Paul, *Schooling the Smash Street Kids*, Macmillan, 1979.
Cotgrove, S.F., *Technical Education and Social Change*, Allen & Unwin, 1958.
Davie, R., Butter, N. and Goldstein, H., *From Birth to Seven*, Longman, 1972.
Davies, Brian, *Social Control and Education*, Methuen, 1976.
Deem, Rosemary, *Women and Schooling*, Routledge & Kegan Paul, 1979.
Douglas, J.W.B., *The Home and the School*, MacGibbon & Kee, 1964.
Douglas, J.W.B., Ross, J.M. and Simpson, H.R., *All our Future: A Longitudinal Study of Secondary Education*, Peter Davies, 1968.
Edward, V., *The West Indian Language Issue in British Schools*, Routledge & Kegan Paul, 1979.
Edwards, A.D., *Language in Culture and Class*, Heinemann, 1976.
Eggleston, John, *The Ecology of the School*, Methuen, 1977.
Eggleston, John, *The Sociology of the School Curriculum*, Routledge & Kegan Paul, 1977.
Entwistle, Harold, *Class, Culture and Education*, Methuen, 1978.
Flew, Anthony, *Sociology, Equality and Education*, Macmillan, 1976.
Ford, Julienne, *Social Class and the Comprehensive School*, Routledge & Kegan Paul, 1969.
Giles, Raymond, *The West Indian Experience in British Schools*, Heinemann, 1977.
Halsey, A.H. and Trow, Martin, *The British Academics*, Faber, 1971.
Hargreaves, David, *Social Relations in a Secondary School*, Routledge & Kegan Paul, 1967.
Hargreaves, David, *Interpersonal Relations and Education*, Routledge & Kegan Paul, 1972.
Hargreaves, David, *Deviance in Classrooms*, Routledge & Kegan Paul, 1975.
Holly, Douglas, *Beyond Curriculum*, Hart-Davis MacGibbon, 1973.
Holly, Douglas, *Society, Schools and Humanity*, Paladin, 1972.
Jackson, Brian, *Streaming: An Education System in Miniature*, Routledge & Kegan Paul, 1964.
Jackson, Brian and Marsden, Dennis, *Education and the Working Class*, Routledge & Kegan Paul, 1962.
Kearney, Hugh, *Scholars and Gentlemen: Universities and Society in Pre-Industrial Britain 1500-1700*, Faber, 1970.
Kelsall, R.K., Poole, Anne and Kuhn, Annette. *Graduates: The Sociology of an Elite*, Methuen, 1972.
Lacey, Colin, *Hightown Grammar*, Manchester University Press, 1970.
Lambert, Royston *et al.*, *The Chance of a Lifetime? A Study of Boarding Education*, Weidenfeld & Nicholson, 1975.
Lambert, R. and Millham, S.L., *The Hothouse Society*, Methuen, 1976.
Lawton, D., *Class, Culture and Curriculum*, Routledge & Kegan Paul, 1975.

Lawton, D., *Social Class, Language and Education*, Routledge & Kegan Paul, 1968.

Levitas, Maurice, *Marxist Perspectives in the Sociology of Education*, Routledge & Kegan Paul, 1974.

MacKinnon, Kenneth, *Language, Education and Social Processes in a Gaelic Community*, Routledge & Kegan Paul, 1977.

Moodie, Graeme C. and Eustace, Rowland, *Power and Authority in British Universities*, Allen & Unwin, 1974.

Nash, R., *Classrooms Observed*, Routledge & Kegan Paul, 1973.

Musgrove, Frank and Taylor, Philip, *Society and the Teacher's Role*, Routledge & Kegan Paul, 1969.

Robinson, Philip, *Education and Poverty*, Methuen, 1979.

Rosen, H., *Language and Class: A Critical Look at the Theories of Basil Bernstein*, Falling Walls Press, 1972.

Rulter, Michael, Maugham, Barbara, Mortimore, Peter and Ouston, Janet, *Fifteen Thousand Hours. Secondary Schools and their Effects on Children*, Open Books, 1979.

Sharp, R. and Green, A.G., *Education and Social Control*, Routledge & Kegan Paul, 1975.

Tapper, Ted and Salter, Brian, *Education and the Political Control*, Macmillan, 1978.

Tyler, William, *The Sociology of Educational Inequality*, Methuen, 1976.

Vaughan, M. and Archer, M.S., *Social Conflict and Educational Change in England and France, 1789-1898*, Cambridge University Press, 1971.

Wakeford, John, *The Cloistered Elite*, Macmillan, 1969.

Williamson, Bill, *Education, Social Structure and Development*, Macmillan, 1979.

Wiles, Paul, *Learning to Labour*, Saxon House, 1977.

Wootton, Anthony, *Dilemmas of Discourse*, Allen & Unwin, 1975.

Review papers and critiques

Archer, Margaret Scotford. 'Egalitarianism in English and French Educational Sociology', *EJS*, XI, 1, 1970. pp. 116-129.

Banks, Olive, 'The "New" Sociology of Education', *Forum*, autumn, 1974.

Bernstein, Basil, 'Sociology and the Sociology of Education: A Brief Account', in Rex, J. (ed.), *Approaches to Sociology*, Routledge & Kegan Paul, 1974, pp. 145-54.

Best, T., 'New Directions? Some Comments on the "New" Sociology of Education', *Radical Education*, no. 5, 1976.

Byrne, D.S. and Williamson, W., 'The Myth of the Restricted Code', *Durham University Working Papers in Sociology*, no. 1, n.d.

Demaine, Jack, 'On the New Sociology of Education: A Critique of M.F.D. Young and the Radical Attack on the Politics of Educational Knowledge', *Economy and Society*, vol. 6, no. 2, 1977, pp. 111-44.

Evetts, Julia, 'Equality of Educational Opportunity: The Recent History of a Concept', *BJS*, vol. XXI, no. 4, 1970, pp. 425-30.

Floud, J. and Halsey, A.H., 'The Sociology of Education', *Current Sociology*, vol. VII, no. 3, 1958.

Garbutt, D., 'The "New" Sociology of Education', *Education for Teaching*, autumn, 1972.

Hoyle, E., 'Social Theories of Education in Contemporary Britain', *Social Science Information*, vol. 9, no. 4, 1969.

Whitty, Geoff, 'Sociology and the Problem of Radical Educational Change: Notes towards a Reconceptualisation of the "New" Sociology of Education', in Young and Whitty, op. cit., 1977, pp. 26-58.

Williamson, Bill, 'Continuities and Discontinuities in the Sociology of Education', in Flude and Ahier, op. cit., 1974.

Health and medicine

Texts

Robinson, David, *Patients, Practitioners and Medical Care*, Heinemann, 1973.

Readers and edited collections

Cox, Caroline and Mead, Adrian (eds.), *A Sociology of Medical Practice*, Collier-Macmillan, 1975.

Dingwall, R., Heath, C., Reid, M. and Stacey, M (eds.), *Health Care and Health Knowledge*, Croom Helm, 1977.

Halmos, P. (ed.), *Sociology and Medicine*, Sociological Review Monograph no. 5, 1962.

Stacey, M. (ed.), *The Sociology of the NHS*, Sociological Review Monograph no. 22, 1976.

Stacey, M., Reid, M., Heath, C. and Dingwall, R. (eds.), *Health and the Division of Labour*, Croom Helm, 1977.

Tuckett, D. and Kaufert, J.M. (eds.), *Basic Readings in Medical Sociology*, Tavistock, 1978.

Tuckett, David, *An Introduction to Medical Sociology*, Tavistock, 1976.

Wadsworth, Michael and Robinson, D., *Studies in Everyday Medical Life*, Martin Robertson, 1976.

Woodward, John and Richards, David (eds.), *Health Care and Popular*

Medicine in Nineteenth Century England, Croom Helm, 1977.
Wallis, Roy and Morley, Peter (eds.), *Marginal Medicine*, Peter Owen, 1976.

Specific studies and monographs

Brown, G. and Harris, T., *The Social Origins of Depression*, Tavistock, 1978.
Cartwright, Ann, *The Dignity of Labour? A Study of Child-bearing and Induction*, Tavistock, 1979.
Davis, A. and Horobin, G., *Medical Encounters*, Croom Helm, 1977.
Dingwall, R., *The Social Organisation of Health Visitor Training*, Croom Helm, 1977.
Dennison, J., *Midwives and Medical Men: A History of Inter-Professional Rivalries and Women's Rights*, Heinemann, 1977.
Hall, J. and Stacey, M. (eds.), *Beyond Separation: Further Studies of Children in Hospital*,
Horobin, G., *Experience with Abortion' A Case Study of North-East Scotland*, Cambridge University Press, 1973.
Klein, R., *Complaints Against Doctors: A Study in Professional Accountability*, Charles Knight, 1973.
Leeson, Joyce and Gray, Judith, *Women and Medicine*, Tavistock, 1978.
MacIntyre, Sally, *Single and Pregnant*, Croom Helm, 1977.
O'Connor, J., *The Young Drinkers: A Cross-National Study of Social and Cultural Influences*, Tavistock, 1978.
Parry, N. and J., *The Rise of the Medical Profession*, Croom Helm, 1976.
Plant, Martin, *Drinking Careers*, Tavistock, 1979.
Raffel, Stanley, *Matters of Fact. A Sociological Inquiry*, Routledge & Kegan Paul, 1979.
Robinson, David, *The Process of Becoming Ill*, Routledge & Kegan Paul, 1971.
Stimson, G. and Webb, B., *Going to See the Doctor*, Routledge & Kegan Paul, 1975.
Voysey, Margaret, *A Constant Burden: The Reconstitution of Family Life*, Routledge & Kegan Paul, 1975.

Review papers and critiques

Butler, J.R., 'Sociology and Medical Education', *SR*, vol. 17, no. 1, 1969, pp. 87-96.
Frankenberg, Ronald, 'Functionalism and After? Theory and Developments in Social Science Applied to the Health Field', *International Journal of Health Services*, no. 4, 1974.
Gerhardt, U., 'The Parsonian Paradigm and the Identity of Medical Sociology', *SR*, vol. 27, no. 2, 1979, pp. 229-51.
Gold, Margaret, 'A Crisis of Identity: The Case of Medical Sociology',

Journal of Health and Social Behaviour, no. 18, 1977, pp. 160-8.
Johnson, Malcolm, 'Medical Sociology and Sociological Theory', *Social Science and Medicine*, no. 9, 1975, pp. 227-32.
Johnson, Malcolm (ed.), 'Medical Sociology in Britain: A Register of Research and Teaching', *Medical Group of British Sociological Association*, 1974.
Murcott, Anne, 'Blind Alleys and Blinkers: The Scope of Medical Sociology', *Scottish Journal of Sociology*, vol. 1, no. 2, 1977, pp. 155-71.
Reid, Margaret, 'The Development of Medical Sociology in Britain', *University of Glasgow Discussion Papers in Social Research*, no. 13, 1975/6.
Stacey, Margaret and Homans, Hilary, 'The Sociology of Health and Illness: Its Present State, Future Prospects and Potential for Health Research', *Sociology*, vol. 12, no. 2, 1978, pp. 280-307.

History of sociology and classical theorists

Texts

Fletcher, Ronald, *The Making of Sociology* (2 vols), Nelson, 1972.
Giddens, Anthony, *Capitalism and Modern Social Theory: An Analysis of the Writings of Marx, Durkheim and Weber*, Cambridge University Press, 1971.
Hawthorn, Geoffrey, *Enlightenment and Despair. A History of Sociology*, Heinemann, 1976.
Keat, Russell and Urry, John, *Social Theory as Science*, Routledge & Kegan Paul, 1975.
Poggi, G., *Images of Society. Essays on the Sociological Theories of Tocqueville, Marx and Durkheim*, Oxford University Press, 1973.
Sahay, Arun, *Sociological Analysis*, Routledge & Kegan Paul, 1972.

Readers and edited collections

Andreski, S. (ed.), *Auguste Comte*, Croom Helm, 1974.
Andreski, S. (ed.), *Herbert Spencer*, Michael Joseph, 1971.
Bottomore, Tom (ed), *Karl Marx*, Blackwell, 1979.
Bottomore, Tom and Nisbet, Robert (eds.), *A History of Sociological Analysis*, Heinemann, 1979.
Bottomore, T.B. and Rubel, Maxmilien, *Karl Marx. Selected Writings in Sociology and Social Philosophy*, Penguin, 1963.
Eldridge, J.E.T. (ed.), *Max Weber: The Interpretation of Social Reality*, Nelson, 1972.
Finer, S.E. (ed.), *Vilfredo Pareto. Sociological Writings*, Pall Mall Press, 1966.
Fletcher, R. (ed.), *John Stuart Mill: A Logical Critique of Sociology*, Nelson, 1973.

Giddens, Anthony (ed.), *Positivism and Sociology*, Heinemann, 1974.
Giddens, Anthony (ed.), *Emile Durkheim: Selected Writings*, Cambridge University Press, 1972.
Jordan, Z.A. (ed.), *Karl Marx: Economy, Class and Social Revolution*, Nelson, 1972.
Runciman, W. (ed.), *Max Weber. Selections in Translation*, Cambridge University Press, 1978.
Sahay, A. (ed.), *Max Weber and Modern Sociology*, Routledge & Kegan Paul, 1971.
Thompson, Kenneth A. (ed.), *Auguste Comte*, Nelson, 1976.

Specific studies and monographs
Abrams, Philip, *The Origins and Growth of British Sociology, 1834-1914*, University of Chicago Press, 1968.
Beetham, David, *Max Weber and the Critique of Modern Politics*, Allen & Unwin, 1974.
Bottomore, Tom, *Marxist Sociology*, Macmillan, 1975.
Burrow, J.W., *Evolution and Society: A Study in Victorian Social Theory*, Cambridge University Press, 1966.
Dahrendorf, R., *Essays in the Theory of Society*, Routledge & Kegan Paul, 1968.
Giddens, Anthony, *Durkheim*, Fontana, 1978.
Giddens, Anthony, *Politics and Sociology in the Thought of Max Weber*, Macmillan, 1972.
Hirst, P.Q., *Durkheim, Bernard and Epistemology*, Routledge & Kegan Paul, 1975.
Lukes, Steven, *Emile Durkheim: His Life and Work: A Historical and Critical Study*, Allen Lane, 1973.
MacRae, D.G., *Max Weber*, Fontana, 1973.
Peel, J.D.Y., *Herbert Spencer: The Evolution of a Sociologist*, Heinemann, 1971.
Rex, John, *Key Problems of Sociological Theory*, Routledge & Kegan Paul, 1961.
Runciman, W.G., *Social Science and Political Theory*, Cambridge University Press, 1963.
Sayer, Derek, *Marx's Method*, Harvester Press, 1979.
Simey, T.S. and M.B., *Charles Booth: Social Scientist*, Oxford University Press, 1960.
Torrance, John, *Estrangement, Alienation and Exploitation: A Sociological Approach to Historical Materialism*, Macmillan, 1977.

Review papers and critiques
Bryant, Christopher G.A., 'Positivism Reconsidered', *SR*, vol. 23, no. 2, 1975, pp. 95-106.
Collison, Peter and Webber, Susan, 'British Sociology 1950-70: A Journal Analysis', *SR*, vol. 19, no. 4, 1971, pp. 521-42.

Farmer, Mary E., 'The Positivist Movement and the Development of English Sociology', *SR*, vol. 15, no. 1, 1967, pp. 5-20.

Giddens, Anthony, 'Recent Works on the History of Social Thought', *EJS*, no. 11, 1970, pp. 130-54.

Hall, John A., 'The Curious Case of the English Intelligentsia', *BJS*, vol. XXX, no. 3, 1979, pp. 291-306.

Halliday, R.J., 'The Sociological Movement, the Sociological Society and the Genesis of Academic Sociology in Britain', *SR*, vol. 16, no. 3, 1968, pp. 377-98.

Hawthorn, Geoffrey, 'The History of Sociology', *Sociology*, vol. 6, no. 2, 1972, pp. 279-85.

Lukes, Steven, 'On the History of Sociological Thought', *BJS*, vol. XVII, no. 2, 1966, pp. 198-203.

MacRae, D.G., 'Towards a History of Sociology: A Discussion Paper', in Archer, M.S. (ed.), *Current Research in Sociology*, Mouton, 1974.

Peel, J.D.Y., 'Two Cheers for Empiricism; or What is the Relevance of the History of Sociology to Current Practice?', *Sociology*, vol. 12, no. 2, 1979, pp. 346-59.

Rex, J., 'Social Structure and Humanistic Sociology: the Legacy of the Classical European Tradition', in Rex, J., *Approaches to Sociology*, 1974, pp. 187-204.

Swingewood, Alan, 'Origins of Sociology: The Case of Scottish Enlightenment', *BJS*, vol XXI, no. 2, 1970, pp. 164-80.

Swingewood, Alan, 'Comte, Marx and Political Economy', *SR*, vol. 18, no. 3, 1970, pp. 335-49.

Torrance, John, 'Max Weber: Methods and the Man', *EJS*, vol. XV, 1974, pp. 127-65.

Ziff, Maurice L., 'From Mill to Hobhouse: the Radical Progressive Origins of British Sociology', *University of Leeds Occasional Papers in Sociology*, no. 7, 1978.

Knowledge/science

Texts

Hamilton, Peter, *Knowledge and Social Structure*, Routledge & Kegan Paul, 1974.

Readers and edited collections

Barnes, Barry (ed.), *Sociology of Science*, Penguin, 1972.

Blackburn, R. (ed.), *Ideology in Social Sciences*, Fontana, 1972.

Halmos, P. (ed.), *The Sociology of Science*, Sociological Review Monograph no. 18, 1972.

Horton, Robin and Finnegan, Ruth (eds.), *Modes of Thought*, Faber, 1973.

Wallis, Roy (ed.), *On the Margins of Science: The Social Construction of Rejected Knowledge*, Sociological Review Monograph no. 27, 1979.

Wilson, Bryan (ed.), *Rationality*, Blackwell, 1970.

Specific studies and monographs

Barnes, Barry, *Scientific Knowledge and Sociological Theory*, Routledge & Kegan Paul, 1974.

Barnes, Barry, *Interests and the Growth of Knowledge*, Routlledge & Kegan Paul, 1978.

Bloor, David, *Knowledge and Social Imagery*, Routledge & Kegan Paul, 1976.

Cotgrove, Stephen and Box, Steven, *Science, Industry and Society: Studies in the Sociology of Science*, Allen & Unwin, 1970.

Gellner, E., *Legitimation of Belief*, Cambridge University Press, 1974.

Harris, N., *Beliefs in Society*, Penguin, 1971.

Jarvie, I.C., *Concepts and Society*, Routledge & Kegan Paul, 1972.

Madge, Charles, *Society in the Mind: Elements of Social Eidos*, Faber 1964.

Mulkay, M.J., *The Social Process of Innovation*, Macmillan, 1972.

Rose, H. and Rose, S., *Science and Society*, Allen & Unwin, 1969.

Sklair, Leslie, *Organised Knowledge*, Paladin, 1973.

Stark, W., *The Sociology of Knowledge*, Routledge & Kegan Paul, 1968.

Review papers and critiques

Barnes, S.B. and Dolby, R.G.A., 'The Scientific Ethos: A Deviant Viewpoint', *EJS*, vol. 11, no. 1, 1979, pp. 3-25.

Barnes, S.B., 'Sociological Explanation and Natural Sciences: A Kuhnian Re-appraisal', *EJS*, vol. 13, no. 2, 1972, pp. 371-93.

Cotgrove, S., 'The Sociology of Science and Technology', *BJS*, vol. XXI, no. 1, 1970, pp. 1-15.

Elias, Norbert, 'Sociology of Knowledge: New Perspectives, Part I, *Sociology*, vol. 5, no. 2, 1971, pp. 149-68; Part II, *Sociology*, vol. 5, no. 3, 1971, pp. 353-70.

Elias, Norbert, 'Theory of Science and History of Science', *Economy and Society*, vol. 1, no. 2, 1972, pp. 117-33.

Law, John and French, David, ''Normative and Interpretive Sociologies of Science', *SR*, vol. 22, no. 4, 1974, pp. 581-95.

Lovell, Terry, 'Weber, Goldmann and the Sociology of Beliefs', *EJS*, vol. XIV, no. 2, 1973, pp. 304-23.

Martin, David, 'The Sociology of Knowledge and the Nature of Social Knowledge', *BJS*, vol. XIX, no. 3, 1968, pp. 334-42.

Urry, John, 'Thomas S. Kuhn as a Sociologist of Knowledge', *BJS*, vol. XXIV, no. 4, 1973, pp. 462-73.

Leisure and sport

Texts

Parker, Stanley, *The Sociology of Leisure*, Allen & Unwin, 1977.

Parker, Stanley, *The Future of Work and Leisure*, MacGibbon & Kee, 1971.

Roberts, Kenneth, *Leisure*, Longmans, 1970.

Roberts, Kenneth, *Contemporary Society and the Growth of Leisure*, Longmans, 1979.

Readers and edited collections

Dunning, Eric (ed.), *The Sociology of Sport*, Cass, 1971.

Smith, Michael *et al.* (eds.), *Leisure and Society in Britain*, Penguin, 1972.

Specific studies and monographs

Dunning, Eric and Sheard, Kenneth, *Barbarians, Gentlemen and Players: A Sociological Study of the Development of Rugby Football*, Martin Robertson, 1974.

Rappoport, Rhona and Rappoport, Robert, *Leisure and the Family Life Cycle*, Routledge & Kegan Paul, 1975.

Salamaan, Graeme, *Community and Occupation: an Exploration of Work/Leisure Relationships*, Cambridge University Press, 1974.

Review papers and critiques

Critcher, Charles and Willis, Paul, 'Women in Sport', *CS*, no. 5, 1974, pp. 1-26.

Parker, Stanley, 'The Sociology of Leisure: Progress and Problems', *BJS*, vol. XXVI, no. 1, 1975, pp. 91-101.

Giddens, A., 'Notes on the Concepts of Play and Leisure', *SR*, no. 12, 1964, pp. 73-89.

Rappoport, R. and R.E., 'Four Themes in the Sociology of Leisure', *BJS*, vol. XXV, no. 1, 1974, pp. 215-29.

Mass media

Texts

Chaney, David, *Processes of Mass Communication*, Macmillan, 1972.

Gallagher, M. and Murdock, G., *Media Organisations*, Open University, 1977.

Golding, P., *The Mass Media*, Longmans, 1974.

Hood, Stuart, *The Mass Media*, Macmillan, 1972.

McQuail, D., *Towards a Sociology of Mass Communications*, Collier-Macmillan, 1969.

McQuail, D., *Communications*, Longmans, 1975.

Readers and edited collections
Beharrell, Peter and Philo, Greg, *Trade Unions and the Media*, Macmillan, 1977.
Blumler, Jay and Katz, Elihu, *the Uses of Mass Communications*, Sage, 1974.
Cohen, Stanley and Young, Jock (eds.), *The Manufacture of News: Social Problems, Deviancy and the Mass Media*, Constable, 1973.
Curran, James (ed.), *The British Press*, Macmillan, 1978.
Curran, James, Gurevitch, Michael and Woollacott, Janet (eds.), *Mass Communication and Society*, Edward Arnold, 1977.
Halmos, P. (ed.), *The Sociology of Mass Media Communicators*, Sociological Review Monograph, no. 13, 1969.
McQuail, D. (ed.), *Sociology of Mass Communications*, Penguin, 1972.
Tunstall, J. (ed.), *Media Sociology*, Constable, 1970.

Specific studies and monographs
Belson, W.A., *The Impact of Television*, Crosby Lockwood, 1967.
Blumler, J., Gurevitch, M. and Ives, J., *The Challenge of Election Broadcasting*, Leeds University Press, 1978.
Blumler, J. and McQuail, D., *Television in Politics*, Faber, 1968.
Brundsdon, Charlotte and Morley, David, *Everyday Television: 'Nationwide'*, BFI Television Monograph, no. 10, 1978.
Burns, Tom, *The BBC: Public Institution and Private World*, Macmillan, 1978.
Cleverley, Graham, *The Fleet Street Disaster*, Constable, 197 .
Collins, Richard, *Television News*, BFI Television Monograph, no. 5, 1976.
Dunn, Gwen, *The Box in the Corner. Television and the Under-Fives*, Macmillan, 1977.
Elliott, P., *The Making of a Television Series*, Constable, 1972.
Fiske, John and Hartley, John, *Reading Television*, Methuen, 1978.
Garnham, Nicholas, *Structures of Television*, BFI Television Monograph no. 1, rev. edn. 1978.
Glasgow University Media Group, *Bad News*, Routledge & Kegan Paul, 1976.
Golding, Peter and Elliott, Philip, *Making the News*, Longmans, 1979.
Halloran, J., Elliott, P. and Murdock, G., *Demonstrations and Communication: A Case Study*, Penguin, 1970.
Hartmann, Paul and Husband, Charles, *Racism and the Mass Media: A Study of the Role of the Mass Media in the Formation of White Beliefs and Attitudes in Britain*, Davis-Poynter, 1974.
Hoggart, Richard, *Speaking to Each Other*, Chatto & Windus, 1970.
Jarvie, I., *Towards a Sociology of the Cinema*, Routledge & Kegan Paul, 1970.
Murphy, David, *The Silent Watchdog: The Press in Local Politics*,

Constable, 1976.
Noble, Grant, *Children in Front of the Small Screen*, Constable, 1975.
Piepe, A., Emerson, M. and Lannon, J. *Television and the Working Class*, Saxon House, 1975.
Schlesinger, Philip, *Putting 'Reality' Together*, Constable, 1978.
Seymore-Ure, C., *The Political Impact of the Mass Media*, Constable, 1974.
Smith, Anthony, *The Shadow in the Cave. The Broadcaster, the Audience and the State*, Allen & Unwin, 1973.
Smith, Anthony, *The Politics of Information*, Macmillan, 1978.
Tracey, M., *The Production of Political Television*, Routledge & Kegan Paul, 1978.
Tunstall, J., *The Westminster Lobby Correspondents*, Routledge & Kegan Paul, 1970.
Tunstall, J., *Journalists at Work*, Constable, 1971.
Tunstall, J., *The Media are American*, Constable, 1977.
Whale, J., *The Half-Shut Eye: Television and Politics in Britain and America*, Macmillan, 1967.
Whale, J., *The Politics of the Media*, Fontana, 1977.
Williams, R., *The Long Revolution*, Chatto & Windus, 1961.
Williams, R., *Communications*, Penguin, 1971.
Williams, R., *Television: Technology and Cultural Form*, Fontana, 1974.

Review papers and critiques

Agassi, Judith, 'The Worker and the Media', *EJS*, no. 11, 1970, pp. 26-66.
Ellis, Connie, 'Current British Research on Mass Media and Mass Communication', Centre for Mass Communication Research, University of Leicester, 1976.
Golding, P. and Murdock, G., 'Theories of Communication and Theories of Society', *Communications Research*, vol. 5, no. 3, 1978, pp. 339-56.
Hall, Stuart, 'Culture, the Media and the "Ideological Effect" ', in Curran, J. *et al.* (eds.), 1977, pp. 315-48.
Hall, Stuart, 'Encoding and Decoding the TV Discourse', *Culture and Education*, Council of Europe, 1974.
Halloran, J., 'Mass Communication Research: State of the Art — Where We are and Where We Should be Going', in International Association for Mass Communication Research, *Mass Media and Man's View of Society*, Adams Bros & Shardlow, 1978, pp. 71-21.
Halloran, J. and Gurevitch, M. (eds.), *Mass Communication Research*, Kavanagh & Sons, 1971.
Katz, Elihu, *Social Research on Broadcasting: Proposals for Further Development*, BBC, 1977.
Williams, R., 'Communications as Cultural Science', *Journal of*

Communication, vol. 23, no. 4, 1974, pp. 17-25.
Williams, R., 'Base and Superstructure in Marxist Cultural Theory', *New Left Review*, no. 82, 1973, pp. 3-16.

Methods and problems of research

Texts

Easthope, G., *History of Social Research Methods*, Longmans, 1974.
Hughes, John A., *Sociological Analysis: Methods of Discovery*, Nelson, 1976.
Moser, C. and Kalton, G., *Survey Methods in Social Investigation*, Heinemann, 1971.
Stacey, Margaret, *Methods of Social Research*, Pergamon, 1967.
Wakeford, John, *The Strategy of Social Enquiry*, Macmillan, 1968.

Readers and edited collections

Archer, Margaret, S. (ed.), *Current Research in Sociology*, Mouton, 1974.
Bell, Colin and Newby, Howard (eds.), *Doing Sociological Research*, Allen & Unwin, 1977.
Bulmer, M. (ed.), *Sociological Research Methods*, Macmillan, 1977.
Bulmer, M. (ed.), *Social Policy Research*, Macmillan, 1978.
Bulmer, M. (ed.), *Censures, Surveys and Privacy*, Macmillan, 1979.
Gittus, Elizabeth (ed.), *Key Variables in Sociological Research*, Heinemann, 1972.
Halmos, P. (ed.), *The Sociology of Sociology*, SR Monograph no. 11, 1970.
Rex, John (ed.), *Approaches to Sociology: An Introduction to Major Trends in British Sociology*, Routledge & Kegan Paul, 1975.
Shipman, Martin (ed.), *The Organisation and Impact of Social Research*, Routledge & Kegan Paul, 1976.
Stacey, Margaret (ed.), *Comparability in Social Research*, Longmans, 1973.
Turner, Roy (ed.), *Ethnomethodology*, Penguin, 1974.

Specific studies and monographs

Allen, V.L., *Social Analysis*, Longmans, 1975.
Andreski, S., *Social Sciences as Sorcery*, Penguin, 1975.
Baldamus, W., *The Structure of Sociological Inference*, Martin Robertson, 1976.
Barnes, J.A., *Who Should Know What?*, Penguin, 1979.
Bryant, Christopher G.A., *Sociology in Action*, Allen & Unwin, 1976.
Cherns, Albert, *Using the Social Sciences*, Routledge & Kegan Paul, 1979.
Coxon, Anthony P.M. and Jones, Charles L., *Measurement and Mean-*

ings, Techniques and Methods of Studying Occupational Cognition, Macmillan, 1979.

Fletcher, Colin, *Beneath the Surface. An Account of Three Styles of Social Research*, Routledge & Kegan Paul, 1974.

Ford, Julienne, *Paradigms and Fairy Tales* (2 vols), Routledge & Kegan Paul, 1975.

Gellner, E., *Cause and Meaning in the Social Sciences*, Routledge & Kegan Paul, 1973.

Giddens, Anthony, *New Rules of Sociological Method*, Hutchinson, 1977.

Glass, David, *Numbering the People*, Saxon House, 1973.

Hindess, Barry, *The Use of Official Statistics in Sociology. A Critique of Positivism and Ethnomethodology*, Macmillan, 1973.

Hindess, Barry, *Philosophy, Methodology and the Social Sciences*, Harvester Press, 1977.

Krausz, Ernest, *Sociology in Britain: A Survey of Research*, Batsford, 1969.

Lessnoff, Michael, *The Structure of Social Science: a Philosophical Introduction*, Allen & Unwin, 1974.

Outhwaite, William, *Understanding Social Life: the Method Called Verstehen*, Heinemann, 1972.

Platt, Jennifer, *Realities of Social Research. An Empirical Study of British Sociologists*, Chatto & Windus, 1976.

Platt, Jennifer, *Social Research in Bethnal Green. An Evaluation of the Work of the Institute of Community Studies*, Macmillan, 1971.

Rein, Martin, *Social Science and Social Policy*, Penguin, 1976.

Rex, John, *Discovering Sociology: Studies in Sociological Theory and Method*, Routledge & Kegan Paul, 1973.

Runciman, W.G., *Sociology in its Place and Other Essays*, Cambridge University Press, 1970.

Sandywell, Barry *et al.*, *Problems of Reflexivity and Dialectics in Sociological Inquiry*, Routledge & Kegan Paul, 1976.

Simey, T.E., *Social Science and Social Purpose*, Constable, 1968.

Townsend, Peter, *Sociology and Social Policy*, Penguin, 1976.

Research papers and critiques

Baldamus, W., 'Sociological Trends', *BJS*, vol. XXV, no. 3, 1974, pp. 378-83.

Barnes, S.B., 'Sociological Explanation and Natural Sciences: a Kuhnian Re-appraisal', *EJS*, vol. 13, no. 2, 1972, pp. 371-93.

Bechofer, Frank, 'Current Approaches to Empirical Research: Some Central Ideas', in Rex, J. (ed.), *Approaches to Sociology*, 1974, pp. 70-91.

Bulmer, Martin, 'Social Survey Research and Postgraduate Training in Sociological Method', *Sociology*, vol. 6, no. 2, 1972, pp. 267-74.

Bulmer, Martin, 'Some Neglected Problems of Sociological Research',

BJS, vol. XXV, no. 2, 1974, pp. 244-51.
Bulmer, Martin, 'Problems, Theories and Methods in Sociology', *Durham University Working Papers in Sociology*, no. 7, 1974.
Burns, Tom, 'Sociological Explanation', *BJS*, vol. XVIII, no. 4, 1967, pp. 353-69.
Carter, M.P., 'Report on a Survey of Sociological Research in Britain', *SR*, vol. 16, no. 1, 1968, pp. 5-40.
Cohen, Percy, 'Models', *BJS*, vol XVII, no. 1, 1966, pp. 70-8.
Cohen, Percy, 'Social Attitudes and Sociological Inquiry', *BJS*, vol. VXII, no. 4, 1966, 341-52.
Coulter, Jeff, 'Decontextualised Meanings: Current Approaches to *Verstehende* Investigations', *SR*, vol. 19, no. 3, 1971, pp. 301-23.
Goldthorpe, John H., 'A Revolution in Sociology?' *Sociology*, vol. 7, no. 7, 1973, pp. 449-62.
McSweeney, Bill, 'Meaning, Context and Situation', *EJS*, vol. XIV, no. 1, 1973, pp. 137-53.
Platt, Jennifer, 'Survey Data and Social Policy', *BJS*, vol. XXIII, no. 1, 1972, pp. 77-92.
Sayer, Derek, 'Method and Dogma in Historical Materialism', *SR*, vol. 23, no. 4, 1975, pp. 779-810.
Town, Stephen W., 'Action Research and Social Policy: Some Recent British Experiences', *SR*, vol. 21, no. 4, 1973, pp. 573-96.
Wilkinson, Philip and Grace, Clive, 'Reforms as Revolutions', *Sociology*, vol. 9, no. 3, 1975, pp. 396-418.

Military

Specific studies and monographs

Finer, S., *The Man on Horseback: The Role of the Military in Politics*, Pall Mall, 1962.

Review papers and critiques

Abrams, Philip, 'Armed Forces and Society: Problems of Alienation', in Wolfe, J.N. and Erickson, J. (eds.), *The Armed Services and Society, Alienation, Management and Integration*, Edinburgh University Press, 1970.
Ashworth, A.E., 'The Sociology of Trench Warfare, 1914-1918', *BJS*, vol. XIX, no. 4, 1968, pp. 407-23.
Money, W.J., 'Do We Need a New Model Army?', *SR*, vol. 23, no. 3, 1975, pp. 577-605.
Otley, C.B., 'The Educational Background of British Army Officers', *Sociology*, vol. 7, no. 2, 1973, pp. 191-209.
Otley, C.B., 'The Social Origins of British Army Officers', *SR*, vol. 18, no. 2, 1970, pp. 213-39.

Organisations, industrial relations, professions and economic life

Texts

Banks, J.A., *Trade Unionism*, Collier-Macmillan, 1974.

Burrell, Gibson and Morgan, Gareth., *Sociological Paradigms and Organisational Analysis*, Heinemann, 1979.

Clegg, H.A., *The System of Industrial Relations in Great Britain*, rev. edn., Blackwell, 1979.

Crouch, C.J. *The Politics of Industrial Relations*, Fontana, 1979.

Crouch, C.J. (ed.), *The Resurgence of Class Conflict in Western Europe since 1968*, Macmillan, 1978.

Crouch, Colin (ed.), *State and Economy in Contemporary Capitalism*, Croom Helm, 1979.

Eldridge, J.E.T., *Sociology and Industrial Life*, Nelson, 1973.

Eldridge, J.E.T. and Crombie, A.D. *A Sociology of Organisations*, Allen & Unwin, 1974.

Elliott, Philip, *The Sociology of the Professions*, Macmillan, 1972.

Fox, A., *A Sociology of Work in Industry*, Collier-Macmillan, 1971.

Fox, A., *Beyond Contract: Work, Power and Trust Relations*, Faber, 1974.

Hindess, Barry (ed.), *Sociological Theories of the Economy*, Macmillan, 1977.

Hyman, R., *Industrial Relations, a Marxist Introduction*, Macmillan, 1975.

Jackson, Michael P., *Industrial Relations, A Text Book*, Croom Helm, 1977.

Johnson, T., *Professions and Power*, Macmillan, 1972.

Mouzelis, N.P., *Organisations and Bureaucracy: An Analysis of Modern Theories*, rev. edn, Routledge & Kegan Paul, 1975.

Parker, S.R., Brown, R.K., Child, J. and Smith, M.A., *The Sociology of Industry*, rev. edn, Allen & Unwin, 1977.

Salaman, Graeme, *Work Organisations, Resistance and Control*, Longmans, 1979.

Silverman, D., *The Theory of Organisations*, Heinemann, 1970.

Turner, Barry A., *Exploring the Industrial Sub-Culture*, Macmillan, 1971.

Readers and edited collections

Abell, Peter (ed.), *Organisations as Bargaining and Influence Systems*, Heinemann, 1975.

Blackburn, R. and Cockburn, A. (eds.), *The Incompatibles: Trade Union Militancy and the Consensus*, Penguin, 1967.

Brannen, P. (ed.), *Entering the World of Work: Some Sociological Perspectives*, Department of Employment, HMSO, 1975.

Bulmer, Martin (ed.), *Mining and Social Change*, Croom Helm, 1977.

Burns, Tom (ed.), *Industrial Man*, Penguin, 1969.

Child, John (ed.), *Man and Organisation*, Allen & Unwin, 1973.
Clarke, Tom and Clements, Laurie (eds.), *Trade Unions under Capitalism*, Fontana, 1977.
Clegg, Stewart and Dunkerley, David (eds.), *Critical Issues in Organisations*, Routledge & Kegan Paul, 1977.
Esland, Geoff, Salaman, Graeme and Speakman, Mary-Ann (eds.), *People and Work*, Open University Press, 1975.
Fraser, Ronald (ed.), *Work: Twenty Personal Accounts*, Penguin, 1968.
Jackson, John A. (ed.), *Professions and Professionalisation*, Cambridge University Press, 1970.
Salaman, Graeme and Thompson, Kenneth (eds.), *People and Organisations*, Longmans, 1973.
Warner, Malcolm (ed.), *The Sociology of the Workplace*, Allen & Unwin, 1973.
Weir, D.T.H. (ed.), *Men and Work in Modern Britain*, Fontana, 1973.
Williams, W.M. (ed.), *Occupational Choice*, Allen & Unwin, 1974.
Woodward, Joan (ed.), *Industrial Organisations: Behaviour and Control*, Oxford University Press, 1970.

Specific studies and monographs
Albrow, Martin, *Bureaucracy*, Macmillan, 1970.
Allen, V.L., *Militant Trade Unionism*, Merlin Press, 1966.
Allen, V.L., *The Sociology of Industrial Relations*, Longmans, 1971.
Anthony, P.D., *The Ideology of Work*, Tavistock, 1977.
Ashton, D.N. and Field, David, *Young Workers*, Hutchinson, 1976.
Bain, G.S., *The Growth of White Collar Trade Unionism*, Clarendon Press, 1970.
Baldamus, W., *Efficiency and Effort*, Tavistock, 1961.
Banks, J., *Marxist Sociology in Action: A Sociological Critique of the Marxist Approach to Industrial Relations*, Faber, 1970.
Batstone, Eric, Boraston, Ian and Frankel, Stephen, *Shop Stewards in Action: The Organisation of Workplace Conflict and Accommodation*, Blackwell, 1977.
Batstone, Eric, Boraston, Ian and Frankel, Stephen, *The Social Organization of Strikes*, Blackwell, 1978.
Beynon, Huw, *Working for Ford*, Allen Lane, 1973.
Beynon, Huw and Blackburn, R., *Perceptions of Work: Variations Within a Factory*, Cambridge University Press, 1972.
Beynon, Huw and Wainwright, Hilary, *The Workers' Report on Vickers*, Pluto Press, 1979.
Blackburn, R.M., *Union Character and Social Class*, Batsford, 1968.
Blackburn, R.M. and Mann, M., *Working Class in the Labour Market*, Macmillan, 1979.
Boraston, Ian, Clegg, H.A. and Rimmer, Malcolm, *Work-place and Union: A Study of Local Relationships in Fourteen Unions*, Heinemann, 1975.

Bowen, Peter, *Social Control in Industrial Organisations*, Routledge & Kegan Paul, 1976.

Brannen, P., Batstone, E., Fatchett, D. and White, P., *The Worker Directors*, Hutchinson, 1975.

Brown, G., *Sabotage*, Spokesman Books, 1977.

Burns, Tom and Stalker, G.M., *The Management of Innovation*, Tavistock, 1961.

Carter, M.P., *Into Work*, Penguin, 1966.

Child, J., *The Business Enterprise in Modern Industrial Society*, Collier-Macmillan, 1969.

Clegg, H.A., *Trade Unionism under Collective Bargaining: A Theory Based on a Comparison of Six Countries*, Blackwell, 1976.

Clegg, Stewart, *Power, Rule and Domination*, Routledge & Kegan Paul, 1975.

Clegg, Stewart, *The Theory of Power and Organisations*, Routledge & Kegan Paul, 1979.

Cotgrove, Stephen, Dunham, Jack and Vamplew, Clive, *The Nylon Spinners*, Allen & Unwin, 1971.

Crouch, C.J., *Class Conflict and the Industrial Relations Crisis*, Heinemann, 1977.

Cunnison, Sheila, *Wages and Work Allocation*, Tavistock, 1966.

Dore, Ronald, *British Factory — Japanese Factory: The Origins of National Diversity in Industrial Relations*, Allen & Unwin, 1973.

Dunkerley, David, *The Foreman: Aspects of Task and Structure*, Routledge & Kegan Paul, 1975.

Edelstein, David J. and Warner, Malcolm, *Comparative Union Democracy*, Allen & Unwin, 1975.

Eldridge, J.E.T., *Industrial Disputes: Essays in the Sociology of Industrial Relations*, Routledge & Kegan Paul, 1968.

Flanders, Allan, *The Fawley Productivity Agreements*, Faber, 1964.

Flanders, Allan, *Management and Unions. The Theory and Reform of Industrial Relations*, Faber, 1970.

Flanders, Allan, Pomeranz, Ruth and Woodward, Joan, *Experiment in Industrial Democracy. A Study of the John Lewis Partnership*, Faber, 1968.

Fricke, Peter H., *The Social Structure of Crews of British Dry Cargo Merchant Ships: A Study of the Organisation and Environment of an Occupation*, UWIST, 1974.

Friedman, Andrew L., *Industry and Labour: Class Struggle at Work and Monopoly Capitalism*, Macmillan, 1977.

Fryer, Bob, Fairclough, Andy and Manson, Tom, *Organisation and Change in the National Union of Public Employees*, University of Warwick, Department of Sociology, 1974.

Gamble, Andrew and Walton, Paul, *Capitalism and Crisis*, Macmillan, 1976.

Gough, Ian, *The Political Economy of the Welfare State*, Macmillan,

1979.

Hemingway, John, *Conflict and Democracy: Studies in Trade Union Government*, Clarendon Press, 1978.

Heraud, Brian, *Sociology in the Professions*, Methuen, 1978.

Hill, Stephen, *The Dockers: Class and Tradition in London*,Heinemann, 1976.

Hollowell, Peter, *The Lorry Driver*, Routledge & Kegan Paul, 1968.

Hyman, R., *Strikes*, Fontana, 1972.

Hyman, R., *Marxism and the Sociology of Trade Unions*, Pluto Press, 1973.

Hyman, R. and Brough, I., *Social Values and Industrial Relations*, Blackwell, 1975.

Ingham, Geoffrey K., *Size of Industrial Organisations and Worker Behaviour*, Cambridge University Press, 1970.

Ingham, Geoffrey K., *Strikes and Industrial Conflict: Britain and Scandinavia*, Macmillan, 1974.

Jacques, E., *A General Theory of Bureaucracy*, Heinemann, 1976.

Kelly, Joe, *Is Scientific Management Possible? A Critical Examination of Glacier's Theory of Organisation*, Faber, 1968.

Land, Hilary, *The Family, the State and the Labour Market*, Blackwell, 1979.

Lane, David and O'Dell, Felicity, *The Soviet Industrial Worker*, Martin Robertson, 1978.

Lane, T., *The Union Makes Us Strong*, Arrow Books, 1974.

Lane, T. and Roberts, K., *Strike at Pilkingtons*, Fontana, 1971.

Lupton, Tom, *On the Shop Floor*, Pergamon, 1963.

McNally, Fiona, *Women for Hire: a Study of the Female Office Worker*, Macmillan, 1979.

Mann, M., *Workers on the Move*, Cambridge University Press, 1973.

Marsden, Dennis and Duff, Ewan, *Workless. Some Unemployed Men and Their Families*, Penguin, 1975.

Martin, R. and Fryer, R.M., *Redundancy and Paternalist Capitalism*, Allen & Unwin, 1973.

Millerson, Geoffrey, *The Qualifying Associations*, Routledge & Kegan Paul, 1964.

Moran, Michael, *The Union of Post Office Workers: A Study in Political Sociology*, Macmillan, 1974.

Mumford, Enid, *The Computer and the Clerk*, Routledge & Kegan Paul, 1967.

Musgrave, P.W., *Technical Change, the Labour Force and Education: A Study of the British and German Iron and Steel Industries*, Pergamon, 1967.

Nichols, Theo, *Ownership, Control and Ideology: an Inquiry into Certain Aspects of Business Ideology*, Allen & Unwin, 1969.

Nichols, Theo and Armstrong, Peter, *Workers Divided. A Study in Shop Floor Politics*, Fontana, 1976.

Nichols, Theo and Byenon, Huw, *Living with Capitalism*, Routledge & Kegan Paul, 1976.
Oakley, Ann, *The Sociology of Housework*, Martin Robertson, 1974.
Pahl, J.M. and R.E., *Managers and their Wives*, Allen Lane, 1971.
Panitch, Leo., *Social Democracy and Industrial Militancy: The Labour Party, the Trade Unions and Incomes Policy, 1945-74*, Cambridge University Press, 1976.
Peil, Margaret, *The Ghanaian Factory Worker: Industrial Men in Africa*, Cambridge University Press, 1972.
Poole, Michael., *Workers' Participation in Industry*, Routledge & Kegan Paul, 1975.
Pugh, D.S. and Hickson, D.J., *Organisational Stucture in its Context, The Aston Programme I*, Saxon House, 1976.
Pugh, D.S. and Payne, R.L., *Organisational Behaviour in its Context: The Aston Programme II*, Saxon House, 1977.
Reiner, Robert, *The Blue-Coated Worker. A Sociological Study of Police Unionism*, Cambridge University Press, 1979.
Rose, Michael, *Industrial Behaviour: Theoretical Development Since Taylor*, Penguin, 1975.
Rose, Michael, *Servants of Post-Industrial Power*, Macmillan, 1974.
Ryrie, A.C. and Weir, A.D., *Getting a Trade*, Hodder & Stoughton,1978.
Scott, John, *Corporations, Classes and Capitalism*, Hutchinson, 1979.
Scott, W.H., Mumford, Enid, McGivering, I.C. and Kirby, J.M., *Coal and Conflict*, Liverpool University Press, 1963.
Silverman, David and Jones, Jill, *Organisational Work*, Collier-Macmillan, 1976.
Sinfield, A., *The Long-Term Unemployed*, OECD, 1968.
Sofer, Cyril, *Men in Mid-Career: A Study of British Managers and Technical Specialists*, Cambridge University Press, 1970.
Trist, E.L., Higgin, G.W., Murray, H. and Pollock, A.B., *Organisational Choice. Capabilities of Groups at the Coal Face under Changing Technologies*, Tavistock, 1963.
Tunstall, J., *The Fisherman*, MacGibbon & Kee, 1962.
Turner, H.A., *Trade Union Growth Structure and Policy: A Comparative Study of Cotton Unions*, Allen & Unwin, 1962.
Turner, H.A., Clack, G. and Roberts, G., *Labour Relations in the Motor Industry: A Study of Industrial Unrest and an International Comparison*, Allen & Unwin, 1967.
Warner, Malcolm and Stone, Michael, *The Data Bank Society*, Allen & Unwin, 1970.
Watson, Tony, *The Personnel Managers*, Routledge & Kegan Paul, 1978.
Wedderburn, Dorothy, *Enterprise Planning for Change*, OECD, 1968.
Wedderburn, Dorothy and Crompton, Rosemary, *Workers' Attitudes and Technology*, Cambridge University Press, 1972.
Wilson, David F., *Dockers, The Impact of Industrial Change*, Fontana, 1972.

Woodward, Joan, *Industrial Organisation: Theory and Practice*, Oxford University Press, 1965.
Zweig, F., *The Worker in an Affluent Society*, Heinemann, 1961.

Review papers and critiques

Ackroyd, Stephen, 'Economic Rationality and the Relevance of Weberian Sociology to Industrial Relations', *BJIR*, vol. XII, no. 2, 1974, pp. 236-48.
Albrow, Martin, 'The Study of Organisations — Objectivity or Bias?' in Gould, J. (ed.), *Penguin Social Science Survey, 1968*, Penguin, 1968.
Bain, G.S. and Woolven, G.B., *A Bibliography of British Industrial Relations*, Cambridge University Press, 1979.
Brown, R.K., 'Participation, Conflict and Change in Industry', *SR*, vol. 18, no. 3, 1965.
Brown, R.K., 'Research and Consultancy in Industrial Enterprises: a Review of the Contribution of the Tavistock Institute of Human Relations to the Development of Industrial Sociology', *Sociology*, vol. 1, no. 1, 1967, pp. 33-60.
Brown, R.K., 'The Growth of Industrial Bureaucracy — Change, Choice or Necessity?', in *Human Figurations. Essays for Norbert Elias*, 1977, pp. 19-210.
Brown, R.K., 'Women as Employees: Some Comments on Research in Industrial Sociology', in Barker, D.L. and Allen, S. (eds.), *Dependence and Exploitation in Work and Marriage*, Longmans, 1976, pp. 21-46.
Brown, R.K., 'From Donovan to Where? Interpretations of Industrial Relations in Britain since 1968', *BJS*, vol. XXIX, no. 4, 1978, pp. 439-61.
Child, John, 'Organisational Structure, Environment and Performance, the Role of Strategic Choice', *Sociology*, vol. 6, no. 1, 1972, pp. 2-22.
Child, John, 'British Management Thought as a Case Study within the Sociology of Knowledge', *SR*, vol. 16, no. 2, 1968, pp. 217-39.
Clegg, H.A., 'Pluralism in Industrial Relations', *BJIR*, vol. XIII, no 3, 1975, pp. 309-16.
Coulson, Margaret, Keil, E. Teresa, Riddell, David S. and Struthers, John S., 'Towards a Sociological Theory of Occupational Choice', *SR*, vol. 15, no. 3, 1967, pp. 301-9.
Cousins, J.M., 'Values and Value in the Labour Market', *Durham University Working Papers in Sociology*, no. 9, n.d.
Ditton, Jason, 'The Problem of Time: Styles of Time Management and Schemes of Time-Manipulation amongst Machine-Paced Workers', *Durham University Working Papers in Sociology*, no. 2, n.d.
Eldridge, J.E.T., 'Industrial Conflict: Some Problems of Theory and Method', in Child, John (ed.), *Man and Organisation*, 1973, pp. 158-184.

Eldridge, J.E.T., 'Sociological Imagination and Industrial Life', in Warner, Malcolm (ed.), *The Sociology of the Workplace*, Allen & Unwin, 1973, pp. 274-86.

Eldridge, J.E.T., 'Panaceas and Pragmatism in Industrial Relations', *IRJ*, vol. 1, no. 1, 1975, pp. 4-13.

Eldridge, J.E.T., 'Industrial Relations and Industrial Capitalism', in Esland, Geoff *et al.* (eds.), *People and Work*, 1975, pp. 306-24.

Elger, A.J., 'Industrial Organisations: A Processual Perspective', in McKinley, J.B. (ed.), *Processing People: Cases in Organisational Behaviour*, Holt, Rinehart & Winston, 1975, pp. 91-149.

Elger, A.J., 'Valorisation and "Deskilling": a Critique of Braverman', *Capital and Class*, no. 7, 1978, pp. 58-99.

Ford, Julienne and Box, Steven, 'Sociological Theory and Occupational Choice', *SR*, vol. 15, no. 3, 1967, pp. 287-99.

Fox, Alan, 'Industrial Sociology and Industrial Relations', HMSO, 1966.

Fox, Alan, 'Industrial Relations: a Social Critique of Pluralist Ideology', in Child, John (ed.), *Man and Organisation*, 1973, pp. 185-233.

Goldthorpe, John H., 'The Social Action Approach to Industrial Sociology', *JMS*, May 1970, pp. 199-208.

Goldthorpe, John H., 'Industrial Relations in Great Britain: A Critique of Reformism', in Clarke, Tom and Clements, Laurie (eds.), *Trade Unions under Capitalism*, 1977, pp. 184-224.

Goldthorpe, John H., 'The Current Inflation: Towards a Sociological Account', in Hirsch, Fred and Goldthorpe, John H. (eds.), *The Political Economy of Inflation*, Martin Robertson, 1978, pp. 186-216.

Hickson, D.J., 'A Convergence in Organisation Theory', *ASQ*, vol. II, 1966, pp. 224-37.

Hill, Stephen and Thurley, Keith, 'Sociology and Industrial Relations', *BJIR*, vol. XII, no. 2, 1974, pp. 147-60.

Mackenzie, Gavin, 'The "Affluent Worker" Study: An Evaluation and Critique', in Parkin, Frank (ed.), *The Social Analysis of Class Structure*, 1974, pp. 237-56.

Mackenzie, Gavin, 'World Images and the World of Work', in Esland, Geoff *et al.* (eds.), *People and Work*, 1975, pp. 170-85.

Martin, Roderick, 'Union Democracy: An Explanatory Framework', *Sociology*, vol. 2, no. 2, 1968, pp, 205-20.

Musgrave, P.W., 'Towards a Sociological Theory of Occupational Choice', *SR*, vol. 15, no. 1, 1967, pp. 33-46.

Pugh, D.S., Mansfield, Roger and Warner, Malcolm, *Research in Organisational Behaviour*, Heinemann, 1975.

Salaman, Graeme, 'Towards a Sociology of Organisational Structures', *SR*, vol. 26, no. 3, 1978, pp. 519-54.

Silverman, David, 'Formal Organisations or Industrial Sociology: Towards a Social Action Analysis of Organisations', *Sociology*, vol. 2, no. 2, 1968, pp. 221-37.

Watson, Tony J., 'Industrial Sociology: Theory, Research and Technology — Some Problems and Proposals', *JMS*, vol. 16, no. 2, 1979, pp. 9-138.

Westergaard, John, 'The Re-discovery of the Cash-Nexus', in Miliband, R. and Saville, John (eds.), *Socialist Register*, Merlin Press, 1970.

Race, ethnicity and nationalism

Texts

Allen, Sheila, *New Minorities, Old Conflicts: Asian and West Indian Immigrants in Britain*, Random House, 1972.

Banton, Michael, *Race Relations*, Tavistock, 1967.

Kahn, Verity Saifullah (ed.), *Minority Families in Britain*, Macmillan, 1979.

Krausz, Ernest, *Ethnic Minorities in Britain*, MacGibbon & Kee, 1971.

Mason, Philip, *Patterns of Dominance*, Oxford University Press, 1970.

Mason, Philip, *Race Relations*, Oxford University Press, 1970.

Rex, John, *Race Relations and Sociological Theory*, Weidenfeld & Nicolson, 1970.

Readers and edited collections

Bowker, Gordon and Carrier, John (eds.), *Race and Ethnic Relations*, Hutchinson, 1976.

Crewe, Ivor (ed.), *The Politics of Race: British Political Sociology Yearbook Vol. 2*, Croom Helm, 1975.

Miles, Robert and Phizaclea, Annie (eds.), *Racism and Political Activism in Britain*, Routledge & Kegan Paul, 1978.

Richardson, Ken and Spears, David (eds.), *Race, Culture and Intelligence*, Penguin, 1972.

Richmond, A. (ed.), *Readings in Race and Ethnic Relations*, Pergamon, 1972.

Verma, G.K. and Bagley, C. (eds.), *Race, Education and Identity*, Macmillan, 1974.

Verma, G.K. and Bagley, C. (eds.), *Race and Education Across Cultures*, Heinemann, 1975.

Wallman, Sandra (ed.), *Ethnicity at Work*, Macmillan, 1974.

Zubaida, S. (ed.), *Race and Racialism*, Tavistock, 1970.

Specific studies and monographs

Allen, Sheila, Bentley, Stuart and Bornat, Joanna, *Work, Race and Immigration*, University of Bradford, 1977.

Bagley, Christopher, *Social Structures and Prejudice in Five Boroughs*, Institute of Race Relations, 1970.

Bagley, Christopher, *The Dutch Plural Society. A Comparative Study in Race Relations*, Oxford University Press, 1973.

Banton, Michael, *Racial Minorities*, Fontana/Collins, 1972.
Banton, Michael, *The Idea of Race*, Tavistock, 1977.
Berger, John and Mohr, Jean, *A Seventh Man*, Penguin, 1975.
Bolt, Christine, *Victorian Attitudes to Race*, Routledge & Kegan Paul, 1971.
Brooks, Denis, *Race and Labour in London Transport*, Oxford University Press, 1975.
Burney, Elizabeth, *Housing on Trial: a Study of Immigrants and Local Government*, Oxford University Press, 1967.
Cashmore, Ernest, *Rastaman. The Rastafanian Movement in England*, Allen & Unwin, 1979.
Castles, Stephen and Kusack, Godula, *Immigrant Workers and Class Structure in Western Europe*, Oxford University Press, 1973.
Daniel, W., *Racial Discrimination in England*, Penguin, 1968.
Davison, R.B., *Black British: Immigrants to England*, Oxford University Press, 1966.
Dummett, Ann, *Citizenship and Nationality*, Runneymede Trust, 1976.
Glass, Ruth, *Newcomers*, Allen & Unwin, 1970.
Foot, P., *Race and Immigration in British Politics*, Penguin, 1966.
Gerrard, John A., *The English and Immigration: A Comparative Study of the Jewish Influx, 1880-1910*, Oxford University Press, 1971.
Hepple, Bob, *Race, Jobs and the Law in Britain*, Penguin, 1970.
Hill, Michael J. and Issachasoff, Ruth M., *Community Action and Race Relations: A Study of Community Relations Committees in Britain*, Oxford University Press, 1971.
Hiro, Dilip, *Black British, White British*, Eyre & Spottiswood, 1971.
Jackson, John A., *The Irish in Britain*, Routledge & Kegan Paul, 1963.
James, Alan G., *Sikh Children in Britain*, Oxford University Press, 1974.
John, Augustine, *Race in the Inner City*, Runneymede Trust, 1972.
Kiernan, V.G., *The Lords of Human Kind, European Attitudes Towards the Outside World in the Imperial Age*, Weidenfeld-Nicolson, 1969.
Lambert, John R., *Crime, Police and Race Relations*, Oxford University Press, 1970.
Lawrence, Daniel, *Black Migrants: White Natives. A Study of Race Relations in Nottingham*, Cambridge University Press, 1974.
Lee, Trevor R., *Race and Residence: the Concentration and Dispersal of Immigrants in London*, Oxford University Press, 1977.
Moore, Robert, *Slamming the Door*, Martin Robertson, 1975.
Mullard, Chris, *Black Britain*, Allen & Unwin, 1973.
Nairn, Tom, *The Break-Up of Britain: Crisis and Neo-Nationalism*, New Left Books, 1977.
Patterson, Sheila, *Immigration and Race Relations in Britain 1960-67*, Oxford University Press, 1969.
Patterson, Sheila, *Dark Strangers: a Study of West Indians in London*, Penguin, 1965.

Peach, Ceri, *West Indian Migration to Britain*, Oxford University Press, 1968.

Pryce, Ken, *Endless Pressure*, Penguin, 1979.

Rex, John, *Race, Colonialism and the City*, Routledge & Kegan Paul, 1973.

Rex, John and Moore, Robert, *Race, Community and Conflict*, Oxford University Press, 1967.

Rex, John and Tomlinson, Sally, *Colonial Immigrants in a British City*, Routledge & Kegan Paul, 1979.

Richmond, Anthony, *Migration and Race Relations in an English Town A Study in Bristol*, Oxford University Press, 1973.

Rimmer, Malcolm, *Race and Industrial Conflict*, Heinemann, 1972.

Rose, E.J.B. *et al.*, *Colour and Citizenship. A Report on British Race Relations*, Oxford University Press, 1969.

Smith, Anthony D., *Theories of Nationalism*, Duckworth, 1971.

Smith, D., *Racial Disadvantage in Britain*, Penguin, 1977.

Tinker, Hugh, *Race, Conflict and the International Order: From Empire to United Nations*, Macmillan, 1977.

Wright, Peter L., *The Coloured Worker in British Industry*, Oxford University Press, 1968.

Review papers and critiques

Banton, M., 'Analytical and Folk Concepts of Race and Ethnicity', *Ethnic and Racial Studies*, vol. 2, no. 2, 1979, pp. 127-38.

Campbell-Platt, K., *Ethnic Minorities in Society: A Reference Guide*, Runnymede Trust, 1976.

Cohen, Percy S., 'Need There be a Sociology of Race Relations?', *Sociology*, no. 6, 1972, pp. 101-8.

Gabriel, Jon and Ben-Tovium, Gideon, 'The Conceptualisation of Race Relations in Sociological Theory', *Ethnic and Racial Studies*, vol. 2, no. 2, 1979, pp. 190-212.

Halsey, A.H., 'Sociology and Race Relations', *EJS*, vol. 12, no. 2, 1971, pp. 301-11.

Moore, Robert, 'Race Relations and the Re-discovery of "Sociology"', *BJS*, vol. XXII, no. 1, 1971, pp. 97-104.

Sivanandan, A., 'Race, Class and State', *Race and Class*, vol. XVII, no. 4, 1976, pp. 347-68.

Smith, Anthony D., 'Nationalism: A Trend Report and Bibliography', *Current Sociology*, vol. XXI, no. 3, 1973.

Ward, Robin, 'Race Relations in Britain', *BJS*, vol. XXIX, no. 4, 1978, pp. 464-80.

Religion/morals

Texts

Budd, Susan, *Sociologists and Religion*, Collier-Macmillan, 1973.

Hill, Michael, *A Sociology of Religion*, Heinemann, 1973.
Robertson, Roland, *The Sociological Interpretation of Religion*, Blackwell, 1970.
Scharf, Betty, *The Sociological Study of Religion*, Hutchinson, 1970.
Towler, Robert, *Homo Religiousus: Sociological Problems in the Study of Religion*, Constable, 1974.
Wilson, Bryan, *Religion in Secular Society*, Watts, 1966.

Readers and edited collections
Hill, M. (ed.), *A Sociological Yearbook of Religion*, nos 3-8, SCM, 1970-5.
Martin, D. (ed.), *A Sociological Yearbook of Religion*, nos 1-2, SCM, 1968-9.
Martin, D. and Hill, M. (eds.), *A Sociological Yearbook of Religion*, no. 3, SCM, 1970.
Robertson, Roland (ed.), *Sociology of Religion: Selected Readings*, Penguin, 1969.
Wallis, Roy (ed.), *Sectarianism: Analyses of Religious and Non-Religious Sects*, Peter Owen, 1975.
Wilson, Bryan R. (ed.), *Patterns of Sectarianism*, Heinemann, 1967.

Specific studies and monographs
Barnsley, John H., *The Social Reality of Ethics. A Comparative Analysis of Moral Codes*, Routledge & Kegan Paul, 1972.
Beckford, James A., *The Trumpet of Prophecy: A Sociological Study of Jehovah's Witnesses*, Blackwell, 1975.
Brothers, Joan, *Church and School*, Liverpool University Press, 1964.
Budd, Susan, *Varieties of Unbelief: Atheists and Agnostics in English Society 1850-1960*, Heinemann, 1977.
Calley, M.J.C., *God's People: West Indian Pentecostal Sects in England*, Oxford University Press, 1965.
Campbell, Colin, *Towards a Sociology of Irreligion*, Macmillan, 1971.
Currie, Robert, *Methodism Divided: A Study in the Sociology of Ecumenicalism*, Faber, 1968.
Currie, Robert, Gilbert, Alan and Horsley, Lee, *Churches and Churchgoers, Patterns of Church Growth in the British Isles since 1700*, Clarendon Press, 1978.
Douglas, Mary, *Purity and Danger. An Analysis of Concepts of Pollution and Taboo*, Routledge & Kegan Paul, 1966.
Douglas, Mary, *Natural Symbols: Explorations in Cosmology*, Barrie and Jenkins, 1973.
Gill, Robin, *The Social Context of Theology*, Mowbray, 1975.
Glasner, Peter E., *The Sociology of Secularisation. A Critique of a Concept*, Routledge & Kegan Paul, 1977.
Henderson, Ian, *Power Without Glory: A Study in Ecumenical Politics*, Hutchinson, 1967.

Hill, Michael, *The Religious Order. A Study of Virtuoso Religion and its Legitimation in the Nineteenth-Century Church of England*, Heinemann, 1973.

Inglis, K.S., *Churches and the Working Classes in Victorian England*, Routledge & Kegan Paul, 1963.

Kadt, E. de, *Catholic Radicals in Brazil*, Oxford University Press, 1970.

Lane, C., *Christian Religion in the Soviet Union: a Sociological Study*, Allen & Unwin, 1979.

MacIntyre, Alasdair, *Secularisation and Moral Change*, Oxford University Press, 1967.

MacLaren, Allan A., *Religion and Social Class: the Disruptive Years in Aberdeen*, Routledge & Kegan Paul, 1974.

McLeod, Hugh, *Class and Religion in the Late Victorian City*, Croom Helm, 1974.

Martin, David, *Pacifism: A Sociological and Historical Study*, Routledge & Kegan Paul, 1965.

Martin, David, *The Religious and the Secular*, Routledge & Kegan Paul, 1969.

Martin, David, *A Sociology of English Religion*, SCM, 1967.

Martin, David, *The Dilemmas of Contemporary Religion*, Blackwell, 1978.

Martin, David, *A General Theory of Secularisation*, Blackwell, 1978.

Moore, Robert, *Pitmen, Preachers and Politics: the Effects of Methodism in a Durham Mining Community*, Cambridge University Press, 1974.

Musgrove, Frank, *Ecstasy and Holiness: Counter Culture and Open Society*, Methuen, 1974.

Nelson, G.K., *Spiritualism and Society*, Routledge & Kegan Paul, 1969.

O'Day, Rosemary, *The English Clergy: The Emergence and Consolidation of a Profession 1558-1642*, Leicester University Press, 1979.

Peel, J.D.Y., *Aladura: A Religious Movement Among the Yoruba*, Oxford University Press, 1969.

Ranson, Stewart, Hinings, Bob and Bryman, Alan, *Clergy, Ministers and Priests*, Routledge & Kegan Paul, 1978.

Sharot, Stephen, *Judaism: A Sociology*, David and Charles, 1976.

Stark, W., *The Sociology of Religion* (5 vols), Routledge & Kegan Paul, 1966-72.

Thomas, Keith, *Religion and the Decline of Magic*, Weidenfeld & Nicholson, 1971.

Thompson, Kenneth A., *Bureaucracy and Church Reform: the Organisational Response of the Church of England to Social Change, 1800-1965*, Clarendon Press, 1970.

Towler, Robert and Coxon, A.P.M., *The Fate of the Anglican Clergy*, Macmillan, 1979.

Turner, Bryan S., *Weber and Islam*, Routledge & Kegan Paul, 1974.

Wallis, Roy, *The Road to Total Freedom. A Sociological Analysis of Scientology*, Heinemann, 1977.
Wallis, Roy, *Salvation and Protest*, Frances Pinter, 1979.
Ward, C.K., *Priest and People*, Liverpool University Press, 1961.
Whitworth, J.M., *God's Blueprints: A Sociological Study of Three Utopian Sects*, Routledge & Kegan Paul, 1975.
Wilson, Bryan, *Sects and Society*, Heinemann, 1961.
Wilson, Bryan, *Magic and the Millennium*, Heinemann, 1973.
Wilson, Bryan, *Contemporary Transformations of Religion*, Oxford University Press, 1976.
Wilson, Bryan, *The Noble Savages: The Primitive Origins of Charisma and its Contemporary Survival*, University of California Press, 1976.
Yeo, Stephen, *Religious and Voluntary Organisations in Crisis*, Croom Helm, 1976.

Review papers and critiques
Beckford, James, 'Religious Organisation: A Trend Report and a Bibliography', *Current Sociology*, vol. XXI, no. 2, 1973.
Martin, David, 'The Sociology of Religion: A Case Study of Status Deprivation', BJS, vol. XVII, no. 4, 1966, pp. 353-9.
Robertson, R. and Campbell, C.B., 'Research Strategies', *Social Compass*, no. 19, 1972, pp. 185-97.
Wilson, Bryan, 'Establishment, Sectarianism and Partisanship', SR, vol. 15, no. 2, 1967, pp. 213-20.

Sex, gender, generation

Texts
Farmer, Mary, *The Family*, Longmans, rev. edn, 1978.
Fox, R., *Kinship and Marriage*, Penguin, 1967.
Harris, C.C., *The Family*, Allen & Unwin, 1969.
Mair, L., *Marriage*, Penguin, 1971.
Morgan, D.H.J., *Social Theory and the Family*, Routledge & Kegan Paul, 1975.
Oakley, A., *Sex, Gender and Society*, Temple Smith, 1972.
Woods, P., *Youth, Generation and Social Class*, Open University, 1977.

Readers and edited collections
Allen, Sheila and Barker, Diana (eds.), *Dependence and Exploitation in Work and Marriage*, Tavistock, 1976.
Anderson, Michael (ed.), *Sociology of the Family*, Penguin, 1971.
Barker, Diana and Allen, Sheila (eds.), *Sexual Divisions and Society: Process and Change*, Tavistock, 1976.
Hall, Stuart and Jefferson, Tony (eds.), *Resistance through Rituals:*

Youth Sub-Cultures in Great Britain, Hutchinson, 1976.
Mungham, Geoff and Pearson, Geoff. (eds.), *Working Class Youth Culture*,
Munn, Annette and Wolpe, Ann-Marie (eds), *Feminist Materialism*, Routledge & Kegan Paul, 1978.
Shanes, Ethel *et al.* (eds.), *Old People in Three Industrial Societies*, Routledge & Kegan Paul, 1968.
Smart, Carol and Barry (eds.), *Women, Sexuality and Social Control*, Routledge & Kegan Paul, 1978.

Specific studies and monographs

Anderson, Michael (ed.), *Family Structure in Nineteenth-Century Lancashire*, Cambridge University Press, 1972.
Banks, J.A. and Banks, O., *Feminism and Family Planning in Victorian England*, Liverpool University Press, 1964.
Bell, Colin, *Middle-Class Families*, Routledge & Kegan Paul, 1968.
Bott, Elizabeth, *Family and Social Network*, rev. edn, Tavistock, 1971.
Cook-Gumperz, J., *Social Control and Socialisation: A Study of Class Differences in the Language of Social Control*, Routledge & Kegan Paul, 1973.
Firth, Raymond, Hubert, Jane and Forge, Anthony, *Families and their Relatives. Kinship in a Middle-Class Sector of London: An Anthropological Study*, Routledge & Kegan Paul, 1970.
Fletcher, Ronald, *The Family and Marriage in Britain*, Penguin, 1966.
Fogarty, M. *et al.*, *Sex, Career and Family*, PEP, 1971.
Gavron, Hannah, *The Captive Wife: Conflicts of Housebound Mothers*, Routledge & Kegan Paul, 1966.
Hunt, Pauline, *Gender and Class Consciousness*, Macmillan, 1979.
James, Alan G., *Sikh Children in Britain*, Oxford University Press, 1974.
Klein, Josephine, *Samples from English Cultures* (2 vols), Routledge & Kegan Paul, 1965.
Klein, Viola, *Britain's Married Women Workers*, Routledge & Kegan Paul, 1965.
Laslett, Peter, *Family Life and Illicit Love in Earlier Generations*, Cambridge University Press, 1977.
Mitchell, J., *Women's Estate*, Penguin, 1971.
Musgrove, F., *Youth and Social Order*, Routledge & Kegan Paul, 1964.
Myrdal, Alva and Klein, Viola, *Women's Two Roles. Home and Work*, Routledge & Kegan Paul, rev. edn, 1968.
Newson, John and Newson, Elizabeth, *Infant Care in an Urban Community*, Allen & Unwin, 1963.
Newson, John and Newson, Elizabeth, *Four Years Old in an Urban Community*, Allen & Unwin, 1968.
Newson, John and Newson, Elizabeth, *Seven Years Old in the Home Environment*, Allen & Unwin, 1976.

Parker, Howard J., *View from the Boys: A Sociology of Down-Town Adolescents*, David & Charles, 1974.

Plummer, Kenneth, *Sexual Stigma. An Interactionist Account*, Routledge & Kegan Paul, 1975.

Rappoport, Rhona and Rappoport, Robert, *Dual-Career Families*, Penguin, 1971.

Rigby, A., *Alternative Realities*, Routledge & Kegan Paul, 1974.

Rosser, C. and Harris, C.C., *The Family and Social Change. A Study of Family and Kinship in South Wales*, Routledge & Kegan Paul, 1965.

Rowbotham, S., *Hidden from History*, Pluto Press, 1973.

Rowbotham, S., *Women's Consciousness, Men's World*, Penguin, 1973.

Townsend, Peter, *The Family Life of Old People*, rev. edn, Penguin, 1963.

Tunstall, J., *Old and Alone*, Routledge & Kegan Paul, 1966.

Willis, Paul, *Profane Culture*, Routledge & Kegan Paul, 1978.

Willmott, Peter, *Adolescent Boys of East London*, Routledge & Kegan Paul, 1966.

Young, M. and Willmott, P., *Family and Kinship in East London*, Routledge & Kegan Paul, 1962.

Young, M. and Willmott, P., *Family and Class in a London Suburb*, Routledge & Kegan Paul, 1960.

Young, M. and Willmott, P., *The Symmetrical Family*, Routledge & Kegan Paul, 1973.

Review papers and critiques

Allen, Sheila, 'Class, Culture and Generation', *SR*, vol. 21, no. 3, 1973, pp. 437-46.

Allen, Sheila, 'Some Theoretical Problems in the Study of Youth', *SR*, vol. 16, no. 3, 1968, pp. 319-31.

Ashworth, J.E. and Walker, W.M., 'Social Structure of Homosexuality: A Theoretical Approach', *BJS*, vol. XXIII, no. 2, 1972, pp. 146-58.

Chester, R., 'Contemporary Trends in the Stability of English Marriage', *Journal of Biosocial Science*, no. 3, 1971, pp. 389-402.

Crawford, Marion P., 'Retirement: A Rite de Passage', *SR*, vol. 21, no. 3, 1973, pp. 447-61.

Edgell, Stephen, 'Marriage and the Concept of Companionship', *BJS*, vol. XXIII, no. 4, 1972, pp. 452-61.

Gibson, Colin, 'Research Note: A Note on Family Breakdown in England and Wales', *BJS*, vol. XXIII, no. 3, 1971, pp. 322-5.

Keil, Teresa, Riddell, D.S. and Green, B.S.R., 'Youth and Work: Problems and Perspectives', *SR*, vol. 14, no. 2, 1966, pp. 117-37.

Mitchell, J., 'Women: The Longest Revolution', *New Left Review*, no. 40, 1966, pp. 11-37.

Pearce, F. and Roberts, A., 'The Social Regulation Of Sexual Behaviour and the Development of Industrial Capitalism in Britain', in Bailey, R.V. and Young, J. (eds.), *Contemporary Social Problems in Britain*, Saxon House, 1973.

Rowbotham, Sheila, *Women's Liberation and Revolution: a Bibliography*, Fallings Wall Press, 1972.

Smith, David M., 'Adolescence: A Study of Stereotyping', *SR*, vol. 18, no. 2, 1970, pp. 197-211.

Wainwright, Hilary, 'Women and the Division of Labour', in Abrams, P. (ed.), *Work, Urbanism and Inequality*, Weidenfeld & Nicolson, 1978., pp. 160-205.

Women's Study Group Centre for Contemporary Cultural Studies, *Women Take Issue: Aspects of Women's Subordination*, Hutchinson, 1978.

Social change, transition, development, underdevelopment

Texts

Goldthorpe, J.E., *The Sociology of the Third World: Disparity and Involvement*, Cambridge University Press, 1975.

Hoogvelt, Ankie M.M., *The Sociology of Developing Societies*, Macmillan, 1976.

Poggi, Gianfranco, *The Development of the Modern State*, Hutchinson, 1978.

Roxborough, Ian, *Theories of Underdevelopment*, Macmillan, 1979.

Smith, Anthony, *Social Change: Social Theory and Historical Processes*, Longmans, 1976.

Taylor, John G., *From Modernisation to Modes of Production. A Critique of the Sociologies of Development and Underdevelopment*, Macmillan, 1979.

Readers and edited collections

Bernstein, H., *Development and Underdevelopment: The Third World Today*, Penguin, 1973.

Cohen, Robin, Gutkind, Peter C.W. and Brazier, Phyllis (eds.), *Peasants and Proletarians*, Hutchinson, 1979.

Halsey, A.H. (ed.), *Trends in British Society*, Macmillan, 1972.

Ionesen, G. and Gellner, E. (eds.), *Populism: Its National Characteristics*, Weidenfeld & Nicolson, 1969.

Jackson, John A. (ed.), *Migration*, Cambridge University Press, 1969.

Jarvie, I. (ed.), *Hong Kong: A Society in Transition*, Routledge & Kegan Paul, 1969.

Kadt, Emmanuel de and Williams, Gavin (eds.), *Sociology and Development*, Tavistock, 1974.

Oxaal, Ivor, Barnett, Tony and Booth, David (eds.), *Beyond the Sociology of Development: Economy and Society in Latin America and Africa*, Routledge & Kegan Paul, 1975.

Sandbrook, R. and Cohen, R. (eds.), *The Development of an African Working Class*, Longmans, 1976.

Shanin, T. (ed.), *Peasants and Peasant Societies*, Penguin, 1971.

Specific studies and monographs

Anderson, Perry, *Passages from Antiquity to Feudalism*, New Left Books, 1975.

Anderson, Perry, *Lineages of the Absolute State*, New Left Books, 1975.

Andreski, S., *The African Predicament*, Michael Joseph, 1968.

Andreski, Stanislav, *Parasitism and Subversion*, Weidenfeld & Nicolson, 1975.

Banks, J.A., *The Sociology of Social Movements*, Macmillan, 1972.

Butler, David and Stokes, Donald, *Political Change in Britain*, Macmillan, 1974.

Cross, Malcolm, *Urbanisation and Urban Growth in the Caribbean: An Essay on Social Change in Dependent Societies*, Cambridge University Press, 1979.

Elias, Norbert, *The Civilising Process* (2 vols), Blackwell, 1979.

Florence, P. Sargant, *Economics and Sociology of Industry: A Realistic Analysis of Development*, Watts, 1964.

Gellner, E., *Thought and Change*, Weidenfeld & Nicholson, 1964.

Hindess, B. and Hirst, P.Q., *Pre-Capitalist Modes of Production*, Routledge & Kegan Paul, 1975.

Hopkins, Keith, *Sociological Studies in Roman History*, vol. I, Cambridge University Press, 1979.

Jenkins, Robin, *Exploitation*, Paladin, 1971.

Kumar, Krishan, *Prophecy and Progress*, Penguin, 1978.

Laslett, Peter, *The World We Have Lost*, Methuen, 1965.

Leys, C., *Underdevelopment in Kenya: the Political Economy of Neo-Colonialism, 1964-1971*, Heinemann, 1971.

Lloyd, P.C., *Africa in Social Change*, Penguin, 1967.

Lloyd, P.C., *Classes, Crises and Coups: Themes in the Sociology of Developing Countries*, MacGibbon & Kee, 1971.

Lloyd, P.C., *Power and Independence: Urban Africans' Perceptions of Inequality*, Routledge & Kegan Paul, 1974.

Lloyd, P.C., *Slums of Hope? Shanty Towns of the Third World*, Penguin, 1979.

Mouzelis, Nicos P., *Modern Greece: Facets of Underdevelopment*, Macmillan, 1978.

Nettle, P. and Robertson, R., *International Models of Modernity*,

Faber, 1968.
Newby, Howard, *Green and Pleasant Land. Social Change in Rural England*, Hutchinson, 1979.
Peil, M., *Consensus and Conflict in African Societies*, Longmans, 1977.
Pons, V., *Stanleyville*, Oxford University Press, 1969.
Roberts, Bryan, *Cities of Peasants*, Edward Arnold, 1978.
Shanin, T., *The Awkward Class: Political Sociology of Peasantry in a Developing Society, Russia 1910-1925*, Oxford University Press, 1972.
Smith, Anthony D., *The Concept of Social Change*, Routledge & Kegan Paul, 1973.
Thompson, E.P., *Whigs and Hunters*, Penguin, 1975.
Urry, John, *Reference Groups and the Theory of Revolution*, Routledge & Kegan Paul, 1973.
Worsley, Peter, *The Trumpet Shall Sound*, rev. edn, MacGibbon & Kee, 1968.
Worsley, Peter, *The Third World*, rev. edn, Weidenfeld & Nicolson, 1967.

Review papers and critiques

Allcock, J.B., ' "Populism": A Brief Biography', *Sociology*, vol. 5, no. 3, 1971, pp. 371-87.
Bulmer, Martin, 'Sociology and History: Some Recent Trends', *Sociology*, vol. 8, no. 1, 1974, pp. 138-50.
Cohen, Robin, Shanin, Teodor and Sorj Bernando, 'The Sociology of Developing Societies: Problems of Teaching and Definition', *SR*, no. 25, 1977, pp. 351-75.
Dore, Ronald, 'Making Sense of History', *EJS*, no. 10, 1969, pp. 295-315.
Foster-Carter, Aidan, 'Marxism versus Dependency Theory? A Polemic', *University of Leeds Occasional Papers in Sociology*, no. 9, 1979.
Gellner, E., 'Our Current Sense of History', *EJS*, no. 12, 1971, pp. 159-79.
Gellner, E., 'Democracy and Industrialisation', *EJS*, no. 8, 1967, pp. 47-70.
Goldthorpe, John H., 'Theories of Industrial Society: Reflections on the Recrudescence of Historicism and the Future of Futurology', *EJS*, vol. 12, no. 2, 1971, pp. 263-88.
Hobsbawm, E.J., 'Peasants and Politics', *Journal of Peasant Studies*, vol. 1, no. 1, 1973.
Kumar, Krishan, 'The Sociology of the Future', *Sociology*, vol. 7, no. 2, 1973, pp. 277-88.
MacEwan, Alison M., 'Stability and Change in a Shanty Town: A Summary of Some Research Findings', *Sociology*, vol. 6, no. 1.

1972, pp. 43-57.
Nettle, J.P. and Robertson, R., 'Industrialisation, Development or Modernisation', *BJS*, vol. XVII, no. 3, 1966, pp. 274-91.
Payne, Geoff, 'Comparative Sociology: Some Problems of Theory and Method', *BJS*, vol. XXIV, no. 1, 1973, pp. 13-29.
Peel, J.D.Y., 'Cultural Factors in the Contemporary Theory of Development', *EJS*, vol. XIV, 1973, pp. 283-303.
Roxborough, Ian, 'Dependency Theory in the Sociology of Development. Some Theoretical Problems', *West African Journal of Sociology and Political Science*, vol. 1, no. 2, 1976, pp. 116-33.
Streeten, Paul, 'An Institutional Critique of Development Concepts', *EJS*, no. 11, 1970, pp. 69-80.

Social stratification: class, status and party

Texts

Bottomore, Tom, *Classes in Modern Society*, Allen & Unwin, 1965.
Bottomore, Tom, *Elites and Society*, Watts, 1964.
Bottomore, Tom, *Political Sociology*, Allen & Unwin, 1979.
Dowse, Robert E. and Hughes, John A., *Political Sociology*, Wiley, 1972.
Kelsall, R.K., *Stratification*, Longmans, 1974.
Littlejohn, J., *Social Stratification*, Allen & Unwin, 1972.
Martin, R., *The Sociology of Power*, Routledge & Kegan Paul, 1977.
Noble, Trevor, *Modern Britain: Structure and Change*, Batsford, 1975.
Parkin, Frank, *Class Inequality and Political Order*, MacGibbon & Kee, 1971.
Westergaard, John and Resler, Henrietta, *Class in a Capitalist Society: A Study of Contemporary Britain*, Heinemann, 1975.

Readers and edited collections

Archer, Margaret S. and Giner, S. (eds.), *Contemporary Europe: Class, Status and Power*, Weidenfeld & Nicolson, 1971.
Bechofer, Frank and Elliott, Brian (eds.), *The Petite Bourgeoisie. Comparative Studies of the Uneasy Stratum*, Macmillan, 1979.
Bulmer, Martin (ed.), *Working Class Images of Society*, Routledge & Kegan Paul, 1975.
Butterworth, Eric and Weir, David (eds.), *The Sociology of Modern Britain*, Fontana, 1975.
Clarke, John, Critcher, Chas. and Johnson, Richard (eds.), *Working-Class Culture*, Hutchinson, 1979.
Coxon, A.P.M. and Jones, C.L. (eds), *Social Mobility*, Penguin, 1975.
Crewe, Ivor (ed.), *British Political Sociology Yearbook Vol. I. Elites in Western Democracy*, Croom Helm, 1974.
Giner, S. and Archer, Margaret S. (eds.), *Contemporary Europe. Social*

Structures and Cultural Patterns, Routledge & Kegan Paul, 1978.
Hope, Keith (ed.), *The Analysis of Social Mobility. Methods and Approaches*, Clarendon Press, 1972.
Hunt, A. (ed.), *Class and Class Structure*, Lawrence & Wishart, 1977.
Jackson, John A. (ed.), *Social Stratification*, Cambridge University Press, 1968.
Littlejohn Gary, Smart, Barry, Wakeford, John and Yurel-Davis, Niro (eds.), *Power and the State*, Croom Helm, 1978.
MacLaren, Allan A. (ed.), *Social Class in Scotland: Past and Present*, John Donald, 1976.
Parkin, F. (ed.), *The Social Analysis of Class Structure*, Tavistock, 1974.
Ridge, J.M. (ed.), *Mobility in Britain Reconsidered*, Clarendon Press, 1974.
Scase, Richard (ed.), *Industrial Society: Class, Cleavage and Control*, Allen & Unwin, 1977.
Stanworth, Philip and Giddens, Anthony (eds.), *Elites and Power in British Society*, Cambridge University Press, 1974.
Urry, John and Wakeford, John (eds.), *Power In Britain*, Heinemann, 1973.
Wedderburn, Dorothy (ed.), *Poverty, Inequality and Class Structure*, Cambridge University Press, 1974.

Specific studies and monographs

Bain, George, Coates, David and Ellis, Valerie, *Social Stratification and Trade Unionism: A Critique*, Heinemann, 1973.
Berry, D., *The Sociology of Grass-Roots Politics*, Macmillan, 1970.
Burton, Frank, *The Politics of Legitimacy. Struggles in a Belfast Community*, Routledge & Kegan Paul, 1978.
Chapman, Richard A., *The Higher Civil Service in Britain*, Constable, 1970.
Coates, K. and Silburn, R., *Poverty: The Forgotten Englishmen*, Penguin, 1973.
Coxon, A.P.M. and Jones, C.L., *The Images of Occupational Prestige: A Study in Social Cognition*, Macmillan, 1978.
Coxon, A.P.M. and Jones, C.L., *Class and Hierarchy. The Social Meaning of Occupation*, Macmillan, 1979.
Crompton, Rosemary and Gubbey, Jon, *Economy and Class Structure*, Macmillan, 1977.
Dahrendorf, R., *Society and Democracy in Germany*, Weidenfeld & Nicolson, 1968.
Dahrendorf, R., *The New Liberty*, Routledge & Kegan Paul, 1975.
Davis, Howard, *Beyond Class Images*, Croom Helm, 1979.
Foster, John, *Class Struggle and the Industrial Revolution*, Methuen, 1977.

Frankel, H., *Capitalist Society and Modern Sociology*, Lawrence & Wishart, 1970.

Friedmann, Andrew L., *Industry and Labour: Class Struggle at Work and Monopoly Capitalism*, Macmillan, 1977.

Gallie, D., *In Search of the New Working Class*, Cambridge University Press, 1978.

Giddens, Anthony, *The Class Structure of the Advanced Societies*, Hutchinson, 1973.

Goldthorpe, John H., Lockwood, David, Bechofer, Frank and Platt, Jennifer, *The Affluent Worker in the Class Structure*, (3 vols), Cambridge University Press, 1968-9.

Gray, Robert Q., *The Labour Aristocracy in Victorian Edinburgh*, Oxford University Press, 1976.

Guttsman, W.L., *The British Political Elite*, MacGibbon & Kee, 1971.

Halsey, A.H., *Change in British Society*, Oxford University Press, 1978.

Harris, Nigel, *Competition and the Corporate Society. British Conservatism, the State and Industry 1945-64*, Methuen, 1972.

Hindess, B., *The Decline of Working-Class Politics*, MacGibbon & Kee, 1971.

Jessop, Bob, *Traditionalism, Conservatism and British Political Culture*, Allen & Unwin, 1974.

Kincaid, J., *Poverty and Equality in Britain*, Penguin, 1973.

Lane, David, *The End of Inequality? Stratification under State Socialism*, Penguin, 1971.

Lane, David, *Politics and Society in the USSR*, Weidenfeld & Nicolson, 1970.

Lane, David, *The Socialist Industrial State: Towards a Political Sociology of State Socialism*, Allen & Unwin, 1976.

Mackenzie, Gavin, *The Aristocracy of Labour: The Position of Skilled Craftsmen in the American Class Structure*, Cambridge University Press, 1973.

McKenzie, Robert and Silver, Allen, *Angels in Marble: Working Class Conservatives in Urban England*, Heinemann, 1968.

Mann, M., *Consciousness and Action among the Western Working Class*, Macmillan, 1973.

Marceau, J., *Class and Status in France: Economic Change and Social Immobility, 1945-1975*, Clarendon Press, 1977.

Marshall, T.H., *Sociology at the Crossroads and Other Essays*, Heinemann, 1963.

Miliband, R., *The State in Capitalist Society*, Weidenfeld & Nicolson, 1968.

Newby, Howard, *The Deferential Worker: A Study of Farm Workers in East Anglia*, Allen Lane, 1977.

Newby, Howard, Bell, Colin, Rose, David and Saunders, Peter, *Property, Paternalism and Power*, Hutchinson, 1978.

Newton, Kenneth, *The Sociology of British Communism*, Allen Lane, 1969.

Nordlinger, Eric A., *The Working Class Tories*, MacGibbon & Kee, 1967.

Parkin, Frank, *Middle Class Radicalism*, Manchester University Press, 1968.

Parkin, Frank, *Marxism and Class Theory. A Bourgeois Critique*, Tavistock, 1979.

Robertson, K., Cook, S.C. and Semeonoff, Elizabeth, *The Fragmentary Class Structure*, Heinemann, 1977.

Runciman, W.G., *Relative Deprivation and Social Justice*, Routledge & Kegan Paul, 1966.

Scase, Richard, *Social Democracy in Capitalist Society*, Croom Helm 1977.

Stewart, A., Prendy, Ken and Blackburn, R.M., *Social Stratification and Occupational Structure*, Macmillan, 1979.

Thompson, E.P., *The Making of the English Working Class*, Gollancz, 1965.

Titmuss, Richard, *Income Distribution and Social Change*, Allen & Unwin, 1962.

Townsend, Peter, *The Social Minority*, Allen Lane, 1973.

Townsend, Peter, *Poverty in the United Kingdom*, Pelican, 1979.

Review papers and critiques

Bechofer, Frank and Elliott, Brian, 'An Approach to the Study of Small Shop-keepers and the Class Structure', *EJS*, no. 9, 1968, pp. 180-202.

Bechofer, Frank, Elliott, Brian, Rushforth, Maurice and Bland, Richard, 'Small Shopkeepers: Matters of Money and Meaning', *SR*, vol. 22, no. 4, 1974, pp. 465-82.

Box, Steven and Ford, Julienne, 'Some Questionable Assumptions in the Theory of Status Inconsistency', *SR*, vol. 17, no. 2, 1969, pp. 187-201.

Carter, Ian, 'Agricultural Workers in the Class Structure: A Critical Note', *SR*, vol. 22, no. 2, 1974, pp. 271-9.

Chamberlain, C.W. and Moorhouse, H.F., 'Lower-Class Attitudes Towards the British Political System', *SR*, vol. 22, no. 4, 1974, pp. 503-25.

Chivers, T.S., 'The Proletarianisation of Service Workers', *SR*, vol. 21, no. 4, 1973, pp. 633-56.

Cotgrove, Stephen and Vamplew, Clive, 'Technology, Class and Politics: The Case of Process Workers', *Sociology*, vol. 6, no. 2, 1972, pp. 169-85.

Cousins, J.M. and Brown, R.K., 'Patterns of Paradox: Shipbuilding Workers' Images of Society', *Durham University Working Papers in Sociology*, no. 4, n.d.

Critcher, Charles, 'Capital and Culture' The Post-War Working Class Re-visited', in Clarke, John, Critcher, Charles and Johnson, Richard (eds.), *Working Class Culture*, Hutchinson, 1979, pp. 238-53.

Doreion, Patrick and Stockman, Norman, 'A Critique of the Multidimensional Approach to Stratification', *SR*, vol. 17, no. 1, 1969, pp. 47-65.

Fulcher, James, 'Class Conflict in Sweden', *Sociology*, vol. 7, no. 1, 1975, pp. 477-84.

Garnsey, Elizabeth, 'Occupational Structure in Industrialised Societies' Some Note on the Convergence Thesis in the Light of Soviet Experience', *Sociology*, vol. 9, no. 3, 1975, pp. 437-58.

Goldthorpe, John H., 'Social Stratification in Industrial Society', in Halmos, P. (ed.), *The Development of Industrial Societies*, Sociological Review Monograph, no. 8, 1964, pp. 97-122.

Goldthorpe, John H., 'Class, Status and Party in Modern Britain: Some Recent Interpretations, Marxist and Marxisant', *EJS*, vol. 13 13, no. 2, 1972, pp. 342-72.

Goldthorpe, John H., 'Social Inequality and Social Integration in Modern Britain', in Wedderburn, Dorothy (ed.), *Poverty, Inequality and Class Structure*, 1974, pp. 217-38.

Goldthorpe, John H. and Bevan, Phillipa, 'The Study of Social Stratification in Great Britain *1945-1974*', Nuffield College Oxford mimeo, 1975.

Goldthorpe, John H. and Llewellyn, Catriona, 'Class Mobility in Modern Britain: Three Theses Examined', *Sociology*, vol. 11, no. 2, 1977.

Goldthorpe, John H. and Llewellyn, Catriona, 'Class Mobility: Intergenerational and Worklife Patterns', *BJS*, vol. XXVIII, no. 3, 1977, pp. 269-302.

Goldthorpe, John H., Payne, Clive and Llewellyn, Catriona, 'Trends in Class Mobility', *Sociology*, vol. 12, no. 3, 1978, pp. 440-68.

Hall, S., 'The "Political" and "Economic" in Marx's Theory of Classes', in Hunt, A. (ed.), *Class and Class Structure*, 1977.

Halsey, A.H., 'The Sociology of Poverty', *Sociology*, vol. 5, no. 3, 1971, pp. 401-6.

Johnson, R.W., 'The British Political Elite, 1955-1972', *EJS*, vol XIV, no. 1, 1973.

Jones, Bryn, 'Max Weber and the Concept of Social Class', *SR*, vol. 23, no. 4, 1975, pp. 729-57.

Kahan, Michael, Butler, David and Stokes, Donald, 'On the Analytical Division of Social Class', *BJS*, no. XVII, no. 2, 1966, pp. 122-32.

Lockwood, David, 'Sources of Variation in Working-Class Images of Society', *SR*, vol. 14, 1966, pp. 249-67.

Mackenzie, Gavin, 'The Economic Dimensions of Embourgeoisement', *BJS*, vol. 18, no. 1, 1967, pp. 29-44.

Mackenzie, Gavin, 'The Class Situation of Manual Workers in the

United States and Britain', *BJS*, vol. XXI, no. 3, 1970, pp. 333-42.
Moorhouse, H.F., 'The Marxist Theory of the Labour Aristocracy', *Social History*, vol. III, no. 1, 1978, pp. 61-82.
Moorhouse, H.F., 'The Political Incorporation of the British Working Class: An Interpretation', *Sociology*, vol. 7, no. 3, 1973, pp. 341-59.
Moorhouse, H.F. and Chamberlain, C.W., 'Lower-Class Attitudes to Property: Aspects of the Counter Ideology', *Sociology*, vol. 8, no. 3, 1974, pp 387-405.
Noble, Trevor, 'Social Mobility and Class Relations in Britain', *BJS*, vol. XXIII, no. 4, 1972, pp. 422-36.
Noble, Trevor, 'Research Note: Intergenerational Mobility in Britain: A Criticism of the Counter-balance Theory', *Sociology*, vol. 8, no. 3, 1974, pp. 475-83.
Oldman, David and Illsley, Raymond, 'Measuring the Status of Occupations', *SR*, vol. 14, no. 1, 1966, pp. 53-72.
Parkin, Frank, 'Working-Class Conservatives: A Theory of Political Deviance', *BJS*, vol XVIII, no. 3, 1967, pp. 278-90.
Payne, Geoff, 'Typologies of Middle-Class Mobility', *Sociology*, vol. 7, no. 3, 1973, pp. 417-28.
Piepe, Anthony, Prior, Robin and Box, Arthur, 'The Location of the Proletarian and Deferential Worker', *Sociology*, vol. 3, no. 2, 1969, pp. 239-44.
Reid, Ivan, *Social Class Differences in Britain: a Source-Book*, Open Books, 1977.
Rose, Richard, 'Class and Party Divisions: Britain as a Test Case', *Sociology*, vol. 2, no. 2, 1968, pp. 129-62.
Webb, David, 'Research Note: Some Reservations on the Use of Self-Rated Class', *SR*, vol. 21, no. 2, 1973, pp. 321-34.
Wolpe, Harold, 'The "White Working Class" in South Africa', *Economy and Society*, vol. 5, no. 2, 1976, pp. 197-240.

OTHER REFERENCES CITED IN THE TEXT

Aron, Raymond, *German Sociology*, Heinemann, 1957.

Banks, J.A., 'Moving up in Society', *Twentieth Century*, May 1960.

Banks, Olive, *Parity and Prestige in English Secondary Education*, Routledge & Kegan Paul, 1955.

Bendix, R., *Nationbuilding and Citizenship*, Wiley, 1964.

Bernstein, Richard J., *Restructuring Social Theory*, Methuen, 1976.

Banton, M., *The Coloured Quarter*, Cape, 1955.

Baran, Paul A., *The Longer View*, Monthly Review Press, 1969.

Barratt-Brown, Michael, *The Economics of Imperialism*, Penguin, 1974.

Bell, Daniel, *The Cultural Contradictions of Capitalism*, Heinemann, 1976.

Berger, Peter, *Invitation to Sociology*, Penguin, 1963.

Berger, Peter, *The Social Reality of Religion*, Faber & Faber, 1969.

Berger, Peter, *The Heretical Imperative*, Anchor Press/Doubleday, 1979.

Berger, Peter and Luckmann, Thomas, *The Social Construction of Reality*, Allen Lane, 1967.

Birnbaum, Norman, 'Monarchs and Sociologists', *Sociological Review*, 3 January 1955.

Blau, Peter M. (ed.), *Approaches to the Study of Social Structure*, Free Press, 1975.

Blauner, Robert, *Alienation and Freedom*, University of Chicago Press, 1964.

Bott, Elizabeth, *Family and Social Network*, Tavistock, 1957.

Bottomore, T., *Sociology*, Allen & Unwin, 1962.

Carr, E.H., 'What is history?', *Listener*, 4 July 1961.

Castells, M., *The Urban Question*, Edward Arnold, 1977.

Castells, M. and Godard, F., *Monopolville*, Mouton, 1974.

Cicourel, A., *Method and Measurement in Sociology*, Free Press, 1964.

Clarke, John *et al.*, *Working-Class Culture*, Hutchinson, 1979.

Clegg, Hugh, *The System of Industrial Relations in Great Britain*, Blackwell, 1972.

Crozier, M., *The Bureaucratic Phenomenon*, Tavistock, 1964.

Dahrendorf, R. *Class and Class Conflicts in an Industrial Society*, Routledge & Kegan Paul, 1959.

Delamotte, Yves and Walker, Kenneth F., 'Humanisation of Work and the Reality of Working Life — Trends and Issues', *International*

Institute of Labour Studies, vol. II, 1973.

Dennis, N., Henriques, F. and Slaughter, C., *Coal is our Life*, Eyre & Spottiswoode, 1956.

Douglas, J., *The Social Meanings of Suicide*, Princeton University Press, 1967.

Dunlop, J., *Industrial Relations Systems*, Henry Holt, 1958.

Dunlop, J., 'Future Trends in Industrial Relations in the United States', International Industrial Relations Association, 3rd World Congress, 1973.

Durkheim, E., *Professional Ethics and Civic Morals*, Routledge & Kegan Paul, 1957.

Durkheim, E., *Lectures on Socialism*, Collier, 1962.

Elias, Norbert, *What is Sociology?*, Hutchinson, 1978.

Eversley, David, *The Planner in Society*, Faber & Faber, 1973.

Eysenck, H.J., *Race, Intelligence and Education*, Temple Smith, 1971.

Flander, Allan, *Management and Unions*, Faber & Faber, 1970.

Flanders, Allan and Clegg, Hugh (eds.), *The System of Industrial Relations in Great Britain*, Blackwell, 1954.

Frank, A.G., *Latin-America: Underdevelopment or Revolution?*, Monthly Review Press, 1969.

Frank, A.G., Lumpenbourgeoisie: Lumpendevelopment, *Monthly* Review Press, 1972.

Galbraith, J.K., *American Capitalism*, Hamish Hamilton, 1957.

Galbraith, J.K., *The Affluent Society*, Hamish Hamilton, 1958.

Gellner, E., *Words and Things*, Gollancz, 1959.

Gerth, Hans and Mills, C.W. (eds.), *From Max Weber*, Routledge & Kegan Paul, 1948.

Ginsberg, M., 'Interchange Between Social Classes', *Economic Journal*, 1929.

Glass, David *et al.*, *Social Mobility in Britain*, Routledge & Kegan Paul, 1954.

Glass, Ruth, Verbal Pollution, *New Society*, 29 September 1977.

Gluckman, M. and Devons, E. (eds.), *Closed Systems and Open Minds*, Oliver & Boyd, 1964.

Gouldner, Alvin, *Wildcat Strike*, Routledge & Kegan Paul, 1955.

Gouldner, Alvin, *Patterns of Industrial Bureaucracy*, Routledge & Kegan Paul, 1959.

Gouldner, Alvin, *The Coming Crisis of Western Sociology*, Routledge & Kegan Paul, 1970.

Gouldner, Alvin, *For Sociology*, Penguin, 1973.

Gouldner, Alvin, *The Dialectics of Ideology and Technology*, Macmillan 1976.

Gouldner, Alvin, *The Future of Intellectuals and the Rise of the New Class*, Macmillan, 1979.

Henriques, F., 'The Miner and his Lass', *Twentieth Century*, May 1960.

Hill, Christopher, *The World Turned Upside Down*, Penguin, 1972.

Hobhouse, L.T., *Morals in Evolution*, Chapman & Hall, 1906.
Hobhouse, L.T., *Liberalism*, Hutchinson, 1911.
Hobhouse, L.T., *Social Development*, Allen & Unwin, 1924.
Hobhouse, L.T., *Sociology and Philosophy*, G. Bell, 1966.
Hobhouse, L.T., Wheeler, G.C., Ginsberg, M., *The Material Culture and Social Institutions of the Simpler People*, Chapman & Hall, 1930.
Hobsbawm, E., *Primitive Rebels*, Manchester University Press, 1959.
Hobsbawm, E., *Labouring Men*, Weidenfeld & Nicolson, 1964.
Hobsbawm, E. and Rudé, G., *Captain Swing*, Pelican, 1969.
Hoggart, Richard, *The Uses of Literacy*, Chatto & Windus, 1958.
Homans, George, *The Human Group*, Routledge & Kegan Paul, 1950.
Homans, George, *Sentiments and Activities*, Routledge & Kegan Paul, 1962.
Homans, George and Horowitz, Irving (eds.), *Sociological Self-Images*, Pergamon, 1967.
Horowitz, Irving (ed.), *The New Sociology*, Oxford University Press, 1964.
Hoselitz, B.F., *Sociological Factors in Economic Development*, Free Press, 1969.
Hughes, John, 'Giant Firms and British Trade Union Responses', in Coates, K. *et al.* (eds.), *Trade Union Register*, Merlin Press, 1970.
Hunnius, G. *et al.* (eds.), *Workers Control*, Vintage Books, 1973.
Hymes, Dell, *Foundations in Sociolinguistics*, Tavistock, 1977.
Kerr, C., *Labour and Management in Industrial Society*, Doubleday, 1964.
Kersler, S. and Weekes, B. (eds.), *Conflict at Work*, BBC, 1971.
Kuper, Adam, *Anthropologists and Anthropology. The British School 1922-72*, Allen Lane, 1973.
Lenin, V. 'What is to be done?', in *Collected Works*, vol. 5, Moscow, 1961.
Lindsay, Kenneth, *Social Progress and Educational Waste*, Routledge & Kegan Paul, 1926.
Lipset, S. *et al.*, *Union Democracy*, Free Press, 1956.
Little, Kenneth, *Negroes in Britain*, Routledge & Kegan Paul, 1947.
Lockwood, D. *The Blackevated Worker. A Study in Class Consciousness*, Allen & Unwin, 1958.
McCarthy, W. and Ellis, N., *Management by Agreement*, Hutchinson, 1973.
McClelland, D., *The Achieving Society*, Van Nostrand, 1961.
MacRae, D.G., 'Between Science and the Arts', *Twentieth Century*, May 1960.
Mallet, Serge, *The New Working Class*, Spokesman Books, 1975.
Mannheim, Karl, *Ideology and Utopia*, Routledge & Kegan Paul, 1936.
Mannheim, Karl, *Man and Society in an Age of Reconstruction*, Routledge & Kegan Paul, 1940.
Mannheim, Karl, *Diagnosis of Our Time*, Routledge & Kegan Paul, 1943.

Mannheim, Karl, *Freedom, Power and Democratic Planning*, Routledge & Kegan Paul, 1951.

Marcuse, Herbert, *Soviet Marxism*, Penguin, 1958.

Marcuse, Herbert, *One Dimensional Man*, Routledge & Kegan Paul, 1964.

Marshall, T.H., *Sociology at the Crossroads and Other Essays*, Heinemann, 1963.

Marx, Karl, *Economic and Philosophical Manuscripts of 1844*, Lawrence & Wishart, 1970.

Marx, Karl, *Communist Manifesto*, in Fernback, D. (ed.), *Karl Marx: The Revolutions of 1848*, Pelican, 1973.

Marx, Karl, *Capital*, Allen & Unwin, 1957.

Marx, Karl, *Grundrisse*, Pelican, 1973.

Merton, R.K., *Social Theory and Social Structure*, Free Press, 1957.

Mezaros, I. (ed.), *Aspects of History and Class Consciousness*, Routledge & Kegan Paul, 1971.

Michels, R., *Political Parties*, Collier, 1962.

Mills, C.W., *The New Men of Power*, Harcourt Brace, 1948.

Mills, C.W., *White Collar*, Oxford University Press, 1951.

Mills, C.W., *The Power Elite*, Oxford University Press, 1956.

Mills, C.W., *The Sociological Imagination*, Oxford University Press, 1959.

Mills, C.W., *The Marxists*, Penguin, 1963.

Mills, C.W., *Power, Politics and People*, Oxford University Press, 1963.

Mitchell, Clyde (ed.), *Social Networks in Urban Situations*, Manchester University Press, 1969.

Myrdal, Gunnar, *An American Dilemma*, Harper, 1944.

Nisbet, Robert, *Social Change and History*, Oxford University Press, 1969.

O'Connor, James, *The Fiscal Crisis of the State*, St Martins Press, 1973.

Parker, Julia, *Social Policy and Citizenship*, 1975.

Parsons, Talcott, *The Structure of Social Action*, Free Press, 1937.

Parsons, Talcott, *Societies: Evolutionary and Comparative Perspectives*, Prentice-Hall, 1966.

Plowden Report, *Children and their Primary Schools*, HMSO, 1967.

Popper, Karl, *The Open Society and its Enemies*, Routledge & Kegan Paul, 1941.

Popper, Karl, *The Poverty of Historicism*, Routledge & Kegan Paul, 1957.

Popper, Karl, *The Logic of Scientific Discovery*, Hutchinson, 1959.

Popper, Karl, *Objective Knowledge: an Evolutionary Approach*, Oxford University Press, 1972.

Popper, Karl, *Unended Quest*, Fontana, 1976.

Rice, A.K., *Productivity and Social Organisation. The Ahmedabad Experiment*, Tavistock, 1958.

Richardson, Ken and Spears, David (eds.), *Race, Culture and Intelligence*, Penguin, 1972.

Richmond, Anthony, *Colour Prejudice in Britain*, Routledge & Kegan

Paul, 1954.

Roethlisberger, F. and Dickson, W.J., *Management and the Worker*, Harvard University Press, 1939.

Rostow, W.W., *Stages of Economic Growth*, Cambridge University Press, 1960.

Ryan, Alan, *The Philosophy of the Social Sciences*, Macmillan, 1970.

Ryle, Gilbert (ed.), *The Revolution in Philosophy*, Macmillan, 1956.

Samuel, R. (ed.), *Village Life and Labour*, Routledge & Kegan Paul, 1975.

Scott, W. *et at.*, *Technical Change and Industrial Relations*, Liverpool University Press, 1956.

Smelser, N., *Social Change in the Industrial Revolution*, Routledge & Kegan Paul, 1959.

Spencer, Herbert, *The Study of Sociology*, Ann Arbor, 1961.

Stein, Maurice and Vidich, Arthur (eds.), *Sociology on Trial*, Prentice-Hall, 1963.

Sprott, W.J.H., *Sociology at the Seven Dials*, Athlone Press, 1962.

Stretton, Hugh, *The Political Sciences*, Routledge & Kegan Paul, 1969.

Shils, E., 'On the Eve', *Twentieth Century*, May 1960.

Thomis, M.I., *The Town Labourer and the Industrial Revolution*, Batsford, 1974.

Tawney, R.H., *The Agrarian Problem in the Sixteenth Century*, Longman Green, 1912.

Tawney, R.H., *The Acquisitive Society*, Bell, 1921.

Tawney, R.H., *Secondary Education for All*, Allen & Unwin, 1922.

Tawney, R.H., *Religion and the Rise of Capitalism*, Murray, 1926.

Tawney, R.H., *Equality*, Allen & Unwin, 1931.

Thompson, E.P., *Whigs and Hunters*, Pelican, 1975.

Titmuss, Richard, *Essays on the Welfare State*, Allen & Unwin, 1958.

Touraine, A. *et al.*, *Workers Attitudes to Technical Change*, OECD, 1965.

Turner, H.A., The Royal Commission Research Papers, *BJIR*, 6 March 1968.

Walker, Charles R., *Steeltown: An Industrial Case History of the Conflict and Security*, Harper & Row, 1950.

Walker, Charles R., *Towards the Automatic Factory*, Yale University Press, 1957.

Warner, W. and Low, J., *The Social System of a Modern Factory*, Yale University Press, 1946.

Watson, W., 'The Managerial Spiralist', *Twentieth Century*, May 1960.

Waxman, Chaim I. (ed.), *The End of Ideology Debate*, Simon & Schuster, 1968.

Webb, S. and B., *Industrial Democracy*, privately published, London, 1911.

Webb, S. and B., *Methods of Social Study*, privately published, London, 1932.

Weber, Max, *The Protestant Ethic and the Spirit of Capitalism*, Allen & Unwin, 1920.

Weber, Max, *Economy and Society*, Bedminster Press, 1968.

Winch, Peter, *The Idea of a Social Science and its Relation to Philosophy*, Routledge & Kegan Paul, 1958.

Woodward, Joan, *Management and Technology*, HMSO, DSIR, 1958.

Young, M. and Shils, E., 'The Meaning of the Coronation', *Sociological Review*, 1 February 1953.

Young, M. and Willmott, P., Research Report No. 3. Institute of Community Studies: Bethnal Green, *Sociological Review*, July 1961.

Zweig, F., 'The New Factory Worker', *Twentieth Century*, May 1960.